The
Steelband
Movement

The Forging of a National Art in Trinidad and Tobago

Stephen Stuempfle

University of Pennsylvania Press

Philadelphia

Permission is acknowledged to reprint previously published material excerpted from the following sources:

Michael Anthony, *Port-of-Spain in a World at War, 1939-1945*. Port of Spain: Ministry of Sport, Culture and Youth Affairs. Reprinted by permission of the Trinidad and Tobago Ministry of Community Development, Culture, and Women's Affairs.

Franz Fanon. *The Wretched of the Earth*. New York: Grove Press, 1963. Reprinted by permission of Grove Press, Inc.

Lionel Mordaunt Fraser, *History of Trinidad*, vol. 1. London: Frank Cass & Co. Ltd., 1971 [1891]. Reprinted by permission of Frank Cass & Co. Ltd.

Patrick Leigh Fermor, *The Travellers' Tree: A Journey Through the Caribbean Islands*. London: John Murray, 1950. Reprinted by permission of John Murray (Publishers) Ltd.

Earl Lovelace, *The Dragon Can't Dance*. Harlow: Longman, 1981. Reprinted by permission of Earl Lovelace.

Bertie Marshall, "The Bertie Marshall Story: Pan is Mih Gyul," *Tapia* 2, nos. 1-10 (1972); interview of Ian Jones by Lennox Grant, "Pan and Ian," *Trinidad and Tobago Review* 5, no. 3 (1981). Reprinted by permission of the *Trinidad and Tobago Review*.

Lennox Pierre, "History and Development of Steelband." Video tape of lecture delivered at West Indian Reference Section, Central Library of Trinidad and Tobago, 1987. Reprinted by permission of the Trinidad and Tobago Ministry of Education.

Raymond Quevedo, *Atilla's Kaiso: A Short History of Trinidad Calypso*. St. Augustine, Trinidad: Department of Extra Mural Studies, University of the West Indies, 1983. Reprinted by permission of the University of the West Indies—St. Augustine.

W. Austin Simmonds, *Pan: The Story of the Steelband*. Maraval, Trinidad: BWIA International, n.d.[1959]. Reprinted by permission of BWIA International.

John E. Slater, *The Advent of the Steel Band and My Life and Times with It*. Reprinted by permission of John E. Slater.

Selwyn Tarradath, *Pan Trinbago's Information Booklet*. 1987. Reprinted by permission of Pan Trinbago.

Articles from the *Daily Express, Sunday Express*, and *Trinidad Express*, 1967-1993. Reprinted by permission of Trinidad Express Newspapers Ltd.

Articles from the *Trinidad Guardian* and *Sunday Guardian*, 1920-1988. Reprinted by permission of the Guardian Newspapers.

Library of Congress Cataloging-in-Publication Data

Stuempfle, Stephen.
    The steelband movement / the forging of a national art in Trinidad and Tobago / Stephen Stuempfle.
        p.   cm.
    Includes bibliographical references, discography, and index.
    ISBN 0-8122-3329-8 (cloth : alk. paper). — ISBN 0-8122-1565-6 (pbk. : alk. paper)
    1. Steel bands (Music)—Trinidad and Tobago—History and criticism.
784.6´8—dc20   95–38564
                                                                                   CIP
                                                                                   MN

Cover photograph: Members of Invaders at the Queen's Park Oval, Port of Spain, early 1950s. Junia Browne collection.

The Steelband Movement

To Denise
and
the Panmen and Panwomen
of
Trinidad and Tobago

Contents

Photographs begin on page 125

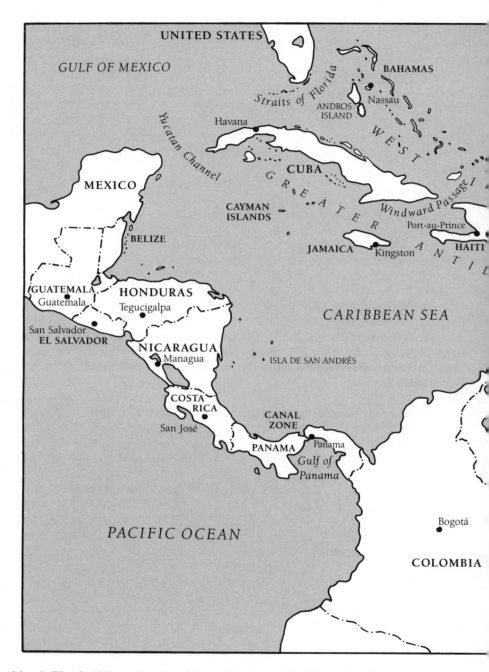

Map 1. The Caribbean. Reprinted from *The Modern Caribbean*, edited by
Franklin W. Knight and Colin A. Palmer. Copyright © 1989 by the University
of North Carolina Press. Used by permission of the publisher.

ATLANTIC OCEAN

TURKS &
CAICOS ISLANDS

I E S

DOMINICAN
REPUBLIC

LEEWARD ISLANDS

Canal de la Mona

VIRGIN
ISLANDS

San
Juan

ANGUILLA

Santo
Domingo

PUERTO
RICO

E S

SAINT
KITTS-NEVIS
MONTSERRAT

BARBUDA

ANTIGUA
St. Johns

Basse-Terre

GUADELOUPE

Roseau

DOMINICA

LESSER ANTILLES

Fort-de-France

MARTINIQUE

Castries

SAINT LUCIA

WINDWARD ISLANDS

SAINT
VINCENT
Kingstown

BARBADOS
Bridgetown

NETHERLANDS
ANTILLES

ARUBA   CURAÇAO

BONAIRE
Willemstad

GRENADA
St. George's

ISLA DE MARGARITA

Port-of-Spain

TRINIDAD & TOBAGO

Caracas

VENEZUELA

Georgetown

Paramaribo

Cayenne

GUYANA

FRENCH
GUIANA

SURINAME

BRAZIL

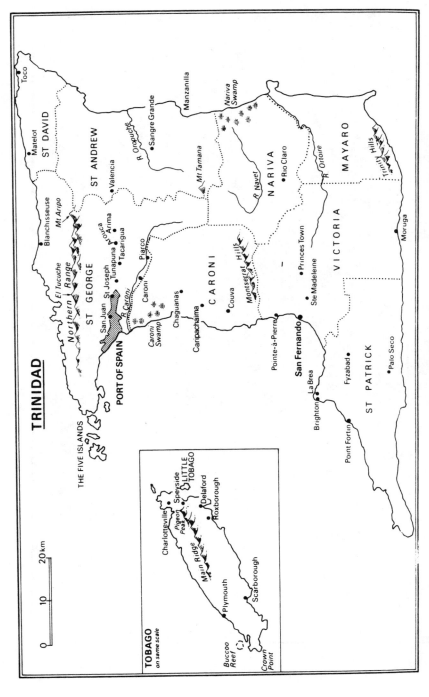

TRINIDAD

THE FIVE ISLANDS

Toco

ST DAVID

Matelot

ST ANDREW

Blanchisseuse

Mt Aripo

El Tucuche

Northern Range

ST GEORGE

San Juan

St Joseph

Tunapuna

Arouca

Arima

Tacarigua

Piarco

Caroni

Chaguanas

Caripachaima

Caroni Swamp

PORT OF SPAIN

R Caroni

CARONI

Couva

Montserrat Hills

Ste Madeleine

Pointe-à-Pierre

San Fernando

La Brea

Brighton

Point Fortin

Fyzabad

Palo Seco

ST PATRICK

R Orouche

Sangre Grande

Manzanilla

Nariva Swamp

Valencia

Mt Tamana

NARIVA

Rio Claro

R Navet

R Ortoire

Princes Town

VICTORIA

Moruga

MAYARO

Trinity Hills

TOBAGO
on same scale

Charlotteville

Speyside

LITTLE TOBAGO

Pigeon Peak

Delaford

Roxborough

Main Ridge

Plymouth

Scarborough

Buccoo Reef

Crown Point

0   10   20 km

Map 2. Trinidad and Tobago. Reprinted from *A History of Modern Trinidad, 1783–1962*, by Bridget Brereton. Copyright © 1981. Used by permission of Heinemann Publishers and Bridget Brereton.

Preface

Above the eastern edge of Port of Spain, Trinidad, rises Laventille Hill, with densely built houses clinging to its steep slopes. A narrow road winds up the hill, and from it radiates a maze of paths that lead to individual locations with names that only the inhabitants know. On top of the hill, across from the Laventille Shrine, are a spacious lot and an open concrete block community center which together serve as the *pan-yard*, or practice site, for the Desperadoes Steel Orchestra. On a Sunday morning during the busy Carnival season, the band can be found at rehearsal. Its beautifully chromed *pans* are grouped in sections, from the rich basses through the pure, high-pitched tenors. The performers in each section move in unison, negotiating complex phrases and chord progressions under the guidance of the musical arranger. Soon they will be appearing in Panorama, a nationwide steelband competition where they have claimed many victories. Scattered about the yard are young men from the neighborhood, some of whom observe the band intently while others banter among themselves. In the yards of nearby houses, people tend to laundry and other morning chores. Boys fly small homemade kites that rise so high as to almost disappear in the cloudless sky. Below, the Gulf of Paria stretches out to the hazy shore of Venezuela.

To the west of Laventille Hill, downtown Port of Spain extends from the Gulf to the Queen's Park Savannah. Two blocks above the wharves is Independence Square, presided over by the Cathedral of the Immaculate Conception. The square is always jammed with pedestrians, cars, and *maxi-taxis*, privately owned taxi vans with booming sound systems and often lush interior decor. In the commercial district surrounding and above the square, banks, fabric stores, clothing shops, dry goods emporia, jewelry stores, and restaurants vie with street vendors selling shirts, shoes, sunglasses, kitchen utensils, newspapers, lottery tickets, herbs, hot peanuts, and an array of fruits, vegetables, and fish. People come downtown not only to shop but for the conviviality. On the crowded sidewalks, one is sure to encounter friends and acquaintances.

Two blocks north of Independence Square is Woodford Square, a shady park surrounded by Trinity Cathedral, the Courthouse, and the elegant Red House where Parliament meets. It was in this square that Dr. Eric Williams, Trinidad and Tobago's first Prime Minister, addressed the masses in the years preceding independence from Britain. The consequences of colonialism and other political topics continue to be enthusiastically debated there by street orators and the audiences that gather spontaneously. Meanwhile, Spiritual Baptists in long robes sing hymns, ring bells, and offer libations.

A few blocks from Woodford Square, at the corner of George and Duke Streets, is the panyard of the Trinidad All Stars Steel Orchestra. Nearby is the old Hell Yard on the edge of the East Dry River where the band was formed over fifty years ago. The front of the band's current yard is wedged between two buildings and some sheds for storing pans and equipment. The practice space is jammed with pans mounted on mobile metal frames which the band uses to parade the streets for Carnival. During evening rehearsals the sounds of the pans reverberate from the adjacent buildings at a tremendous volume. Outside on the pavement, people *lime* (hang out) and enjoy beers or sweet drinks from the band's refreshment stand. There are always a few All Stars "old boys" around, reminiscing about the band's illustrious past and imagining its future. Drivers of passing cars slow down for a chat or to hear a little of the rehearsal.

All Stars is a real downtown band, supported by the patrons of nearby bars and recreation clubs and by the late-night denizens of the surrounding streets. However, it also counts among its followers some of the most prominent members of Trinidadian society. In fact, All Stars, like other top bands, attracts players and fans from throughout the island.

On Duke Street one can catch a maxi-taxi for a trip to the west side of Port of Spain. One passes along Tragarete Road through the residential neighborhood of Woodbrook, where there are still some airy wooden houses from the colonial era with large jalousied windows and ornate fretwork on the gables and eaves. Also on Tragarete Road are the old Lapeyrouse Cemetery, with its legends of scandalous grave-side occurrences, and the Queen's Park Oval where Test level cricket attracts huge crowds. Across the street from the Oval is the panyard of the Invaders Steel Orchestra, who like All Stars and Desperadoes is among the oldest bands in Trinidad. After passing the nineteenth-century police barracks and Starlift's panyard, one enters St. James, another residential neighborhood with a chaotic main road of bars, fast-food joints, stores, and racing pools. On leaving St. James, one passes by the Gulf of Paria, where perhaps a large tanker carrying Trinidadian oil or small schooners full of fruit from Grenada or St. Vincent can be spotted.

To the northwest lies the Diego Martin Valley. Though this was one of the most fertile areas in Trinidad during the plantation era, it is now filled with suburban housing developments. At the end of the valley, however, are a few old villages which maintain an existence somewhat separate from the new neighborhoods. One such place is Green Hill Village, home of the Merrytones Steel Orchestra. Merrytones' panyard is situated near a crossroads to the north of the village and is built into the slope of one of the verdant hills which surround the valley. Across from the yard is a spacious savannah for football (soccer) and cricket, and farther up the road is a large squatter community of migrants from other islands or from elsewhere in Trinidad. The hills above the yard are covered with dense vegetation, occasionally broken by family gardens maintained by residents of the nearby villages. These hills are also the site of the mysterious cave of St. Hilaire Begorrat, the most notorious planter of the old Diego Martin Valley. To the north, the hills plunge sharply into the Caribbean Sea. Though the surf pounds dangerously against the rocks that lie at the bottom of the cliffs, men from the area sometimes go there to fish.

Merrytones' panyard attracts a steady stream of visitors, due to its prominent crossroads location. Young members of the band often lime there during the day, practicing tunes and tending to the upkeep of the yard. Toward the end of the day, they sometimes prepare a communal meal of provisions gathered from nearby gardens. At nightfall band members drift in from the neighboring communities and soon pan music rings out across the valley, easily drowning out the intense noise of the frogs. Supporters of the band come by to listen, and orange and peanut vendors provide them with refreshments. Over the years Merrytones have experienced many hardships. In earlier days there was the effort to gain social acceptance and recognition; in recent times there has been an ongoing attempt to obtain the funds necessary to maintain a large orchestra. In addition, there is the daily personal struggle of individual band members, the majority of whom are unemployed. While these struggles continue, the band's music fills the night with a sheer brilliance, a sort of testimony of Green Hill Village, which has managed to survive for a century and a half.

There are over one hundred steelbands in Trinidad and Tobago, each with its own story of struggle and achievement. Though the highest concentration is in the Port of Spain area, bands can be found in towns throughout the twin-island state. Pan (steelband music) becomes a particularly prominent part of public life during the annual Carnival season, which extends from early January to Carnival Monday and Tuesday. During this period the bands rehearse nightly for the multi-round Panorama competition that culminates on the Saturday before Carnival. The steelbands then join masquerade bands on the streets for the two days of Carnival itself. Steelbands also perform at the biennial Steelband Music Festival and at various smaller competitions, concerts, and community functions throughout the year. One of the most impressive aspects of the bands is their sheer size: many perform for Panorama with eighty to one hundred players, and thus are among the largest musical ensembles in the world. The presence of a great number of steelband musicians in Trinidad and their resourcefulness have resulted in much innovation in *tuning* (pan making), musical arranging, and performance technique since the inception of the music in the late 1930s.

Though the steelband originated in Trinidad and continues to have its most vibrant manifestation there, during the 1940s and 1950s it spread with migrants to other parts of the Caribbean and to West Indian communities in North America and England. Dissemination of steelband music has also occurred through performances by top Trinidadian bands overseas, the distribution of steelband recordings, and in more recent years the occasional use of pan soloists by popular singers and musical ensembles in the United States. This growing exposure of pan has inspired some formation of bands among people who are not of West Indian descent. In the United States, for example, there are numerous small steelbands connected with colleges and high schools. Steelbands can also be found in South America, Europe, Africa, and Asia.

The dissemination of the steelband has produced some serious international appreciation of the music. Still, the impression of the steelband held by the average North American is remote from the reality of the tradition as it exists in Trinidad. Many North Americans, if they are familiar with steelbands at all, first encountered one on a vacation to one of the more tourist-oriented islands of the Caribbean, or perhaps saw one in a movie or television show that reflected this milieu. In contrast to the huge and highly skilled bands of Trinidad that play for devoted national audiences, the steelband of the tourist hotel is often a handful of men in brightly colored shirts hired to provide light music for dining and dancing. In fact the steelband continues to be an integral part of the North American and European fantasy of the Caribbean: it is the soundtrack for an exotic experience of tropical, palm-fringed beaches and carefree living. People from the North generally go to the Caribbean for pleasure and play, and it is difficult for them to conceive of the region in any other terms. The West Indians they meet there exist for them mainly in a service capacity, as part of the set for the fantasy. It is forgotten that the inhabitants of the Caribbean have a history and a life outside the resorts.

Tourism is not a major industry in Trinidad: there are no large beach-front hotels and visits by cruise ships are relatively infrequent. For the most part, Trinidad has depended on its oil resources for economic development and has intentionally avoided the social and economic hazards that mass tourism has brought to some of the other Caribbean islands. With the decline of the oil industry since the early 1980s, however, there has been a growing interest in tourism, particularly in Tobago. Some tourists do come to Trinidad, especially during the Carnival season, and often they arrive with a vague sense of Trinidad as "The Land of Carnival, Steelband, and Calypso." Trinidadians are well aware of these perceptions. In general they are proud of the international attention to their achievements in music and masquerade. Yet they also believe that a superficial understanding of the Carnival arts contributes to a stereotype of Trinidad as a land of frivolity. Fortunately, travelers to Trinidad are able to encounter steelbands, calypso, and masquerade not in shows produced for tourists but at events attended by the local population. Thus they have the opportunity to gain some awareness of the deeper significance of the Carnival arts to this Caribbean nation.

My own interest in the steelband developed during the 1980s while I was a graduate student in the Department of Folklore and Folklife at the University of Pennsylvania. For years I had been intrigued by what the folk and popular music traditions of the United States reveal about diverse American experiences. At Penn it became clear to me that the examination of the musical styles of the Caribbean could provide a much broader understanding of processes of cultural creativity and identity formation in New World societies. Thus I started attending the Labor Day Carnival festivities in Brooklyn's West Indian community, and conducted some research with a small Trinidadian steelband in Houston known as the Caribbean Steeltones. During this same period I discovered the work of J. D. Elder, a scholar from Trinidad and Tobago who had received a doctorate in folklore from Penn in the 1960s. Elder's vivid and insightful writing opened up for me the complexity of Trinidadian musical styles and raised a number of questions concerning the steelband, Carnival traditions, and social relations.

By 1986 I had decided to write my doctoral dissertation on the steelband *movement*: the whole social and artistic phenomenon as it has developed in Trinidad over time. I was particularly impressed by the fact that the steelband was a relatively new musical form. Since it originated during the late 1930s, most of the individuals who played key roles in its invention were still alive. Thus it seemed that it would be possible to obtain direct accounts of how a new type of music came into existence—of how artistic creativity was shaped by both cultural traditions and historical circumstance. Furthermore, it appeared that the development of the steelband movement was closely linked to the process of decolonization. I hoped that documentation and interpretation of the history of the movement would reveal new aspects of Trinidad and Tobago's transition to independence and formation of a national identity. Finally, I was intrigued by the vitality of the steelband movement: the number and size of the bands and the integral role that they played in community life. Through ethnographic investigation, I expected to learn more about how a popular music tradition was perpetuated and what types of meanings it had for performers and audiences.

The primary research for this study was conducted in Trinidad from October 1987 through April 1989 and included field observation, interviewing, and archival work. In the course of my stay, I attended countless steelband performances, rehearsals, meetings, and other events, mainly in Port of Spain and its environs. Numerous formal and informal interviews were conducted with panmen, panwomen, and other participants in the movement. I was careful to talk with pannists from different neighborhoods and bands and with ones who ranged in age from the early pioneers down to the young players of today. The perspectives of many of the key pan innovators and influential figures in the movement are included in the following chapters.

I complemented my fieldwork with extensive research in libraries and archives. Though I read through a variety of Carnival booklets, travel literature, record album liner notes, and other publications, I found newspapers to be the most valuable primary source. Only a few brief remarks were made about pans in newspapers during the 1930s but, as the movement grew in importance, coverage gradually expanded. From the newspapers, it was possible to obtain descriptions of events and exact dates that could be correlated with the oral history I was gathering. In addition, letters to the editor, editorials, and columns proved to be a wonderful source of information on perceptions of and attitudes toward this new musical form.

The account of the steelband offered here is derived from a comparison and synthesis of material from this range of sources. The interpretations of the steelband's significance are based on the identification of patterns in the social usage of the music and in the local discourse about it from the late 1930s to the present.

Over the years the steelband has attracted commentary from a number of outside observers as well as from local researchers. This is inevitable, given the growing awareness of the music. Pan musicians themselves conceive of their music not only as Trinidadian but as international. It is international both in repertoire and in its performance by musicians from a variety of countries around the world. International interest in the steelband is perceived by Trinidadian pannists as a tribute to its uniqueness and excellence. Though they want the world to remember that the music originated in Trinidad and are concerned that some other country may be the first to develop a successful method of mass-producing pans, they remain dedicated to the promotion of the steelband as a transnational art. In the light of this orientation, the present study is offered as a contribution to an increasing global appreciation of this important musical tradition.

It should also be noted that a researcher like myself can learn some valuable lessons about the United States in Trinidad. The United States has had a substantial economic and cultural impact on the island since the 1940s. In fact it was during World War II, when many American servicemen were stationed in Trinidad, that the steelband began to take shape. The early panmen were fascinated by these servicemen, as well as by American movies and music, and incorporated what they saw and heard in their own expressive practices. Since the war a variety of American corporations have operated in Trinidad and there is an overwhelming American presence in the media. Most of the movies and television programs and much of the music on the radio continues to emanate from the United States. So the American researcher arriving in Trinidad is clearly a familiar figure. In such surroundings, the researcher stands to learn much about what happens to American cultural styles overseas: how they are adopted, transformed, parodied, and resisted.

North American and European anthropological research in the colonial and post-colonial world has historically had an imperialistic dimension in terms of the control of representations of peoples and access to information. However, scholars and other intellectuals in the countries under examination have their own traditions of cultural research. The anthropological projects of the North today have value to the extent that they are part of a dialogue. The present study of the steelband has been shaped by several years of discussion with pan musicians, supporters, and researchers from Trinidad. Ideally, it will expand the international discourse on the steelband tradition and generate some new questions for further research.

I am indebted to many individuals and institutions for the assistance they provided in the course of my study. Funding for the field research and writing of the dissertation included a grant from the Wenner-Gren Foundation for Anthropological Research, a Mellon Graduate Fellowship from the University of Pennsylvania, and a fellowship from the Philadelphia Folksong Society. Library privileges at the Main Library of the University of the West Indies, Trinidad and Tobago, were arranged by Eric St. Cyr, Dean of the Faculty of Social Sciences. The revision of the dissertation was facilitated by access to New York University's Bobst Library during my term as a Visiting Scholar in the Department of Performance Studies from 1991 to 1993.

Of the numerous individuals who assisted me while in Trinidad and Tobago, first thanks must go to Kendall Lewis, a seasoned pan musician and leader, who took a keen interest in my project from the very beginning. Kendall helped me navigate the steelband world and could always be relied on for insightful commentary, amusing anecdotes, and general encouragement. I owe many thanks also to Pan Trinbago, the steelband association of Trinidad and Tobago. This organization graciously invited me to their general meetings, facilitated many contacts, and always kept me informed about what was happening in the movement. I am grateful to all of the organization's officers, especially Owen Serrette, Richard Forteau, Nestor Sullivan, Roy Henry, and Selwyn Tarradath.

While in Trinidad and Tobago, I spent time with a number of steelbands. Special thanks are due to Merrytones, both for their help with the study and for all the good times. Liming in their panyard was always a welcome retreat from long days of research. I am also particularly grateful to Harmonites, Tokyo, Trinidad All Stars, Starlift, Pamberi, Desperadoes, Hummingbirds Pan Groove, Laventille Sounds Specialists, Phase II, Renegades, and East Side.

There are numerous panmen and panwomen whom I must thank individually for their assistance: Patricia Adams, Merle Albino-de Coteau, Leo Alfred, John Babb, Mayhew Bain, Dawn Batson, Prince Batson, Wellington Bostock, Clive Bradley, Glenford Broomes, Melville Bryan, Eric Charles, David Chow-Quan, Michael Cupidore, Michelle Dennis, Allison Dyer, Nicholas Fermin, Ken Flaverney, George Goddard, Ray Holman, Brenda James, Benjamin Job, Anthony Johnson, Neville Jules, McDonald Kinsale, Eric McAllister, Leon McPherson, Andrew Mader, Vernon Mannette, Alfred Mayers, Peter Mercer, Maureen Clement Moe, Maurice Muir, Curtis Pierre, Oscar Pile, McDonald Pinder, Junior Pouchet, George Prescott, Anthony Prospect, Joseph Renaud, George Richardson, Selwyn St. Clair, Kelvin St. Rose, Sylvan Salandy, McKeller

Sandiford, Selwyn Scott, Jerry Serrant, Bryon Serrette, Johnny Serrette, Michael Sheriffe, Les Slater, Lytton Stewart, Conrad Victor, Lincoln Waldron, Leo Warner, Anthony Williams, Gilbert Williams, Patti Wilson, Victor Wilson, Lloyd Woods, Steve Yearwood, George Yeates, and Errol Zephyrine. I am also grateful to Lennox Pierre, Beryl McBurnie, J. D. Elder, Lloyd Braithwaite, Eileen Guillaume, and Vivian Ventour for sharing their memories of the steelband movement. In addition, Jason Griffith provided much useful information on sailor masquerade and Ricky Ali helped familiarize me with tassa drumming.

Further thanks are due to a number of institutions in Trinidad: the West Indiana Division, Main Library, University of the West Indies, Trinidad and Tobago; the West Indian Reference Section, Central Library of Trinidad and Tobago; the West Indian Reference Division, Trinidad Public Library; the recently established National Heritage Library of Trinidad and Tobago; the National Archives of Trinidad and Tobago; the National Broadcasting Service; the Educational Television Unit, Ministry of Education; and the Ministry of Community Development, Culture, and Women's Affairs. The helpfulness and patience of the staff at these institutions made arduous archival work considerably easier. I also appreciate the assistance of the staff at the Research Institute for the Study of Man in New York.

Nydia Daniel and family provided me with a perfect home in St. James. I especially looked forward to the Sunday dinners and lively living room conversations. I will also always be grateful for the hospitality of Errol and Rhona Stephenson and family, Grace Steele, and Richard and Noreen Groden. All the holiday visits, evenings on the town, and excursions to the countryside were among my best times in Trinidad.

While writing the dissertation, I received much support and useful advice from my committee members: Roger Abrahams, Kenneth Goldstein, Sandra Pouchet Paquet, and John Roberts. When I was still in Trinidad, I benefited greatly from conversations with Gordon Rohlehr of the English Department of the University of the West Indies. I am also grateful to a number of individuals who offered valuable information or commented on portions of the manuscript: Ray Allen, Patricia Alleyne, Vaneisa Baksh, Daniel Crowley, Ivor Ferriera, Ray Funk, Don Hill, Danny Jagan, Kim Johnson, Aisha Khan, Ann Lee, Mario Montaño, Valerie Taylor, Jeffrey Thomas, and Kevin Yelvington. Special thanks to Patricia Smith and Alison Anderson of the University of Pennsylvania Press for their suggestions for improving the manuscript, and to Junia Browne for providing the majority of the photographs included with the text.

I must mention my parents, who over the years have provided the encouragement and advice that help make a study of this kind possible. Final thanks go to Denise Stephenson Stuempfle, whose years of experience in both the library system and the music world of Trinidad contributed immeasurably to this study. From the early days of the research through the final revision, she offered good-natured support, made countless suggestions, and shared my devotion to pan from J'Ouvert with Merrytones in Port of Spain to Desperadoes in concert in New York.

Introduction

When steelbands first appeared on the streets of Port of Spain and other towns in Trinidad, they astonished the colony's populace. In the years to come this astonishment would turn to disdain and eventually to pride. The occasion of the steelbands' birth was Carnival—the annual contest of the imagination in Trinidad in which competitors creatively utilize all available resources. It was during the intense, festive moments of Carnival street performance, or at least in preparation for such moments, that the first pans were forged. The subsequent development of these instruments was very rapid. It took only a little over a decade to transform an assortment of metal containers into an orchestra of high-precision instruments with bell-like tones. Today, immense steelbands with multiple sections perform intricate arrangements of local calypsos, North American and Latin American popular tunes, and European classical pieces.

The panmen's transformation of objects from their environment into musical instruments is one representation of the whole creative process by which Trinidadians have defined themselves as a people. In fact, the emergence of the steelband and its development up to the present parallel the emergence and development of Trinidad and Tobago itself as a nation. To a large extent, nation-building has involved negotiations between Trinidad and Tobago's various ethnic groups and socioeconomic classes; and patterns of conflict and consensus in these negotiations have, at the same time, been played out in the dramas of the steelband movement. Similarly, the problems and successes of nation-building are paralleled by a sense of struggle and achievement among panmen. Parallels such as these suggest that pan embodies some of the essential contours of the Trinidadian experience and can be interpreted as one of the central symbols of the nation. In festive steelband performances and in discussions about these performances, many Trinidadians find a means of exploring various visions of themselves.[1]

The steelband is derived from the Trinidadian *tamboo bamboo* band, an ensemble consisting of different sized pieces of bamboo that were struck together or stamped on the ground during Carnival street processions. During the 1930s members of these ensembles began beating on metal containers and other objects, and by around 1940 a few of the bands in Port of Spain had discarded their bamboo altogether. Soon it was discovered that the bottoms of containers could be pounded into different shapes to produce musical tones when struck with sticks. A period of great experimentation followed and the early steelband began to take form.

The creators of the steelband were generally young and of African descent.[2] In addition, they belonged to that sector of society that Trinidadians refer to as *grass-roots*: the working class, the marginally employed, and the unemployed. Their bands were based in different neighborhoods and villages and intense rivalries ensued as they developed their new instruments. The grass-roots basis of the music and the violent clashes in which bands sometimes engaged evoked much hostility from the middle and upper classes and even from many members of the grass-roots class itself. Essentially the new music was perceived as a threat to the social order and legal restrictions were soon placed on its performance.

By the late 1940s, however, some civic leaders, artists, and politicians with nationalist sentiments were defending the panmen, encouraging them to form an association, and presenting their bands in shows that highlighted local music and dance to primarily middle class audiences. By the 1950s panmen were performing at a wide variety of social occasions, some middle class youths had begun forming bands of their own, and the movement as a whole had received the official support of the government. When Trinidad and Tobago gained its independence from Britain in 1962, pan was already a national symbol. This institutionalization of the movement was paralleled by further musical developments. The fabrication of pans from large-sized oil drums was initiated, repertoires were expanded, and musical arrangements became more complex.

During the 1960s businesses began to sponsor steelbands and state involvement in the movement increased. By the 1970s pan instruction was being offered in a number of schools, and women began joining bands. Today there are scores of steelbands in Trinidad and Tobago that appear in Carnival and other competitions and in community and concert settings. In addition, there are a number of virtuoso pan soloists who perform and record with conventional musical ensembles. These soloists and some of the best-known steelbands regularly perform overseas and have been attracting wider audiences to pan.

The story of the steelband movement outlined above is a version of a narrative on pan that is ubiquitous in Trinidad. This master narrative highlights the transformation of the steelband from a widely condemned form of grass-roots leisure into a respected national art and symbol. Emphasis is placed both on the panmen's struggle and on their achievements. Since Trinidadians tend to comprehend the steelband experience through this master narrative, some version of the story occurs in most oral and written discussions of the movement.

Many of the individuals who were involved in the actual creation of the first pans are still alive, and their reminiscing and debating have generated a lively oral history tradition full of rich, though often conflicting, details. Recently there has been a growing effort to record what these early panmen have to say. The publication of the reminiscences of some of the pan innovators and close observers of the movement constitutes one of the types of literature available on the steelband. These accounts provide a vivid sense of places, bands, personalities, and important occasions in steelband history, and tend to emphasize themes of individual creativity, struggle, and accomplishment. The fullest example of this genre of steelband literature is George Goddard's *Forty Years in the Steelbands,* which includes not only Goddard's personal experiences but his newspaper and oral history research.[3]

Analytical study of pan has its roots in the work of three scholars from Trinidad and Tobago: J. D. Elder, Errol Hill, and Lloyd Braithwaite.[4] The writings of these individuals demonstrate a keen appreciation and advocacy of the steelband as a local art. Pan is examined in the context of other Carnival artistic traditions and attention is given to the gradual social acceptance of the movement, the consequences of class and color, and the music's national significance. The concerns of these three scholars have continued to influence the anthropological, sociological, and historical research on the steelband that has since occurred.[5] Unfortunately, relatively little musicological research on pan has been published. Part of the problem here is that no known recordings of steelbands were made before the early 1950s, by which time the ensembles were already quite developed. So it is difficult to know, let alone analyze, what the early steelbands sounded like.[6]

The present study follows the steelband master narrative and the themes outlined by Elder, Hill, and Braithwaite. However, my discussion attempts to provide both greater historical and ethnographic detail on the steelband and a fuller analysis of how the movement is interrelated with the social, political, and economic developments that have shaped Trinidad and Tobago as a nation. Special attention is given to pan's relationship to the grass-roots uprisings of the late 1930s and 1940s, the American presence in the colony during World War II, the nationalist movement of the 1940s and 1950s, the aftermath of independence in 1962, the Black Power protests of 1970, the oil boom in the 1970s, and the recession in the 1980s and 1990s. Though I attempt to provide some sense of the panmen's particular experiences and goals over the years, I do not present accounts of all of the individuals and bands who have made significant contributions to the movement. Rather, I focus on describing and interpreting patterns in the emergence and institutionalization of pan. It should be noted that my discussion is for the most part restricted geographically to the capital city of Port of Spain, since it is here that the movement originated, was first institutionalized, and continues to have its fullest manifestation.

My examination of the steelband devotes considerable attention to steelband performances: those occasions where pannists have presented their music to audiences, ranging from the streets at Carnival to the concert hall stage. The musical dimensions of these performances are not examined at any length. Though I do deal with some basic patterns in instrumentation, repertoire, and style, this study includes no musicological analysis. Instead, I focus on the social and symbolic aspects of performances—on how people use pan at social occasions and what it means to them. Essentially I attempt to reveal how performance practices have been shaped in the course of the movement's development and what they express about Trinidadian social relations and notions of national identity.

In short, the present study is intended to be a history of the steelband movement as a cultural phenomenon, with culture conceived of as a temporal and flexible system of symbols which is enacted and manifested in practices. This perspective is in some respects similar to the type advocated by Marshall Sahlins in his historical essays on Hawaii, in which he elucidates how history is culturally ordered, while cultural schemes are historically ordered. In other words, people organize their projects in life in accordance with their cultural understandings, while the specific circumstances of action lead them to alter their cultural schemes. So human action or history always involves both cultural reproduction and cultural change. Such concerns have recently been developed by Renato Rosaldo, who articulates a form of social and cultural analysis that emphasizes subjectivity, action, particularity, and history. Instead of searching for law-like generalizations or treating events as programmed cultural routines, Rosaldo suggests a focus on how specific events unfold in time through human agency and spontaneity.[7]

In the following chapters I examine the steelband movement in terms of the interrelatedness of culture and history. I outline the various Trinidadian cultural traditions that have structured developments in the steelband movement and detail the historical circumstances that have in turn altered cultural patterns. My basic objective is to reveal how continuity and innovation in the pan movement are related to particular social, political, and economic conditions, trends, and events. Ideally the reader will gain a sense of the steelband as a historically situated cultural process, that is, an expressive tradition that has been created, perpetuated, and changed through the practical actions of specific groups and individuals.

In focusing on pan as symbol and performance, I draw on the theoretical frameworks of Victor Turner and Roger Abrahams. Turner, in his discussions of symbolism and the dynamics of social life, argues that symbols are not units in abstract, atemporal systems but resources that are creatively used by actors with particular, and often differing, intentions and goals. He uses the concept of "social dramas" to describe those sequences of events in history in which competing parties employ symbols in the expression and resolution of conflicts. In a somewhat similar fashion, Abrahams utilizes the concept of performance to describe the special occasions in social life in which the enactment of expressive traditions is subject to evaluation by audiences. At these occasions, performers creatively adapt traditions to accomplish specific aesthetic and social goals—to move their audiences in particular ways. Performances are not simply static reflections of the social order but events in which the social order is produced, examined, and contested.[8]

Since the 1970s there has been an increasing amount of anthropological study of music as symbol and performance. Researchers have investigated the characteristics of musical events and their meanings and have revealed how musical performances play an active role in maintaining and changing social values and relationships. Considerable attention has been given to music and social conflict: to how musical styles can serve as expressions of ethnic and class based concerns and to how the meanings of musical practices are subject to negotiations between different groups.[9]

In the present study I elucidate the ways in which steelband performance practices and their meanings have been created and re-created in the course of time. Performances are examined both as innovative responses to specific social conditions and as an active force in shaping Trinidadian life. In addition, I suggest that the history of the steelband movement can be thought of as a series of negotiations or social dramas in which different ethnic groups, classes, organizations, alliances, and individuals have all attempted to define and use the steelband according to their own particular values and interests.[10] Sometimes these dramas have taken the form of struggles. At other times they have involved accommodation and collaboration rather than intense and irreconcilable conflict. In both cases it is apparent that the meanings that the steelband carries are complex: different groups in the society have interpreted and continue to interpret pan in different ways.

In order to comprehend the essential characteristics of the steelband movement, it is crucial to keep in mind that the music emerged under colonialism and developed during a period of decolonization. For readers not familiar with Trinidad's history, some brief comments on the island's colonial past and transition to independence will be helpful.

When Christopher Columbus reached Trinidad in 1498, the island was inhabited by Caribs and Arawak-related peoples. The first permanent Spanish settlement was not established until 1592, and for the following two centuries Trinidad was neglected and undeveloped. In 1783 Spain issued a Cedula of Population that opened the island up to settlement by Catholics from elsewhere in the Caribbean. French and free colored planters and their enslaved Africans began arriving from islands such as Grenada, St. Lucia, Martinique, and Guadeloupe. By the end of the century Trinidad had become a full-scale plantation society with sugar as its primary product, and Port of Spain had developed into a bustling commercial and residential center. The Africans who worked the plantations belonged to a range of peoples from the western and central regions of the African continent and greatly outnumbered the French and Spanish planters. The French and Spanish were also outnumbered by the population of free coloreds and free Africans, which included slave-holding planters, small farmers, artisans, and servants.

In 1797 Trinidad was captured by Britain, and in the following years British officials, merchants, planters, and their enslaved Africans contributed to the island's growing population. For the remainder of the nineteenth century, the British and French struggled over the institutions and the dominant cultural orientation of the colony. Though the British controlled the government, French cultural influence remained strong. In fact, *Patois,* a French- and African-derived Creole language, was the primary means of communication for the majority of Africans throughout the nineteenth century.

Emancipation was initiated in 1834 and completed in 1838, following a four-year apprenticeship period. Though Africans continued to provide some labor on the sugar plantations, many established small independent farms. These African peasants, along with Venezuelan "peons" (immigrants of "mixed" Spanish, Amerindian, and African descent), played a major role in the development of the cocoa industry in Trinidad during the second half of the nineteenth century. During this same period a growing number of Africans migrated to Port of Spain and other towns, where they worked as tradesmen and laborers or remained unemployed.

As Africans left the plantations, a serious labor shortage developed. In an effort to preserve the colony's sugar economy, planters and officials recruited Africans from more populated West Indian islands as well as Old World Africans who had been liberated from the slave trade, Portuguese from Madeira, and Chinese. However, most members of these groups soon left the plantations to engage in other economic pursuits. Many of the Portuguese and Chinese eventually became shopkeepers.

An abundant source of labor for the plantations was finally found in India. Between 1845 and 1917 over 140,000 Indians were brought to Trinidad as indentured laborers to serve on the sugar estates. By the end of the century most had left the estates to become small cultivators, due to the decline of the sugar industry and to the expiration of their periods of indentureship. Though some Indians returned to India, the majority stayed and gradually began to conceive of Trinidad as a home. Indian cultural traditions were perpetuated and re-created, and the extended family, religious institutions (Hindu and Muslim), and the village were foci of Indian life and vehicles for maintaining some degree of social distance from the rest of the colony's population. To a large extent, Indians were denigrated by other ethnic groups because of their engagement in what were considered low-status types of agricultural work and because of their foreign cultural practices. At the same time, Indians continued to value their own traditions and resisted assimilation.

This history of voluntary and forced migration made Trinidad one of the most ethnically complex places in the world. As the diverse African, European, and Asian groups settled in the colony, they all began to participate in what Edward Kamau Brathwaite and other scholars have described as a process of creolization.[11] Creolization is the cultural interaction and convergence (or "interculturation") that accompanied the ongoing social interactions between the variety of peoples in the plantation regions of the Americas. Members of the different populations creatively drew on their diverse cultural heritages in adjusting to their new natural and social environments. In each setting, a creole culture consisting of both reinterpreted Old World and distinctively local cultural symbols and practices gradually emerged.

A creole culture can be conceptualized, in somewhat simplified terms, as a set of continua. In a locale like Trinidad, the continua reflected varying degrees of interculturation within and between the different African, European, and Asian populations. Though creolization is an ongoing process and cultural forms are continually altered through action, Trinidadians constructed and maintained different ethnic categories to refer to the range of practices in their society. Hence different customs could be labeled in terms of categories such as "African," "Indian," or "British," in spite of cultural change. In a similar fashion, Trinidadians placed themselves in such categories according to perceptions of phenotypes, ancestries, and behaviors.

Creolization did not occur in a harmonious manner, however, but within the context of oppression that is intrinsic to any colonial society. The paramount concerns of a colonial society are order and control. To a substantial extent the perpetuation of the colonial system is dependent on political and economic control and on the brute force of the militia and the police. However, the dominant group is usually vastly outnumbered by the dominated and thus must depend not only on force but on cultural influence for its continued existence. Though Raymond Williams utilizes the concept of cultural domination or hegemony primarily in reference to metropolitan societies, this concept is also applicable to colonial societies.[12] Cultural hegemony is the process whereby the system of meanings, values, and practices of the dominant group permeates the whole society to the extent that day to day action and experience of even the most mundane type are affected. In a colonial society like Trinidad, European cultural values and beliefs, including an ideology of European superiority, were imposed on the whole society via such institutions as plantation management, colonial administration, courts, churches, and schools.

Williams stresses, however, that a hegemony is never total or exclusive. There are always cultural practices outside the hegemonic order which may become forms of resistance. Thus a hegemony must be continually defended and redefined. Certainly the European hegemony in Trinidad was never all-encompassing: African- and Indian-derived practices and emergent local customs continued to flourish. To the extent that some of these practices became counter-hegemonic or tools of resistance, cultural struggles developed within the society. Grass-roots Africans and Indians asserted themselves through cultural practices ranging from festivals to peasant agriculture, while the dominant European groups attempted to suppress or contain such practices. The result was creole cultural continua structured by relationships of power. To a substantial extent, the dominant groups succeeded in maintaining a cultural orientation in the society in which European-derived practices were perceived as having a high status while African- and Indian-derived practices were considered to be of low status.

Trinidad's cultural hegemony, social structure, and plantation economy have been gradually altered in the course of the twentieth century. Though the island has continued to produce sugar, cocoa, and other agricultural goods, its economy during the past century has been increasingly dominated by oil. British, American, and local firms have all participated in oil production and refining over the years, and the industry has provided Trinidad with a standard of living relatively higher than that found in most other parts of the Caribbean. Since World War II manufacturing has been a significant part of the economy, and at present there is production of a range of commodities such as steel, chemicals, and fertilizer. In the post-independence period, much of Trinidad's oil, sugar, and manufacturing industries became state-owned. Though there have been some efforts at privatization in recent years, Trinidad continues to have a large public sector. As mentioned in the Preface, Trinidad has never relied heavily on tourism. With the decline in the oil industry, however, there has been increasing interest in developing this source of income.

Economic growth during the twentieth century and progress toward independence affected all of Trinidad's ethnic groups and classes.[13] From the peasants, laborers, and artisans of the nineteenth century, an African and colored grass-roots class developed that was increasingly urbanized and continued to include a substantial number of unemployed persons. Meanwhile, the expansion of educational opportunities in the latter part of the nineteenth century was instrumental to the growth of an African and colored middle class that included teachers, lawyers, doctors, civil servants, and clerks. It was the African and colored grass-roots and middle classes that were most prominent in the growing resistance to colonial rule during the twentieth century. The middle class actually engineered the process of decolonization during the 1950s and early 1960s and assumed political power from the British.

The majority of Indians have remained in rural areas in the course of the twentieth century, though there has been increasing urban migration. Improved access to education since the 1930s contributed to the gradual rise of an Indian middle class. Indians moved into the professions, became quite successful in the commercial sector, and eventually obtained jobs in the civil service. With decolonization during the 1950s, tensions between Indians and Africans increased due to competition over political power and economic opportunities.

By the beginning of the twentieth century, the local French and British had to a large extent resolved their differences and merged into a single anglophone class known as "French Creoles."[14] This upper class lost its political power during the 1950s but continues to wield considerable economic influence in business, finance, and landholding. Other elements of Trinidad's population include the Chinese, who remain active in business, and Syrians and Lebanese, who immigrated in the early part of the century as peddlers and have since become merchants.

Trinidad's current population of approximately 1.2 million is 41 percent African, 40 percent Indian, 17 percent "mixed," and 2 percent European, Chinese, Syrian, or Lebanese. Virtually the entire population speaks Trinidadian Standard and/or Creole English as a primary language and the adult literacy rate is 96 percent. Due to a depressed economy since the early 1980s, over 18 percent of the population is unemployed.[15]

Though economic growth, the expansion of the middle class, intermarriage, and creolization have all helped integrate Trinidadian society, there is still considerable cultural diversity, with people engaging in a wide range of cultural projects and styles. In recent years anthropologists have vigorously questioned the traditional concept of culture as a self-contained, unified, and homogeneous system within a particular society and have emphasized the substantial differentiation and flexibility of cultural schemes. It has also been stressed that societies have never existed in isolation with independent cultures, but have long histories of mutual influence. Such interaction obviously increased dramatically over the past five centuries with the development of global imperialism.[16]

If a revision of the concept of culture as self-contained and unified is necessary in the study of societies in general, it is emphatically required for any analysis of Caribbean societies. Caribbean societies are places where almost everyone has roots somewhere else. These are new societies, formed over the last few hundred years, by diverse peoples with differing interests and objectives. In the course of their histories, Caribbean societies have been intimately connected with their metropoles and in more recent years with North America, through trade, the mass media, and cyclical migration. In the Caribbean it is exceedingly difficult to define cultural units or boundaries of any type.

Though Trinidad is one of the most culturally diverse Caribbean societies, members of its population do have varying degrees of awareness of each other's way of life and there is a considerable body of local notions and practices that most people share.[17] It is from perceptions of distinctively local cultural practices that a sense of national identity has gradually developed. However, there is no single conception of this identity. Rather, debate rages over exactly what constitutes the national culture. A nation of course is always an invention—the product of a population imagining a single community and selecting symbols of this community.[18] In a new and diverse nation like Trinidad, this process of imagination and selection is particularly vibrant and contentious.

It is in terms of this history of colonialism and decolonization, class hegemony and resistance, and ethnic diversity and creolization that the development of the steelband movement must be understood. The steelband was a grass-roots African creation that incorporated elements of a range of cultural traditions in the society. Though it originated under an oppressive colonial system in which everything grass-roots and African was denigrated, it was gradually championed as an important local art as Trinidad underwent decolonization, and the concern with defining a national identity grew. Today the majority of pannists continue to be of African descent, but steelbands also include individuals of other ethnic backgrounds and the music receives strong support from at least some members of all ethnic groups. Still, a number of Indians, in particular, do not identify with pan and do not accept it as a national symbol.

This questioning of the steelband's national significance is examined in more detail in the concluding chapter of this study. At this point, however, I should note that my intention is not to suggest that pan is *the* symbol of Trinidad. Rather, I argue that pan's significance has been contested in one manner or another since its inception and that these contestations and their accompanying social dramas provide a window into Trinidad's social and cultural history.

Such a perspective on pan is in some ways similar to C.L.R. James's examination of cricket in his classic *Beyond a Boundary*.[19] James demonstrates that cricket can be used as a vehicle for insights into West Indian social structure and history, particularly color and class relations and nationalism. Certainly the development of West Indian cricket in the course of the twentieth century was closely connected to the gradual emergence of independent West Indian nations, in that both involved local accomplishment and pride in response to imperial hegemony. A similar case can be made for the steelband and Trinidad. The development of the steelband movement and the process of decolonization in Trinidad were intertwined, and the movement has continued to encompass many of the tensions and aspirations of the new nation.

Works such as James's demonstrate the value of the study of popular culture for a fuller understanding of Caribbean societies. In the 1970s Kamau Brathwaite lamented the insufficient attention in Caribbean scholarship to the "inner plantation." Brathwaite noted that scholars generally concentrated on the major economic and political aspects of Caribbean societies without paying enough attention to the expressive life of the masses.[20] Though there has been some study of traditional cultural forms in the Caribbean for decades, such research has increased since the 1970s. In recent years there has been considerable study of musics such as calypso, reggae, salsa, and zouk; religions such as Santería, Vodou, and Rastafari; celebrations such as Carnival, saints' festivals, and East Indian religious observances; and the range of Caribbean Creole languages and verbal genres.[21]

Now social and cultural researchers are realizing what Caribbean novelists, poets, playwrights, and essayists have understood for years: that traditional forms of expressive culture provide a means for disclosing fundamental aspects of the Caribbean experience. Through studying such expressive forms, we can gain not only an appreciation of their aesthetic qualities but a much broader and nuanced sense of how Caribbean peoples have perceived their worlds in the course of their histories of slavery, emancipation, peasantry formation, urbanization, and decolonization.

Much of the study of decolonization and nationalism in the Caribbean continues to focus on political figures, movements, and ideologies, and on institutional change. There is still insufficient attention to the role of local expressive forms in the creation and negotiation of national identities. Throughout the Caribbean and the Americas as a whole, societies have selected various emergent, creolized art forms to represent themselves. The present examination of the steelband will ideally contribute to further comparative research on the convergence of African, European, Asian, and Amerindian cultural heritages in the creation of New World national identities.

The following chapters are organized chronologically. Chapter One provides a sketch of the festive and musical traditions in nineteenth- and early twentieth-century Trinidad that were precursors of the steelband movement. Some comparisons with similar creolized cultural traditions from other parts of the Caribbean are also offered. Chapter Two deals with the emergence of the steelband as a creative adaptation of traditional cultural practices. Attention is given to the characteristics of the early steelband, the range of performance contexts, the panmen's cultural style, and the condemnation of their music.

Chapter Three examines the institutionalization of the steelband: nationalist advocacy of the music, the formal organization of the movement, new performance settings, musical developments, and the rise of middle class bands. These developments are considered in the context of decolonization. Chapter Four deals with the steelband movement in the post-independence period of the 1960s and 1970s. The focus here is on state and corporate involvement in the movement and the expanding musical dimensions of the bands. The various dilemmas faced by the newly independent nation and the pan movement, including the challenges posed by the Black Power uprising of 1970, are also discussed.

Chapter Five is an overview of the steelband movement in contemporary Trinidad. Ethnographic observations and interviews from the late 1980s provide the basis for a description of the pan life, the growing involvement of women in pan, relationships between steelbands and communities, the continued roles of the state and the corporate sector in the movement, and the range of steelband performance contexts. I have returned to Trinidad for several brief visits since the original period of research, and I occasionally refer to more recent events. By and large the essential characteristics of the steelband movement in the 1980s have continued into the 1990s.

In Chapter Six I outline the complex symbolism of the steelband today in terms of cultural continuity and change in the course of the movement's history. I suggest that pan's multiplicity of meanings has resulted from a process in which colonial hegemony has been disrupted by local creativity and initiative, and in which different ethnic groups and socioeconomic classes have advocated diverse conceptions of a national identity in their negotiation of political power. Like Jamaican reggae, Dominican merengue, and Haitian dance music, the steelband is an expressive tradition through which a Caribbean people has attempted to sort out its complicated past and define its place in the global order of nations. Over the years steelband performances have been occasions in which Trinidadians have re-created and affirmed their various cultural traditions and in which local innovation and achievement have assumed international significance.

Chapter One
Festive and Musical Traditions in Trinidad

The creators of the steelband in the 1930s and 1940s drew on musical and festive traditions that had been developing in Trinidad for well over a century. Their bands as social organizations were a new manifestation of a long lineage of local associations with festive orientations, while their pans were modeled on bamboo instruments, which in an earlier era had been modeled on skin drums. The symbolic significance of the music was similarly rooted in tradition. African percussion in Trinidad, and elsewhere in the plantation regions of the Americas, was generally associated with celebration, power, resistance, and identity, and these themes became an integral part of the steelband experience. At the same time, public condemnation of the steelband derived from a well-established discourse on the immorality and disruptiveness of African percussion and related forms of festive expression. Given these continuities, an examination of the nineteenth- and early twentieth-century musical and festive traditions that preceded the advent of the steelband is crucial to an understanding of the particular characteristics of this new art form and to how it was perceived and utilized by its inventors and others in the society. Two particularly salient aspects of the development of these traditions in Trinidad were intercultural exchange, and conflict between efforts to maintain a colonial social and cultural order and the rise of local social groupings and cultural practices.

The Emergence of Creole Festivity

By the beginning of the nineteenth century, Trinidad had developed into a full-scale plantation society structured by hegemonic European-derived cultural traditions and alternative African-derived traditions. Elite festivity and music were dominated by the French, who had managed to establish something of an aristocratic cultural style in this frontier colony. Planters lived in comfortable houses, dressed fashionably, and enjoyed a full schedule of balls, dinners, concerts, and other recreations, particularly from Christmas to Carnival. Sophisticated Port of Spain featured dramatic companies, dance halls, and soirées in private homes with music provided by pianos, harpsichords, or harps.[1]

Meanwhile, the enslaved inhabitants of Trinidad drew on West and Central African heritages to develop their own artistic and recreational practices. The high points of Afro-Trinidadian social life were the dances held during periods outside the plantation work routine: times of leisure (Saturday nights and Sundays) or times of festivity (especially Christmas and Easter). These dances generally occurred in spaces outside the land directly controlled by the planters: either in the Africans' yards and homes or on the provision grounds where they grew their own food. Among the dance types were the *kalinda*, the *bel air* or *bele*, the *jhouba*, and the *bamboula*, while the accompanying instruments included various types of skin drums and *chac-chacs* (gourd rattles). Little is known about the characteristics of these dances in pre-emancipation Trinidad since recorded descriptions are scant and since the dance names mentioned have been used to refer to a range of dance styles in different parts of the Caribbean at different points in time.[2]

Some of the Africans' dance events were primarily religious in nature while other occasions were basically recreational. For example, Africans from different estates often took turns hosting weekend *fetes* or parties. According to one observer,

> They dress in their best clothes, dance both Creole and African dances, drink lemonade and rum and water; but on particular occasions they have subscription balls, or what they call boquet balls, so named from the king and queen of the night wearing a nosegay, which they present, when leaving the table, to two others, who preside at the next entertainment in the same capacity. . . .[3]

The planters had mixed attitudes toward African dances and the accompanying drumming. To some extent they viewed them as amusing pastimes that improved the Africans' morale. At the same time they perceived them as "barbaric" and "lewd"—as threats to European cultural values. Such perceptions were heightened by the fact that the dances often occurred on the Christian Sabbath. There was also an underlying fear that the drumming and dancing could inspire rebellion; in fact these activities had been connected with revolts at various times and places in the New World. Some restrictions were placed on dances, but apparently had limited effect in discouraging or containing the events.

In pre-emancipation Trinidad, Christmas was the celebration that involved the greatest participation by the diverse segments of the population. Africans were given considerable freedom to enjoy themselves during the Christmas season, but it was also believed that this freedom sometimes led to insurrections. Thus every year at this time martial law was declared, business came to a halt, and all freemen were required to enlist in a militia. There were a variety of corps, with names like "Royal Trinidad Light Dragoons," "St. Anne's Hussars," "Diego Martin's Chasseurs and Infantry," and "St. Joseph's Light Cavalry." By 1820 tents and refreshments were even provided for spectators when the Governor reviewed the regiments' drills. Obviously the militia not only was a means of maintaining order but had become a spectacle in which there was much aesthetic appreciation of uniforms, maneuvers, and weaponry. In addition to the drills, the members of the militia and their ladies indulged in a series of balls and dinners. This association between festivity and military display was to have lasting significance in Trinidad.

Though enslaved Africans were excluded from the affairs of the militia, they were encouraged to celebrate the Christmas season. Mrs. A. C. Carmichael, the wife of a planter in Trinidad during the 1820s, describes scenes of Christmas festivity that consisted of all-night dancing to the accompaniment of drums and chac-chacs. Dress for the women included muslin trimmed with colored satin and ribbons, silk stockings, kid shoes, Madras handkerchiefs, necklaces, and earrings; the men wore embroidered trousers, white jackets, and high collars. Mrs. Carmichael also recollects a Christmas morning when Africans from the plantation came to her door to make "long speeches, full of good wishes," and another occasion when a group from a neighboring estate, including two fiddlers whose hats and fiddles were decorated with multicolored ribbons, arrived to offer entertainment.[4]

Christmas was celebrated in a similar fashion elsewhere in the British West Indies. For example, there are reports from Jamaica of Africans arriving at planters' homes where they were treated to punch. Men wore white waistcoats, silk stockings, cocked hats, and other finery, while women dressed in muslin and cambric. Along with exuberant dancing accompanied by fiddle and drum ensembles, there were parodies of British minuet steps and performances of satirical songs about the masters.[5] Clearly Christmas in the West Indies was a time when plantation social conventions were partially suspended and Africans and Europeans imitated and experimented with each other's cultural styles. Though creolization was integral to plantation life throughout the year, cultural exchange intensified at festive occasions such as Christmas, when the crossing of social boundaries became possible.

While Africans participated in the planters' celebrations, they also pursued their own agendas during the Christmas season. The planters' fear that Christmas festivity could lead to rebellion almost became a reality in Trinidad in 1805. That December a series of events occurred that reveal the Afro-Trinidadian world in all of its complexity and grandeur. On different occasions planters heard Africans shaking chac-chacs and singing a song:

> The bread we eat
> Is the white man's flesh,
> The wine we drink
> Is the white man's blood.

Various individuals were picked up by authorities and an inquiry followed. During the inquiry it was discovered that enslaved Africans throughout the island, but particularly in districts around Port of Spain, were organized into secret regiments. Some of these regiments consisted only of Creoles (locally born Africans), some consisted of Old World Africans, while others comprised individuals from particular islands such as Martinique and Grenada. The regiments had names like "Convoi de St. Georges," "Regiment Macaque," and "Regiment Danois," and included kings and queens, princes and princesses, dauphins and dauphines, and other official personnel. The kings of these associations had flags and elaborate uniforms. At night they and other figures visited each other, exchanged courtesies, and consumed food. Initiation rites, mock communions, dances, and martial games were also part of the regiments' activities. Eventually the authorities determined that a rebellion had been planned for Christmas Day. According to witnesses, the regiments intended to behead a couple of planters, have a pork dinner, dance in a plantation sugar mill, drink holy water at another estate, and finally pillage and burn their way into Port of Spain. The inquiry was soon followed by executions and other forms of punishment.[6]

The Trinidadian underground regiments are an example of African associations that have existed throughout the Americas. These associations were often rooted in African nations such as the Congo, Yoruba, Ewe, or Mandingo. However, Roger Bastide has noted that, with the suppression of the slave trade and intermarriage among different African peoples, associations gradually lost their ethnic basis and became cultural traditions that attracted peoples of different ancestries.[7]

African associations had various functions such as religious observance, artistic performance, recreation, and mutual aid. Much of their activity occurred in private though they also engaged in public displays, particularly during holidays.

In Cuba, for example, associations were known as *cabildos* and included both enslaved and free Africans. They held private festivities in members' houses and for *Dia de Reyes* (Epiphany) elected kings and queens and engaged in masked processions on the streets behind official banners. In Peru cabildos bought houses on the outskirts of Lima and had kings, queens, ladies-in-waiting, and orchestras. There were also organizations in Brazil that owned suburban houses where they engaged in religious ceremonies and planned rebellions. At Christmas time in St. Thomas, enslaved Africans on each estate elected a king, queen, prince, and princess. Dances were held to the accompaniment of drums and singing while maids of honor waved flags over the heads of the queens.[8]

Africans in St. Lucia were organized into two "societies": the Roses and the Marguerites, named after their patron saints. Each society had three kings and three queens and rented a house in Castries for periodic meetings. At these meetings members rehearsed *belairs*, songs which praised their own society and attacked the opposing group, and were censured by kings if they engaged in improper conduct. During festive occasions men and women wore expensive outfits and danced and sang to the accompaniment of drum ensembles. The circle of dancers was marked by blazing flambeaux and red or blue flags and banners with gilt letters.[9]

A similar type of festive association existed in Jamaica. At Christmas young women organized themselves into rival "sets," the Blues and the Reds (or Yellows), and each group chose a queen. They dressed in matching finery and jewelry that was often provided by their mistresses. Sometimes sets were also differentiated by skin color. Processions in the towns and between estates featured distinguishing flags, singing, and such instrumentation as drums, tambourines, fiddles, and fifes. Members of the sets would stop and dance at houses along the way, including those of masters or managers.[10]

The characteristics of these various types of New World African associations help place the Trinidadian underground regiments in perspective. The regiments and other associations had hierarchies of royal personnel, displayed elaborate costumes and identifying flags, and engaged in a range of expressive activities. In essence, they constituted an alternative social and cultural order to that of the dominant plantation regime. They were vehicles through which Africans organized themselves on their own terms and for their own purposes. While Africans were defined as slaves by Europeans, in their own associations they had the identity and power of royalty. In these settings they drew on African and European traditions of hierarchy, dress, and performance to forge creole festive practices. For example, both the royal processions of the Congo and the "march-pasts" of French military regiments were among the models for the associations' elaborate processions in the New World.[11]

The associations' relationships with the dominant social classes varied. The Jamaican sets were patronized by the planters and maintained a congenial orientation. The Cuban cabildos were originally supported by authorities but this support was gradually withdrawn as the associations' autonomy and power increased.[12] The Trinidadian regiments were secret and subversive. Though they were suppressed after their attempted uprising, they appear to have provided a foundation for subsequent forms of festive organizations. A number of their festive characteristics (such as hierarchies, percussion, and flags) have reappeared over the years in various Carnival organizations, including steelbands.

Carnival in Trinidad

Though Christmas was important to Africans in pre-emancipation Trinidad in both the public and private spheres of their lives, they were virtually excluded from participation in Carnival, the other major festival in the yearly plantation cycle. Carnival was primarily a celebration for the French planter class. Free coloreds also observed Carnival but were prohibited from engaging in festivities with Europeans. For the French planters, Carnival season followed directly from Christmas and included masquerade balls with European and African music and dancing, promenading on the streets of Port of Spain with masks, house-to-house visiting, and general buffoonery. One popular masquerade of the period was the *nègre jardin* (field black) which was inspired by activities that occurred during sugar-cane fires. When a fire broke out at night on a plantation, gangs of Africans from the neighboring estates would march to the scene with torches, while drivers blew horns and cracked whips. Planters replicated the drama of these events at Carnival by dressing up as field laborers and *mulâtresses*, forming bands, parading with torches and drums, and performing Afro-Caribbean dances such as the kalinda and bamboula.[13]

Carnival, like Christmas, was thus a time of permissiveness and boundary-crossing in which the planter class could enact imagined versions of African dress, music, dance, and work. This playful inversion of the plantation social order through masquerade perhaps explains why Africans were excluded from Carnival: the potential for rebellion would have been even greater than at Christmas.

After emancipation (1834-1838) Carnival began to assume a very different orientation. During the 1834 Carnival, before emancipation even went into effect, a band of Africans masqueraded as and parodied one of the Christmas militia regiments. By the time of the 1838 Carnival, the editor of the *Port-of-Spain Gazette* described Africans in the streets enacting "disgusting and indecent scenes," "carrying a stuffed figure of a woman on a pole" and "yelling out a savage Guinea song."[14] In the following years Africans increasingly dominated Carnival and, in response, the European elite and the colored middle class withdrew from the street celebration of the festival. The elite continued to hold private balls, while the middle class engaged in house-to-house visits in which they played stringed instruments.

During this period Africans also developed a celebration held on August 1 to commemorate the emancipation. The festival was known as *Canboulay* (*Cannes Brulées*) and, like the planters' nègre jardin masquerade, was based on the scenes of the cane fires. In a manner similar to that of the pre-emancipation regiments, Africans organized themselves into bands with kings, queens, and other royal figures. Public processions were held in which participants dressed in the nègre jardin fashion, carried torches and hardwood sticks, and sang songs accompanied by drumming.[15]

Sometime during the 1840s Canboulay was moved from August 1 to Carnival, with processions beginning immediately after midnight of Carnival Sunday. In 1847 there was a report of a band of maskers covered with black varnish who carried hardwood sticks and dragged one member along by a chain and padlock; and an observer of the 1858 Carnival described how "commencing with the orgies on Sunday night, we have the fearful howling of a parcel of semi-savages emerging God knows where from, exhibiting hellish scenes and the most demoniacal representations of the days of slavery."[16] Along with these creole images and forms of expression, Carnival revelers played European characters such as Punchinellos, Pierrots, pirates, and Turks. There was also much parodying and ridiculing of the upper class, in both masque and song. For several decades after emancipation, the upper class and the press generally condemned Carnival as an obscene and immoral outrage, and periodically there were unsuccessful attempts to suppress the event through ordinances and police action.

During the 1860s and 1870s Carnival was taken over by the *jamettes* (*diamètres*), a term used at the time to refer to people who lived beneath the "diameter" or line of respectability. This was a period of substantial population growth in Port of Spain, due to migration of Africans from rural districts and from other West Indian islands. Many migrants ended up in overcrowded *barrack yards* [17] and shanty towns, and there was massive unemployment (defined as "vagrancy" by the upper class). These impoverished inhabitants of the city often lived off prostitution, petty crime, gambling, and odd jobs, and a whole underworld lifestyle developed that existed in opposition to the dominant culture of respectability. The jamettes organized themselves into rival territorial bands (with kings and other personnel) and engaged in violent clashes with each other, particularly during Carnival.[18]

In his study of crime in nineteenth-century Trinidad, David Trotman comments on the violence of the jamette world:

> Unemployed youths in their prime, condemned to a life of marginality because of the color of their skin and their refusal to be subjected to unrewarding employment on the plantation, were the major perpetrators of this violence. They used their untapped energies and endless time to focus on what they considered to be invasions of their territory, insults to their manhood, and alienation from the favors of their women by those whom they designated as rivals. Minor insults became major reasons for strife. They found many areas of activity in which they competed, and this rivalry resulted in numerous violent clashes.[19]

Trotman adds that those individuals "who were famed for their mastery in sticks, knives, or fists were able to take advantage of the companionship of the female population."[20]

The primary means by which the jamette bands expressed their rivalry was the kalinda, a dance that by this time had evolved into a form of stickfighting. Bands paraded the streets with sticks, torches, and drums, while a *chantwell* (lead singer) and a chorus performed songs that boasted of their stickfighters' abilities and challenged the fighters of rival bands. The stickfights themselves were bloody affairs in which flamboyantly dressed combatants struck each other with hardwood sticks to the accompaniment of drumming and singing. In his discussion of the territorial nature of these bands and their violence, Gordon Rohlehr proposes that migration and unemployment intensified conflict situations that were then ritualized in stickfights. The landless "were defining their territorial boundaries, making ritual claim to the land into which they had been so harshly indigenized, but to which they had no legal title." The stickfights themselves were games in which "manhood, status, identity within the group and on rare occasions life itself were at stake."[21]

During the 1870s public uproar concerning the "degeneration" of Carnival intensified, due both to the widespread violence and to the fact that "obscene" songs and masques, by then traditional to Carnival, were performed with even greater gusto by the jamettes. In 1881 the Chief of Police led 150 policemen in an attempt to suppress the bands. The force was met by a concerted attack from the bands in which 38 policemen were injured. Later in the day the Governor assured the revelers that he did not mean to interfere with their customs. The 1882 Carnival was peaceful, but a resurgence of violence in 1883 led to the passing of a Peace Preservation Ordinance in 1884, which empowered the Governor to prohibit by proclamation torch processions, drumming, dances, and assemblies of ten or more persons with sticks. Though such activities continued to exist in some form, the Canboulay tradition in Carnival was seriously curtailed.[22]

In the final years of the nineteenth century, other efforts were made to "improve" Carnival. With a decrease in violence and sexual explicitness in the festival, the middle and upper classes began once more to participate actively on the streets. Some middle and upper class individuals of French ancestry had retained a fondness for Carnival as an old French creole custom and resented the more blatant efforts by British officials to abolish the festival. Essentially they interpreted these efforts to be part of the general British program of anglicizing the island. At the same time businessmen began to realize that Carnival could be a valuable source of income. By the 1890s Ignacio Bodu, one businessman who was also an enthusiast of creole customs, was organizing and funding competitions for masquerade bands with the objective of improving the "moral tone" of Carnival.

Bodu was also a patron of calypso and during this period the calypso tradition was subjected to "improvement" as well. Calypso developed out of the French Patois song forms used in kalinda fights, Carnival processions, and a variety of traditional dances, all of which were accompanied by drums and chac-chacs. By the turn of the century some chantwells began performing in tents during the Carnival season for audiences that included middle and upper class patrons as well as grassroots folk. These calypsonians began to sing in English instead of Patois and started to use string bands instead of drums as accompaniment.[23] String bands were a Venezuelan-derived musical tradition and consisted of such instruments as guitars, four-stringed *quatros*, mandolins, violins, flutes, clarinets, and chac-chacs. These ensembles were also used as musical accompaniment for masquerading, particularly by the middle and upper classes.[24]

Though the middle and upper classes had reentered the street Carnival and were attempting to re-create the festival according to their own aesthetic preferences, the grass-roots class continued to perform and develop its Carnival traditions. The Peace Preservation Ordinance was only partially successful in suppressing the various elements of Canboulay. For example, an observer of Carnival during the early years of the twentieth century mentions a "torch-lit crowd" roaming the streets on Carnival Sunday night and describes a major clash between two stickfighting bands on Carnival Tuesday.[25] But stickfighting in the twentieth century generally involved individuals rather than bands and occurred in yards instead of in the streets. Drumming also continued to exist, particularly at more private sacred and secular occasions such as *Orisha* (*Shango*) feasts and beles. [26] However, the restrictions on drumming did encourage the development of new forms of percussion for Carnival. Errol Hill states that for a number of years after 1883 chac-chacs along with old boxes and bits of metal were used to accompany Carnival revelers.[27] Sometime around the turn of the century, *tamboo bamboo* (*tambour bamboo* —"bamboo drum") became the primary type of Carnival percussion.

The use of bamboo percussion occurs both in Africa and in other parts of the Caribbean. Among the Ga people of Ghana, for example, bamboo tubes are tuned to three different pitches and are stamped on slabs of stone. Three different rhythms are produced to accompany female choruses. In Venezuela bamboo stamping tubes known as *quitiplas* are made in four different sizes and accompany Afro-Venezuelan songs. Such instruments, in varying sizes, are known as *ganbos* in Haiti and became particularly popular during the United States military occupation (1915–1934), when drums were often seized and destroyed. In addition, different sized pieces of bamboo are cut to make *vaccines,* which are blown into and tapped with sticks. In Jamaica, striking or scraping bamboo with small sticks has been reported for festive occasions known as "tea meetings."[28]

Given this widespread occurrence of bamboo percussion among African peoples, it is likely that the tradition either existed in Trinidad on a limited scale during the nineteenth century or that it was introduced from elsewhere in the region. In any case, Trinidadians had developed tamboo bamboo bands with a distinctive format by the early twentieth century. Hill describes three basic bamboo instruments—the *boom, foulé,* and *cutter*—and suggests that they had roles similar to those of the three different sizes of drums common in Afro-Trinidadian drum ensembles. The boom was a piece of bamboo about five feet long and five inches in diameter, which was stamped on the ground (either on a hard-surfaced road or on a stone in a yard) to provide the bass line. The foulé consisted of two pieces of bamboo, twelve inches long and two or three inches thick, which were struck end to end and produced a sound higher in pitch than the boom. Finally, the cutter was a thin piece of bamboo (apparently of varying lengths), which was held over the shoulder and struck with a hardwood stick to create a high-pitched counter-rhythm to the rhythms of the foulé and boom.

The instruments in the tamboo bamboo band and their uses were by no means standardized. For example, Lennox Pierre, a solicitor who was an early advocate of the steelband movement, describes a three-foot boom; a *buller* and *fuller* (foulé), which consisted of pieces of the same length but with different numbers of joints; and a cutter that was tapped with a stick and, when a band was stationary, was also struck on the ground. In addition, Anthony Prospect, a Trinidadian musicologist, mentions a *chandler*, which was a little longer than the cutter, and states that the boom was simultaneously struck with a stick while being stamped on the ground in order to produce two different rhythms. Along with these various bamboo instruments, every tamboo bamboo band had bottles that were struck with spoons to keep time. The sturdy Dutch gin flask was the preferred type, and these bottles were sometimes filled to different levels so that they would emit different tones. Chac-chacs and scrapers were also sometimes employed. Though the tamboo bamboo ensembles included a range of tones, they did not play melodies. Their objective was to create an intense polyrhythmic background to the call and response singing of a chantwell and chorus.[29]

The earliest description of a tamboo bamboo band performance appeared in the *Trinidad Guardian* in 1920. Of all things, the writer had stumbled upon a group of policemen attempting to prepare their horses for the sounds of Carnival:

> . . . the music struck up. It began with the booming sound of the bass bamboo which serves to regulate the time, and after a few beats, a number of the band who played the lighter reeds joined in. The "cutting" (beating) of the finer reeds in rhythmic percussion between the booms of the bass bamboo was really surprising. The shac-shac players and the bottle-and-spoon operators completed the orchestra, and the music was furnished to the chanting of a "single re" by the director in a high-pitched tenor, and then taken up in chorus by the other members of the band, not excluding the orchestra.[30]

In Port of Spain tamboo bamboo bands were associated with particular neighborhoods such as Charlotte Street, George Street, John John, Laventille Hill, Newtown, and St. James. During the Carnival season these bands performed in yards that were centers for a range of Carnival activities: calypso performances, masquerade preparation, and stickfighting. The calypsonians whom the bands accompanied were the old-style chantwells who sang short verse-and-refrain calypsos, as opposed to the "oratorical" calypsos with longer verses and string band accompaniment that appealed to wider audiences. Stickfights in the yards were held during the daytime so that the combatants could see. Victor "Totee" Wilson, a tamboo bamboo man and early panman, describes how fights in the "Big Yard" in Newtown occurred for about a month before Carnival and began at three o'clock in the afternoon. People paid six cents to enter the yard and formed a ring around the fighters. The tamboo bamboo band was on one side of the ring and, along with the singing, provided a background for the fights.[31]

Alfred "Sack" Mayers, another early panman, describes how in Corbeaux Town, the neighborhood where he grew up, tamboo bamboo and stickfighting were performed every Saturday throughout the year:

> I could remember the tamboo bamboo around 1937, '38. It was some people who used to play the tamboo bamboo every Saturday afternoon. Let's say from after lunch, they would buy two, three bottles of rum and they would all assemble in a yard. And they would have their regular chants. They would chant certain songs and play the bamboo. In those days, well, that was the music of the day. . . . And people just drinking and dancing, you know, jumping up and having a good time. . . .
>
> Every Saturday used to have stickfighting, bamboo and stickfighting. . . . You'd have the people and them chanting different songs and people answering and all kind of thing. It used to be nice, you know. But you see, the busting of the head—I didn't like to see that.[32]

In many areas of Trinidad tamboo bamboo was also used at wakes and at Christmas—two occasions that like stickfights previously included drumming.

It was for the two days of Carnival itself, however, that the tamboo bamboo bands were most prominent. They came out on the streets in greatest numbers for *J'Ouvert* (*Jour Ouvert*—"break of day"), the early Monday morning opening of Carnival. Basically, J'Ouvert was a reinterpretation of the old Canboulay tradition and featured percussion, aggressive action, eerie figures, and satirical commentary. With the banning of Canboulay, Carnival officially opened at 6:00 a.m. However, revelers apparently would come out early and take advantage of the darkness. Andrew Carr, an accountant and folklorist, and Errol Hill state that, in the early part of the century, folklore characters such as Soucouyant, La Diablesse, Loup Garou, and Papa Bois scurried about the streets making weird noises before the break of dawn.[33] In later years these figures were replaced by *ol' mas* (old masquerade) portrayals, which involved people dressing up in odd assortments of old clothing. Others parodied doctors, lawyers, and aristocratic ladies, or played characters who demanded money from onlookers. ˙

In the midst of these J'Ouvert masquerades, the tamboo bamboo bands moved through town with their followers chanting *lavways* (short Carnival street songs) such as "We want a thousand gen-er-al, to follow de Kaiser fun-er-al" and "Dingo-lay-yo, tie me monkey down town." Victor Wilson states that the Newtown tamboo bamboo band might have had as many as twelve cutters, twelve foulés, six booms, five bottles and spoons, and two scrapers. Though J'Ouvert was the primary time for tamboo bamboo, a few bands perhaps performed during the day on Monday and Tuesday and more came out again at night. While these bands were popular among grass-roots Trinidadians, the middle and upper classes (who masqueraded with string bands) perceived them as inferior and annoying. Tamboo bamboo was never outlawed, but attempts were made to suppress it. In 1919, for example, a Carnival competition was held in which masqueraders accompanied by bamboo music were excluded.[34]

Various types of metal objects were also utilized as Carnival percussion during this period. Like bamboo, metal percussion is widespread in Africa and the diaspora. Among the metallic instruments employed in Africa are iron bells (with and without clappers), bell-like iron castanets, iron cymbals, and hoe blades. African-style bells have also been made in Haiti, Cuba, and Brazil, while hoe blades have been used as percussion instruments in many parts of the West Indies. In the Big Drum dance in Carriacou, for example, a hoe blade is struck with a piece of steel to invoke ancestors. Old cannisters and pieces of metal were used in *John Canoe* masquerades in Jamaica as early as the eighteenth century, and there are reports of triangles in Tobago, Barbados, and St. Vincent in the early nineteenth century. During the nineteenth century metal containers were also utilized as percussion in street processions in Cuba and for dances in Louisiana.[35]

Metallic percussion in Trinidad dates back at least to the mid-nineteenth century. A report on the 1848 Carnival in the *Port-of-Spain Gazette* includes a reference to "bands of music (soi-disant) including those inelegant instruments, the tin kettle and salt box, the bangee and shack shack." J. D. Elder discusses how people of Congolese descent in Trinidad, some of whom arrived after emancipation, fashioned a percussion instrument from an olive oil container called a *marli-doundoun*. One of Elder's informants also states that it was old African-born men from Hell Yard (on Charlotte Street) and La Cour Harpe who switched from drums to tamboo bamboo after the Carnival riot in 1881. According to Elder's informant, these men introduced large biscuit drum basses into the bands as well.[36]

In addition to this evidence of metallic percussion, Hill cites references to Carnival music including "old tins, graters and other discordant instruments" in 1909 and to tamboo bamboo bands including "tin pans" in 1911 and 1912. Another report on Carnival in the early years of the century describes revelers "singing, leaping and dancing to the insistent rattle of painted chac-chacs, tuneful pot covers and kerosene tins" for J'Ouvert, and mentions a band on a Carnival Tuesday that produced "a veritable babel of sound from drums, tubs, triangles, buckets, bamboos and bottles." Finally, Prince Batson, a veteran of Hell Yard, points out that metal containers were used to accompany specific masquerade characters such as *Jab Molassis* (molasses devils), cows, and "knock-about" or "all-about" sailors.[37]

The Jab Molassi was firmly rooted in the old Canboulay tradition. Individuals playing this masque (which is still common today) coated their bodies with black grease or tar and wore horns, tails, and sometimes chains. During J'Ouvert Jab Molassis danced erotically on the streets to the accompaniment of a vigorous rhythm beat out on a "pitch oil" (kerosene) tin and smeared their bodies against cleanly-dressed onlookers. The pitch oil tin, a rectangular container used to hold lard as well, also accompanied the cow masque. This masque involved wearing horns obtained from an abattoir and dancing on clogs that imitated hoofs. It should also be noted that pitch oil tins were traditionally used in a Good Friday custom in which an effigy of Judas (called a *bobolee*) was hung from a tree. Children circled around the tree, struck both the effigy and the tins with sticks, and shouted: "Beat the bobolee, beat the bobolee."[38]

The sailor masque has a complex history and deserves special attention because of its later connection with the steelband movement. As mentioned above, the first military masquerade occurred in the Carnival of 1834 when a band of Africans parodied the local militia. Hill states that, though militia laws were suspended in 1846, military parades and mock battles continued to be held during the pre-Carnival season up until the end of the nineteenth century and thus provided models for masqueraders. In the Carnival of 1886, for example, there was a full-scale naval masquerade. A band of workers from the wharves dressed in naval uniforms (including wooden swords) and performed drills while pulling a large model of a ship on wheels.[39]

At the turn of the century there were many military masquerades. Bands during this period were partially inspired by the Boer War and much rivalry existed between them. They had names such as "Artillery," "Cavalry," "Admirals," and "Lancers," and included kings and queens who were sometimes crowned at public ceremonies. During Carnival the bands marched through the streets carrying large banners designed with their names and related emblems and scenes. In 1907 the United States Atlantic Fleet visited Trinidad, and from that point on masquerades of American sailors in Carnival became common.[40] Bands of "military sailors" or "ships' crews," with names like "Texas," "Wisconsin," and "Hit the Deck," represented all the ranking officers and other personnel of particular American ships. While parading the streets in full uniform, these bands performed drills and were often accompanied by string bands or brass bands playing military music.

At least by the 1920s, all-about or knock-about sailors began to appear on the streets. In elucidating the origin of these sailors, and their characteristic dance and percussion, Prince Batson states:

> When the Americans came here around the First World War of 1914, the people here saw the American sailors; and . . . between World War I and World War II, there were a lot of visiting man-of-war . . . German, French, English and all the like.'Cause the Americans had a way: their behavior was worse than all the others. And they had a peculiarity in their display which the people took pattern from and create a dance. So that is the history of the sailor dance on the street. They took that dance and they brought it in. Because the same uniform, the same bell-bottom pants and the cap and the jumpers and so on, they utilize that and they create a dance. So they'd be dancing on the street and this is the birth of the fancy sailor.
>
> In the ordinary days, we call it knock-about or all-about. Because they would have a cane. They get cane. They get bananas. Just as the sailors when they came about. When they came to town. The same basket and the same attitude. They'll dance in the streets. And they say: "Hey Joe. Hey Joe. How are you? How are you? What you doing, man?" Everything that the Americans. But they had a dance that emulate the behavior. They used to get their bladders from the abattoir and dry it and inflate it so it would come as a balloon. And they would take that and strike the bottom of [the women]. . . . And when they

strike them, they would sing . . . "Hey Joe. Have you seen that big boom-boom? What a big backside. That's a lovely boom-boom. Ha, ha, ha, ha, ha, ha." And smoking their pipes and thing. It's from that they evolved this same mas.

So those are the first set of people I saw beating pans on the streets. . . . They used what you would call a chamber [pot]. . . . That was mostly on their head. . . . And they have two small tins beating it together. And they're dancing and jigging. . . .[41]

Knock-about sailor bands had other features as well. Additional personnel included "stokers" or firemen who wore goggles and gloves and carried long stoking rods. Around the same time that the sailor dance was developed, these firemen created their own dance that incorporated mimes of various boiler room activities. The sailor band from Hell Yard, "Bad Behavior," was perhaps the most famous contingent of knock-about sailors. Along with other antics, they would roll in coal dust to dirty their uniforms and would then proceed to scare off masqueraders in pretty costumes. Sometime before 1930, knock-about sailors began wearing masks. According to Jason Griffith, a master of sailor mas, the common practice of wearing masks with long noses attached was introduced during the 1930s by Jim Harding, the leader of "S. S. Mischievous." Masks opened up even more opportunities for misbehavior since the sailors could antagonize women and steal items from roadside vendors without fear of recognition. As Prince Batson describes above, these knock-about sailors also sang songs that they made up, and accompanied themselves by banging on chamber pots. Jerry Serrant, another veteran of Hell Yard, recalls that Bad Behavior occasionally utilized tamboo bamboo.[42]

By 1930 there already was considerable public uproar concerning sailors and their activities. Though the Trinidadian elite had resumed participation in the street Carnival, they still maintained a distance by masquerading on the backs of lorries (trucks) rather than parading and dancing on the street with everyone else. But even on their lorries they were not entirely safe and were frequently attacked by sailors. For the Carnival of 1930, regulations pertaining to sailors were made under the Summary Conviction Offences Ordinance: "It shall not be lawful for any person to carry any bladder or chamber utensil"; and "It must be clearly understood that improper conduct of those disguised persons locally known as 'Drunken Sailors' who usually carry these articles will not be permitted and that any person acting in disobedience of this Regulation will be immediately arrested."[43] This regulation motivated the following letter to the editor of the *Port-of-Spain Gazette*.

Dear Sir,—Just a few lines to thank the Constabulary on its prompt attitude in preventing "bladders" from being used in the forthcoming Carnival, especially by that class of hooligans who disguise as "sailors." As one who has been about in lorries for years, it is disgraceful how these hoi poloi take advantage of their disguise on the two days and indiscriminately hit respectable people. Many thanks to your correspondents who suggested this rule, and I hope the next thing that will be stopped is "confetti" bundled together, in a hard ball, which, when flung, hurts very much.

Yours truly,
X[44]

Clearly, sailors and their performances had assumed class significance. The grass-roots class was using outrageous costume and behavior, crude percussion and weapons, and lewd songs to produce a concerted attack on the middle and upper classes and the values of respectability. The authorities responded with legislation but the efforts to restrict sailor mas were not successful. It flourished in spite of the 1930 regulations, and during the 1940s became attached to an even more assertive and powerful form of percussion—the steelband.

The conflict over sailor mas was typical of the social struggles that had occurred over Carnival since the early nineteenth century. Over the years the diverse components of Trinidad's population conceived of the festival in different ways. Originally the French elite utilized Carnival as a means of defining and celebrating their community and cultural heritage. The free coloreds and the enslaved Africans were relegated to the margins of public festivity. Following emancipation, however, Africans appropriated the event and re-created it in terms of Canboulay—a celebration of their new freedom. As the nineteenth century progressed, Africans increasingly used Carnival as an occasion to publicly display their autonomy and identity and to threaten and ridicule the middle and upper classes. The French in turn resented the "degeneration" of their festival, while the British were thoroughly baffled and offended by this culturally foreign affair. A discourse on the immorality of Carnival became established and legal restrictions were employed in an effort to maintain the colonial social and cultural order. The Peace Preservation Ordinance of 1884 suppressed the elements of African culture which the dominant classes found particularly disturbing such as drumming, torch processions, and stickfighting. Thus it became more difficult for African organizations to display themselves in public.

The upper and middle classes' efforts at "improving" Carnival at the end of the nineteenth century demonstrate how cultural hegemony is expanded and reaffirmed through the incorporation of oppositional cultural practices. The chaos and threat of the grass-roots street festival could best be controlled by redefining the event as a traditional Trinidadian celebration suitable for the enjoyment of the general public. This re-definition in turn paved the way for the commercialization of Carnival. The grass-roots class, however, refused to surrender the festival that they had been cultivating for decades. Essentially they re-created the Canboulay tradition in J'Ouvert, tamboo bamboo, and sailor mas, and through these new expressive forms continued to assert their presence on the streets in resistance to the "improvement" program.

The development of Carnival in Trinidad was thus a process of ongoing negotiations in which groups with differing positions and interests in the colony pursued their particular agendas. The colliding of these agendas in the context of public festivity produced a wide array of new performance practices. Innovations in music, dance, costume, and verbal art were a means by which the various groups examined, parodied, and challenged each other. It was through this process of negotiation, competition, and cultural exchange that Carnival became a distinctively creole festival that embodied the tensions and diverse aesthetics of Trinidadian society.[45]

Chapter 2
The Emergence of the Steelband:
The 1930s and 1940s

The steelband developed in Trinidad in the late 1930s and 1940s as a new way of making music. There was much excitement in the streets and yards during this period as actual notes, and then even whole tunes, began to be heard on pans. News of discoveries traveled fast, and more and more youths began searching around for empty containers with which to equal or surpass the accomplishments of their rivals. Soon the emerging panmen of different neighborhoods and villages formed themselves into bands and began to parade the streets with their new instruments, particularly at festive occasions. The response of the public to this disconcerting form of musical expression was mixed. To some extent people were intrigued by the novelty of the pans and felt that the music brought a new thrill to traditional celebrations. At the same time there was condemnation of the music as "noise" and of the musicians as "hooligans." Despite opposition and even legal restrictions, panmen continued to appear on the streets and, through their musical performances, began to assert themselves as a distinctive group in the society. Trinidad was undergoing fundamental change during this period with increasing political consciousness among the grass-roots class, widespread labor uprisings, and a massive American military presence during the war years. In the midst of these changes, pan was a focal point of youth expression and became symbolic both of social disorder and of grass-roots aspirations.

Metallic Percussion and the Early Steelband

Accounts of the origin of the steelband often state that metal containers were introduced into tamboo bamboo bands during the 1930s. Given that there are references as early as 1911 to metal containers being combined with bamboo instruments, it would be more accurate to say that the 1930s was a period during which these containers were included in tamboo bamboo bands with increasing regularity. The various legends about the origin of the steelband cannot be verified, but they are suggestive of the types of chance occurrences that may have encouraged the use of metallic percussion.

One of the best-known legends features the Newtown tamboo bamboo band and Carlton "Lord Humbugger" Forde at a Carnival during the mid-1930s. Forde himself states that, while the band was moving down the street, a bottle broke and everybody scattered, presumably believing that a fight had broken out. According to different versions of the story, Forde or another member of the band then picked up a paint can from the side of the road and started beating it as a replacement for bamboo. The band then took the can back to their yard for future use.[1] Another legend is set in a yard in the neighborhood of Gonzales in 1937. According to an article written by Oscaret Claude for the *Trinidad Guardian*, the surprise abdication of King Edward did not give the fellows time to prepare their bamboo instruments for celebrating the coronation of the new king. Thus, "The old motorcar and cycle which had lain in Tantie Willie's yard—the rendezvous and opera house of Gonzales Place—fell victims of circumstance to frontal attack of the revellers which resulted in a hairraising rhythmic tintinabulation."[2]

Though chance events such as these may have occurred, it appears that metal objects were adopted by tamboo bamboo bands with increasing frequency because they were a more convenient and durable form of percussion than bamboo. Alfred Mayers, who played with the Red Army and Merry Makers steelbands, states:

> Well what happened is like this. Sometime you on the road and you hitting the bamboo on the ground all the while, it will pop. And then you catch yourself not doing anything. And if you see a rubbish can, you wouldn't leave it. That gone. Yes, because . . . in the morning, everybody start off with bamboo. But when the band comes back in, it have sometime ten, twelve rubbish can in the band, because the bamboo pop. And the guy want to do something. He want to play something. So whatever rubbish can, whatever it is—anything metal-like—he decided well he taking that . . . banging it in some sort of rhythm.[3]

Victor Wilson, who is often credited with introducing metal into the Newtown tamboo bamboo band, states that he started to employ cans because the bamboo was always breaking and adds that the band was "getting a sweeter melody from steel drum."[4] So the strength of metal containers and the intense sounds that they emit made them particularly suitable for long days of Carnival revelry.

The gradually increasing presence of metal containers and other objects in tamboo bamboo bands can be traced from accounts of Carnival in newspapers during the late 1930s and early 1940s. Until 1937 there were simply references to bamboo bands with bottles and spoons. But for the Carnival of 1937 the *Port-of-Spain Gazette* reported:

> At the break of day, yesterday, King Carnival for 1937 was ushered in by thousands of disguises termed "Old Masks" who paraded the streets of the city, decked in the oddest garments imaginable and giving vent to their highly strung fe[e]lings by jumping, prancing and yelling to their hearts' content—singing or at least shouting refrains such as "Nettie Nettie etc." that were almost meaningless to the accompaniment of noises produced by tin pans etc. As the hours went by, these gave way to more orderly bands which consisted of folks wearing their costumes of previous years and headed by string bands playing popular airs.[5]

The pan phenomenon was not restricted to Port of Spain during the 1937 Carnival. A report from Tunapuna stated that "The Tamboo-Bamboo, the band of the proletariat was fully alive with their spoons and bottles and other primitive instruments." For J'Ouvert in San Fernando, "Old pots, old pans, old umbrellas, old coats and fragments of old garments were all pressed into service."[6] It is not clear in this description whether the old pots and pans were musical instruments or parts of costumes—perhaps, like the sailors' chamber pots, they served as both.

Reports on the Carnival of 1938 suggest even greater geographic distribution of metallic percussion. Along with mention of "instruments of all description" in Port of Spain, there are references to people dancing in odd J'Ouvert costumes to "improvised musical instruments . . . [b]ottle and spoon and bamboo" in Arima and to "bottles and spoons, pans and bamboo" in Princes Town. There are no citations in either the *Port-of-Spain Gazette* or the *Trinidad Guardian* of metal containers in the 1939 Carnival. However, the *Gazette* states that the "Bad Behavior Rag Time Band," led by Eric Stowe, won the "Best Bamboo Band" category at a Carnival band competition.[7] This was the Hell Yard band and they would certainly have employed metal instruments as well as bamboo.

By 1940 pan had become a clearly identifiable part of Carnival festivity. The *Gazette* reported that "masqueraders of all classes sang and danced to the strains of musical instruments, empty cans, bottle and spoon and other noise making articles" in Port of Spain.[8] That year also saw the arrival of representatives of the Decca Records Corporation (U.S.A.) to record calypsonians. In addition, recordings of "local East Indian songs and dances" and "Steel Music" were made as "novelties":

> Then there is the real native music that is so characteristic of the Trinidad Carnival. No longer does the bamboo band hold sway, it having given place to the steel drums with bottle and spoon. This 'Steel Music' as it is called, has also been recorded and thus every feature of our Carnival has been included in the 1940 records that are coming to us through the instrumentality of the Decca Records Corporation.[9]

The above comments suggest that by 1940 metal containers had replaced bamboo instruments in Port of Spain. In districts such as Princes Town and Sangre Grande, however, there were reports of pans still being combined with tamboo bamboo.[10]

The 1941 Carnival was the last one held before a ban on the festival went into effect for the duration of World War II. For J'Ouvert in Port of Spain that year, the "music in the majority of cases was furnished by the biscuit drums and dustbin' orchestras; the performers on which instruments (?) exhibited a degree of skill and brought forth the rhythm which particularly suited the maskers." However, pans were combined with bamboo in Chaguanas, and San Fernando still had a "Best Bamboo Band" category at a Carnival competition.[11]

This series of newspaper articles from 1937 to 1941 demonstrates that metal containers gradually replaced tamboo bamboo instruments throughout Trinidad during this period, but that the process occurred at a faster pace in Port of Spain. The evidence also suggests that it was in Port of Spain that the first all-steel band performed on the streets for Carnival. Today, however, there is considerable controversy surrounding which band was first. In origin narratives of the steelband, the Newtown band is often cited as the first to appear. Carlton Forde relates that it was in either 1934 or 1936 that his band picked up a paint can from the road, and that by the Carnival season of 1935 or 1937 he and other younger members of the band had gathered together similar paint cans. They beat rhythms on these cans and eventually started using a large biscuit drum as a bass. While the older men were rehearsing with bamboo, they gradually eased their pans into the band. After some initial resistance the pans were accepted and the band decided to go out for Carnival that year without any bamboo. They named themselves

"Alexander's Ragtime Band" after a current movie.[12] George Goddard, who was a member of this band, argues that it was really Victor Wilson who introduced the pans and that this must have occurred in late 1938 or 1939, since the movie was copyrighted in August 1938. Goddard recalls that the band went out for the 1939 Carnival but notes that the first newspaper reference to the band did not appear until the Carnival of 1940.[13]

In any case, when Alexander's Ragtime Band emerged on the streets of Port of Spain, it made a major impression. Alfred Mayers, who was associated with the band, recollects that they came out in 1939 or 1940 and that

> they were well-dressed. There was a bandmaster, like a conductor. And he had on all-black scissors-tail coat, top hat and this stick. If you see him conducting the band! This thing caused quite a stir in town, man. . . . [The other members] had on jackets . . . and some of them take cardboard and make fantastic bow ties. Terrible! A lot of people followed them because they actually changed the trend. Because the majority of the other bands was using bamboo. And they came all-metal. It was nice. . . . A lot of people followed them all about J'Ouvert morning. They had everybody with them.[14]

Carlton Forde, who was the conductor, adds that "Every member was equipped with music sheets"; and Lennard Morris, another early panman, mentions that the band had "biscuit drums, old paint cans, old buckets, old bed posts, brassy parts from trucks, and old Gramaphone horns."[15] These descriptions suggest that Alexander's Ragtime Band followed the J'Ouvert ol' mas tradition of outrageousness and parody and that their metal objects had a visual as well as a musical function.

Though Alexander's Ragtime Band was very influential in encouraging bands to discard their bamboo, it is likely that a few other Port of Spain bands had independently become all-steel. In the late 1930s J. D. Elder was living near Hell Yard and recalls seeing young men "idling" in the yard on the embankment of the East Dry River:

> This group could be seen experimenting with discarded motor-car parts, beating out what was mere rhythmic noise, under the tutelage of retired kalinda-men. In time, different lengths of iron were found to produce different pitches. Soon the group which met on that site came to be known as the "Hell Yard Boys;" they called their orchestra "Iron Band." It took the duration of the war for the experiments to come to a head.[16]

Jerry Serrant, an early observer of pan, confirms that the Hell Yard band was all-steel around 1939 and states that the Gonzales band was all-steel by this point as well.[17] In fact, claims have been made that the Gonzales group was the first steelband.[18] The John John band probably also was all-steel around this time. Many members of this band worked at a nearby abattoir; early in the morning and at lunch time, they would beat on metal objects with their butcher knives and "steels."[19] In addition, Victor Wilson states that, when the Newtown band was still playing tamboo bamboo, "goatskin drum and iron bands" came out from places such as John John and Laventille.[20]

It is unlikely that there was any "first" steelband which inspired all others. Rather, the evidence suggests that during the late 1930s young men in a number of different neighborhoods were experimenting with the plenitude of metal containers and other objects that an urban environment like Port of Spain provided. There were various locations around town that were favorite sources of pans. For example, around 1936 construction of a deep-water harbor began, and youths would often go down to the "harbor scheme" to pick up empty cement drums. There they also found paint cans and zinc cans (zinc is an ingredient used in the mixing of paint). Paint and zinc cans were also obtained from the Queen's Park Oval, the stadium in Woodbrook used for cricket matches and other sporting events. A biscuit factory on the east side of town was pillaged for biscuit drums, and caustic soda drums were stolen from two soap factories near John John. The abattoir near John John also provided metal tins and utensils. Dustbins (trash cans) and covers and automobile parts were easily obtained from yards and streets, and many homes had cooking oil tins, pitch oil tins, and buckets. By the mid-1940s panmen began to take advantage of the abundance of large oil drums that Trinidad's industries offered. It was through the combining and manipulating of this diverse assortment of metal objects that the steelband began to take shape.

Just as it is difficult to pinpoint an original steelband, it is unlikely that any particular individual can be designated as the first person to tune notes on a pan. The discovery of variations in pitch on particular pans appears to have been a gradual process which occurred simultaneously in different neighborhoods as band members pounded away on containers in their yards and on the streets. For example, McKeller "Big Mack" Sandiford, an early member of both the Hell Yard band and Bar 20 (from the La Cour Harpe area), recalls that, when a caustic soda drum was repeatedly struck on the bottom, its sound would eventually become "dead." One would then turn the drum ninety degrees or so and begin striking on a different section of the bottom. This led to the realization that denting cans in different ways created different pitches.[21]

Through experimenting with pitch variations on various containers, panmen were eventually able to tune actual notes from the scale on pans. Victor Wilson claims that he was finding notes on zinc cans from the Queen's Park Oval during the 1930s. However, there is a general consensus that Alexander's Ragtime Band first came out with untuned pans, which suggests that Wilson's "notes" were perhaps originally simply rough variations in pitch which he subsequently developed. Meanwhile, Prince Batson states that the first person he observed obtaining notes on a pan was Hamilton "Big Head" Thomas of the Hell Yard band. Thomas also used zinc cans and, like Wilson and others, would burn these containers to remove the remaining zinc. After discovering that burning the cans changed their pitch when struck, he started to fashion notes on the cans.[22]

At the same time, progress was being made over in John John and a member of this neighborhood's band, Winston "Spree" Simon, is often represented as the "father of the steelband." The story here, related by pan observer Anthony Rouff, is that Spree lent a pan to Wilson "Thick Lip" Bartholomew, who was known to have the strength to lift a tub of water and pour it on himself. When the pan was returned, it was badly smashed in. In the process of punching it out again, Spree discovered different pitches. He then began to tune a few notes on a caustic soda drum.[23] Rouff claims that this happened during the 1941 Carnival. What this account and the others suggest is that improvements on accidental discoveries of pitch variations led to the creation of notes on pans in a number of neighborhoods during the early 1940s.

By the early 1940s a basic steelband had emerged that had considerable consistency in instrumentation from neighborhood to neighborhood. The large biscuit drum was used as a *cuff boom* or *slap bass,* which produced one low sound of indefinite pitch when struck with a hand wrapped in cloth, a tennis ball, or a stick wrapped with rubber. Sometimes a player tapped the side of the drum with his other hand or another individual tapped it with two sticks. The lead instrument was the *kittle* (sometimes called a *tenor kittle* or *side kittle*), which was typically made from a zinc or paint can. The original kittle had three notes and phrases were played over and over again with two sticks. The third basic pan was the *bass kittle* or *dud-up,* which was usually made from a caustic soda drum. The bottom of this container was divided to form two notes, and the instrument was played with two sticks to produce a counterrhythm to the rhythms of the kittle and cuff boom. Finally, an *iron* was struck as a time-keeper. At first, this was an angle iron or other piece of metal, while in later years the automobile brake drum became the standard instrument. Chac-chacs and scrapers were also sometimes included as minor rhythm instruments. This basic steelband did not play full tunes but simply provided a polyrhythmic background for revelers who sang call-and-response lavways or other songs. Some time during the war bugles were also introduced into steelbands. The bugles did not serve as lead or melody instruments but played repeated calls or phrases from military tunes.[24]

The early steelband was modeled on a number of different musical ensembles in Trinidad. Most important was the tamboo bamboo band from which it emerged. Big Mack Sandiford notes that each of the basic steelband instruments was a substitute for a tamboo bamboo instrument: the cuff boom for the boom, the kittle for the foulé, the dud-up for the cutter, and the iron for the bottle and spoon. Musicologist Anthony Prospect points out that, in addition to these instrument substitutions, kalinda and Orisha (Shango) drum rhythms were reproduced by the tamboo bamboo band and that these same rhythms were in turn transferred to the early steelband.[25]

Orisha drum ensembles were themselves another model for the steelbands. Both Prince Batson and George Yeates, an early panman in Laventille, assert that steelbands as well as tamboo bamboo bands had a deep connection in terms of musical influence with Orisha centers in East Dry River (eastern Port of Spain). In commenting on the John John steelband, Leo "Little Drums" Alfred, one of the original members, relates:

> Plenty, plenty skin-drum players. I also used to play the skin drum. Now where we got all the practice on the skin drum now, we had a lot of Shango up here. A lot, a lot, a lot of Shango tents and thing. A lot of Shango leaders. So we, now [would play] the drums for the Shango people to dance. . . . So we were very skillful in the drumming of the skin drums.

Prince Batson suggests that the Orisha background of East Dry River explains why steelbands from this area had a strong rhythmic orientation, while bands from western Port of Spain were experimenting more with melody and eventually harmony.[26]

The military marching bands that were prominent in Trinidad provided a third model for the early steelband. Prince Batson states that the kittle was named after the military kettle drum (side drum), that it was suspended around the neck in a similar fashion, and that kittlers sometimes rattled their sticks to produce rhythms like those played on the kettle drum.[27] The cuff boom resembled the military bass drum in appearance and was suspended and struck in a similar manner, while the bugles and the phrases that they played were adopted directly from military bands. Steelbands also followed the military band practice of parading in the streets in orderly rows.

A fourth model for the early steelband was the Indian *tassa* drum ensemble. These ensembles, which perform for *Hosay* (the Muslim observance of *Muharram*) and at other occasions, are similar in structure to tamboo bamboo bands and steelbands. Generally, one tassa drum is employed as a cutter while the others serve as foulés (terms used by tassa drummers). There are also large drums for the bass line and small, high-pitched cymbals that keep time. Tassa ensembles play a variety of distinct *hands* (rhythms), some of which have been influenced by Afro-Trinidadian rhythms. St. James in particular is a neighborhood where there has been considerable African-Indian social and cultural interaction for generations. There tassa groups and steelbands have both included Indians and Africans, and the two percussion traditions have influenced each other. Researcher Noorkumar Mahabir points out that the shells of the Indian bass drums used to be made from biscuit drums, that tassa drums are heated to stretch their skins and raise their pitches, and that the drums in the ensemble are suspended around the neck and played with two sticks. He argues that all of these practices had an influence on the early steelband.[28]

In the course of the 1940s the basic steelband was expanded and tremendous advancements were made in the tuning (fashioning) of pans. The most important breakthrough was the development of the *ping pong*, which replaced the kittle as the lead pan. Spree Simon was one of the key innovators of and performers on this instrument. During the war he hammered the bottoms of containers outward to form convex surfaces. After he obtained up to four notes on caustic soda drums, he switched to using small oil drums on which he is believed to have produced eight notes by around 1945. Another ping pong pioneer was Ellie Mannette who was a member of Oval Boys. Oval Boys' yard was located across the street from the Queen's Park Oval in Woodbrook. During the war Mannette experimented with a 35 gallon sweet oil container and claims to have obtained nine notes by the war's end. He adds that he was friends with Spree and that they used to trade ideas. Meanwhile, over in Hell Yard, Neville Jules was experimenting with the kittle, and by the end of the war had developed a ping pong on which Rudolph "Fish-Eye" Ollivierre became a well-known performer.[29]

At first, panmen could only play simple children's songs such as "Mary Had a Little Lamb" on their ping pongs. Even when steelbands came out on the streets for V-E Day and V-J Day in 1945, they were still only playing children's songs and simple calypso choruses, which suggests that most ping pongs at this point were quite limited in range. By 1946, however, a variety of calypsos, popular tunes, and hymns were being performed on pans. Anthony Williams, a master *tuner* (pan-maker) from St. James, explains that panmen were motivated to expand the range of their ping pongs by the desire to play popular tunes that they heard in the movies or on the radio. Someone would hear a tune and then would fashion a pan with the notes necessary to play that particular piece. The influence of movies had, in fact, begun during the war when early panmen played a phrase on their kittles inspired by the movie *This Gun for Hire*, starring Alan Ladd.[30]

Though the kittle was strapped over the shoulder and played with two sticks, the ping pong was initially held with one hand and played with one stick. Sometime during the mid-1940s, however, two sticks were introduced and this allowed for greater fluidity in the playing of melodies. During this period the wrapping of ping pong sticks with rubber was also introduced and this practice greatly improved the tone quality of pan music. Ellie Mannette, who is often credited with this innovation, states that he began wrapping sticks with bicycle inner tube in 1943. However, steelband supporter Lennox Pierre reports that Mannette once told him that he had previously seen Dudley Smith (another well-known panman) wrapping sticks; while Prince Batson states that panmen were wrapping cuff boom sticks with rubber before this idea was ever applied to ping pongs.[31]

Another important innovation that is often credited to Ellie Mannette is the introduction of the large oil drum for tuning ping pongs. These drums were available in both 44 and 45 imperial gallon sizes (slightly smaller than the 55 U.S. gallon drum). Researcher Jeffrey Thomas points out that the oil drums had a larger diameter and were made of a higher quality metal than other containers. This allowed for the tuning of more notes on a pan and the production of tones that were louder, clearer, and could be sustained longer. Anthony Williams recalls that around late 1945 he and a friend tuned two ping pongs from full-size oil drums obtained from the American base in Mucurapo (on the west side of Port of Spain). In 1945, at least as late as V-J Day, Ellie Mannette states that he was still using 35 gallon sweet oil drums. Neville Jules recalls that the first time he saw a full-size oil drum used as a pan was at a competition in Tunapuna (a town east of Port of Spain) after the war, and states that the idea spread quickly after this event.[32]

Though there is controversy surrounding who introduced the oil drum, there is general consensus that Mannette was the first person to sink the bottom of a drum inward, thus creating a ping pong with a concave shape. This innovation occurred sometime after the war, and in the postwar years panmen made rapid advancements in the tuning of ping pongs. As pans were sunk to deeper levels and the metal became thinner, it was possible to obtain both more and higher-pitched notes. Lennox Pierre recalls that Ellie Mannette had tuned a ping pong with two diatonic scales by 1947.[33]

During the 1940s basic tuning procedures were also developed: the balanced sinking of a pan with a hammer, the grooving of individual sections of different sizes on the face of the pan with a punch, the tempering of the steel by heating the pan in a fire, and the actual tuning of notes by carefully hammering the sections. However, there was much variation between tuners in terms of the arrangement of notes on the face of a pan. The whole development of the ping pong depended both on the exchange of ideas among tuners and on competition. There are many stories of panmen visiting each other's yards, especially during the war years before band rivalry became particularly violent. At the same time, everyone wanted to be the best. If one panman came across another with an eight-note ping pong, he would go back to his yard and try to tune nine notes. Such competition, along with the challenge of playing increasingly difficult music, helped produce a quite sophisticated ping pong by the end of the decade.

While the ping pong was evolving, other new pans were being added to the basic steelband. During the war a larger and heavier version of the kittle, known as a *balay* or *grumbler*, was developed. By around 1946 Neville Jules had created a *tune boom* out of the biscuit drum cuff boom. Jules relates that he modeled this pan on a form of thumb piano:

> In those days there was a place where people used to go to get stuff to eat at night called Tanti's Tea Shop that was right near to where All Stars is now on George Street and Duke Street. And at nights all type of people would come there. . . . Kitchener used to come there and sing sometimes. Different calypsonians. You used to get a lot of guys who could play good guitar would come there and sing and show off. . . . And we had a guy. . . . He had a guitar and he had what you call a box bass. They had this box built with three pieces of spring, spring metal. And he would sit down on this box . . . and he would pluck these three springs. . . . Of course, you're just getting the bom, bom, bom. They're not bringing any chords to coincide with the music

you're playing. . . . And that gave me the idea. And I went and I get the biscuit drum and I put in the notes in that.[34]

The tune boom originally had three notes and more were gradually added. Jules also introduced a caustic soda drum *bass* with three and then four notes that replaced the cuff boom. His first version of this pan was named the "Paul Robeson" after the well-known singer. By the late 1940s Jules had invented a *quatro* pan after observing a family playing *parang*, a Venezuelan-derived Christmas music traditional to Trinidad which is generally performed by vocalists accompanied by guitars, quatros, mandolins, a one-string box bass, chac-chacs, and scrapers. A performer on the quatro pan played chords in a manner similar to the strums of the four-stringed quatro.[35]

During the 1940s steelbands were small: most had under twenty members, though a few may have had thirty or more. The organization of players in a band was quite loose. It was not until well into the decade that efforts were made to tune the various pans to a common pitch or to arrange for some sort of melodic coordination. As pointed out above, the emphasis in the early steelband was on rhythmic accompaniment for singing. Kittles, balays, dud-ups, and booms would play various steady rhythms, while in the front of the band ping pong players tried to pick out their own melodies. Leo Warner, a member of Alexander's Ragtime Band and the founder of Commandoes (another early steelband), provides a sense of what a steelband performance might have sounded like in the mid-1940s:

> To take a picture of what went on. You have the dud-up, dud-up, dud-up, dud-up, dud-up. And a fellow would come in with a strumming pan, and he would strum as to what the notes can bring out. And if the ping pong pan can find itself playing a tune which would be close to that, this is what we had. You probably would have one, two, three people beating a piece of iron or chac-chac or whatever you can put your hands on at the time. And with the hope that the ping pong man is good enough to carry the tune. But he sometimes is drowned out by the various instruments. But the voices then would help. But when he can produce a tune that is known to everyone, this is where he gets the backup from the voices.[36]

During the late 1940s members of a steelband would try to have their pans in tune with each other and would attempt to play chords as well as melodies. Through these experiments panmen transformed the steelband into a percussion ensemble with melodic and harmonic dimensions. Thus Errol Hill suggests that they integrated the two basic Carnival musical traditions: they "merged the percussion music of the drum and the bamboo with the smooth, lilting music of the country string orchestra."[37] In fact, the panmen's achievement was much broader. They had developed a means of re-presenting much of the music existing in Trinidad at the time: African, Indian, and European drum rhythms, and the melodic and harmonic patterns of calypso, parang, European hymns, and American popular tunes. It is in this sense that the steelband was an instrument of creolization. Panmen drew on and synthesized a range of cultural traditions to create a distinctively local musical ensemble and sound. Tuners, in particular, constantly expanded the dimensions of the steelband in order to more fully encompass and express their musical experience. Once pans were able to effectively reproduce the musics popular in Trinidad, the steelband ceased to be a background for singing revelers and became a versatile performing ensemble in its own right.

Steelbands and Steelbandsmen in the 1940s

The steelband emerged in Trinidad in a context of intensifying social conflict that had a profound impact on the performance and reception of the music. A growing sense of working class consciousness in the wake of World War I, including a series of strikes in 1919, paved the way for widespread protests against the colonial socioeconomic system in the 1930s. During this period Trinidadians experienced particularly poor living and working conditions as a result of the world-wide depression and the unscrupulous business practices of many companies in the colony. In 1934 there were riots and demonstrations among sugar workers, including a hunger march to Port of Spain. The following year workers went on strike in one of the oil fields in southern Trinidad and staged a hunger march to Port of Spain under the new charismatic leadership of Uriah "Buzz" Butler. Labor unrest reached a peak in 1937, when an effort to arrest Butler sparked off riots and strikes in the southern oil area that quickly spread throughout the island and to several other sectors of the economy. Political scientist Selwyn Ryan suggests that Butler was simply a catalyst for the uprising and that its fundamental causes included the high cost of living, unemployment and underemployment, low wages, racist hiring practices, the absence of a means for expressing labor grievances, and dissatisfaction with the few elected representatives in the government. Oil workers particularly resented low wages and a low standard of living since they knew that the oil companies were generally making large profits.[38]

The uprising of 1937 was followed by two official commissions of inquiry from Britain, whose recommendations became the basis for a new colonial policy of "social welfare, limited constitutional change, and encouragement of an orthodox trade union movement."[39] Oilfield workers, sugar workers, seamen and longshoremen, and several other groups formed unions that had middle class leadership and received guidance from both the Colonial Office and British trade unions.

The turmoil of the 1930s was followed by another upheaval in the early 1940s: the arrival of the Americans. World War II had begun and Britain agreed to lease land in various parts of the West Indies to the United States for bases. In the course of the war thousands of American Navy, Marine, Army, Army Air Corps, and civilian personnel poured into Trinidad. Construction of bases began in 1941 and proceeded at a rapid pace. The largest installation was Chaguaramas, a naval base on the northwest peninsula close to Port of Spain. But there were also an Army Air Corps base east of Arima (Fort Read), a facility on the harbor in Port of Spain (Docksite), and several other posts around the island and in Tobago. The presence of the Americans created much excitement and a sense of involvement in the drama of the war. Trinidadians were impressed with the soldiers and their equipment and felt that "the wealth which America represented held out the promise of bigger, better and brighter things."[40]

The American presence also opened up extensive employment opportunities in the construction of bases and roads. Particularly appealing was the fact that the American pay scale was much higher than that of local employers. Large numbers of people moved from rural areas to Port of Spain and other centers of activity, and there was heavy migration from Tobago and other islands. Employment with the Americans not only provided much needed cash but further strengthened working class consciousness. Sociologist Lloyd Braithwaite remarks that full employment brought a much greater sense of personal dignity to the working class; and Wenzell Brown, an American writer who visited Trinidad immediately after the war, comments that American Communists were active among the workers and that the discontent of the 1930s became more focused.[41] Though employment opportunities brought a taste of a better life, there was also overcrowding in the city and inflation during this period. Food shortages were another serious problem and rationing eventually became necessary.

Along with providing construction jobs, the American presence in Trinidad created a booming entertainment scene. Though the street

Carnival was banned during the war years for security and financial reasons, the calypso tents were kept open and American servicemen became enthusiastic patrons of these venues. Calypsonians were also featured on the bases and at various functions throughout the year. Raymond Quevedo (Atilla the Hun), an active performer during this period, comments that the calypsonian "was finding himself in a new awakening and discovering that he was now a celebrity."[42] Strips of somewhat seedy nightclubs developed along Wrightson Road by the harbor and on Park Street in town. There and at other locations near bases the servicemen sought not only musical entertainment but the favors of women. Lord Invader immortalized this encounter in his calypso "Rum and Coca-Cola," which describes mothers and daughters carousing with the Americans and collecting Yankee dollars.[43]

Prostitution did become widespread during this period. Quevedo notes that this was inevitable, given the presence of thousands of young men with spare cash in a society where poverty was rampant. Writer Michael Anthony provides a vivid sense of the scene:

A new characteristic—something never seen here before—was the emergence of loose, wayward women swarming in the full light of the sun. Many of these had been respectable young girls and staid housewives. For them life took a sudden dramatic turn, and to the fun-loving crowd, here indeed were the gay times in Port-of-Spain. The bars and nightclubs were full. When the sun went down the roar of the city did not die—it heightened. At such times, laughter, quarrels, fights, took over the city centre. Garish light adorned restaurants, and gramophone music blared out everywhere.[44]

The Americans' behavior produced mixed reactions from the local population. On the one hand, Trinidadians resented their racism, their loud and boisterous manner, and the disruption caused by their consorting with local women. On the other hand, they liked the friendly, easy-going style of the Americans. Occasionally there were brawls between servicemen and local men, but there was also camaraderie in drinking and gambling together. More than anything else, Trinidadians liked the Americans' liberality with money, both in wages and in casual spending. In addition, the sailors would give local people food from the bases (very welcome in a time of rationing), and when asked would give away their caps (very handy for future masquerading). Finally, Trinidadians were disconcerted by watching the Americans work, since they had never before seen whites doing manual labor, and they were astonished by the servicemen's drunken antics. According to Lloyd Braith-waite, such behavior during the war years brought a serious challenge to the colony's color-based social status system, in that whiteness was no longer viewed as synonymous with high status.[45]

It was during this extended period of social chaos in Trinidad—the 1930s and World War II—that the emerging panmen came of age. Though many of the men who introduced metal containers into tamboo bamboo bands were middle-aged, the individuals who actually developed the steelband were young. During the 1940s most were teenagers or in their twenties. Their background was one of poverty: some lived in the crowded barrack yards in the downtown area, while others resided in the depressed neighborhoods on the east side of the city such as John John, Laventille Hill, La Cour Harpe, and Gonzales. Even those in Newtown and Woodbrook (more middle class neighborhoods) were poor and lived in barrack yards or other sub-standard housing. Though there were panmen of Indian or "mixed" ancestry, most were African, and a number of these were the children of people who had migrated from other islands to seek a better life in Trinidad.

The majority of panmen in Port of Spain did not work, even though the arrival of the Americans opened up many opportunities. Generally they lived with their parents and occasionally picked up odd jobs. For example, Leo Alfred states that the panmen in John John might now and then sell a little meat obtained from the abattoir; and Vernon "Birdie" Mannette, an original member of Oval Boys, says that the fellows in Woodbrook occasionally fielded balls at sports events.[46] This was the typical pattern in steelbands as a whole during these years, though there were some panmen who worked as laborers or tradesmen for the Americans or for local employers.

For the most part, panmen had little interest in full-time jobs and some even adopted, to varying degrees, what was known as the *saga boy* life. This lifestyle was a direct response to the presence of the Americans and the dramatic rise in prostitution. With so much money circulating in the society, there was less need to work and a life of stylish leisure became possible. Saga boys essentially were flashy dressers who attempted to live off the earnings of women who engaged in prostitution. Most claimed to have more than one woman, though their relationships with these women varied. A few were full-fledged pimps who exercised considerable control over their women and arrangements with customers. The majority, however, were content to collect money periodically from women whom they considered "theirs." Some saga boys lived with their women and were dependent on them, while others lived with their parents and used the cash from their ladies for gambling and buying clothes.

Dressing in fact was a key activity because it was the means by which the saga boy attracted women and generally cut a profile for himself on the streets. There was no uniform saga boy style. Instead dressing was innovative and competitive. Bell-bottomed pants, tight-bottomed pants, silk shirts, Stetson hats, felt hats, and Brazilian shoes were all parts of saga boy outfits at one time or another, as were the zoot suits, popularized by Cab Calloway, among the most flamboyant dressers. Saga boys reserved their best clothes for the nights on which they took their women to dance clubs.

Some panmen led the lives of saga boys or had more casual relationships with women from whom they occasionally collected money. Most simply liked to dress up—one especially popular practice was to wear naval officers' caps with steelband monograms. Real saga boys who were busy managing and protecting their women generally did not have time to play pan, and individuals who were devoted to pan did not have time for the true saga boy life. There was also variation between bands. For example, there was a substantial number of saga boys in Red Army, a band that was formed from a group of youths who used to lime on Green Corner on Park Street. This corner was in the heart of the nightclub/prostitution district and was a vantage point from which the saga boys could easily observe their women and count the women's tricks.

Wellington "Blues" Bostock, an original member of Red Army, recounts how, after rambling around Trinidad as a youth, he ended up on Green Corner:

> Then I start my life as—well I have to call it a saga boy. Well I had three and four women. I used to gamble. Knock about with all the friends and so forth. We going to dance, fight, and thing coming out in between. We going a little club. . . . We walk out that free. The war started in '39. I was down Green Corner there, gambling, playing dice. And the war break out. England declare war on Germany. . . . And they used to sell a kind of paper they call "What News" for a penny. I used to buy and read and thing while I gambling and thing. Well thing go on. The war going on. I had to line up for bread, sugar, rice with a ration card for my family—104 Charlotte Street. But we fight and we come through. And then the war go and continue, continue. Well we on Green Corner. We gambling. We look on with the Green Corner boys, you understand. And we women: they going out in the night and they making us happy and thing. We living a saga life.[47]

Alfred Mayers, a member of Red Army who was not a saga boy, further describes the saga boy appearance and life:

> He look for the most expensive shirt, the most expensive pants and shoe. And every time you see him, he clean. Well-shaved. Every two days he going to the barber to get a fresh mark. And he does nothing more than pose. Just go, let's say, by Green Corner. That was the headquarters for posing. You'd go by Green Corner and you'd see him posing there. You'd see him call one girl and he'd talk to her. And she'd hand over some money and she gone. And maybe about a half an hour after, you'd see him call the next one. She'd hand over money to him. And he goes over to his friends and says: "Well, boy, I did well. Collect from two of them.". . . So he had no reason to work.[48]

The relationship between saga boys and women obviously was one that created much competition and jealousy. Moreover, the women were often associated with particular neighborhoods and steelbands, and fights would sometimes break out when women from one band were seen cavorting with men from a rival band. Fancy dressing in itself was also a source of jealousy and fights, since it was perceived as a means of stealing women away from a band. Conflicts over the female supporters of steelbands, some of whom engaged in prostitution, were in fact one of the main causes of tension between bands. During the war brawls occurred at clubs and dances; after the war there were steelband clashes on the streets during Carnival.

Though the panmen enjoyed liming on the streets, they also spent a great amount of time at the cinemas. Movies, most of which were American, were very popular in Trinidad, and panmen were among the most devoted patrons. Sometimes they attended several shows a day. They particularly liked war movies but also enjoyed other types of films such as gangster dramas, Westerns, and musicals.

Through these movies the panmen experienced a foreign world of grandeur, battles, and romance that had a major influence on the cultural style that they were developing. They appropriated ways of dressing, walking, and talking from the movies and creatively combined these with parallel practices from the local street culture. Sometimes they even adopted the names of movie stars such as Humphrey Bogart and Cesar Romero, but they used many locally-created nicknames as well. Similarly, during the war and the immediate postwar years, panmen often named their bands after movies: Casablanca (based near La Cour Harp), Destination Tokyo (John John), Cross of Lorraine (Hell Yard), Night Invaders (formerly Oval Boys, Woodbrook), Desperadoes

(Laventille Hill), Sun Valley (St. James), and Bataan (San Fernando). Other names associated with the war were also used by bands such as Hill 60 (Gonzales) and Pearl Harbour (San Fernando). Leo Alfred explains that the John John band took the name "Destination Tokyo" because John John and Japan were both in the east and the fellows liked the way the Japanese fought.[49] Once the war was over and Carnival was again permitted, the movies had a tremendous impact on military masquerades played by steelbands. Uniforms, equipment, and maneuvers observed in the cinema were replicated with great precision on the streets. As noted earlier, the movies were also an important source of tunes for the steelbands, particularly in the postwar years.

When not in the cinema or on the street corner, panmen were usually in their panyards. These yards, which were either vacant lots or the open spaces in barrack yards, served as sites for a range of recreational activities such as wrestling, boxing, football, cricket, kite-flying, and gambling. Hell Yard was a well-known athletic center under the direction of "Captain Sagiator," and organized boxing matches were regularly held in John John. A few yards, such as the Big Yard in Newtown, still had stickfighting during the war, and the fights were now accompanied by pan. Essentially, sports provided panmen and saga boys with additional means of competition. Athletic contests, like musical and sartorial ones, enabled them to cultivate impressive images and achieve status within the street world.[50]

Panyards, of course, were also the locations where the panmen developed and played their new instruments. They spent long hours experimenting with their various metal containers in attempts to hammer out notes and play tunes. While playing pan was focused around Carnival during the years of transition from tamboo bamboo, during the war it became a year-round activity. Legitimate opportunities for public performance were limited by the ban on Carnival and other street festivities. But panmen regularly played on the streets anyway, particularly at night in their own neighborhoods. During these outings they sometimes ended up in confrontations with each other or with the police who were sent to arrest them. In order to elude the police, they often performed in the bed of the East Dry River or up on the steep hills to the east. Holidays, both during and after the war, were a particularly popular time for panmen to parade the streets. Neville Jules recalls:

> Every Christmas, we used to be on the road playing even though we know that the police gonna raid us and we have to run. We did it. If you didn't do that, like there wouldn't be no Christmas. There would

be nights like we just hanging and we liming, nothing to do. And one guy might say "Look, let's go over the hill." "Alright, let's go." Now, just to take your pan out of the yard and walk with it in the street is a chance you're taking, because you don't want the cops to see you because they gonna know you're going somewhere to beat. So we used to take this chance. . . .

Many nights when we're on the street beating, police would come and they would raid and they would hold people. Lock them up and take your instruments and throw them away or whatever. But next day, the next week, more instruments gonna come and we're back on the road again. Steelband in those days come like you're in a boat that have a leak. The bigger the water, the more water coming down. It's something like you couldn't stop.[51]

Prince Batson notes that the police sometimes even harassed panmen in their own yards:

The policemen overstepped their authority. They used to waltz over your wall and come quite in your yard, although you're fenced around, and come and take your pans. And take it to the police station. And if you have anybody in the community, a person of prominence, they take and give him to put garbage in it. Or they put it there and they put plants in it. And they defy you to come and take it.[52]

Occasionally during the war years performances on the streets led to serious clashes with the police. For example, the *Port-of-Spain Gazette* reported that early Carnival Monday morning in 1942 four youths were caught "beating drums and bottles and carrying sticks and stones" and were imprisoned for twenty-one days. These youths were part of a band of around two hundred that paraded through town and, when approached by the police, "threw stones, bottles and other missiles." A court prosecutor noted that such activity had been occurring over the previous few weeks. A similar situation developed on Boxing Day in 1944, when seven men beating "pans, bottles and pieces of steel" were arrested and fined. These individuals belonged to a band one hundred strong that also attacked the police with stones and bottles. Apparently, panmen and their followers were determined to parade the streets for Carnival and at other occasions, regardless of restrictions. Jerry Serrant comments that playing on the streets during the war years was a form of open defiance in which the panmen expressed their resentment of the ban on Carnival.[53] Certainly, it was during the war that a pattern of antagonism and confrontation developed between panmen and authorities. The panmen were in the process of developing a new form of music that they were eager to display in public. But the government considered processions in the streets to be too much of a risk in a wartime society.

When V-E Day arrived in 1945, however, the government declared a two-day holiday and temporarily lifted the ban on processions. The steelbands quickly responded to this opportunity. For example, Mac-Donald "Mack" Kinsale recalls that when V-E Day was announced he and some of the other Green Corner panmen went into town and observed all the flags and bunting that were being sold for the celebration. They came across a Soviet flag with the hammer and sickle and decided to name their band "Red Army." After returning to their yard, they painted their pans red and yellow with hammers and sickles and, early the next morning, marched into town with a Soviet flag.[54] V-E Day in fact turned into the Carnival for which people had been yearning during the war. The *Trinidad Guardian* reported:

> On the streets of Port-of-Spain tramping, yelling, dancing and gesticulating thousands were in a riot of rejoicing over the triumph of the United Nations in Europe.
>
> Giving full vent to their feelings pent up for more than five years, residents formed themselves into large bands and paraded the streets to sing all the songs they could remember.
>
> Carnival costumes, packed away since 1940, were shaken out and men donned housecoats and dresses to join in the fun. Scrap metal heaps were searched for brake drums which were mercilessly pounded all day long under flags of all descriptions.

The *Port-of-Spain Gazette* commented that, as the day wore on, "persons from all walks of life threw caution to the winds unable no longer to restrain the tantalising beat of the old pan and steel."[55]

Panmen were even better prepared to participate in the two-day celebration of V-J Day that August. According to the *Guardian*,

> On both days the steel band boys kept up a deafening din with their improvised instruments which all but crushed recognised orchestras off the streets as revellers showed preference for music t[h]umped out of old iron.

Throwing caution to the wind, as they let themselves go entirely, blushing young women as well as old, their faces painted, in certain cases beyond recognition, shook and twisted their bodies to keep time with the tunes.[56]

V-E Day and V-J Day were the occasions at which the steelbands dramatically presented themselves in the public arena. Of course the bands had come out on the streets for the Carnivals of 1940 and 1941, but they were still at a very early stage of development during those years. They improved during the war, but their appearances on the streets were sporadic and clandestine, and many people in the society would have had limited if any awareness of the new music. By V-E Day and V-J Day, however, steelbands were organized and able to play simple calypsos or lavways. As the above quotations reveal, the public could not help but respond. In fact, by V-J Day the steelbands were apparently the dominant form of musical accompaniment. V-E Day and V-J Day were also important because they reaffirmed and expanded the cultural connection between street celebration and steelband performance. Pan emerged as a form of Carnival music, but it soon became expected at any festive occasion.

Though the end of World War II was greeted with jubilation, Trinidad quickly fell into an economic recession. The Americans' completion of their construction projects and the removal of most of their personnel from the island meant that many people lost their jobs. Widespread unemployment, combined with low wages and a sharp rise in the cost of living, in turn created substantial social unrest. In early 1946 the *Trinidad Guardian* reported that a flogging bill had been passed to suppress a crime wave which was believed to have escalated since the abolishment of this form of punishment in 1941. A few days later the paper reported that the City Council was concerned about the high level of unemployment manifested by recent demonstrations and other signs of disaffection, and noted that the Council requested the appointment of a commission to investigate the unrest. In his examination of the postwar period, political scientist John La Guerre states that the "opening months of 1946 thus contained all the elements of a revolutionary situation—mounting violence, growing militancy on the part of the workers and increasing unionization among them." This was the background for the general elections that year, the first held in Trinidad with universal suffrage. A number of loosely organized political "parties" emerged with labor orientations, but divisiveness among them resulted in a fragmented labor vote and little in the way of political advancement for the working class. Social unrest intensified; by the end of the year there were strikes and riots first in the southern oil fields and then in Port of Spain.[57]

A longshoremen's strike in Port of Spain in late 1946 was of particular significance for panmen. Since panmen were chronically unemployed, the government decided to use them to break the strike. They were invited to register to work at local police stations, and trucks with armed policemen were sent around to the various yards to carry them down to the wharves. Apparently a large number of panmen participated in the scheme, but at least one band refused to cooperate. Mack Kinsale had brothers working on the docks and was able to convince Red Army not to break the strike.[58] Many panmen continued to work on the docks after the strike was over, but the unemployment level among panmen as a group remained high. A large number chose not to work. Though the Americans had withdrawn most of their troops from Trinidad, the saga boy lifestyle persisted in the postwar years. Women engaged in prostitution depended now on the remaining Americans on the bases, on sailors passing through the port, and on the local population. The amount of prostitution and the flow of cash declined, however, and the saga boy life was not as comfortable as it had been during the war. In general, saga boys and panmen, like other grass-roots Trinidadians, experienced considerable hardship during the postwar period.

Though the end of the war helped create a serious economic crisis in Trinidad, it also allowed for the resumption of the celebration of Carnival. After the four-year ban, the level of excitement in 1946 was extremely high. The steelbands were particularly eager to participate in the festival, given their success with the public at the V-E Day and V-J Day celebrations. On certain days during the week or two preceding Carnival, they were granted permission to parade the streets between 6:00 and 9:00 p.m. By the time J'Ouvert arrived, they were in prime form. The *Trinidad Guardian* reported that at 6:00 a.m. "the anxiously awaiting masqueraders poured into the streets and paraded about to the strains of familiar tunes provided by numerous steel bands and other orchestras." In the neighborhood of Belmont, revelers were unable to wait for the official opening of J'Ouvert and "started pounding away on the improvised drums, biscuit pans and other pieces of iron, before it was 6 o'clock."[59] After two days of Carnival festivities, the *Guardian* observed:

> The parade this year was by far the largest ever held . . . [and included] steel bands which lacked no encouragement to supply a constant flow of music.

The greatest rhythm makers of them all during the two days celebrations were the members of the "Red Army," a band of happy-go-
lucky thumpers, who, sporting their red merinoes and white trousers,
took along with them a painting of Stalin.

Other Steel Bands, not to be outdone, paraded in fine style, and afforded in rhythm, everything that was expected of them.[60]

The following year, the *Guardian* reported that "Steel bands are much
in demand this carnival and nearly every street band was headed by a
steel band." In addition, the paper commented that the "infectious
quality of steel band music caught revellers in its spell to make everyone
join hands and dance and sing regardless of colour, class or creed."[61]
So, during the postwar years, the steelband became an integral part of
the Carnival experience and, at least in moments of revelry, appealed to
a cross-section of the population. String and brass bands also remained
popular, however, and generally accompanied masquerade bands that
represented historical themes. It was these mas bands that tended to
have large numbers of middle and upper class members.

On Carnival Monday (after J'Ouvert) and on Carnival Tuesday, steelbands typically accompanied sailor masquerades.[62] These masquerades
became immensely popular among the grass-roots class during the postwar years. Though the presence of a large number of American sailors
in Trinidad during the war perhaps contributed to this popularity, people also liked to play sailor because the same costume could be used for
years and because its light weight allowed for much freedom of movement. In the postwar period the basic ship's crew sailor bands became
very large and continued their elaborate reenactments of maritime
scenes and exercises. At the same time, the long-nosed sailors developed into highly imaginative masques. Even before the war their noses
were beginning to take the shapes of various bird beaks. After the war
innovators such as Jim Harding, Cecil Jobe, and Jason Griffith began to
create noses shaped like different types of airplanes and ships. Uniforms worn by these sailors were elaborately decorated with sequins,
patches, and other ornaments. Leo Warner explains that every sailor
would decorate his uniform in a new way each year and that the competition between individual sailors was another reason that this type of
mas was so popular. Out on the streets, these fantastic long-nosed or
"fancy" sailors continued to perform their intricate dances and bad behavior antics.[63]

These innovations in sailor mas paralleled the outburst of creativity in
the pan movement, and individuals involved in the two areas of expression worked closely together. Often a steelband developed its own sailor

masquerade for Carnival, that is, it arranged for its members and followers to wear a particular type of ship's crew or fancy sailor costume. For example, Casablanca usually played French sailors. For the 1948 Carnival the *Trinidad Guardian* reported that they were around 150 members strong and had "everything to be found in a real Navy." The paper added that "their drummers and trumpeters played the marches well."[64] If a steelband did not present its own masquerade, it might be hired by an established sailor band to provide musical accompaniment. For example, Leo Warner's Commandoes occasionally played for Jim Harding's S. S. Mischievous and Jason Griffith's S. S. Sullivan, two well-known fancy sailor bands.

Though sailor mas was the primary way panmen chose to represent themselves at Carnival, they sometimes played other military masquerades that were made popular by war movies. In 1948, for example, Red Army played its namesake with "officers and high-ranking generals in their red coats and dark trousers." Ju Ju Warrior and other African warrior masquerades were also performed by steelbands during this period. Leo Alfred of Tokyo comments that nobody ever beat them with the Ju Ju mas, since they used to get bones from "the La Basse" (the nearby dump).[65]

A crucial member of every steelband at Carnival was the flagman. This individual identified his band by carrying a flag bearing the band's name and led the band through the crowded streets. Sometimes a band had more than one flagman and, if it was playing a military masque, the appropriate national flag would be included. Flagmen developed elaborate ways of twirling their band flags and performed lively dances. Jerry Serrant suggests that some of the moves in these dances may have been derived from the dances of the fancy or king sailor and the dragon (another Carnival figure).[66] Along with flags, bands carried banners displaying their names, a practice that perhaps has its roots in the identifying banners used by military masquerade bands at the turn of the century.

As noted above, the members of a steelband lined up in rows as they marched through the streets at Carnival. Though there was no standard order, it was common for the flagmen to go first, followed by the bugles, ping pongs, and intermediate pans, with the dud-ups, booms, and irons bringing up the rear. When two bands met on the street, an intense competition began both for space to pass and for musical victory. Each band played as loudly as possible in an attempt to drown out the other and break its rhythm. This would force the defeated band to begin its tune again. The tunes that were played (and sung) in these encounters were the popular lavways or "road marches" of the time, such as "Mary

Ann," "In a Calabash," "Pharaoh," "Ramgoat Baptism," and "Canaan Barrow" ("Canaan Barrow went to town, and a Red Army badjohn lick him down"). Anthony Williams describes how steelbands also composed their own songs during this period. These songs had aggressive lyrics such as Sun Valley's "Sun Valley comin' down, Invaders bound to run," and Casablanca's "Invaders, Invaders too bad, we gonna beat them out of they yard." Invaders, in turn, had responses to these threats such as "Invaders want to use you" and

> Mothers, keep your daughters inside
> Mothers, keep your daughters inside
> Mothers, keep your daughters inside
> Because Invaders' sailors outside.

Invaders also played "We Ain't 'Fraid Nobody," a popular calypso composed by Lord Radio.[67] As the 1940s progressed, steelbands were competing on the streets not only in rhythmic skill and volume but in their ability to play more complex arrangements of these different kinds of Carnival songs.

Though Carnival was the most important context for steelband performances, bands played on other holidays as well. One such occasion was Discovery Day, which was held on the first Monday in August and commemorated Christopher Columbus's arrival in Trinidad. At least by 1946, this holiday had become partially carnivalized. After a special Mass on Sunday, Discovery Day itself opened with the pealing of church bells and the discharging of rockets. Everyone then gathered at Columbus Square to lay wreaths at the statue of Columbus and listen to a speech by the mayor. Once this ceremony was over, the serious tone of the holiday was replaced by revelry on the streets in which some people wore costumes from previous Carnivals. In 1946 the *Trinidad Guardian* reported that "Following the laying of wreaths, revellers danced around, singing old ballads to the strains of the steel bands which played a prominent part in the proceedings." According to the *Guardian,* the most outstanding wreath laid at Columbus' statue was one in the shape of an anchor brought by members of Invaders. After the street celebration, Discovery Day climaxed with a display of fireworks.[68]

In addition to playing an important role in Discovery Day celebrations, steelbands performed for a range of religious holidays. An especially common practice was for small groups of panmen to go serenading at Christmas, sometimes in exchange for Christmas foods. While originally bands simply provided accompaniment for singers, by the late 1940s they were able to play full carols. At Christmas and at

Easter, steelbands also took part in beach "excursions," organized trips in which participants paid for their transportation. For St. Peter's Day, panmen journeyed to the fishing village of Carenage, where a large celebration was (and is) traditionally held. Leo Warner relates how bands used to take over the whole town with performances on all the streets. The feast of La Divina Pastora (a devotion to Mary) in Siparia was another occasion regularly attended by panmen. Victor Wilson recalls taking the train to Siparia and playing pan at every stop along the way. Finally, Leo Alfred describes All Saints' Day festivities in which the people of John John used to proceed up the hills carrying lighted candles and dancing while the members of Tokyo played hymns on their pans. In short, during the 1940s most of the important dates in the Christian calendar in Trinidad became occasions that were celebrated with pan.[69]

Though steelband developed as a type of music that was performed on the streets for Carnival and other holidays, it was also presented in formal competitions, shows, and dances during the 1940s. The organized competitions had rules, judges, and prizes and capitalized on the informal competitiveness that was an integral part of steelband street performance. Apparently, some formal competitions occurred even before the end of the war. For example, George Goddard cites a competition held as early as 1942 at the Queen's Park Oval and notes that it was won by Alexander's Ragtime Band.[70] It was after the war, however, that steelband competitions became quite common. Many of these events were organized by enterprising businessmen who were beginning to recognize the commercial potential of the steelband.

Formal competitions were often held at Carnival. On Carnival Sunday in 1946, for example, a combined calypso and steelband competition took place at Mucurapo Stadium, and this contest subsequently became an annual event. In addition, steelband masquerades were judged at the city's masquerade band competitions. It was at one of these occasions that Winston "Spree" Simon of Tokyo gave his famous performance for Sir Bede Clifford, the governor, and introduced many people to the progress he had made in tuning a ping pong. In its report on the 1946 Marine Square competition, the *Port-of-Spain Gazette* commented:

> His Excellency the Governor and his party showed much amusement at the John John band led by "drummer Springer" who treated the crowd to varied musical tunes. Among the popular tunes this band played were "Lai Fung Lee" "Ave Maria" and ended with "God Save the King."

Anthony Rouff states that Spree also played the hymn "I Am a Warrior" and Lord Kitchener's "Tie Tongue Mopsy."[71]

That same year the public had the opportunity to hear even greater advancements in pan music at an island-wide steelband competition at the Mucurapo Stadium. The event was organized by Ranee Phillips, a local impresario behind many pan contests and shows. Anthony Williams comments that the competing bands worked hard on arrangements of tunes for the occasion. Among the performances were Casablanca's rendition of "Bells of St. Mary's" (from the Bing Crosby movie of the same name) and Sun Valley's arrangements of "Home, Sweet Home" and "La Paloma." Another popular steelband competition in the postwar years was organized by City Councillor Mortimer Mitchell in downtown Port of Spain each J'Ouvert, and beginning in 1949 the *Trinidad Guardian* included a steelband competition at their prestigious Carnival Sunday night show at the Queen's Park Savannah. The first *Guardian* contest was won by Invaders who played "It's Magic" (from the movie *Romance on the High Seas*) in bolero rhythm.[72]

One important aspect of Ranee Phillips's 1946 island-wide pan competition was his decision to take the victor on a tour to British Guiana (Guyana). Sun Valley came in first but apparently was not prepared for a tour. Thus the opportunity went to second-place Red Army, who, under the name of "Russian Symphony," became the first steelband to travel overseas. It appears that they were presented in British Guiana as a novelty act in a variety show:

> Mr. Phillips told the "Trinidad Guardian" yesterday that he will also be taking a troupe, including Rochester and Anelle, popular jiving artistes, "The Singing Cowboy," Johnny Walker and Kenneth Savary, two of Trinidad's oldest comedians; "Lucille," a female acrobat, and Mademoiselle Georgette, the Martiniquan rhumba dancer who was brought out here by Mr. Phillips a few weeks ago.

Mack Kinsale recalls that thirteen members of Red Army went on the tour and that it was a big boost for the band. Before leaving for British Guiana, they performed in theaters, community centers, and schools all over Trinidad.[73] These performances helped pave the way for other presentations of steelbands in stage settings.

In the postwar years it became increasingly common for steelbands to be featured at nightclubs, dance halls, theaters, and community centers. These performances were generally attended by grass-roots Trinidadians, though some venues and occasions attracted wider audiences. The remaining American servicemen also enjoyed the steelbands and would often go to hear them at the clubs on Park Street and Wrightson Road. Occasionally, they even brought bands out to the base at Chaguaramas. In addition, steelbands were sometimes invited to house fetes (such as weddings and christenings) in grass-roots communities. Writer Kim Johnson notes that brothels and funerals were two other settings for pan:

> Two brothels had opened on Bath Street for the American soldiers, attracting all kinds of men and women out for a hustle, and which was their band? Bar 20.
>
> When Ancil Boyce, the Bar 20 Captain, fell into the Dry River and died, his funeral drew hundreds of these villains to the Lapeyrouse Cemetery, all drunk, sporting stolen jackets they'd dyed black. Back in Bath Street, spirits high, the battalion decided to hit the road. Waving flag up front was "Bubulups"—later immortalised in calypso after she beat a policeman and made a jail. . . .[74]

This range of new performance opportunities encouraged panmen both to improve their musical technique and to expand their repertoires. Competitions in particular were an important factor in the rapid musical development made by steelbands in the postwar years. While in 1945 they were still beating out rough versions of children's songs and lavways, by the end of the decade they were playing arrangements of calypsos, carols, hymns, and North American and Latin American popular tunes.

The resumption of Carnival after the war and the increase in steelband competitions brought musical progress, but they appear to have also been factors in the escalation of steelband violence during this period. By the end of the war, many steelbands had become territorial units engaged in rivalries, particularly over women. Gordon Rohlehr suggests that a decline in the prevalence of prostitution and the flow of cash after the war perhaps intensified disputes.[75] At the same time, musical rivalry increased as bands became more skilled at playing pan and as they entered competitions. Bands prided themselves on their musical ability, and any challenge of this ability was taken as an insult. Unpopular decisions by judges at competitions also contributed to the tension that existed between bands.

Carnival, with its focus on street encounters and competition, provided the main opportunity for steelbands to act out their rivalries. Each band paraded into the city with a combative orientation: panmen and followers from their community joined forces, wore military or warrior masques, sang aggressive songs, played music at a high intensity, and attempted to dominate space on the streets. Rival bands in fact sought each other out in order to demonstrate their prowess and the creativity of their music and masquerade. When two bands met tension rose, especially if unsettled disputes existed between them. Onlookers watched with bated breath to see if the bands would pass each other without confrontation. Usually bands did manage to pass with minimal physical turmoil. But sometimes an incident occurred that sparked off a major clash. For example, a woman claimed by one band might be seen in the other band. Or a member of one band might throw a bottle into the rival band. Flagmen were also responsible for many fights, due to the aggressive manner in which they waved their flags and to their determination to create competition over space in the streets. In general it was not the performing panmen but their followers who initiated the violence. However, once an incident occurred everyone became involved. Cutlasses, knives, razors, bottles, stones, and other weapons appeared from nowhere and a bloody battle ensued. Spectators scattered, the police rushed to the scene, and arrests were made, later followed by court cases and sentences. Lennox Pierre suggests that, since fights also sometimes developed outside of court after cases were heard, the cases in effect recycled steelband warfare.[76]

Serious steelband violence really began with the 1947 Carnival. During this period there was considerable unrest in the society as a whole, with strikes and riots occurring in December 1946 and January 1947. In January the level of tension was so high that the Governor delayed his official proclamation of Carnival. Eventually the unrest subsided and Carnival was proclaimed and held as usual. The *Trinidad Guardian* warned in an editorial, however, that Carnival might "present an opportunity for trouble-makers to attempt to create difficulties" and that revelers should "take special care to observe rigidly all the recognised standards of good conduct."[77] Some violence did occur that year, including at least one major steelband clash and at least fifteen reported cases of woundings. The Commissioner of Police stated that "the 'steel band element' could be held responsible for all or nearly all the breaches of the peace." Fighting continued after Carnival, and steelbands were banned from participating in the Discovery Day festivities that year.[78]

Steelband violence sometimes occurred at occasions other than Carnival. For example, the *Guardian* reported that the Christmas weekend in 1948 was the worst in the colony's history and included "a number of dance hall brawls and street clashes in various sections of the city." In one part of East Dry River, "steelbandsmen who were pursued by police on Christmas Day resorted to sticks, stones and bottles which were show-ered indiscriminately about the heads of policemen who attempted to intercept the revellers."[79] Eighteen panmen were charged with "playing steel drums without a license and throwing stones to the danger of per-sons."[80]

There were also fights between panmen at times other than holidays. The strong territorial attitude of bands meant that it was sometimes difficult for panmen from one neighborhood to pass through a hostile neighborhood without being attacked. Furthermore, some bands had long-standing feuds with each other that could flare up at any time. In the late 1940s Invaders (of Woodbrook) and Casablanca (of East Dry River) were continually at war with each other. Vernon Mannette ex-plains that this was due to the perception of Woodbrook as a more pros-perous neighborhood and to the fact that Invaders would dress up and attract women from downtown. In late 1949 and early 1950 a consider-able amount of publicity was given to stabbings and arrests involving these two bands.[81]

Steelband violence was one of the main factors behind ambivalent at-titudes toward the movement in the 1940s. During this period pan music was enjoyed by a fairly wide cross-section of the public at Carnival and, at least by the grass-roots class, at other festive occasions. But pan-men themselves were often perceived by members of all classes as reck-less and belligerent or, in local terms, as *hooligans, badjohns,* and *robustmen.* As fights between bands escalated, panmen as a segment of the society increasingly became feared, even though the majority of them were not instigators of violence. The public also objected to pan-men because of their association with the saga boy lifestyle, which was based on leisure rather than steady employment. In short, panmen were perceived as involved in wayward activities, and these perceptions led many people to have reservations about the music and its performance. Naturally there was somewhat more tolerance for pan and panmen in grass-roots communities, since it was here that band members lived. But even many grass-roots Trinidadians were wary of pan and did not want their families too closely associated with it. In fact, most panmen from this era relate that their parents emphatically did not want them playing pan and tell stories of receiving "licks" when they were caught near pan-yards.

During the postwar years many members of the middle and upper classes viewed the steelband movement as a threat to the social order. The violence and chaos of the steelbands could easily be associated with the demonstrations, riots, and general social unrest that had become so prevalent. Flogging (colloquially known as the "cat") was reinstituted in

1946 as one coercive means of maintaining order in the society. It was subsequently abolished again, but by 1949 there were calls for its return. For example, a pastor from Couva stated in a letter to the *Trinidad Guardian* that "Only shortsighted sentimentalists would oppose return of the 'cat'—the only remedy that could assist in checking the current evil wave and rising tide of local Communism, steelbandism, and hooliganism in Trinidad."[82] Through such perceptions of the steelband as an aggressive grass-roots phenomenon, the movement became symbolic of the whole upsurge of grass-roots militancy during this period.

The fear of steelband violence was also a factor in renewed efforts at Carnival "improvement" during the 1940s. The City Council of Port of Spain had formed a Carnival Improvement Committee before the war; by the postwar years this committee was engaged in a full-scale attempt to "clean up" Carnival. Each year a list of "Carnival Don'ts" was published for the benefit of revelers. Among the guidelines were: "Don't dress in an immodest or scanty costume," "Don't dance in a vulgar way," "Don't sing any immoral or suggestive songs," and "Don't lose your temper and behave in a violent manner."[83] In addition, the committee held Carnival competitions that received support from businessmen. At these events prizes were used to encourage what were considered to be acceptable forms of masquerading. Obviously, steelbands, with their combative practices and bad behavior sailor masquerades, were a primary target of this campaign to "clean up" Carnival, and one means of attempting to contain their objectionable activities was to encourage them to participate in the various masquerade (and music) competitions.

The *Trinidad Guardian* was another important force in the Carnival "improvement" effort and each year wrote editorials calling for restrained behavior. "Shorn of its ugly features," the paper suggested in 1947, "the festival should produce as much clean fun as an afternoon on the Savannah playing cricket or soccer." Moreover, the *Guardian* centered its Carnival Sunday night show around the selection of a Carnival Queen. The contestants in the event were sponsored by businesses and organizations and were always fair-skinned. This competition, the paper argued, "establishes a focal point of interest for the celebrations, tends to raise their general tone, and adds to the attraction of Carnival for visitors and our public." Tourism was in fact increasing in the postwar years, and there was much concern that visitors not be offended. In 1948, a year after the violence of the 1947 Carnival, the *Guardian* stated that, if the festival were to continue to attract tourists, it was necessary "to steer events into safe channels, and away from the evil associations of gang war which have tended to crop up in the past." The paper went on to argue that steelbands were responsible for most of the disturbances in the previous year.[84]

Though steelband clashes were an important factor behind negative perceptions of the movement, the "noise" of the bands was equally a source of concern. Condemnation of pan on this account was by no means restricted to members of the middle and upper classes. The fact that panmen tended to rehearse for several hours every day caused much distress among the residents of their neighborhoods. Often individuals living near panyards would call the police to complain. The bands' habit of marching through the streets at night whenever possible provoked further criticism.

As early as December 1945 the Legislative Council responded to complaints about noise by passing a bill that amended the Summary Offences Ordinance to forbid "the playing of noisy instruments on the streets and other public places except during such time as the Governor shall proclaim or with the permission of the Commissioner of Police." Council member Albert Gomes, who was to become one of the strongest defenders of the steelband, voted against the bill and remarked that it would prevent the strumming of guitars and quatros on the streets. The Attorney General who had proposed the bill responded that its purpose was "to curtail excessive noise." Gomes added that, although the Attorney General had not specified steelbands, the legislation was obviously inspired by them. He went on to state that the individuals who complained to the Attorney General "were guided as much by their social prejudices as they were by their sensitiveness to noise," and argued that the government was becoming remote from the people and did not understand their situation. L. C. Hannays, a council member who voted in favor of the bill, replied to Gomes that steelbands could still play in their yards and that the intention was "to prevent this form of mischief being transferred to a public place." Hannays continued that he "would prefer to see the people who play these drums rise to greater heights" and that, instead of encouraging them to play pans, arrangements should be made with talented local musicians such as Winifred Atwell "to teach these people how to express themselves musically."[85]

This new legislation had only a limited impact on steelbands, and during the postwar years people continued to complain about steelband noise. In a letter to the *Guardian* in 1946, for example, a citizen of San Fernando stated:

> Beating tins and pans today seems to be contagious. Unemployment is not the cause of it, for young people prefer the steel bands to good hard work. . . .

So we must put up with the transformation of earth into bedlam, to the utter disgust of parents, students, tired workmen, troubled people and invalids.

Can beating is pan beating in any language and in any form. It does nobody any good, and when it is indulged in all day all night day in and day out, it is abominable. Why is there no legislation to control it?

If it must continue and if by virtue of its alleged inherent beauty and charm it will someday bring popularity and fame to the island and a fortune to the beaters, then by all means let it go on—but in the forests and other desolate places.

A month before the 1946 elections under universal suffrage, a citizen of Tunapuna wrote to the *Guardian* that steelband music was "a maddening noise on bits of old junk from morn till night" and that "True democracy does not mean giving complete sway to the underprivileged and uneducated."[86]

Letters such as these and the debate in the Legislative Council suggest that objections to the steelband were not simply a matter of "noise" but that issues of class, power, and culture were involved as well. As noted in the Introduction to this study, the maintenance of the colonial order in Trinidad depended in part on the creation and perpetuation of a pattern of perceptions in which European cultural practices were seen as superior and African or local practices as inferior. This ideology was firmly asserted by colonial authorities and British expatriates and was imposed on the colonial population through such means as the educational system and cultural policy (including legal restrictions). Thus notions of European cultural superiority pervaded the entire society. They were especially pronounced, though not entirely accepted, among members of the local middle and upper classes. In order to preserve their own positions in the society, these classes attempted to maintain a distance from the grass-roots class and condemned some of its cultural practices such as African-derived percussion and religion.

Given this cultural hierarchy in colonial Trinidad, European music was highly valued and affirmed while local percussion instruments such as pans were described as disturbing sources of "noise." An incident reported by the *Guardian* in 1946 perfectly captures this situation:

The Rev. Fr. Keenan, presiding over formal opening of a piano at St. Dominic R.C. School, Morvant, last Sunday said he hoped the piano would help the children to understand something of musical notes, and kill the perversity which declared the beating of steel drums was music.

"It is unfortunate," he said, "that so many of our children spend so

much time beating steel drums. I hope now that the war is over, we
will see guitars and other musical instruments in the hands of people
instead of empty cans."

Shortly after the Rev. Fr. Keenan had spoken and the piano was
opened, a very large steel band passed by, holding up the programme
for two minutes drawing smiles from the audience.[87]

Views similar to Fr. Keenan's were expressed in a letter to the
Guardian the following day from "Bust Ear-Drums," a citizen of Port of
Spain:

> Some bright soul suggested recently that steel bands and their pro-
> ducers should be confined to the bush when expressing their particu-
> lar form of "culture", and I heartily endorse the suggestion, for the
> simple fact that of all noises we in Trinidad are heir to, steel bands be-
> long to the bush in more ways than one. Drum-beating in Africa is a
> common heritage and had its use, inasmuch as it was used for the
> sending of messages; but to those who defend the steel bands in our
> midst and cry that by banning them we are denying the people their
> cultural expression, I say "baloney", or if that's the best they can do by
> way of cultural expression by all means let them go into the bush.
>
> There is a terrific amount of rot talked about "culture" these days,
> and if steel bands are to fall into this category, I prefer to remain a
> savage and listen to Mozart.[88]

For many residents of Trinidad, the steelband symbolized a disruption of the society. The bill banning noisy instruments on the streets was
passed in late 1945 and the above letters were written in 1946. This was
precisely the period in which the steelband became a widely known and
heard phenomenon and in which grass-roots Trinidadians were again
expressing considerable discontent over their economic and political
situation. The middle and upper classes were hearing a range of "noise"
in the streets from demonstrations to steelbands and began to associate
these disturbances as a general threat to the social and cultural order.
The perceptions established during this period remained and were re-
inforced by the increase in steelband violence in the late 1940s.

The pattern of valuing European over local cultural practices was not
limited to the middle and upper classes but also influenced many members of the grass-roots class. This produced ambivalent attitudes toward
some Afro-Trinidadian forms of expression. On the one hand, local
Carnival and religious practices were an important source of strength

and identity for grass-roots Trinidadians and had been defended for generations against suppression by the colonial authorities. On the other hand, individuals with aspirations towards "respectability" in the society needed to distance themselves, at least to some extent, from the most objectionable grass-roots activities such as pan. Bertie Marshall, a well-known pan tuner, provides a sense of this in a description of his boyhood in John John and Laventille during the 1940s:

We used to hear the sounds—all the pans playing only three notes— B, D, E, but plenty rhythm and people jumping up [dancing] and waving coconut branches. All this we saw while peeping through the jalousie, and all the time my mother yelling:

"Move from the jalousie before they chook out all yuh eye. Before all yuh say yuh prayers and go to bed all yuh looking at stupidness." And she would then turn down the lamp low to make sure that the neighbors understood on which side of the steelband-line we stood.[89]

Some grass-roots individuals who were especially concerned with respectability might indulge in the steelband at Carnival or certain other special occasions, but on the whole it was something to be avoided and even criticized. In fact panmen encountered so much opposition inside as well as outside their communities that, in the end, they could only depend on each other for encouragement. Mack Kinsale recalls:

It was very rough. Because you had everybody against you. Your mother, your father, your bigger brother and your bigger sister . . . then the police and the public, too. You had to fight all these . . . in order to have this thing moving. Because, remember as I tell you, from the time you was a steelbandman, you becomes a robustman. Your good neighbor see you talking to he daughter, that's it. . . . Because you was an outcast. But the determination we had, we used to choo [ignore] all that. "Call me what you want. Do what you want. But we like we pan." And we had to beat that pan.[90]

So, from the earliest days, the steelband life became one of struggle. The panman's primary concern was to perfect his instrument and his music—to produce something new and valuable and to be somebody in the society. His combativeness was to some extent a response to the public's refusal to recognize his creativity and worth and to the general oppressiveness of the social order. Big Mack Sandiford explains:

We were really not rebellious or violent being left alone. But we didn't used to be left alone. Most of our reaction was being provoked by society. Some privilege that they wouldn't allow us to use our freedom. . . . They wanted to keep us in a certain environment, in a certain yoke. And this caused us frustration. . . .

But I don't know if it was jealousy or dumbness, they hadn't realized that this is a new talent that being originated from mankind. And they couldn't recognize it. But they used to resent it. They never welcomed it and looked on it as something cultural. They were always treat you in that aspect as being wild beasts and you's belong in a jungle. And this is jungle music. This is music from people of the jungle. This is not music which should be associated between human beings. This is how they term it. This is how they had it. They never turned and said: "Well, my gosh. This is extremely . . ."

You have to begin somewhere. . . . Because it come from the lower masses, then, they never think that we were worthy enough, cultivated enough to create such and so on. They treated us as outcasts. It's only beasts and cannibals would look to produce such nuisance, noise.[91]

It was the pervasiveness of sentiments such as these that led the Mighty Sparrow to recount, in his 1964 calypso "Outcast," how a young woman could be thrown out of her family's house, if she were caught talking with a steelbandsman.[92]

In spite of sustained opposition, the steelband became a widespread phenomenon in Trinidad and Tobago during the 1940s as young men throughout the colony formed steelbands and worked at developing their new instruments and music. By V-E Day and V-J Day, steelbands were already prominent in locations as far apart as Cedros, San Fernando, Princes Town, Chaguanas, and Sangre Grande.[93] Though it is possible that advancements in the tuning of pans occurred independently in a number of different areas, Port of Spain was certainly the center of innovation. New ideas spread as individuals from other districts came to live in Port of Spain and as panmen from the city traveled to other parts of the island.

The movement also spread to the rural island of Tobago, and its particular manifestation there further reveals the significance that pan assumed during the war and postwar years. In Trinidad steelbands gradually emerged out of tamboo bamboo bands that had been created due to the prohibition of drumming. In Tobago, on the other hand, there was no similar law and the drumming tradition remained.[94] Pans were introduced to this island during the war years by Tobagonians who had gone to work for the Americans in Trinidad and through interaction with Trinidadians on the wharves in Scarborough (the largest town in Tobago). Lytton "Bomber" Stewart, an early panman from Plymouth, recalls that he first heard a steelband in Scarborough at the Carnival of 1943 (the wartime Carnival ban was not as rigidly enforced in Tobago). This group included a few individuals who had been working in Trinidad and who brought back some three-note pans made from paint cans and some biscuit-drum basses. Pans were also used in the celebration of V-E Day and V-J Day in Tobago; and the *Trinidad Guardian* reported that, a week before the 1946 Carnival, "steel bands paraded the streets of Scarborough with hundreds of revellers behind them."[95]

In the postwar years there were a number of steelbands in Tobago, such as Lucky Jordan (Scarborough), Rhythm Tigers (Glen Road), Desperadoes (Plymouth), Free French (Canaan), and Black Swan (Whim). Often these bands obtained their pans from Trinidad, but some Tobagonians also learned the art of tuning. On Carnival Monday the bands generally marched on the roads in their own districts while on Tuesday they went into Scarborough. Often they played sailor or Ju Ju Warrior masquerades that were introduced with the steelband from Trinidad. There was rivalry between villages and occasional skirmishes, but steelband-related violence in Tobago was minimal compared to Port of Spain. Bands also performed at competitions at the Rex Cinema in Scarborough, at dances, and for wedding marches. Wedding marches were traditionally accompanied by *tamborin* bands, ensembles consisting of the shallow goatskin tamborin drums, a fiddle, and a triangle. With the growing popularity of steelbands, tamborin bands gradually became less common. Though pan was enjoyed at a range of festive occasions, it was also viewed with suspicion by many and with hostility by some, due to its grass-roots basis and its association with violence in Trinidad.[96]

During the war years Tobagonians not only went to work in Trinidad but took advantage of the good wages being offered on two small American bases in Tobago. J. D. Elder describes how the arrival of the steelband in Tobago was associated with a whole experience of an American way of life, including such novelties as Marlboro cigarettes and chewing gum. Similarly, George "Josey" Richardson (an early pan tuner from Plymouth) recalls that, when young Tobagonian fellows returned from working in Trinidad, they often affected a Trinidadian saga boy or an American way of dressing, walking, and talking. People in the community would be impressed and would gather around them, eager to hear their exciting tales of life in Trinidad.[97] The steelband was interrelated with this life of excitement and for young Tobagonians, like young Trinidadians, playing pan was a way of displaying a new identity in keeping with the times.[98]

Steelbands, Festive Traditions, and Social Conflict

Though steelband practices were novel forms of expression, they were at the same time based on creole festive traditions that date back to the nineteenth century. Over the years Trinidadians gradually re-created these traditions in response to changing historical conditions and events. Individuals played out particular festive occasions according to cultural models but the models were gradually altered, due to the historical circumstances of their enactment. Performances were thus simultaneously occasions in which traditions were perpetuated and changed. This ongoing process of cultural reproduction and innovation produced a variety of Carnival and other festive practices in the course of the nineteenth and early twentieth centuries, and the development of the steelband in the 1940s was a further manifestation of the process. Panmen utilized existing cultural models but adapted these models to express their particular experience of the social upheaval of wartime and postwar Trinidad.

Steelbands as social organizations for participation in festive occasions ultimately have their roots in the pre-emancipation underground regiments that privately observed Christmas with royal personnel, uniforms, flags, and percussion. Following the emancipation it became possible for Africans to engage in public street festivity. Bands reappeared as Africans appropriated Carnival and transformed it into a version of their own Canboulay festival. The prohibition of kalinda bands in the 1880s was followed by the emergence of tamboo bamboo bands and other grass-roots Carnival groups, such as the military bands that drew on the masquerade tradition inspired by nineteenth-century Christmas military displays. Kings and queens were still crowned in many Carnival bands, but the royal hierarchies of the pre-emancipation regiments were now more clearly manifested in the array of officers in sailor and other military bands. In terms of personnel and expressive forms, steelbands were essentially a merger of tamboo bamboo bands and sailor bands, and like earlier African organizations they re-created the festivals of the Christian calendar in creole terms.

The steelband rivalry and related elements of the pan life in many ways parallel the kalinda band rivalry and the whole jamette cultural style, which reached its peak during the 1870s. The recurrence of similar social conditions in the 1940s in effect amplified a tradition that had existed to some degree since the nineteenth century. The 1940s, like the 1870s, was a period of extensive migration, urban overcrowding, and more prevalent prostitution. The panmen were landless and in some cases migrants or the children of migrants to Port of Spain. As was true during the jamette period, there was a need to identify with neighborhoods, to belong somewhere, and to stake out territories. Similarly, there was competition over women, with those panmen who were toughest, best-dressed, or most skilled musically having the greatest success.

Disputes over women, as well as other conflicts, were now ritualized in the steelband clash instead of in the stickfight. These clashes were acted out with considerable self-consciousness and drama: there were flamboyant military masques, boastful and antagonistic songs, and aggressive flagmen. Clashes became occasions that were expected in that band members were often well-armed. In addition to being a means of settling disputes, the clashes were public displays of power and a means of carving out an identity in the anonymity of the urban world. A panman was not simply another unemployed man on the streets but a member of Tokyo or Casablanca or Invaders, and there was an array of flags, banners, hand-painted jerseys, caps with monograms, and tattoos that confirmed this. It was partially through victories in clashes that a panman and his band earned their reputations.

Not only were steelbands related to much older social organizations, but the instruments themselves were a direct development from earlier forms of percussion. The pans of the prototypical steelband were substituted for the instruments of the tamboo bamboo band which in turn had been modeled on skin drums. Specific historical circumstances precipitated these substitutions: the disintegration of pieces of bamboo in Carnival street performances, the interest in finding more durable and dynamic replacements, the increasing availability of metal containers, and the chance discoveries of pitch variations. The basic instruments of the early steelband were subsequently expanded or replaced as young men, with spare time and much imagination, sought means of playing increasingly complex melodies and harmonies. In the course of the 1940s the steelband was rapidly transformed by pan tuners engaged in a continual process of replication and alteration.

In addition to musical continuities, the use and symbolism of the steelband resembled uses and symbolic meanings of percussion that had been established in earlier times. Drumming occurred either in the private spaces and times of the Afro-Trinidadian world or as a means of appropriating and remaking European festivals. It also became the accompaniment for stickfighting. For Africans, drumming was not only festive but spiritually empowering and an expression of an identity alternative to the one imposed on them by the planter class. For Europeans, drumming was festive but also a sign of moral corruption and a potential source of rebellion. This general pattern of usage and mean-

ing continued through the tamboo bamboo period and into the steelband era. The steelband existed in yards that panmen claimed as their
own and at grass-roots community fetes, but was also part of the festivals
in which the entire society participated. At times pan was a form of martial music, used occasionally to accompany stickfights in the earlier days
and later as an inspiration for steelband rivalries which sometimes resulted in clashes. For panmen, the music was not only a means of recreation and celebration but an achievement—a creation that was entirely
theirs.[99] Through informal and formal pan competition, they achieved
and asserted reputations that paralleled reputations gained through
sports or fighting. For others, the steelband was often enjoyable at festive occasions but was also a threat to values of respectability and to a
sense of order in the society.

Notions of reputation and respectability were in fact at the foundation of the opposing perceptions of the steelband. These notions have
been explored at a theoretical level by Peter Wilson in his anthropological studies of West Indian societies. Wilson suggests that respectability
and reputation are two principles of thought and sentiment that produce practices and social groupings. Respectability includes such values
as formal marriage, household management, economic success, church
attendance, and proper manners. Among the values related to reputation, on the other hand, are virility and sexual exploits, fighting ability,
male occupational and expressive skills, and recreation. Women and
married or older men tend to be more concerned with respectability,
while reputation is generally the domain of younger or unmarried men.
In terms of social groupings, respectability is associated with formal institutional structures such as the family and the church and has the
home as its primary setting. Reputation, on the other hand, involves
small informal groupings of men (sometimes called "crews") and is
based in the world of the street and the rum shop. Wilson argues that
respectability is European-oriented and externally imposed on the society, while reputation is indigenous. Reputation is related to the way in
which men achieve a sense of self-worth on their own terms. Their crews
and networks of crews are counter-political structures which exist in opposition to the world of respectability and can be used to circumvent,
criticize, and even undermine the legal system.[100]

One problem with Wilson's framework is his description of respectability as European-oriented and externally imposed. Actually,
both respectability and reputation are integral parts of the process in
which West Indians have created and organized their own cultures. As
Roger Abrahams suggests, reputation and respectability are best
thought of as value-complexes for opposing expressive styles within

West Indian societies. Another problem is Wilson's limited account of women's behavior. Jean Besson has demonstrated that West Indian women also participate in some reputation-oriented activities and stresses that their sense of respectability is their own creation and not a mirror image of Eurocentric values.[101] At the same time, it should be emphasized that young and unmarried men are not exclusively concerned with reputation but often embrace some elements of respectability.

With these qualifications, Wilson's framework can provide a useful perspective on some West Indian expressive practices, including pan. The steelband lifestyle of the 1940s was to a significant degree focused around the principle of reputation. Steelbands were indigenous, informal groupings of young men (much larger than crews) that were based in streets and in panyards (which were physical and social extensions of the streets). Much of the pan life revolved around musical performance, recreation, and attracting women. It was through informal competition with each other on their own terms that panmen achieved, challenged, and defended reputations. Meanwhile, the attack on the steelband movement during the 1940s was launched from the world of respectability. The steelband life was perceived as contrary to values of marriage, home, church, hard work, and decorum, and as a threat to the institutional structure of the society. Steelbands were seen as uncontrollable and unpredictable gangs, and efforts were made to contain the movement by designating some of its basic practices as "illegal." Thus a struggle over the steelband ensued. The music was criticized and restricted in terms of values of respectability, but the bands continued to circumvent restrictions and to pose a challenge to these values.

From this perspective, the development of the steelband movement can be interpreted as an expression of the deeply rooted West Indian cultural pattern of an alternative tradition of reputation existing in opposition to a dominant tradition of respectability. Yet the movement was also a distinctive youth lifestyle which owed much to the particular circumstances of wartime and postwar Trinidad. In their analyses of working class youth "subcultures" in Britain, Stuart Hall and other scholars associated with the Centre for Contemporary Cultural Studies in Birmingham discuss how such cultural styles are often focused around territorial spaces, material artifacts (such as clothing), and leisure time pursuits (such as music). Youths draw on a range of working class and dominant cultural practices but rearrange and recombine these practices in unusual ways to form distinctive styles, which exist in opposition to the dominant culture and provide a sense of group identity and belonging in the face of unstable social conditions.[102]

The young panmen of the 1940s lived during a period of extended social disruption in Trinidad: the depression and intolerable living and working conditions of the 1930s; Americanization, increased migration, and temporary economic opportunity during the war; and the decline of the economy again in the postwar years. Urbanization and unemployment contributed to the emergence of the steelband lifestyle, while intensified conflicts in male-female relations (precipitated, in part, by prostitution) contributed to its combative dimension. The symbols of this style were the panmen's creative response to their experience during these years. Americanization seemed to be the trend of the times, and panmen were influenced by American images and behaviors as manifested in the movies and by the American military presence on the island. American styles of dressing, walking, and talking, as well as names, were all appropriated and imaginatively combined with parallel practices from the local alternative culture. American militarism and the bad behavior of servicemen when off-duty were especially appealing and had already been incorporated into the Carnival. Panmen developed these traditions in terms of their expanded awareness of America during the war and combined them with other local traditions of competition and misbehavior, to create an often confrontational stance toward one another and toward authorities. This stance was most explicit at Carnival when the battles from the movies and the bad behavior antics were reenacted on the streets.

It was in the steelband itself, however, that panmen most fully expressed their creative energies, and for them collaborative music making was ultimately of much greater importance than confrontation. Panmen collected from their environment a range of mundane metal objects, from biscuit tins to automobile parts to oil drums, and transformed these objects into musical instruments. Through this process, they symbolically made the urban-industrial world their own and forged a new music that encompassed the experiences of their generation. The use of such an odd assortment of objects to make music was shocking to the public. Steelband performances thus disrupted conventional and respectable notions of music and identified the panmen as an assertive new group in the society.

As discussed earlier, the 1930s and 1940s were a period of growing grass-roots consciousness in Trinidad. The response of many grass-roots Trinidadians during these years was militancy: strikes, demonstrations, hunger marches, and riots. These spectacular displays of resistance in the streets were paralleled by the street performances of steelbands in which panmen dramatically displayed their identities and sense of self-worth. Pan was not an overt protest music, however, but a symbolic expression of the discontent and militancy of the times as experienced by unemployed youths. This significance was certainly not lost on the middle and upper classes, who as already noted often spoke about steelbands in the same vein that they described other signs of disorder in the society.

Though pan was disruptive, it was also festive and could, at special moments, attract much of the population. The steelband developed in the context of Carnival and was yet another manifestation of the inventiveness that lies at the heart of this event. The openness and freedom of Carnival encourage much creativity in Trinidad, including the creation of alternative cultural practices and identities. Through Carnival, Trinidadians explore new visions of themselves. The steelband was one of these new visions and was an initiator of social change as well as a response to socioeconomic conditions. As an indigenous music performed by indigenous social organizations, it was one prefiguration of the emergence of a new society, namely, a nation.

Chapter Three
The Institutionalization of the Steelband: The 1940s and 1950s

As Trinidad and Tobago progressed toward independence from Britain during the late 1940s and 1950s, the steelband movement was gradually integrated into the formal institutional structure of the society. This process of institutionalization was motivated both by the panmen themselves and by certain members of the middle class who developed a special interest in the movement. The panmen asserted the fundamental worth of their music and their desire for an accepted place in the society, while a growing number of middle class Trinidadians affirmed the steelband as a local art and a potential symbol of national identity. Grass-roots assertion combined with middle class nationalist promotion thus helped propel this indigenous form of expression into the cultural mainstream.

The transformation of the use and significance of the steelband was a very slow, arduous, and convoluted process. A number of social dramas affecting the steelband's fate were played out simultaneously, and the new music only acquired some degree of respectability after a variety of changes had occurred in the movement. The negotiations over the future of pan involved several parties: grass-roots panmen, middle class steelband advocates, opponents of the steelband, new middle class panmen, businessmen, and the government. All of these parties were pursuing particular goals in relation to the steelband, and their interactions with each other included both conflict and collaboration. At the same time, the various steelband dramas were interrelated with the whole process of decolonization during this period. In fact, the institutionalization of the steelband can be seen as one expression of the complex development of Trinidad and Tobago as an independent nation.

In the course of the past century, nationalism has assumed a variety of forms in Trinidad. Definitions of cultural identity and assertions of political autonomy have been conceived both in specifically Trinidadian

terms and in terms of a broader West Indian nation. These ideas of national identity based on place or region have in turn been accompanied
by movements of ethnic nationalism. Africans and Indians have com-
petitively promoted their cultural heritages and have often differed in
their views of what a Trinidadian or West Indian nation might be. Class
agendas have been important as well. Nationalist sentiments have developed among both the middle and the grass-roots classes and have been
shaped by the particular interests of these classes.

Nationalism first became a significant force in Trinidad in the late
nineteenth century. By this point an urban colored and African middle
class had developed, consisting primarily of professionals, teachers, and
office workers. Members of this class had a firm sense of local identity
that they utilized as a basis for organized political resistance to some aspects of colonial rule. One of their primary grievances was the colonial
government's placement of foreigners at the higher levels of the civil
service. The local middle class felt that these positions rightfully belonged to them and protested with the slogan "Trinidad for Trinidadians."[1] They also objected to the absence of any elected members in
Trinidad's Legislative Council. After colonial authorities abolished the
partially elected Port of Spain Borough Council in 1898, the middle
class began to pursue more militant action and was able to elicit the support of the grass-roots class. The most dramatic display of resistance to
colonialism during this period was the riot of 1903 in which the Red
House (the seat of the colonial government) was destroyed by fire.

The nationalist sentiments of the grass-roots class became more pronounced with the growth of the Trinidad Workingmen's Association
(TWA) which had been established around 1897. This organization
played a role in the strikes of 1919 and its newspaper, the *Labour Leader,*
reflected ideas of Garveyism, Pan-Africanism, and socialism which were
increasingly influential among the urban African working class in the
years after World War I.[2] A. A. Cipriani, a popular ex-captain of the
West Indian Regiment, became president of the TWA in 1923, and in
1925 won a seat in the then partially elected Legislative Council. As a
council member, Cipriani consistently defended working class interests
and advocated self-government within the framework of the British Empire. Though the conservative orientation of the Council thwarted most
of his efforts, he was immensely popular with the Trinidadian people
and was a seminal figure in the development of a sense of national consciousness. Selwyn Ryan argues that Cipriani "succeeded in awakening
the 'barefooted man' to the relevance of national politics in his daily
routine" and "was the instrument by which large numbers of individuals
who had previously experienced no basic attraction towards one an-

other came to develop feelings of national kinship and identification."[3] In 1934 the TWA became the Trinidad Labour Party in order to pursue political goals more effectively. By this time, however, Cipriani and his party were being eclipsed by a more militant labor movement led by individuals such as Uriah Butler.

The strikes and riots of the 1930s were the most vigorous and effective assault on the colonial system that Trinidad had ever experienced. These events were primarily a manifestation of grass-roots discontent. During this same period, however, some members of the middle class were pursuing nationalist interests through literary means. In the late 1920s and early 1930s an important group of writers emerged, including C. L. R. James, Alfred Mendes, Albert Gomes, and R. A. C. de Boissière. Initially this group published much of their creative writing and social and political commentary in a small magazine called *The Beacon*. There they challenged European literary conventions and focused attention on West Indian, African, and Indian history and culture. James, Mendes, and, later de Boissière also published novels on the life of grass-roots Trinidadians. James's *Minty Alley,* for example, portrays the dilemmas of a young middle class man who lives in a grass-roots yard and experiences a sense of alienation from and attraction to yard life.[4] For the middle class writers of this period, folk culture became a realm to be explored as a source of a new identity.

During the post-World War II years nationalist sentiments gradually became more widespread in Trinidad and constitutional reform became a primary concern. In 1946 universal suffrage was instituted and the number of elected members in the Legislative Council was increased. By 1950 there was a majority of elected representatives. However, there were no stable political parties that could take full advantage of these constitutional changes. Political parties were numerous, short-lived, and to a considerable extent the expressions of individual personalities. Albert Gomes, the *Beacon* group writer and a trade unionist, became the dominant figure in Trinidadian politics during this period and, from 1950 to 1956, occupied the powerful position of Minister for Labour, Commerce, and Industry in the Executive Council. While in 1946 Gomes had been affiliated with a labor party that advocated working class interests and self-government, by 1950 he was aligned with business interests and argued for a more cautious approach to constitutional reform.

Political advancements in the postwar years were accompanied by further developments in cultural nationalism. As the African and colored middle class became more prominent, it increasingly sought new symbols with which to define itself. Gradually more attention was given to Afro-Trinidadian folklore. Beryl McBurnie, for example, presented interpretations of folk dances in her Little Carib Theatre, while Olive Walke's La Petite Musicale performed arranged versions of folksongs. However, with continued attraction to foreign cultural styles, it would be some time before efforts like these became widely accepted by the middle class. Meanwhile, the independence of India in 1947 and a growing Indian middle class gave a boost to the Indian nationalism that had been developing in Trinidad at least since the 1930s. There was increased construction of temples, mosques, and Hindu and Muslim schools. Musicians, dancers, and religious figures from India were enthusiastically received in Trinidad, while some Indo-Trinidadians returned to India for visits. Bridget Brereton comments that: "On the whole, articulate Indians in the 1950s considered 'Creole culture' [Afro-Trinidadian culture] to be inferior to that of India, and they objected to the widespread idea . . . that Indians would inevitably be creolized."[5] In the course of the 1950s, ethnic nationalism and competition were also manifested in the tendency of Africans and Indians to vote along ethnic lines in elections.

The Advocacy and Organization of the Steelband Movement

Nationalist sentiments in postwar Trinidad played an increasingly important role in debates concerning the significance and value of the steelband. As discussed in the previous chapter, the growing steelband movement generated considerable public hostility. For the majority of Trinidadians, particularly members of the middle and upper classes, the steelband represented social disruption and degeneration. However, there were some more open-minded and progressive members of the middle class who were impressed by the inventiveness and uniqueness of the steelband. For them this new musical style was not something to suppress but an unusual phenomenon worthy of examination and even encouragement. They recognized the steelband as an indigenous form of creative expression and sensed its potential as a symbol of national identity as Trinidad, and the West Indies as a whole, moved toward political autonomy.

Certainly the most prominent advocate of the steelband in the immediate postwar years was Albert Gomes. The fascination with local folk culture that Gomes shared with other members of the *Beacon* group of writers continued into his political career, and he became a strong defender of steelband, calypso, and the Spiritual Baptist faith.[6] In addition to expressing his views in the Legislative Council, he wrote a weekly column for the *Sunday Guardian* entitled "Behind the Curtain."[7] With eloquence, verve, and a romantic sensibility, Gomes persistently attempted to jar the Trinidadian public into recognizing what was truly theirs. As early as June 1946, for example, he was commenting on the steelband's significance:

> Most of the critics of the steel orchestra miss the real point. What is important is not whether the steel orchestra offends the ear, edifies or outrages good taste. Such considerations are irrelevant. It is as a social phenomenon that the steel orchestra must be viewed—and within its own, natural context. Is it any argument against this rather bizarre method of self-expression to insist that its votaries are drawn from the dregs of the social milieu? So what if they are? It is because they belong to the vast army of forgotten men that their method of music expression becomes so exciting and arresting. What approach is this that expects apples from mango trees? . . .
>
> Perhaps what we ought to say of the steel orchestra is that it offers a picturesque example of the infinite resourcefulness of the creative urge that, in this case, finds its way even through the ugly bric-a-brac of the junk-heap.

Gomes concluded:

> Why is the average, educated Trinidadian such a prissy milksop as regards all forms of self-expression that are indigenous to his native land? . . . The day some enterprising Trinidad businessman finances a tour of the steel orchestra abroad, the world outside will be presented with yet another means of identifying a rather small island lost in the Caribbean Sea.[8]

Gomes frequently used his column to address the issue of Trinidad's cultural identity. In 1949, for example, he engaged in a debate with the British Council, an organization designed to disseminate British culture throughout the empire. He pointed out that the motives of the Council were suspect among most Trinidadians and argued that West Indians needed to define their own culture.[9] The following week, Stanley Best, the Council's representative in Trinidad, replied in a letter to the *Trinidad Guardian* that West Indian artists should not slavishly copy

British models but should look to Britain for standards until a strong local culture developed its own standards.[10] These comments further enraged Gomes, and the next week he fired his retort in a letter to the *Guardian*:

> The Englishman must face the fact that from now onwards the West Indian will be less and less willing to respect anything but his own. His interest in his native dances, his discovery of the wealth of his country's folklore, the recognition of the artistic merit of the calypso—all indicate that the Trinidadian is no longer willing to be merely an emulator of someone else. He is, indeed, rapidly becoming culturally nationalistic. Both his outlook and his personality will be changed in time by the impact of these hitherto neglected influences.
>
> The West Indian whose deep-seated sense of inferiority permitted him to be transformed into a parody of the perfect Englishman, is another anachronism that is bound to disappear. . . .
>
> In a short time we will reach the stage where it will be more important for an organisation like the British Council to send abroad the new and exciting art and culture of the West Indies than to direct their energies to bringing British art and culture here.[11]

Gomes was particularly impressed with the Carnival arts, and every year during the Carnival season he wrote about the festival's significance for Trinidad. Generally he emphasized Carnival's creative exuberance and its potential for uniting the society's diverse population. Following the 1948 Carnival, for example, he argued:

> Carnival is the one common denominator in our community life. For two days of each year we are riotously and supremely what we are not for the rest of the year—a united community.

He added that: "It was a tingling, tangling music of tin-pans that produced this miracle of unity and mass tolerance."[12] This conception of Carnival as a unifying force and genuinely national fete became increasingly common as Trinidad approached independence.

Gomes's nationalist perspective on the steelband was shared by many individuals who wrote letters to the *Guardian* during the late 1940s and 1950s. As soon as the steelband was attacked, there were citizens who came to its defense. In fact, the debate over the steelband's significance became a lively exchange full of witty attacks (a local verbal strategy known as *picong*). In 1946, for example, a writer from St. James stated:

I am constrained to reply to an article which appeared in your columns on June 6, headed "Forests Suggested For Steel Band." [See Chapter Two, pp. 64–65.]

The author of that pernicious, fat-witted, vituperation sets forth to claim for himself the plaudits of the unhappy group who wear glasses, not to aid the sight but to adorn the nose, and to whom the obvious is not obvious.

The tone and burden of this peevish scribe's complaint is that the steel band is a nuisance encouraged by members of the public credited with a quality which he (the writer), perhaps, does not possess (intelligence), for we see an attempt to condemn indiscriminately the advent of the steel orchestra as the beating of tin pans.

Art is not restricted to any particular realm or sphere and must be appreciated for its aesthetic value as a soul expression. The steel band viewed as an innovation in music has much to be admired, and, in my humble opinion, will leave its mark in the annals of our local history and culture.

There is a regrettably persistent desire to crush any and everything local; this in itself is responsible for the lack of development to any marked degree in local talent. The beating of steel pans is an art which requires practice, and if we denounce it as an abomination we deny ourselves an expression of art.[13]

A week later another writer responded, favorably, to Gomes:

"Ubiquitous" asks: "Why is the educated Trinidadian such a prissy milksop as regards all forms of self-expression that are indigenous to his native land?" The answer is this: The term "educated Trinidadian" is too good a compliment to be paid to those who are so blind, mentally, morally and spiritually, as not to see in the steel orchestra the dawn of a new musical age in Trinidad and the subtle expression of an almost inexhaustible storehouse of untapped musical talent. . . .

The steel orchestra is still in its embryonic stage, and with good management and direction as regards the number, quality and type of pieces that should comprise a band no one can predict how far it will reach in world recognition.[14]

An important accomplishment of the steelband advocates during this period was the promotion of the concept of pan as art when most of the society still perceived it as noise and a nuisance. For its advocates the steelband was an ingenious fabrication of old metal containers and a vital form of self-expression. Furthermore, it was an "orchestra"—a legitimate musical ensemble that deserved to be treated with seriousness and respect. The fact that the steelband was indigenous added to its significance, and its defenders regularly berated the public for their snobbishness and hostility toward local culture. Even as early as 1946 they were predicting the importance of the steelband for Trinidad's national identity. This was quite prophetic, given the rudimentary state of pans at the time. But the pan advocates recognized that these new instruments were in an "embryonic stage."[15]

While the steelband was being advocated in the press as a new form of art, a few prominent individuals in the society began to present steelbands in concert settings, often as part of programs designed to enlighten the urban middle class about local folk traditions. These stage presentations played an important role in changing the public's perceptions of steelband music. During this period the steelband was associated with the streets and was considered to be simply a form of accompaniment for dancing and revelry at Carnival or at other festive occasions. But in formal concert settings steelband music was presented as something to appreciate for its artistic value and cultural significance. The respectable venues for these concerts and the prominent citizens who were patrons lent further legitimacy to the music.

The first known stage presentation of a steelband was organized by Edric Connor, a folksong collector and vocalist. Lennox Pierre relates that during the war Connor was hired by the government's social welfare department to help resettle people from the rural northwest peninsula of Trinidad where the Americans were establishing their naval base. This project further developed his interest in Trinidadian folk traditions, and in 1943 he gave a lecture-recital on West Indian folksongs and dances. The presentation was first made to the Trinidad Music Association and then to the general public at the Prince's Building (a prestigious social center in Port of Spain) in order to raise funds for the founding of the Trinidad and Tobago Youth Council. Featured in the program were performers of folksongs and of the *bongo* and the *limbo* (two Afro-Trinidadian dances). Errol Hill notes that a steelband from Gonzales was also included. The urban middle class audience were considerably impressed by the event, since they had had little or no awareness of these folk forms. The limbo had never before been presented on a stage, and in 1943 the steelband was still something of a novelty. Pierre refers to the occasion as "by and large the turning point in the development of local culture."[16]

Another central figure in Trinidad's national awakening was Beryl McBurnie. McBurnie had developed a strong interest in dance as a youth and periodically accompanied folklorist Andrew Carr on trips to the countryside where she notated folk dances and songs.[17] During the 1940s she formed a dance troupe that performed interpretations of a range of Caribbean folk dances. She also became intrigued by steelband music and developed a relationship with Invaders, whose panyard was located near her home in Woodbrook. In 1946 she included Invaders in a program which she presented at the Prince's Building in connection with a Youth Council anniversary dance. Albert Gomes attended the performance and later stated in his column:

> I was at the Prince's Building last Saturday evening when the steel band known as "Invaders" held an audience spell-bound for more than half-an-hour. Was there anyone in that audience that doubted the value of the steel orchestra after that performance?[18]

The success of McBurnie's performances necessitated the acquisition of her own venue and in 1948 she opened the Little Carib Theatre in Woodbrook, with Invaders as the featured steelband. The printed program for the opening night contained statements on the significance of West Indian culture and of the new theater by prominent citizens such as Albert Gomes, Eric Williams, Jack Kelshall, C. S. Espinet, Wilson Minshall, and Canon M. E. Farquhar.[19] These individuals would all play roles in the development of the steelband movement.

The Little Carib's clientele in the early days was primarily British expatriates and a small but growing sector of the local middle class who either had an interest in West Indian folk culture or wanted to be seen at this avant-garde venue. McBurnie recalls that at first the audiences responded in a reactionary way to her inclusion of a steelband: "Thought I was going back to Africa with all this hooliganism." But attitudes gradually began to change, due to her persistence and the respectable nature of the Little Carib itself. She continued to employ Invaders until the mid-1950s, at which point she switched to using Merry Makers. These bands played a range of calypsos, Latin American pieces, and European classical selections in her programs, both alone and as accompaniment for the dancers, and typically performed a lively dance number to close each show. The audience was invited to participate in this finale and a period of social dancing to steelband music followed.[20]

There was general agreement among the panmen involved that playing at the Little Carib was a valuable experience. Vernon Mannette of Invaders states that their engagement with McBurnie helped counteract the harassment they received from people in Woodbrook. He also points out that, by playing at the Little Carib, the band was able to meet people from "upper society," some of whom then became Invaders supporters. Sack Mayers of Merry Makers emphasizes the opportunity for musical development that McBurnie provided for his band. They learned something about music theory and became skilled at playing in different keys, since at times they were required to accompany singers. In addition, McBurnie taught them a number of European classical pieces.[21]

Casablanca was another steelband whose stage performances had a significant influence on public opinion in the postwar years. In 1950 the band participated in a concert called "Music of the Caribbean" held at White Hall in Port of Spain. There they played calypsos, rhumbas, popular dance tunes, and marches, while C. S. Espinet, an editor at the *Trinidad Guardian* and a folklorist, provided commentary on the different types of pans. The *Guardian* stated:

> At the same place where concerts of classical music are held regularly, the music of the steel band was heard for the first time. It was the local counterpart of Paul Whiteman's taking jazz to Carnegie Hall, some time during the 1920's.
>
> The band demonstrated the musical scope of the steel orchestra, and the ingenuity and skill of the men who comprise it. . . .
>
> Afterwards, members of the audience danced in ball-room style to the music of the Casablanca Band, proving that steel band music is not restricted to "jumping up" in the streets.[22]

Two weeks later Casablanca had an even greater impact when they played in the steelband competition at the *Guardian's* Carnival Sunday night show in the Queen's Park Savannah. Their first selection was "The Bells of St. Mary's" and the audience responded enthusiastically. An observer of the occasion relates:

> Someone started to clap—soon the whole audience broke into wild cheers. The sedate, the patronizing, the doubtful were convinced. All were shouting for More! More!! More!!! Revelling in the glory of the minute, Russell Manning, the bandleader, lifted his arms. The crowd grew still. A slight movement of the fingers—the response of the band—and jaws fell open in amazement. People looked at one another in wonderment. For here in Trinidad, by musicians who knew not a single note of written music, was a most professional arrange-

ment of Chopin's Nocturne in E Flat. The audience followed the nimble-fingered boys in rapt silence and attention. The steelbandsman was accepted as a musician.[23]

Casablanca won the competition. The following year the band again dazzled the public when they gave a recital in conjunction with Victor Soverall (a tenor) and Professor Katz (a pianist) at the Royal Victoria Institute, under the auspices of the Trinidad and Tobago Youth Council. After the performance Professor Katz remarked that the pans blended well with the piano and added that: "Steelbands excel in calypsoes and other local rhythms, but they have reached a standard undreamt of and can merit their place with the more popular classical instruments."[24]

In colonial Trinidad European classical music was highly regarded, and panmen gained familiarity with this tradition through radio broadcasts and movie soundtracks. The classics were part of their experience and they approached them in the same manner that they approached all other musical styles: as something with which to experiment on pan. Generally they considered classical music to be more "complex" and "difficult" than other types of music and regarded it as a means of developing both their instruments and their musicianship. However, they also understood the symbolic value that this music carried in the society. They realized that they could gain legitimacy as musicians through successfully playing the classics and through effective performance and "blend" with European instruments. Thus they were more than happy to receive instruction in classical music from individuals such as Beryl McBurnie and Professor Katz.

The performance of European music certainly contributed to the steelband's growing respectability as a local art. But respectability also required that the music be removed from the world of the streets and placed in the formal settings of genteel cultural institutions. Essentially the European-oriented staged concert was substituted for the local experience of Carnival revelry. Of course the steelband remained firmly based in the street world and in Carnival, but now there were other ways of conceptualizing and presenting the music. Pan could be self-consciously displayed as a national folk music and also combined with accepted forms of foreign music. These re-presentations of the steelband received approval from at least some of the Trinidadian public in the late 1940s and early 1950s.

The pan movement, however, still faced many obstacles in fully achieving respectability. One major problem was that steelband-related violence was actually increasing. It was readily apparent to the pan advocates that the elimination of steelband clashes was crucial for genuine public acceptance of the music and the musicians. An individual who played a major role in containing this violence and in redirecting the movement was Lennox Pierre. In addition to his work as a solicitor in Port of Spain, Pierre was secretary of the Trinidad and Tobago Youth Council, a classical violinist, and a general music enthusiast. He also co-founded the West Indian Independence Party (a short-lived Marxist party) in 1952 and became actively involved in the labor movement in Trinidad.

As a resident of Newtown, Pierre regularly followed Alexander's Ragtime Band and, later, Invaders for J'Ouvert. In the late 1940s he began to take his violin down to Invaders' yard to assist them with their musical training. He helped Ellie Mannette, the band's well-known tuner, find notes that were missing from his ping pongs and also taught the band new tunes, including some classical pieces. To facilitate this process, he devised a method of designating notes on the pans with numbers which he then called out while playing tunes on his violin. In 1947 Pierre, Edric Connor, and Errol Hill presented Invaders on the Youth Council's radio program called "The Voice of Youth." This was the first time a steelband was heard on the radio. Among the highlights of the program were Mannette's performance of Brahms's "Lullaby" and a demonstration of his ping pong's two full diatonic scales.[25]

In 1948 Edric Connor arranged a music scholarship for Mannette in Birmingham, England. Since additional money was needed to pay for Mannette's passage, Pierre went down to Invaders' yard to see if the band could give some concerts to raise the necessary funds. What he found was "Invaders in war with Casablanca." After reporting the situation to the Youth Council, he and Carlyle Kerr (another Youth Council official) conducted an investigation into steelband violence. They determined that rivalry over girlfriends and poor adjudication at pan competitions were among the main causes of band clashes. With these conclusions, they suggested that the Youth Council propose to the government a more effective means of dealing with steelband problems.[26]

In September 1949 the Youth Council drafted a memorandum that was forwarded to Executive Council member Albert Gomes who was known to be sympathetic to the steelband movement. In this document they suggested that the government appoint a special committee to further investigate the steelband situation. According to the *Trinidad Guardian*, the memorandum recommended

a remedial rather than a punitive approach as being more effective, and states that the tendency in certain quarters to associate hooliganism with the steelbands as an automatic outcome of their activity is the result of misguided opinion and hasty and erroneous judgment.

The Police Department is blamed in this memorandum, as, it is alleged, its actions only tend to result in the destruction and annihilation of an individual band as an organised entity.[27]

A remedial approach to the steelband was also advocated around this same time by C. R. Ottley, a local historian and the head of the government's Education Extension Services. Ottley stated to the press that the steelband was a form of cultural expression and that it actually tended to prevent crime by providing something of interest for young people who otherwise would become involved in illegal pursuits. In this light, he added: "I am convinced that with proper organisation, the steel bands can be used as a means of bringing a change of social attitudes to the young men in them."[28]

The concept of the steelband as a positive force was a distinct alternative to the government's policy regarding steelband affairs. Authorities had generally assumed that steelbands were a breeding ground for violence and vice, and that the appropriate response was firm police and legal action. However, it was clear that this approach did not succeed in reducing steelband violence, and the government was willing to try a different tactic. In November 1949 the acting Governor appointed a committee "to carry out a sociological survey of the steel bands in the Port-of-Spain area, and to make recommendations whereby the cultural and recreational potentialities of the steel bands may be encouraged." The committee's members included

Canon M. E. Farquhar	Chairman
Carlyle Kerr	Youth Council
Lennox Pierre	Youth Council
C. R. Ottley	Senior Education Extension Officer
George Mose	Principal Probation Officer
C. S. Espinet	President, Folklore Society
Bertie Thompson	Colts Football Club
E. Mortimer Mitchell	Friendly Societies
Beryl McBurnie	Little Carib
Pearl Carter	Secretary[29]

The Steel Band Committee members were prominent citizens and several were already well-known pan advocates. The inclusion of individuals engaged in youth and cultural affairs underscores the efforts that were being made to integrate the steelband movement into the institutional structure of the society. Canon Farquhar, the committee's chairman, was a distinguished Anglican priest who, like Albert Gomes, wrote a weekly column for the *Sunday Guardian*. His opinions on current affairs in this column were always expressed with equanimity and caution, and he presumably was a figure who evoked considerable public trust. In the early 1950s he regularly used his column to prod the public into accepting the steelband movement.

The Steel Band Committee held its first meeting in December 1949. Minutes from the meeting record that there was discussion of the committee's purposes and agreement on a proposed plan of action. First, the committee would meet with representatives of Port of Spain steelbands and request that the bands refrain from conflicts over the Christmas season "as a preliminary manifestation of their goodwill and desire to co-operate." Next, they would ask the police to exercise "restraint and tolerance towards the steel bandsmen." Finally, they would publish in the press an account of their actions and make "a special appeal to the public for their co-operation." The committee was of the opinion that negative coverage of steelbands in the press greatly encouraged public condemnation of the movement.[30]

The Steel Band Committee did meet with band representatives. In early January 1950 the Commissioner of Police reported that the holiday season had been "remarkably quiet,"[31] though the press managed to sensationalize a few steelband-related incidents. Then, a few days later, a well-known member of Invaders was arrested for stabbing a member of Casablanca. The Steel Band Committee quickly held an "emergency meeting" in response to these developments. At this meeting and at a subsequent one, Lennox Pierre and Carlyle Kerr proposed that the committee deal with the immediate problems facing steelbandsmen, while continuing to pursue its more long-term goals. Among other recommendations, they called for specific action in reference to panmen who had recently been arrested or were imprisoned. Pierre also again suggested that the press be asked to refrain from highlighting steelband incidents.[32]

Following these meetings Canon Farquhar addressed the plight of panmen in his column in the *Guardian*:

> May I be permitted to suggest with all possible humility and deference, that some of the letters published in the Press, together with the general attitude of the Press itself, with respect to the Steel Bands are likely to do incalculable harm to the social well-being of the Colony. They breathe a spirit of intolerance and prejudice which can only accompany evil. . . .
>
> . . . without the opportunity for adequate assessment, my own ob-

servations and contacts disprove this contention, that the Steel Bands represent young men addicted to vice and crime with little pretensions to ordered decency. . . .

. . . ostracised and estranged from the circumstances and the people who alone could help them, they are driven out like the lepers of old into the wilderness and waste places of society.

In my opinion, it is much to their credit that instead of surrendering to sullen despair or violent retribution, they turn to the escapism of music. . . .

Let us therefore study these people and examine their social disabilities, and instead of reviling them, invite their confidence and goodwill and replace unkind criticism by understanding, a spirit of charity and a desire to help.[33]

During this period Farquhar and other defenders of the panmen argued that the violence associated with steelbands was ultimately rooted in socioeconomic problems and was inflamed by the intolerance and hostility of the public, the press, and the police. One of their strategies of defense was to reveal some of the hardships of the underclass and to appeal to the public and to authorities to demonstrate more consideration toward the panmen. They also attempted to accentuate the positive qualities of the steelband movement and its potential for the well-being of its members and the society as a whole. At the same time, the Steel Band Committee pursued more practical tactics in dealing with steelband violence by bringing representatives of bands together in meetings. At these occasions they could try to identify the more immediate causes of steelband feuds and encourage reason and compromise on the part of the bands involved.[34]

In January and February 1950 the war between Invaders and Casablanca was still raging. Even before Carnival began 17 members of Invaders appeared in court on charges of "malicious wounding, assault and taking part in unlawful assembly." Then, during Carnival, Invaders were attacked, though it is not clear from the report whether their assailants were members of Casablanca. Meanwhile, the Steel Band Committee apparently was attempting to bring an end to the conflicts between the two bands. Finally, on March 2, the *Guardian* announced in a headline: "P-of-S Steelbands Sign 'Non-Aggression Pact' After 2 Weeks' Talks." Two days earlier, representatives of the bands had met with members of the Steel Band Committee at the Public Library to discuss all phases of the feud and to finalize negotiations. According to the *Guardian,* "After a two-hour discussion, representatives decided to put an end to the feud which had existed between the two bands for more than two years and undertook that no further clashes will occur between them." The next day the bands held a formal signing at the Black Lion rum shop, followed by a few hours of drinking to each other's health. Then they retired to Invaders' yard for more refreshments, and Invaders permitted their guests to play the band's pans—a sure sign of friendship. Tokyo attended this session as well and also agreed to cease fighting.[35]

A few days later representatives of eight steelbands met at Old Prison Quarry with three members of the Steel Band Committee (Pierre, Mose, and Espinet) and agreed to end all hostilities until the committee found a means of ensuring a lasting peace. The bands included Invaders, Casablanca, Tokyo, Hill 60, Crusaders, Merry Makers, Desperadoes, and All Stars (the Hell Yard band). The Steel Band Committee hinted that they were attempting to get all outstanding court cases against band members dropped and pointed out that this would require the cooperation of the bands. Representatives of the bands then offered their opinions on the causes of the clashes and on possible means of achieving harmony.[36]

A final resolution came two weeks later in court, when 28 members of Invaders, Casablanca, and Tokyo pleaded guilty to unlawful assembly, wounding, and weapons charges and were put on bonds to keep the peace for six months. In a request for leniency, Mitra Sinanan, the defense attorney, had stated that "if the men were given a chance he was sure they would develop a greater sense of responsibility, and as a consequence they would stop the fighting." The magistrate then admonished the panmen "that the good name of the island depended on their behaviour" and also praised the Steel Band Committee and others who had helped create a peaceful understanding between the bands.[37]

The reconciliation of opposing steelbands paved the way for the formation of an association of bands. In early April 1950 18 bands met at the Youth Council's Cocorite Youth Centre on the western side of Port of Spain and, in conjunction with the Steel Band Committee, issued a statement that they would no longer enter "'mushroom' competitions for steel bands sponsored by individuals in their own interest and not in the interest of steel bands." During the late 1940s local entrepreneurs were hastily organizing competitions in order to capitalize on the growing popularity of steelband music. The adjudication at these events was often poor, and disputed decisions intensified the already existing rivalries between bands. Thus the bands determined to boycott all proposed competitions in order to preserve their new sense of friendship and cooperation. They also agreed to "sponsor different forms of public entertainment in their own interest and for the benefit of the community as a whole" and announced that all future negotiations with bands should be handled through a steelband council.[38] By this point, the panmen were very much aware of the fact that their music had become a valuable resource in the society and that it would be beneficial for them to unite in an association that would defend their interests and regulate the use of steelbands.

One week later the Trinidad and Tobago Steel Band Association was officially organized at the Cocorite Youth Centre. An election of officers was held with the following results: S. Gallop (Crusaders) - President, N. Critchlow (Casablanca) - Vice President, C. Harewood (Crusaders) - Secretary, George Goddard (Invaders) - Assistant Secretary, and C. Biddy (Rising Sun) - Treasurer.[39] In a letter to the *Guardian*, Canon Farquhar appealed to the public to recognize and cooperate with the new association. He stated that the association members were trying "to find some honorable place in the society" without "in any way losing their identity as steel bandsmen." In addition, he commented that "it is confidently hoped that a sense of discipline and the desire to improve themselves will spread to all other bands throughout the Colony."[40]

How did the panmen themselves respond to the Steel Band Committee and the formation of the Steel Band Association? Jerry Serrant of All Stars recalls that at first the panmen viewed the steelband advocates with suspicion because they were used to being taken advantage of by members of the middle class.[41] Sack Mayers of Merry Makers also recollects that panmen were suspicious, but describes how their views eventually changed:

> At first we thought they were trying to change the attitude of the men. But, really and truly, they were behind the music. They were interested in the music. And it's afterwards when we saw the good. Because we had thought: "They only coming to keep you quiet, man."...
>
> And I think that Lennox Pierre . . . he saw already the guys and them, they had the ability to play the music. But there must be someone around . . . to keep them away from thinking the wrong way. So he will come and he will give you a little musical lecture. And he tell you: "Well, when I'm finished, it doesn't end there. When I'm finished, you have the right to make some time and go and take your instrument." And then everybody start leaning toward the music. . . . And the fighting and quarreling and all kind of thing start dying down. Is when them came in.
>
> But Canon Farquhar, he was a priest. And imagine a priest coming and getting involved in steelband. And you wondering what kind of

priest is that. But then afterwards, they saw that he was talking to them . . .

In reference to the Steel Band Association, Mayers states that

> they didn't want to form an association because the talk was, whoever on top as executive, they're going to see about whatever band they're in. But afterwards, everybody start thinking differently. Because they start leaning towards the music and listening to all that Farquhar and Lennox Pierre [were saying].[42]

Leo Warner of Commandoes recalls that the panmen responded well to Albert Gomes, Lennox Pierre, and the others because they were glad to have these individuals championing their cause when the law was giving them a rough time. Similarly, Big Mack Sandiford of All Stars relates that the steelband advocates gave the panmen some hope and the sense that "at least somebody's lending an ear to their needs." John Slater of Crusaders also has favorable memories of the birth of the Steel Band Association and describes what the sessions at the Cocorite Youth Centre were like:

> . . . we used to go down there mostly on week-ends to talk about the future of pan and to amuse ourselves beating pan. Bands like Cairo, Invaders, and the [Katzenjammers], to name a few [who] belong in the West, used to supply the music most of the time. As a result of making such positive moves as forming an Association, and holding Elections, we gained recognition and popularity. People were showering praise, and Reverend Farquhar, an ardent supporter of the steelband movement at the time, was showering prayers for our salvation. . . . We were gaining momentum.[43]

Of course the bands that might have resisted the Steel Band Committee's overtures the most were Invaders, Casablanca, and Tokyo. However, Vernon Mannette of Invaders recalls that his band really wanted peace and thought that organizing the movement was a good idea. He adds, though, that some of the fellows enjoyed the fighting. Leo Alfred recollects that Tokyo responded well to the proposal of a steelband association: "We had always been in favor of something like that—something to take care of the panmen." Finally, Oscar Pile of Casablanca states that Lennox Pierre and his colleagues understood the problems facing panmen and provided genuine support.[44]

The formation of the Steel Band Association had important consequences for panmen. Previously steelbands had been autonomous bodies that charted their own courses of action. Sometimes this action
included confrontations with other bands. With the forming of the association, however, the bands began to shift their attention from enacting disputes to pursuing common interests. Their new sense of unity
made them a more powerful force within the society and enabled them
to be more persuasive with their demands. Though various schemes of
exploiting steelbands continued to flourish, the bands were now in a
stronger position to resist them. But the formal organization of the
bands was also useful to the government. When the bands were autonomous, it had been difficult for the police and the courts to control
them. Now authorities could depend to some extent on the movement's
internal controls. Steelbands that engaged in clashes were reprimanded
and sometimes even expelled by the association. In addition, the association released statements to the press reiterating its commitment to
peacefulness.

The formation of the Steel Band Association also enabled panmen to
develop relationships with prominent individuals in the society. This
provided them with new resources and opportunities. They received assistance and protection in their encounters with the law, learned more
about European classical music, and were given chances to perform in
entirely new types of social settings. The panmen's connections with
prominent citizens also increased the movement's respectability. It was
somewhat more difficult to criticize steelbands when they were appearing at venues like the Little Carib and when figures such as Farquhar
and Gomes were regularly commenting on their progress. The fact that
the steelband movement was now formally organized in turn contributed to a growing public acceptance of the steelband advocates' vision of the music as a national art and a vehicle for youth development.

The Trinidad All Steel Percussion Orchestra

In 1951 the Steel Band Association initiated its first major project: the
preparation for a steelband to travel to London and represent Trinidad
at the Festival of Britain. The festival was being held to mark the cente-
nary of the Great Exhibition of 1851 and to convey to the world "the
message that the old country has lost none of its virility, ingenuity, resourcefulness; and determination to hold its place as one of the great
leaders of mankind in every field of worthwhile endeavor." Though the
focus of the festival was to be Britain itself, presentations from Commonwealth countries and colonies were to be included as well.[45]

   The Steel Band Association's participation in the festival was organized both by its executive committee and by a number of steelband advocates (such as Lennox Pierre, Carlyle Kerr, and Canon Farquhar)
who continued to work closely with the panmen. First an all-star steelband was formed and given the name "Trinidad All Steel Percussion Orchestra" (TASPO). The membership of the band consisted of eleven
top pan musicians chosen from the leading bands of Port of Spain and
South Trinidad (ten of the eleven were also pan tuners). The musical
director/manager selected for TASPO was Lieutenant Joseph Griffith, a
Barbadian who had been a member of the Trinidad Police Band and
was currently Director of Music for the government of St. Lucia.

   Griffith brought to the steelband a vision and rigor that would have
lasting consequences for the movement. One of his primary concerns
was that all the pans used by TASPO be tuned to concert pitch and include all the notes of the chromatic scale. This necessitated the creation
of a number of new pans, since at the time only the ping pong was
chromatically tuned. Anthony Williams, one of the members of TASPO,
states that the band used the 23-note ping pong that Ellie Mannette had
developed. A *second pan* or *alto pan* was being employed by some bands
at the time; TASPO redesigned this pan to include fourteen notes.
Griffith also wanted a pair of tune booms consisting of fourteen notes,
but it was only possible to tune a maximum of five notes on a biscuit
drum, given the size of the container and the low quality of the metal.
Thus Anthony Williams replaced the tune boom with a *tenor boom*, a pair
of pans made from large oil drums, each of which included seven notes.
Finally, a new bass instrument consisting of three oil drums and a total
of thirteen notes was created to replace the existing pair of caustic soda
drum basses.[46]

   This new instrumentation brought a tremendous change to the
sound of steelband music. The steelband now had a much more uniform tone quality, since all the pans were made from large oil drums.
Equally impressive was the fact that the chromatic pans allowed for conventional harmony. For the first time it was possible to arrange tunes
using full and accurate chords. In addition, the musicianship of the
TASPO members improved, due to the instruction that they received
from Griffith on the fundamentals of music. Griffith utilized the num-
ber-note system that had been introduced by Lennox Pierre but also
gave the players the parts of his arrangements on sheets with the numbers written next to the actual notes. Eventually, several members of the
band learned to read standard notation.[47]

   TASPO's repertoire was diverse and obviously designed to demonstrate the versatility and expressive range of the new steelband. Their
primary selections included

"Return of the Allies"   (March)   Composed by Griffith
"Tennessee Waltz"   (Waltz)
"Mango Walk"   (Rhumba)
"Enjoy Yourself"   (Samba)
"Drink to Me Only"   (Morceau)
"Cradle Song"   (Lullaby)   Brahms
"Parang"   (Rhumba)
"Sonny Boy"   (Fox Trot)   Jolson
"Johnny"   (Calypso)
"Golden Earrings"   (Bolero)
"Serenata"   (Serenade)   Toscelli
"Figare"   (Calypso)
"Mambo Jambo"   (Mambo)   Prada[48]

This repertoire provides a sense of the variety of musical traditions that were being incorporated into the steelband by the early 1950s. The increased melodic and harmonic possibilities that TASPO's new instrumentation afforded, along with the steelband's already existing rhythmic dimensions, enabled the panmen to effectively interpret a wide range of musical genres, including the creolized dance styles of Latin America that were becoming increasingly popular in Trinidad.

TASPO's achievements were soon presented to the Trinidadian public in a series of concerts held to raise funds for the trip to Britain. C. Yip Young reported in the *Trinidad Guardian* on the band's first public appearance:

Before an audience whose numbers brought forth visions of the White Cliffs of Dover, 10 steel bandsmen comprising TASPO . . . gave their first public performance at the Globe Theatre, Port-of-Spain, last night.

Their crude, unpainted pans stood in sharp contrast to their shiny musician's stands and printed scores, which were being used for the first time by a steel band. But the music they played had all the polish and brilliance which their instruments lacked.

The band, which hopes to attend the Festival of Britain, treated the enormous crowd to a festival of steel band music, which, in the words of Mr. Jack Kelshall, master of ceremonies, "had never been heard before."

The audience was diverse as the fare provided. Its members ranged from Sir Hubert Rance, first Governor to attend a steel band recital, to several well-known downtown steel band partisans.

All were unanimous, however, in the thought that TASPO must play at the Festival.[49]

TASPO's concerts were only one part of a much wider fundraising effort which was dubbed "Operation Britain." The Steel Band Association and the pan advocates determined that $15,000 was required to send the band to the festival, and they turned to the public for support. Canon Farquhar commented in his column that, if TASPO achieved recognition in Britain, it would reflect well on the whole colony and would "help divert attention from the imported to the home grown article." He also remarked that the Junior Chamber of Commerce was considering participating in the fundraising drive and that, if this occurred, it could be "the beginning of a new understanding between all the classes in the Colony."[50] The Jaycees did in fact join the effort, as did other prominent personages such as the Governor, the Colonial Secretary, and the Mayor of Port of Spain. Even the *Guardian*, whose opinion of the steelband movement was not always favorable, wholeheartedly supported the venture in two editorials.[51] Obviously the colonial government and the business community potentially had much to gain if TASPO proved to be a success in Britain. The Colonial Secretary, the Mayor, and the *Guardian* all suggested that TASPO could help attract more tourists to Trinidad.

As Operation Britain's deadline approached, the *Guardian* dutifully acknowledged members of the public who had recently made contributions and stated the amount still required to reach the campaign goal. Initially the response from the public was rather lukewarm. Anthony Williams recollects:

Before TASPO left, it looked uncertain. It looked like the band wouldn't leave Trinidad and Tobago. But after the band gave a few performances, people started to hear the different sounds. They realized it was a different band and it was something that should be exported. So then they contributed. Because TASPO left Trinidad and Tobago by funds contributed by the public. It was the Governor who came in. It was Governor Sir Hubert Rance, when he said TASPO must go to Britain. So the public contributed and so that became a reality.[52]

Meanwhile, the members of TASPO were becoming local heroes. Both the band's concert appearances and the regular newspaper coverage created considerable public excitement. Panmen with placards asked for donations on the streets, some local businesses placed

"shilling jars" on their store counters, and groups ranging from steelbands to the Little Carib to the Jaycees held fundraising events. The
band members themselves were outfitted with suits and shoes, and it
was decided that their performance costumes should be "bright and gay
to symbolise the colour and elan of the West Indies."[53] A few days before
their departure, they were treated to a five-course luncheon at the high
class Rainbow Terrace restaurant and were individually interviewed by
the press.

Pandemonium broke out at TASPO's bon voyage as a crowd of sup-
porters assembled on the wharf to see the new celebrities board their
ship. Invaders were hired to provide music for the occasion, and the
Tourist Board's reception room was transformed into a dance floor.[54]
The members of TASPO were in high spirits and Sonny Roach, from
Sun Valley, proclaimed:

> By the time we leave, every Englishman will have a pan. We will
> make the Festival of Britain a success. We will so impress them that we
> hope to make even the King come to Trinidad to see us beat at the
> next Carnival.
>
> And by the way, . . . I hope to play for Churchill.[55]

John Grimes, a reporter with the *Guardian,* summed up the affair:

> It was a grand day for the steelbands. The story should be written in
> octaves, semi-quavers and the sharps of the sambas, rhumbas and ca-
> lypsoes. It is the all-time success story of Trinidad[.] From rags to
> riches; from the Dry-River to the Albert Hall; from intolerant non-en-
> tity to world-wide recognition.[56]

Trinidadians eagerly awaited the first reports on TASPO's performances in Britain, and their expectations were fulfilled when the
Guardian began publishing articles with London datelines. One of the
first reports stated:

> A revolution in music reached London today, and experts predict
> it will sweep the country in a new craze.
>
> Trinidad All Steel Percussion Orchestra (TASPO) sat outside the
> Festival Concert Hall at the Festival of Britain exhibition and tapped
> sweet, swingy music out of rusty pans still with steamer labels stuck to
> them after their trans-Atlantic voyage.

> Londoners, hearing a steel band for the first time, passed the verdict: "The music is sweet and liquid similar to the xylophone but not so harsh".
>
> The crowd who heard the band was sceptical that music could come out of pans, but they were soon tapping their feet to the rhythms of the Caribbean music.[57]

The several London newspapers that were on hand for the occasion responded enthusiastically as well.

Though this concert seems to have been TASPO's only appearance at the Festival of Britain, Edric Connor and the West Indian Students' Union in London arranged a variety of other performances. The band gave its official "European Premiere" at London's St. Pancras Town Hall in a program that also included Connor, calypsonian Lord Kitchener, and Boscoe Holder's dance company. In addition, the band obtained a regular engagement at the elite Savoy Hotel, performed at the Lyceum dance hall, and appeared at various other venues. These live performances were complemented by appearances on BBC radio and television. For the television program, they were again joined by Connor, Kitchener, and Holder. After the broadcast, Connor sent a message home to Trinidad: "Now I don't want to hear any West Indian say we haven't got culture."[58]

Though TASPO only existed for a short period of time, it had substantial musical and symbolic significance for the steelband movement. Both the improved range and sound quality of its pans and the higher level of musicianship of its members made a profound impression on the Trinidadian public. At the same time, the whole effort of sending TASPO to Britain gave the steelband a social prominence that it had not previously enjoyed. Support of Operation Britain by top government officials and leading business figures sanctioned the project and helped generate wider interest. Never before had such a cross-section of the society rallied around the movement. For some this support was linked to a sense that the steelband was a resource with which Trinidad could represent itself as a unique place in the world. But for most people such feelings were still tentative. Reevaluation of the steelband was to a large extent dependent upon TASPO's success abroad. Trinidadians were highly impressed by TASPO's appearance at the Festival of Britain and in other prestigious settings. Since British artistic taste was widely respected and often taken more seriously than local judgments, the critical acclaim that the band received in the course of its tour brought greater legitimacy to steelband music at home. The local pan advocates' definition of the steelband as art could now be given more consideration.

A change in attitudes toward pan was given further impetus by the significant musical improvement among steelbands as a whole in the years after TASPO. Lennox Pierre points out that, when the members of TASPO returned from Britain and rejoined their original bands, their new knowledge and skills gradually spread throughout the pan movement.[59] TASPO's instrumentation was eventually incorporated by steelbands in general, and Lieutenant Griffith's musical arrangements set a new standard for future arrangers. With the growing versatility and quality of steelbands, the public became more willing to attend and commend their performances.[60]

College Boy Steelbands

By the late 1940s and early 1950s, some middle class youths were becoming attracted to pan. Since many attended elite secondary schools such as Queen's Royal College and St. Mary's College, they were typically referred to as "college boys." They differed from grass-roots panmen not only in class background and educational level but in ethnicity and skin color. Many were brown-skinned and some were fair-skinned or white. By the late 1950s and 1960s, increasing numbers of Chinese and Indian youths became involved in pan as well.

College boys were torn between the worlds of respectability and reputation. They came from families who had a firm sense of superiority to the grass-roots class, and they were well aware of the importance of maintaining respectability. Yet the world of the street held an irresistible lure. The streets were filled with creative and exciting activities, and it was there that college boys, like grass-roots youths, could engage in competition with their peers and achieve reputations. College boys were intrigued by the powerful grass-roots steelbands and their music and were also impressed with the panman's machismo image and ability to attract women. Junior Pouchet, an early college-boy pan musician, recalls:

> The time boys of that era—school or college—pick up and beat a pan, all of us out there feel they're bad. Turned up their collar. Putting their sticks in their [back pocket]. You have a special way of walking. . . . It was an era. It was a feeling about it. Well, you're in a war zone. You're against guys of your age. And that sort of rivalry and competition was very serious at that time.[61]

The process of decolonization may have also encouraged middle class youths' interest in pan. As Trinidad progressed toward independence, the middle class was increasingly identifying with local arts. Pan was becoming a particularly popular and vibrant form of street expression, and college boys wanted to be part of the trend of the times. The steelband thus provided them with both a new creative outlet and a means of constructing an impressive, locally-based image.

College boys, however, were faced with a serious dilemma: how to play pan without incurring the wrath of their parents and teachers. Even though the steelband was beginning to appear in more respectable contexts, panmen themselves were still widely condemned because of their social background and lifestyle. In spite of the objections of their parents and teachers, college boys continued to pursue their new interest by liming in panyards and cultivating relationships with experienced panmen. Over the years a number of college boys played with Invaders in Woodbrook. In most cases, however, they did not join grassroots steelbands but formed bands of their own. Ray Holman, a panman from Queen's Royal College who played with Invaders, explains:

> I think they wanted to get involved in it. They probably had liked the instrument and so. But maybe they didn't feel comfortable playing in the traditional bands. Because it wasn't their element. They went to college and so on. Most of the fellows in these other bands were uneducated . . . just primary level. And [the] social strata they came from was different. So these fellows felt more comfortable in a band of their own.[62]

During the 1950s college boys formed numerous steelbands such as Dixieland, Silver Stars, Starland, Dixie Stars, Hit Paraders, Nightingale, Tropitones, Saigon, Starlift, Dem Boys, and Stromboli. Often these bands were associated with particular neighborhoods and schools. For example, one of the first college-boy bands was Dixieland, and a number of its original members attended St. Mary's College. Curtis Pierre, one of the leaders of Dixieland, recalls how he became interested in pan in 1949 and eventually formed a band:

> One of the guys from the College [St. Mary's], he's now a Roman Catholic priest, called me to his home in Cascade one day and showed me this pan that he had. Probably had about twelve notes. I'll never forget it. It was a green and black Casablanca tenor pan [ping pong]. And I was amazed and I was fascinated by it. . . . So that I took the pan home. Well, my mother didn't see a pan. She saw a symbol of

rabs, as she used to call it. "I don't want you mixing with the rabs—
that is not for you." And I said "You know, everybody is going to like
this eventually." She said "I don't care if the King's son beat pan, . . . I
don't want you beating pan."

So, I had to get rid of it. And I came with a group of boys who eventually started a band called Melody Makers which became Dixieland.
I went down there and everybody had got hold of a tenor pan. So, it
was a band of tenor pans. There must have been about six of us. . . . It
was a cacophony, a real, real pure noise. No attempt to form a band
leader. And no knowledge of music and nobody guiding us. . . . Occasionally, some guy would pick out a tune and everybody would play
the tune on the pans. But there was no effort to make a band sound
out of it.

And then we realized that very close by was Red Army, who became
Merry Makers. They were Red Army then. So, we convinced some of
the boys to go and talk to particularly Alfred Mayers, Sack, and . . . the
captain, Morris. And they sort of befriended us. And they lent us
some other pans. And we realized there was a bigger range.[63]

Sack Mayers recalls that he used to teach members of Dixieland how
to play different pans and that he often performed with the band once
they started obtaining engagements.[64] College-boy bands in general
learned their skills from grass-roots panmen and typically included a
few of these more experienced players when they needed to strengthen
their sound. These bands also depended on grass-roots panmen to tune
their pans.

Gradually middle class parents became more receptive to the idea of
college-boy steelbands and, once the bands improved musically, they
were invited to perform at fetes. At these occasions the bands developed
strong followings of middle class youths. Junior Pouchet, the leader of
the popular Silver Stars, relates:

In those days, when the band went out, all the parents came along the
side-lines to see the kids didn't get into trouble. It was a real PTA affair. So anyway, we passed that stage and they got to trust us after a
while. And then, well, we became popular among what you might call
the college set. The convents [elite Catholic secondary schools for
girls], the girls, the little teenage sets—where people [could] relate.
They could not relate to Laventille Desperadoes or bands like that.
But they could relate to Silver Stars or Dixieland or Dixie Stars.[65]

Basically, the college-boy bands provided pan music in a safe and respectable environment. It was now possible for the middle class (partic-

ularly middle class youths) to enjoy steelbands without becoming
closely associated with grass-roots panmen and the street world. Yet the
college-boy bands maintained the competitiveness of the grass-roots
bands. There were strong rivalries between them, and occasionally
these rivalries even erupted in skirmishes. For example, Nightingale frequently fought with Stromboli over girls.[66] But the clashes of college-boy
bands were much milder than those of their grass-roots counterparts,
and on the whole these bands were perceived as well-behaved and respectable.

There was also some degree of rivalry between college-boy and grass-
roots bands. At present, however, panmen vary greatly in their accounts
of the relations between these two groups. Junior Pouchet, for example,
recalls a considerable amount of tension. He describes how the grass-
roots panmen felt that college boys were trying to appropriate their
form of music:

> . . . the guys who invented the steelband—the Spree Simons and Ellie
> Mannettes . . . the Invaders and Casablancas and what have you—they
> did not accept us. We were sort of like Johnny-Come-Lately, little col-
> lege boys, little so-called white kids. They don't know anything about
> this. . . . And here we were getting pressure from these guys because
> they didn't consider us to be musically inclined or to be able to play
> like them. Upstarts, as you might call it.[67]

One possible cause of tension between college-boy and grass-roots
bands was competition over opportunities to perform at fetes and clubs.
By the mid-1950s college boys may have been obtaining both more and
better-paying jobs. According to Pouchet, college boys were often given
engagements by individuals who were friends of their families:

> In the late '50s . . . steelband was accepted by a lot of people. Well,
> O.K., it didn't matter you're playing pan any more. But who you play-
> ing with was the big thing. You know, what band. What band repre-
> sented who. Either you're in a devil band, a bad band, or you're in a
> decent band or what band have you. Trinidadians . . . love fetes, love
> parties. . . . And you found that the people that really had the money
> was the middle class and rich people. And when they wanted steel-
> band music, who did they hire? Not Desperadoes. Silver Stars or Cur-
> tis Pierre and Dixieland. . . . In other words, if they want a steelband .
> . . they would quicker trust ten fellows from Silver Stars than not
> knowing—the unknown factor from Desperadoes or Tokyo. Whether
> we better than them or not did not mean musically. . . . So that's why
> we did get a lot of jobs.[68]

On the other hand, some panmen argue that, though there were fears that college-boy bands would be given more jobs, this did not in fact occur. For example, both Sack Mayers and Ray Holman point out that Merry Makers and Invaders continued to be very successful at obtaining engagements after the emergence of college-boy bands.[69] The same was true for All Stars. But these were all bands that developed relationships with socially prominent individuals. It seems quite likely that some grass-roots bands did lose opportunities. However, if there were jealousy and resentment, they were rarely manifested in any kind of physical confrontation. For the most part, grass-roots panmen felt that it was beneath them to attack college boys.

Many panmen, from both grass-roots and college backgrounds, recall that relations between the two types of bands were fairly harmonious and that grass-roots panmen generally even welcomed the college boys. The college boys certainly brought new opportunities and benefits. Their bands needed pans, instruction, and skilled players for playing at public engagements. For these services, the grass-roots panmen received money and sometimes even obtained jobs through the college boys' families.

The most far-reaching consequence of college-boy involvement in pan was increased acceptance of the steelband movement as a whole. Ray Holman states:

> Well, I think they gave it a greater measure of respectability. People began to look at it now, to have a little more regard for it, because they see people of a different level coming into it. So they began to accept it. . . . I think more people started to follow it. It wasn't now just something where, you know, badjohns and them. . . . Respectable people playing it so. They gave it more acceptance. And also I think it brought more discipline to it. So it played an important role.[70]

Much of the Trinidadian public originally believed that the steelband was intrinsically connected with unemployment, crime, and street life. But, when college boys started playing pan, people were forced to reinterpret the music's significance. There was a growing perception of pan as an acceptable pastime and form of entertainment for youth, and acceptance of college-boy bands eventually brought more tolerance of grass-roots bands.

College-boy participation in pan also further developed pan's potential as a national symbol. Though grass-roots Africans still represented the great majority of panmen, the movement had now expanded to include members of other classes and ethnic groups. Pan could no longer be perceived as exclusively an expression of one sector of the society—it had become a practice that evoked much wider identification. This expanded presence of pan in the society also had consequences for the control of the movement. Now middle class performers, as well as middle class advocates, joined grass-roots panmen in shaping the usage and meaning of the steelband.

Steelbands in Stage and Street Settings

One of the most important performance contexts for steelbands during the 1950s was the prestigious Trinidad Music Festival. This biennial event was held under the auspices of the Trinidad Music Association, an organization founded for the development of European classical music in Trinidad. The association's festivals included competition in a range of vocal and instrumental categories and adjudication by a British musical expert. Though the first festival was held in 1948, a steelband class was not added until 1952. Initially, there were some reservations concerning the quality of steelband music. However, Anthony Williams states that May Johnstone, the association's president, was open-minded about pan and was eventually able to overcome this resistance.[71]

For the 1952 festival, steelbands were limited to a maximum of twelve members each. In the preliminary round of the competition, they were required to play two selections from four categories of music: calypsos, mambos, rhumbas, and classics. Most bands chose to play a mambo and a classical piece. The festival also included a category for ping pong soloists who were required to perform one selection of any type of music. Six bands and six soloists were then chosen for the finals. At this point the bands played a tune of choice and a folksong as a test piece, while soloists played only a tune of choice.[72] The level of musicianship at the festival was quite high and impressed both the audiences and Dr. Sidney Northcote, the English adjudicator. The *Trinidad Guardian* described the evening of the finals:

> The drums of the steelband throbbed out their heady, exciting rhythms for Dr. Sidney Northcote and a huge, mixed crowd of stiff highbrows and noisy "pan" enthusiasts at the Globe Cinema last night.
> This was the first time that these local percussion outfits were tak-

ing part at a Music Festival; and the bold experiment of the organizers paid off, as not even standing room was available.

Last night's hot steel interlude provided a colourful contrast with the classical type music heard at the Festival so far.

The pans were sweet; the beaters capable; the music rich and varied; and the audience appreciative (too audibly so).

But melodious though the music was, the greatest interest of the night, for most of the audience, lay in the observations of Dr. Northcote. They were anxious to hear his opinion of "pan" music.[73]

Northcote complimented the pan musicians on their ingenuity but added that it would "take patience to build up the technique and purity of the steel band to make it really effective."[74] He also criticized the bands for playing European classics. Anthony Williams, who led North Stars in the festival, recalls how Northcote reprimanded Free French for their performance of Handel's "Largo":

He told them: "Why change this music?" In those days, we used to learn the melody by ear, mainly on the radio or record. And then we would put anything we want in the harmony. And that was wrong. So he criticized that approach to the classics. So we learned that in order to play the classics then, we had to follow the scores. This means reading music.[75]

Williams points out that Northcote also suggested that steelbands not attempt the classics because of their inability, at the time, to play sustained notes. (Later, panmen perfected rolls.) In addition, Northcote stated that steelbands should play "indigenous music" and that they should be used to create an "indigenous culture."[76]

In 1956 Northcote returned to Trinidad to judge that year's festival. At the steelband finals he commended the champions, Katzenjammers of Woodbrook, for their performances of "The Breeze and I" (a popular tune) and "For Steel Orchestra" (a test piece composed by Ozie George, a San Fernando panman). Northcote stated that the "technical skill of it all proved that there are possibilities of acquiring with the steelband, an orchestral precision." A few days later the steelband finalists performed a special concert for Northcote so that he could further evaluate the movement's progress since his last visit. At the end of this event he again advised bands to avoid playing European classics. Since the steelband was indigenous and unique to Trinidad, he argued, it should concentrate on playing its own music.[77] However, another observer of the concert, Canon Farquhar, offered a different opinion. Farquhar was impressed with the steelbands' musical advancements and was particularly captured by a soloist's performance of Bach's "Jesu, Joy of Man's Desiring." "Why should he be precluded the right to the inspiration of Bach, Mozart and Beethoven," Farquhar wondered, "just because of the temporary limitation of his instrument?"[78]

The question of whether steelbands should play European classics was regularly debated in Trinidad, but the debate did not dampen the panmen's interest in playing this type of music. Curtis Pierre of Dixieland explains:

> We were playing anything we could think of. We were attempting anything. That has been basically the success of the steelband. Not confining itself to calypsos only. . . . I realized that the steelband could attempt heavy classical music. Of course, we were criticized and they said we were tampering. Strauss must be rolling in his grave and all that kind of crap. But the steelbands always have been attempting to do a little more than what people expected them to do. And that is the spirit of the steelbandsman. . . . We wanted to show people that we were going to do something different.[79]

Panmen took criticisms of their ability to play the classics as a further challenge. At the same time, they did not perceive any contradiction between playing music from foreign countries and the development of the steelband as a local musical ensemble. Though the adjudicators of the Trinidad Music Festival utilized foreign aesthetic criteria, panmen were always eager to hear their comments. Anthony Williams states that the festival "caused improvement in making and tuning the pans, improvement in arranging and orchestration, improvement in playing the pans, and improvement in the appearance of the instruments."[80]

The festival contributed to the growing social acceptance of the steelband movement as well. It further established pan as a type of music that could be listened to and carefully evaluated in a formal and decorous setting. As the quality of the musical performances improved and as more middle class bands competed, a wider cross-section of the public began attending the festival's steelband section. In 1956 Canon Farquhar observed:

> Six years ago, steelband entertainment would have been limited in audience to a few hardy optimists and a wide mo[t]ley range of those who prefer their music hot and tumultuous. Two Fridays ago—and thanks again to the vision, imagination and audacious courage of the T.M.A. [Trinidad Music Association]—the Roxy Theatre was com-

pletely sold out to an audience that would have graced any more sophisticated and conventional entertainment.[81]

The Trinidad Music Festival was the most prestigious of a range of indoor settings for steelband performances during the 1950s. The growing interest in pan enabled bands to find employment at hotels such as
the Normandie, the Bel Air, and the Hilton; downtown nightclubs such
as the Miramar; and the rougher clubs along Park Street and Wrightson
Road. At some of these venues steelbands were featured in variety shows
that included dancers, novelty performers, and other musicians. They
also played alone or at times alternated sets with popular *brass bands*.[82]
In addition to their hotel and nightclub appearances, steelbands played
at local dance halls and private clubs. Social and sports clubs ranging
from the Trinidad Country Club and Casuals Club to grass-roots organizations regularly hired steelbands (as well as brass bands) for fetes. During the Carnival season, in particular, top bands such as Invaders, All
Stars, Casablanca, North Stars, Merry Makers, Ebonites, Silver Stars, and
Dixieland were in great demand. Frequently bands had to split into
multiple sections in order to accommodate all of their fans.

Outside the Carnival season, steelbands were often employed for special occasions in communities. For example, Owen Serrette relates that
when he belonged to Ebonites, the band played not only in dance halls
and clubs but in private homes:

> It was a major feature of weddings and christenings . . . to have a steel-
> band. I remember playing at many such occasions, particularly in
> Morvant and also around the East Dry River area. . . . We'd have a
> party in Morvant. Two-bedroom house they're playing in. They'd
> clear one bedroom for the steelband and have the drawing room
> where the people dance in. So, those days, the steelband was a major
> part of the whole community festivities.[83]

When steelbands played in stage or indoor settings, they generally utilized between five and fifteen players. By the late 1950s or early 1960s
the standard pans were the ping pong (eventually referred to as a *tenor
pan*), the *double second*, the *double guitar*, the *cello*, and the bass. The double second was a two-pan set, introduced by both Dixieland and North
Stars during the early 1950s.[84] Other innovations of the 1950s included
the development of the guitar pan (and then the double guitar), which
imitated the strumming of a conventional guitar, the expansion of Anthony Williams's two-pan tenor boom into a three-pan cello, and the expansion of TASPO's three-pan bass to five pans. This expansion in

numbers of pans gave steelband instruments greater range and versatility. Furthermore, at the 1954 Trinidad Music Festival Anthony Williams introduced the idea of mounting the upper pans on stands. Previously, a performer either suspended a pan around his neck or, when sitting, rested it on his legs. The use of stands greatly facilitated playing and allowed for the doubling of the second and the guitar.

The repertoires of steelbands in the 1950s included a range of genres: calypsos, boleros, mambos, rhumbas, sambas, waltzes, fox trots, American pop songs, and European classics. The arrangements of tunes during this period became increasingly elaborate and included such elements as more complex harmonies, counterpoint, arpeggios, tempo changes, and bridges.[85] Perhaps the most remarkable innovations occurred in the area of rhythm. Steelbands often recast their tunes in new rhythms. Big Mack Sandiford of All Stars explains:

> So when you hear a tune, you used to try to take that tune and turn it from a waltz to a mambo, from a waltz to a samba, or from a waltz to a kaiso [calypso]. And it takes a lot of doing to do that. . . . You're disarranging the whole of the fellow's composition. You are disarranging it and rearranging it to suit your mentality. . . . You break down the foundation of the tune all over and you start re-building it with some sort of magical growth of your's.[86]

Rhythm was a means by which panmen re-created foreign music on their own terms and made it their own possession. American and European tunes were localized in that they were given new forms that were consistent with the panmen's aesthetics and were more suitable for dancing.

Improvisational skills were another manifestation of the panmen's creative spirit. Tourists and sailors at nightclubs frequently requested unfamiliar tunes, and the most talented panmen were able to work out their own renditions of these tunes on the spot. Improvisational skills were also displayed by highly admired virtuoso soloists such as Emmanuel "Cobo Jack" Riley of Green Eyes and Invaders. These soloists were able to use pans for individual expression in what was generally an ensemble-oriented music guided by tight arrangements.

Though steelbands were increasingly appearing in stage settings during the 1950s, they remained rooted in the world of the streets and an integral part of Carnival, Discovery Day, and other celebrations. This continued association with the streets considerably hampered efforts to redefine pan as a respectable art form. When on the streets, steelbands were uncontrollable and symbolic of disorder. In competitive street per-

formances, there was a potential for violence, and fighting among steelbands continued in the 1950s despite the Steel Band Association's attempt to maintain peaceful relationships. There were a number of
dramatic Carnival clashes, such as one between Invaders and Tokyo in
1950 which the calypsonian Lord Blakie sang about in "Steelband
Clash."[87]

The most serious manifestation of steelband violence during the
1950s actually occurred during the celebration of the Coronation of
Queen Elizabeth II in 1953. In Trinidad the Coronation was observed
with a week of parades, church services, parties, dances, sports events,
youth rallies, bonfires, and fireworks. The climax of the festivities was a
"Coronation Carnival," a distinctively local expression of this imperial
event. The *Trinidad Guardian* reported that steelbands were painting
their pans red, white, and blue for the occasion and that masqueraders
were preparing to play "Coronation Sea-bees" and "Coronation
Sailors."[88]

The Coronation Carnival was a splendid affair except for the out-
break of violence: eight steelband clashes and an estimated two hundred injuries. In addition, the driver of a car was beaten to death with a
baseball bat in the midst of a steelband fight. Needless to say, the public
was shocked by the violence. The Governor quickly banned Carnival for
Discovery Day and appointed a Carnival Improvement Committee. In
the meantime commentators struggled to determine why the festivities
went awry. The *Guardian* stated:

> Nearly every "bourgeois" steel band—Dixie Stars, Dixieland, Dem
> Boys, etc.—was attacked, beaten and had their pans either destroyed
> or taken away from them by the "rango" bands.
>
> What was the reason for all the disorder? A steel band enthusiast,
> who has been following the pans since the dustbin days, supplied the
> following analysis of the situation:
>
> "In the early days when pan-beating was not socially acceptable, the
> steel bands were made up entirely of unemployed young men from
> the lower classes. . . .
>
> "During the past two or three years, however, the middle and
> upper classes have taken up pan-beating. College boys, civil servants,
> store clerks and other white-collar workers have formed themselves
> into bands—Dixieland, Dem Boys, Hit Paraders, etc.
>
> "Not only have these bands learned to play as well, or even better,
> than many of the old bands, but they have been getting all the en-
> gagements at the clubs, dances, etc.

"The proletarian bands, jealous of the prowess of what they call the 'social' bands, and resentful at their encroachment on what were formerly their exclusive preserve[s], have openly resolved to 'run all the social bands off the road.' . . .

"On Saturday, every 'social' band, unarmed, unsuspecting and not looking for trouble, was attacked in broad daylight by hooligans with baseball bats, big sticks, bottles, cowhide whips, and even razors and cutlasses, and put to flight.

"Many of them did not dare venture out in the night. Some have vowed never to beat on the road again."[89]

This commentary provides evidence that there was considerable class tension between steelbands during the early 1950s. On the other hand, Curtis Pierre claims that, though his college-boy band (Dixieland) was attacked by a grass-roots band (Ebonites) at the Coronation Carnival, this assault was not class motivated. In any case, the violence of the Coronation Carnival generated a public uproar against pan that surpassed even the condemnations of the 1940s. Just two years after its coverage and support of TASPO, the *Guardian* stated unequivocally that "in spite of all that has been done to reform them, by and large, steelbands are still harbingers of trouble and violence whenever they parade the streets and even when they do not." Meanwhile, the *Port-of-Spain Gazette* editorialized that the steelband was not characteristically West Indian and called for "a firm hand in the endeavor to rout out the hooliganism that has been sweeping the island."[90]

Over the course of the following weeks dozens of letters to the editor appeared in the *Guardian* and the *Gazette* about the Carnival. Some of the writers suggested that steelbands should be banned from the streets or even abolished entirely. Carnival in general was also widely criticized as decadent and unruly. The following excerpt from a letter is but one example of how vehement the attacks on pan became:

I appeal to decent people to support all proposals that may be made to suppress steel bands, as they appear to be the prime cause for the alarming prev[a]lence of crimes of violence and indecency, not only at Carnival, but all through the year.

I know that there are very many who do not want steel bands banned[.] Trinidad's "Culture," they say. I would ask these people w[h]ether they do not fear for themselves or their families on Carnival days, should they have to walk along a street the same time as a band of our "students of culture," who rum-maddened, hypnotised

and inflamed by the savage primitive beat of the steel pans, are
turned into beasts. Even decent people have been heard to say that
this savage beat "does something" to them.

Steel band fanaticism is a savage, bestial cult and must be recognised as such and completely wiped out, for there can be no compromise with unlawful killings. Control is not the answer, for it would
only stop for awhile and then break out again worse than before.
Steel bandsmen are 90 per cent the loiterers and the unemployable
who do not want to work. They are able to obtain cash by robbery and
violence throughout the year, and are bound together by hatred, jealousy, violence and unnatural rivalry.[91]

A new defense of the steelband was mounted as well. At a public
forum several prominent citizens suggested that the Coronation violence had its roots in class tensions, lack of a "proper" home and family
life, the after-effects of World War II, and corrupt political leadership. It
was also proposed that the steelband was again being used as a scape-
goat for a more general crime wave.[92]

Though steelband performances on the streets continued to evoke
fear and criticism during the 1950s, the actual music the bands were
playing was undergoing dramatic changes and was creating much public interest. Essentially, the music was increasingly influenced by innovations associated with stage performances. This influence was facilitated
by Anthony Williams's idea of mounting pans on wheels. Traditionally,
steelbandsmen paraded the streets with pans suspended around their
necks. This meant that individuals could not play more than one pan
and that it was very difficult to use full-size oil drums as bass pans. In
1956 Williams's North Stars came out for Carnival with wheels attached
to their bass pans. By the following Carnival, other bands were experimenting with mounting bass pans. For example, Crossfire of St. James
placed their basses on a mobile wooden platform. During the next few
years mobile metal frames were developed, and by the late 1950s or
early 1960s most bands were mounting all of their pans on these frames.
Lennox Pierre points out that previously there had been a clear distinction between the concert stage steelband and the Carnival steelband.
But with the innovation of mobile frames the concert band "went on the
road." It was now possible for individuals to play multiple pans such as
double seconds, three-pan cellos, and five-pan basses; and the elaborate
harmonies that had been developed for the concert band were now employed by panmen on the streets.[93]

In Carnival street processions steelbands continued to play the calypsos that were performed by calypsonians in tents in the course of the

Carnival season. As steelbands improved musically and became the favorite type of musical accompaniment for masquerade bands, they became increasingly important to calypsonians who were trying to popularize their compositions. The tune that was played by the greatest number of steelbands and brass bands on the streets for Carnival was designated the *road march* for the year, and the composer of this piece received much acclaim. By the 1960s the Mighty Sparrow and Lord Kitchener were battling each other for the status of road march king by composing calypsos well-suited for steelband performance.

Though calypso was the primary musical expression of local Carnival revelry, steelbands also performed other types of music for the festival. In fact, during the 1950s and early 1960s, bands devoted their greatest effort to arrangements of foreign selections that became known as *bombs.* A bomb was a tune that a band prepared for J'Ouvert with the objective of surprising and impressing other bands with its musical ability. The practice appears to have originated with All Stars, who in the 1940s came out for J'Ouvert playing Latin American tunes. Eventually other bands also began playing Latin pieces for J'Ouvert. According to Prince Batson and Jerry Serrant, All Stars and Crossfire confronted each other with Latin bombs for J'Ouvert in 1955 and almost ended up in a physical clash. But before any violence broke out, the police ordered All Stars to turn back. Crossfire interpreted All Stars' move as an admission of defeat and ridiculed the band. At the next Carnival All Stars emerged for J'Ouvert with a dazzling rendition of Beethoven's "Minuet in G" in calypso rhythm in order to demonstrate to Crossfire that they had in no way been defeated.[94]

In the following years steelbands typically prepared calypso versions of classical selections such as Liszt's "Liebesträume," Mascagni's "Intermezzo," and Handel's "Ev'ry Valley Shall Be Exalted." All Stars, Invaders, Ebonites, Highlanders, and North Stars were a few of the bands that became particularly well-known for their bombs. These tunes were always rehearsed in secret so that they would have a startling impact for J'Ouvert. In 1958 John Grimes, a *Guardian* reporter with a keen interest in pan, stated:

> In many respects the bands regard this tune as far more important to them, particularly in prestige, than the road march. They practise this in the deep silence of the night, and well removed from listening ears.

Grimes goes on to describe how All Stars' bomb rehearsal followed several hours of public practicing of calypsos:

Then at midnight, or thereabout, the band goes into private session. In two and threes they go through the motions without sound, shadow-playing the tune—that will "hit" the road on Jour Ouvert morning.

That melody is top secret. [I]t will not be discussed even among members of the band, for fear that sharp ears may be listening. What will be the road march, to a great extent, does not depend on the bands alone. Other factors may influence its selection. But the tune for Jour Ouvert, is their own individual creation.[95]

Bomb competitions between steelbands often occurred near All Stars' headquarters on Charlotte Street in downtown Port of Spain and at Green Corner on the western side of the downtown area. Anthony Williams describes the western steelbands' approach to Green Corner for J'Ouvert:

Their best tunes would be played from the time they reached Green Corner. They would play a calypso coming up the road. And when we reached there, we'd drop—that's what the bomb thing was all about. You'd drop your bomb. You'd drop your best tune. This was what it was all about—so to let the people hear what you have.[96]

Classical pieces were used as bombs because they were believed to be more challenging than other types of music and thus were the best way a band could display its skill. Furthermore, since most of the music played on the streets for Carnival was calypso, the bombs stood out and were a means by which steelbands could attract attention. Bombs also reflected the openness of Carnival: the desire to represent cultural traditions from throughout the world—but in local terms. Steelbands drew on European music but reinterpreted this music in calypso rhythm and utilized it for their own purposes. The same music that helped bring respectability in stage settings became, in its creolized form, a means of achieving reputations in competitive street encounters.[97]

The panmen's expansion of Carnival music during the 1950s was accompanied by elaborations in their masquerades. Steelbands typically played a simple sailor mas such as Seabees in jeans and jerseys for Carnival Monday. For Carnival Tuesday, however, their masquerades were quite varied. First of all, there were new developments in fancy sailor mas. Instead of using long noses to represent themes, mas men began to fashion large headpieces with bent-wire frames. One of the earliest practitioners of this idea was Leo Warner, whose Commandoes steelband/sailor band came out for the 1950 Carnival with cobra head-pieces. In the following years fancy sailor mas men created headpieces with themes ranging from fruits and flowers to signs of the zodiac to Walt Disney characters. In 1959 Noble Williams's fancy sailor band from Laventille used enormous headpieces that represented modes of trans-port, including a rickshaw, a dromedary, horse-drawn buggies, a loco-motive, a Mississippi river boat (12 feet long), balloons, and a jet plane.[98] Elaborate headpieces were accompanied by increasingly color-ful and varied sailor uniforms to the point where some bands tran-scended the sailor genre altogether. Leo Warner describes Comman-does' development in this regard:

> As time went by, we changed the headpiece. The first was the "Cobra." Then we played the "Octopus.". . . And I think the last one was "Things to Come." It was sailor, yes, in a sense. But, then again, the costumes were modified to meet with certain requirements. Be-cause we're playing spacemen and all that sort of thing. . . . People who played robots and so on—they wear different costumes. . . . Most of the mas had moving parts. . . . That was the year I got a lot of fame because mechanical mas was not well-known. It was not popular at the time. . . . From after 1956, following, many bands started to indulge in moving parts of the costume. . . .
> [My "Godzilla"] was 20 feet high by about 30 feet long. . . . "Godzilla" had moving parts. . . . That was the turning point. . . . We carried the name [sailor], yes. But there was no objection on my part of they playing in whatever costume they think suitable. . . . Many of the sailor bands are doing their own thing. They're coming almost semi-historical.[99]

While some steelbands played fancy sailor mas or accompanied fancy sailor bands, many played other types of mas. Some continued with tra-ditional ship's crew, sailors-on-shore-leave, and other military and war-rior themes. American Indian and Mexican masquerades were also quite popular. Some steelbands even created costumes that focused on themes like those portrayed by large historical bands. For example, Des-peradoes recruited Leo Warner to design "Primitive Man and Extracts from the Animal Kingdom" in 1958 and "Highlights of Noah's Ark" in 1959. These same two years, Starlift played "Nursery Rhymes" and "The Greatest Show on Earth."

This expansion in the types of masquerade played by steelbands dur-ing the 1950s suggests changes in the ways in which panmen conceived of their position in the society. As the role and significance of the steelband in the society broadened, panmen began to search for new ways in which they could represent themselves. The oppositional character of the steelband continued and was manifested in sailor mas, but the rebel image was no longer entirely adequate or desirable as bands moved toward the cultural mainstream. A changing vision of the steelband is also apparent in the fact that panmen began to select a new kind of name for their bands. Instead of drawing on the war imagery of the 1940s, they frequently adopted musical names such as Dixieland, Tropical Harmony, and Merry Tones.

Steelbands and the People's National Movement

As the steelband grew in social importance during the late 1940s and 1950s, politicians began to recognize its value as a vehicle for mobilizing political support. Many residents of particular neighborhoods developed strong loyalties towards their steelbands and took great pride in the bands' accomplishments. Because of these attachments, politicians realized that they could obtain more votes by giving assistance to neighborhood steelbands and by hiring the bands for performances.

Albert Gomes was one of the first politicians to show a strong interest in steelbands. Though he obviously had a genuine concern for the development of indigenous arts, he undoubtedly also sensed that his advocacy of the steelband movement could increase the political support that he received from grass-roots Trinidadians. By the early 1950s a number of other politicians were courting the steelband movement. The best known was Norman Tang of Woodbrook. Tang used to arrange for steelbands to parade the streets of his district on trucks in order to advertise his campaigns and attract people to his rallies. One of the bands that he recruited was Merry Makers. Sack Mayers recalls that Tang would buy instruments and equipment for the band and obtain jobs for unemployed members. Then at election time, he would ask the band members to acknowledge his assistance and canvass their families and friends for votes. Mayers says that he knew that he was being used and that he went about his campaigning rather half-heartedly.[100]

While individual politicians employed steelbands in the early 1950s, political usage of pan became much more systematic with the rise of Eric Williams and the People's National Movement (PNM). An appreciation of the impact of the PNM on the steelband requires consideration of the development of this political party and its central role in the process of decolonization. Eric Williams was an Oxford-educated historian who returned to Trinidad in 1948 to assume a senior position with the Caribbean Commission, a research and development organization. Soon he became connected with an association of local teachers and for several years led study groups and delivered public lectures that gave him a devoted following among the middle class. His vast knowledge of Caribbean history had a profound effect on his audiences; by 1955 it became clear to some of his closest associates that a new political party could be organized around his leadership. In June 1955 Williams addressed the Trinidadian masses for the first time in Woodford Square, a central gathering place in Port of Spain. The following month he renamed this location "The University of Woodford Square" and proceeded to give detailed lectures there and elsewhere on the evils of colonialism. His scholarship and eloquence, as well as his combativeness and sense of style, made him immensely appealing to both the grass-roots and middle classes. Political scientist Ivar Oxaal suggests that Williams's charismatic authority "was the *deus ex machina* which propelled the independence movement forward, revolutionized the political life of the colony almost overnight, and shattered the complacency of the sputtering transition to self-government."[101]

In January 1956 the People's National Movement was officially launched with Williams as the leader. The party's objective was to be truly national in scope: to transcend the various ethnic and class divisions of the society. Its platform included self-government in internal affairs, internal economic development, and the refashioning of the educational system in a manner that would make it more attuned to the local culture and would help build a sense of national identity. The PNM won the elections held in September 1956, due to its success at eliciting widespread support from both middle class and grass-roots Africans. But the party fell short of its goal of being truly national. The majority of Indians and French Creoles gave their support to other parties. In spite of the PNM's attempt to create a national image, Indians tended to perceive the party as an effort by Africans to achieve political dominance, while the business sector viewed it as a threat to its power and privileged position in the society. Ethnic political tension increased in Trinidad in the aftermath of the 1956 elections, with Indians and French Creoles eventually joining together to form a united opposition in the Democratic Labour Party (DLP).

Though the PNM had broad-based African support, its leadership was largely middle class. Furthermore, though Williams sometimes utilized a leftist perspective in his writing and speaking, in practice he was generally moderate and accommodational. In fact the PNM government continued the Gomes regime's pioneer industries program which utilized tax concessions and other incentives to attract foreign investors to

Trinidad. Economic growth continued under the PNM, particularly in the oil sector which became dominated by Texaco, Shell, and British Petroleum. But since the oil industry and the new factories did not require large amounts of labor, unemployment remained high.

In 1958 Trinidad and Tobago joined with nine other West Indian colonies to form the Federation of the West Indies. It was during this period that the PNM government assumed its most militant anti-imperialist stance. Williams decided that the continued occupation of the Chaguaramas naval base by the United States was unjust and demanded that the land be returned to Trinidad. When Britain and the United States refused to negotiate, the PNM, with the assistance of C. L. R. James, launched a full-scale campaign to intensify public sentiments against colonialism. The climax of the protest occurred one rainy day in 1960 when Williams held a mass meeting at Woodford Square and ceremoniously burned documents representing the "Seven Deadly Sins of Colonialism." The meeting was followed by the "March in the Rain" to the United States consulate. These protests had their intended effect: soon afterwards the United States and Britain began negotiations on Chaguaramas directly with Trinidad.

In 1961 elections were again held in Trinidad and were plagued by ethnic tension and blatantly racist political tactics on the part of both the PNM and the DLP. The PNM emerged victorious and returned to its efforts at decolonization. By the end of 1961 the Federation of the West Indies had virtually collapsed due to an array of disputes among its members, and Trinidad decided to seek independence on its own. There was considerable controversy between the PNM and DLP over the drafting of an independence constitution. Negotiations with Britain were smooth, however: apparently the Colonial Office had been anxious to divest itself of the West Indies. An agreement between all parties was reached in May 1962, and on August 31, 1962, Trinidad and Tobago became an independent nation-state.[102]

Steelbands were closely involved in the political ascent of the People's National Movement. Williams thoroughly understood the functions and symbolic value of steelbands in communities and established firm relations with the steelband movement in order to elicit and maintain grassroots support. Steelband leaders became his personal assistants, and he regularly visited panyards. Soon after the PNM won the 1956 elections, Williams developed a particularly close relationship with Desperadoes and Laventille, a predominantly grass-roots African neighborhood that was currently plagued by steelband-related gang warfare. The key figure in this alliance was George Yeates, the captain of Desperadoes and a Laventille youth and community leader. During the 1950s Yeates worked hard to bring an end to violence and to open up opportunities for panmen and other young men in the community. By the late 1950s he realized that the new PNM government could offer assistance by creating jobs:

> This was one of the possible solutions to the solving of the gang warfare. Because when Dr. Williams came up the [Laventille] Hill and spoke to us, that was one of the proposals that we had put forward to him. That there were too many young people, right, that were idle. And an idle brain is a devil's workshop. And we thought that if Government could have put aside some money—not as a dole—some money that could be spent to provide communal amenities. . . . We in the villages would be able to look around and see areas that need repair works. And have it attended to. Potholes and road surfacing, drainage repairs and so on. And so the whole thing became a national idea, employing thousands of people in areas where there were large pockets of unemployment.[103]

This was one of the original projects of the PNM government's "Crash" program to curb unemployment. The program was initiated in 1957, first in sugar cane areas and then in Laventille and San Juan.[104] Over the years it was expanded and given new names: "Special Works" and the "Development and Environmental Works Division" (DEWD). In the course of its existence, this program provided employment for thousands of panmen and other individuals in low-income communities of Trinidad and Tobago and, at the same time, helped develop strong community loyalties to the PNM.

In addition to providing maintenance jobs, the PNM regularly used panmen in its political campaigns. Williams employed members of Desperadoes for protection when he was on the campaign trail, and many steelbands were recruited to perform at political rallies. Bertie Marshall recalls how he and several other Laventille panmen became a PNM band:

> Not far from where we practiced was the PNM office in Laventille. I remember those times well. Donald Granado was the big man, and I used to carry chairs from our house . . . to the office whenever meetings were held.
>
> We were called the 'PNM' band simply because we played at everything the PNM had in Laventille. . . .
>
> Granado used to compliment the band whenever they appeared, and one time at a meeting he announced that he was giving us a

cheque to buy a pair of cymbals which were then a big thing in the steelband world. I never got those cymbals as I have never gotten any of the things promised me by members of government over the last 15 or 16 years. Still, we played as the PNM band.[105]

Though the PNM utilized steelbands to gain grass-roots African political support, it also promoted the steelband as a national symbol. The steelband was conceptualized and presented as an indigenous cultural form in which all ethnic groups and classes in Trinidad could take pride. In order to facilitate the development of the steelband movement and its symbolic value, the PNM government collaborated with the Steelband Association and included bands in a range of official occasions, including visits by foreign dignitaries.

This support of the steelband movement was related to a more general effort to promote Carnival. In late 1956 the government formed a Carnival Development Committee (CDC) whose purpose, according to Dr. Williams, was "to make proposals to organise Carnival on a more national basis."[106] Originally, the CDC did not intend to implement its plans in time for the 1957 Carnival. But a crisis occurred that forced it into action. A number of masquerade bands threatened to boycott the masquerade competitions organized by the *Trinidad Guardian* at the Queen's Park Savannah on Carnival Monday and Tuesday. Their grievance was that the prize monies for these competitions were meager in comparison with the lavish prizes awarded to the Carnival Queen on Carnival Sunday night. The protest was also linked to general resentment over the elitist and racist orientation of the *Guardian's* Queen competition.

This crisis was in fact the culmination of a long-standing tension in Carnival between the forces of "Downtown" and those of the Savannah. Downtown Port of Spain was traditionally the grass-roots domain for the celebration of Carnival, while the festivities at the Savannah had for years been controlled by the Trinidadian elite. The crowning of the Carnival Queen on Sunday night at the Savannah and the awarding of her prizes was a particularly prominent public display of this class and its power. Gordon Rohlehr states:

By the mid-fifties, then, the Carnival Queen competition which had begun as a pleasant if irrelevant ornament to Carnival, had become a means whereby the substantial Caucasian segment of the commercial class advertised, celebrated and applauded itself. . . . It illustrated nothing more or less than the power of Money, which was being flaunted in the face of irate Mas men, bitterly sarcastic calypsonians and smouldering steelbandsmen, the last of whom had for a decade been stigmatized as the living antithesis of what the Queen was supposed to symbolise: beauty, charm, personality and, according to some, holiness; the very genius and spirit of "clean Carnival."[107]

In response to the protest, the CDC assumed the management of the Monday and Tuesday masquerade competitions and raised the prizes. The *Guardian* replied in an editorial that it was no longer interested in running the competitions and warned about government control of Carnival. As Rohlehr notes, Carnival had been under the proprietorship of assorted middle class groups for decades.[108] The formation of the CDC by the PNM government continued this pattern and led to new ways of channeling the passions and commitments that the festival evoked.

In 1958 the CDC replaced the *Guardian*'s Queen competition with a Sunday night show of its own ("Dimanche Gras") which included a Calypso King competition along with other performances. The following year the CDC began to hold a steelband competition on Friday night in conjunction with the Steelband Association called "Carnival Bacchanal." Through these competitions and numerous smaller ones all over Trinidad and Tobago, the PNM government was able to exercise considerable influence over Carnival and its participants. While the government appears to have been sincere in its effort to build the festival into a symbol around which the nation could rally, it undoubtedly also realized that prize monies were a effective means of encouraging political support.

The Steelband Movement, Respectability, and National Identity

The steelband movement assumed entirely new dimensions during the late 1940s and 1950s. Certain middle class individuals defended and redefined the music, a steelband association was formed, bands began performing in a wide range of indoor or stage settings, and panmen developed relationships with political figures and the government. Meanwhile the movement expanded beyond its foundation in grass-roots African communities to include youths of other class and ethnic backgrounds. This institutionalization of the steelband movement was linked to the negotiations between different classes and ethnic groups that accompanied decolonization in Trinidad.

Observers of the colonial world have often commented on how postwar nationalist movements were generally not expressions of whole colonial peoples but of discontented middle classes. In *The Wretched of the Earth,* for example, Franz Fanon discusses how middle classes received some benefits from colonialism and sought to improve their lot by essentially taking over the role of the colonists. The nationalist political parties that they formed were designed to further their own interests. At the same time, nationalist aspirations depended on new cultural assumptions. Middle class intellectuals turned away from Western cultures and determined to "renew contact once more with the oldest and most pre-colonial springs of life of their people." The claim of a national culture in the past served as "a justification for the hope of a future national culture."[109]

The development of nationalism in postwar Trinidad, particularly as it was articulated by the African and colored middle class, was a variation of this general pattern. During the late 1940s and 1950s, this class became much more assertive in its reaction against the limits placed on its economic and political advancement by the colonial hegemony. Its aspirations were expressed not only in political action but in a nascent interest in Afro-Trinidadian folk culture. While the middle classes of Africa, on whom Fanon focuses, could renew their ties with pre-colonial African cultures, Trinidadians had no pre-colonial past in Trinidad. Thus they turned to the local traditions that had developed alongside the imposed European cultures. Folk music and dance were researched and presented and, according to Lloyd Braithwaite, even observation of Orisha ceremonies became permissible. In addition, Barbara Powrie states that there was increased participation on the part of the middle class in Carnival in the postwar years and that it was "at last inclined to take pride in something which is Trinidadian."[110] This exploration and celebration of local folk culture was part of an effort by the African and colored middle class to define a Trinidadian cultural identity which in turn could help justify claims for political autonomy.

During this same period, however, there was a growing Indian middle class which had a strong sense of ethnic identity and increasing economic and political aspirations of its own. One of the strategies of the African and colored middle class for obtaining and maintaining power in this competitive arena was to define Afro-Trinidadian culture as the national culture on the grounds that it was indigenous to the island. While Indians emphasized their cultural continuity with India, Africans tended to stress the local re-creation of African-derived culture. The affirmation of Afro-Trinidadian folk culture was also a means by which the African and colored middle class identified itself with the African grass-roots class and recruited its support. This class alliance, based on a growing sense of a common culture, was a crucial factor in the rise to power of the People's National Movement.

The advocacy and re-presentation of the steelband in postwar Trinidad was shaped by the nationalist goals of the African and colored middle class. Though the steelband advocates were not necessarily operating according to an explicit political plan, a nationalist orientation did make them particularly receptive to the emerging steelband and quick to perceive its potential as a national symbol. But the steelband, like many other grass-roots expressive forms, posed certain problems for nationalist promotion. Lloyd Braithwaite notes that

> the search for a distinctive and national form of expression which would both symbolize and give unity to the society was not altogether easy. The areas in which the lower class seemed to have the most to contribute were areas heavily associated with the more despised forms of lower class behaviour.[111]

Many Trinidadians continued to associate steelbands with unemployment, violence, and crime. Thus efforts to reform the pan movement were necessary before it could be widely accepted as a national symbol. The formation of a steelband association and the presentation of steelbands in concert settings were ways of redirecting the movement toward youth development and musical advancement.

It was the middle class leadership of the PNM that initiated systematic political usage of the steelband. Both the PNM and the Democratic Labour Party recruited members along ethnic lines, while using nationalist rhetoric to maintain legitimacy and broaden their support. The steelband became a particularly useful political symbol for the PNM because of the dual significance it had assumed by the 1950s. On the one hand, it was an expression of grass-roots Africans and was an effective means of mobilizing support from this sector of the population. On the other hand, the fact that it was a new and indigenous cultural form made it an effective national symbol. This nationalist representation gained more influence in the course of the 1950s as the steelband movement became somewhat more diverse in terms of class and ethnicity, due to the rise of college-boy bands.

Middle class nationalism had a profound influence on the institutionalization of the steelband movement, but this transformation was also shaped by the panmen themselves. Panmen were seeking opportunities and a respected position in the society and believed that they could more easily achieve these goals if they cooperated with middle class supporters and the government. Though pan advocates encouraged the formation of a steelband association, the creation and development of this organization depended on the panmen's own efforts. Furthermore, panmen aggressively pursued the opportunities to perform in indoor stage settings that the middle class was making available. So the institutionalization of the steelband was essentially a collaborative effort. However, grass-roots panmen were only willing to collaborate if they were certain that their basic control of the movement was not being threatened. They continued to conceive of and use the music as an expression of their own identity, and their bands remained rooted in the street world and in grass-roots communities.

Similarly, panmen sought respectability, but on their own terms. The process by which the steelband gradually gained respectability was one in which the meanings and expressions of respectability were changed. Panmen were aware that they might achieve respectability by playing European classics. But they primarily perceived the classics as a means of expanding their musical ability, and by playing the classics on pans they gave this music a new sound. This reinterpretation in terms of local cultural models was extended even further when classics were played in calypso rhythms on the streets. In addition, when panmen performed at the Trinidad Music Festival and at other elite occasions, they were not simply achieving respectability but fundamentally changing the character of these events. Essentially the steelband movement contributed to the localization of criteria of respectability and to the establishment of indigenous cultural forms as a source of value in the society. The movement's institutionalization was not simply a form of appropriation but a response to the panmen's assertion of the importance of their music. Steelband music was a locally created art that helped redefine the cultural mainstream. It is in this sense that its development during the 1950s was one symbolic manifestation of the whole process of decolonization. As the steelband became more prominent and significant in the society, Trinidad and Tobago transformed itself from a colony to an independent nation.

Figure 1. Revelers with pans, probably at Carnival in Port of Spain, c. 1940. Photo courtesy Y. De Lima & Co. Ltd. and Dave Sofa.

Figure 2. Unidentified steelband, Christmas season 1950. Note automobile brake drum and tune boom in center. Photo courtesy Trinidad Guardian Newspapers and Junia Browne.

Figure 3. Members of Invaders at the Queen's Park Oval, Port of Spain, early 1950s. Photo courtesy Junia Browne.

Figure 4. Lieutenant Joseph Griffith conducting the Trinidad All Steel Percussion Orchestra (TASPO) in London, 1951. Photo by British Broadcasting Corporation. Courtesy Errol Hill.

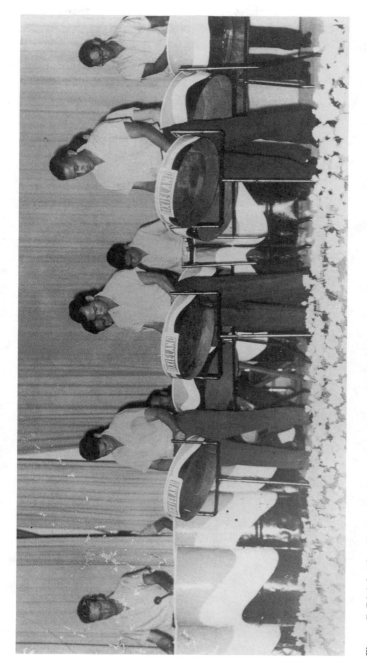

Figure 5. Dixieland at Fatima College, Port of Spain, 1960. Photo courtesy Curtis Pierre.

Figure 6. Cordettes, c. 1968. Note sponsor's name on sign, pans, and jackets. Photo courtesy People's National Movement and Junia Browne.

Figure 7. Prime Minister Eric Williams (left center) with Rudolph Charles, leader of Desperadoes, during the "Meet the Panmen" tour, 1970. Photo courtesy Pan Trinbago and Junia Browne.

Figure 8. Pat Bishop conducting Desperadoes at the 1988 Steelband Music Festival in the Jean Pierre Complex, Port of Spain. Photo by Junia Browne.

Figure 9. Phase II in concert outside the Central Bank, Port of Spain, 1990. Photo by Junia Browne.

Figure 10. Wynton Marsalis and Len "Boogsie" Sharpe at the 1986 Pan Jazz Festival in the Hilton Hotel, Port of Spain. Photo by Junia Browne.

Figure 11. Section of Tokyo at the 1989 Panorama Preliminaries in the Queen's Park Savannah, Port of Spain.

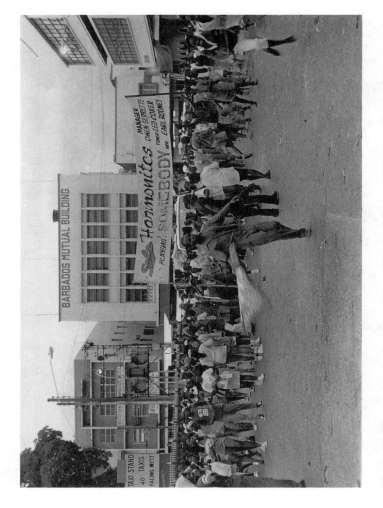

Figure 12. Harmonites in downtown Port of Spain, J'Ouvert 1989. Note flagman in foreground.

Figure 13. Jab Molassi band in downtown Port of Spain, J'Ouvert 1989.

Figure 14. Jason Griffith's sailor band in Belmont, Carnival Tuesday 1989. Note fancy sailors in background, left and right.

Figure 15. Merrytones' panyard in Diego Martin, 1989.

Figure 16. On break from rehearsal in Merrytones' panyard, 1988. Left to right: Byron Serrette, Anthony Johnson, Sylvan Salandy, and Noel Adams.

Chapter Four
The Steelband in the Post-Independence Era: The 1960s and 1970s

By the end of August 1962, Trinidad and Tobago was prepared for the celebration of its independence from Britain. A national flag and coat of arms had been approved, a national anthem composed, and a motto chosen: "Together We Aspire! Together We Achieve!" Dignitaries from over fifty foreign nations were to attend the occasion, along with the Princess Royal who would represent the Queen and open the new Parliament on Independence Day. In conjunction with the official ceremonies, there would be events of a more festive nature such as a state banquet and ball, an Independence Youth Festival, and a gala show at Queen's Hall portraying the variety of African, Indian, European, and Chinese derived cultural traditions in Trinidad. An independence calypsonian had been selected at a competition, and the Prime Minister-designate, Eric Williams, proclaimed the steelband to be one of Trinidad's foremost products, and thus deserving of a prominent role in the celebrations. Local arts were also highlighted in a Carnival, Calypso, and Steelband Exhibition at the Royal Victoria Institute. In addition to this range of preparations and artistic events, the press provided educational commentary on the meaning of independence and on what would be required of the citizens of the new nation.

Finally, the eve of independence arrived. The *Trinidad Guardian* announced:

> Midnight tonight is Trinidad and Tobago's moment of destiny. At this hour, the country and its 830,000 people, aflutter with the fever of Independence, will inhale their first breath of political freedom as the national flag of red, white and black is hoisted on the floodlit forecourt of the Red House, Port-of-Spain, ancestral home of the Territory's legislature.

The Union Jack, flying over the country for the past 165 years, will come down for the last time, signifying "the achievement of a new relationship with Her Majesty and with the Commonwealth."[1]

Independence posed new challenges both to the nation and to the steelband movement. Leaders of the nation were faced with such problems as local economic development, the creation of a national community that fully included all segments of the diverse population, and the forging of a national identity. At the same time, leaders of the steelband movement were forced to consider what the movement's position would be in the new national order. Specifically, they had to make choices concerning the steelband's relationships with the state and the corporate sector. In fact, negotiations between panmen, government officials, and businessmen became the central dramas in the steelband movement in the post-independence period. Both the government and businesses devised ways of assisting steelbands that furthered their own interests, while panmen continued to seek support that was consistent with their particular goals. These negotiations, along with the economic trends of the post-independence period, had a profound impact on steelband performance contexts, pan production, and the music itself.

The Steelband, the State, and the Corporate Sector

In the years after independence, the PNM government's promotion of the steelband movement was interrelated with an elaborate system of patronage and material rewards used to maintain political power. In many respects, this system was an example of what Carl Stone refers to as "clientelism" in his analysis of the political sociology of Jamaica. Stone suggests that clientelism is a characteristic of most post-colonial nation-states that have competitive electoral political systems:

> Clientelism as a power structure usually emerges in Third World countries when imperialist interests disengage from the management of state power, handing over the machinery of government to the emergent politically dominant petty bourgeois party leaders. These leaders harness the state as a resource from which to establish a power structure that competes with and parallels the old and continuing power structure rooted in the ownership of the forces of production by local and foreign capitalist interests.

The party leaders become patrons who use the resources of the state to maintain the support of their followers or clients:

> The dominant basis of political and party allegiance in a clientelistic party system is personal loyalty to individual political actors who have or are perceived to have a high capability to allocate and distribute divisible material and social benefits as well as indivisible sectoral class or communal benefits.[2]

By the 1960s the PNM government in Trinidad and Tobago had developed a system of clientelism that was closely linked to the idea of community development. In 1963 Eric Williams began a "Meet the People Tour" in which he visited communities throughout the nation in order to learn about their problems and to give them a sense of participation in the political process. In her discussion of this community development program, sociologist Susan Craig notes:

> During the tour, the potential of the voluntary organizations—in particular the village councils—for mobilizing support, and as a channel for benefits to the villages was clearly recognized. The Prime Minister, followed by senior members of the ruling party, seized the opportunity, therefore, to urge the members of the PNM to join and influence these organizations.[3]

The village councils then became the vehicles through which the government directed local projects such as building community centers, improving water supplies, and introducing health, library, and postal services.[4] Moreover, the "Crash" program that the government had initiated in the late 1950s to curb unemployment was renamed the "Special Works" program, and specific projects were put under the control of the village councils. In many districts preference was given to panmen in the recruitment of labor for these projects, and in some cases whole projects were allotted to steelbands.

Williams also introduced an annual Best Village competition which highlighted various aspects of community life. In 1965 the competition featured steelbands, with a requirement that the bands be affiliated with village councils. This regulation was undoubtedly designed to foster closer contacts between the PNM-controlled councils and the steelband movement. Sixty-six bands competed in the event and the victor's prize went to Desperadoes who represented the Northwest Laventille Community Council.[5] In the years after 1965 the Best Village competition was devoted to interpretations of folk music, dance, and theatrical traditions by troupes associated with village councils. Though it became immensely popular in PNM constituencies, only a small percentage of Indians ever participated.

In addition to cultivating relationships with individual steelbands, the PNM government assisted the steelband organization which in 1962 assumed a new name: the National Association of Trinidad and Tobago Steelbandsmen (NATTS). In 1963 NATTS organized a National Steelband that included members of bands from throughout Trinidad and Tobago. Some oil companies provided oil drums and the government paid Ellie Mannette to tune the pans. Over the next few years the band performed at various state occasions, including visits by foreign dignitaries, and represented the nation abroad at special events such as the Commonwealth Arts Festival in Britain in 1965 and Expo '67 in Montreal.[6] During this same period the government's Carnival Development Committee (CDC) collaborated with NATTS in staging Panorama, the large steelband competition held during each Carnival season, while the Secretariat of the PNM selected top steelbands to perform at an annual concert during the Christmas season entitled "Carols and Classics On Steel." In the course of the 1960s Williams also formed a number of committees to investigate the problems facing the steelband movement, and appointed George Goddard, the President of NATTS, to the position of Advisor on the Improvement of Steelband Music in the Ministry of Planning and Development.[7]

The PNM government's provision of funds, jobs, and opportunities to the steelband movement both strengthened the movement and advanced the PNM's vision of a national identity in which Afro-Trinidadian cultural traditions were given prominence. In addition, the assistance helped the PNM effectively to maintain the political allegiance of the panmen and their communities and fend off challenges from opposing political parties. Panmen as a group were content with this arrangement in which votes were exchanged for patronage: they welcomed the opportunities and enjoyed the prestige that accompanied government support.

During the 1960s panmen also pursued another means of gaining funds: sponsorship by businesses. In a sponsorship arrangement, a firm assisted a band with expenses such as oil drums, paint, uniforms, and transportation. In return, the band attached the firm's name to its own. The combined name was then prominently displayed on signs, pans, and jerseys at performance occasions, thus providing the firm with a unique form of advertising and public relations. Sponsored steelbands were generally also expected to play periodically at company functions.

The earliest relationships between businesses and steelbands actually occurred during the 1950s. In the early 1950s, for example, Esso Standard Oil recruited a small number of panmen from Southern Symphony to form what became known as the Esso Steelband. Though Esso also assisted other small steelbands from time to time during the 1950s, this kind of support did not carry the significance of the sponsorship arrangements of later years.[8] The first instance of formal sponsorship of an established steelband occurred in 1960 when Invaders became Shell Invaders. By 1965 many prominent steelbands had gained sponsors, such as Pan Am North Stars, Coca Cola Desperadoes, Angostura Starlift, Texaco Sundowners, Guinness Cavaliers, Chase Manhattan Savoys, BWIA West Side, Trinidad Hilton All Stars, Esso Tripoli, Carib Tokyo, Solo Harmonites, and Kirpalani San Juan All Stars. By 1966, 26 out of the 90 steelbands belonging to NATTS were sponsored.[9]

During the mid-1960s many steelbands succeeded in obtaining sponsors through the personal efforts of Eric Williams. The Prime Minister aggressively convinced numerous firms that they could increase their contributions to the nation by providing funds for the steelband movement. Multinationals were certainly indebted to the PNM government, since it continued a plan of economic development that offered many incentives to foreign investors. Then in 1965 the government passed the Industrial Stabilization Act in an attempt to curb growing militancy in the labor movement.[10] Thus Williams's drive for steelband sponsorship may have been one means of softening an economic policy that appeared to favor capital over labor. Through sponsorship, a small percentage of business profits was channeled into the hands of an increasingly restless grass-roots class. More significantly, sponsorship helped corporations create an impression that they cared about local communities, and it provided Williams with another means of maintaining steelbands as political clients.

As sponsorship developed, it began to have a substantial impact on the steelband movement. First of all, it greatly increased steelbands' financial resources which, in turn, facilitated further musical advancements. Anthony Williams, who was the captain of Pan Am North Stars, has positive recollections of the consequences of sponsorship:

It helped in the development because steelbandmen wanted to experiment. We wanted pans to experiment. So if the sponsor just supplied drums alone, that was good enough. And, of course, paint and things like that—the other accessories to help. Later on, they assisted in paying for tuners and, in this way, a tuner then could do that work full-time. . . .

The festivals demanded expert arrangers because the adjudicators started to condemn steelbands for playing the classics, because the way steelbands played the music—playing bad chords and so on. So steelbands had to look for musicians, good qualified musicians, to arrange for them. And, with the sponsors, they were able to pay for that service. Before that, they couldn't afford that. . . . But Trinidadians at the time, I don't think they were interested to be associated with steelband. . . . But by the sponsors coming in—giving a different image to the steelband and of course putting out money—this provided a different sort of atmosphere. So they could come in and assist in the steelband.[11]

Junior Pouchet, who was the captain of Coca Cola Silver Stars, adds that musical development was also encouraged by the sponsors' prohibition of fighting:

Now they had a very deterring effect when sponsorship came into being. First of all, the sponsors made it clear: "Alright fellows. You need some pans? We going to give you some money to buy pans, uniforms, stands, what you need. But our name is on the band. . . . We have an image to keep now. We don't want no fighting." So you found that the bands that got sponsored had a tendency to clean up their act. They sort of discouraged violence from their band. . . . They were more interested in . . . how they sounded and how they looked and things like that. So, in that one respect alone, you find that sponsorship made a tremendous, tremendous contribution in getting the bands to go concentrate on their musical productions rather than continuing in this fighting-days kind of thing.[12]

On the whole panmen responded favorably to sponsorship, since they desired the money and opportunities that businesses could offer. Panmen were constantly searching for new ways of improving their pans and their music, and during the 1960s the full-time tuners and formally trained arrangers provided by sponsors further increased the musical scope of the steelband. There was also a certain prestige in being associated with well-known companies. When a band gained a sponsor, its musical ability was confirmed in the eyes of the panmen. In 1966 Raoul Pantin reported in the *Trinidad Guardian*:

The majority of steelbands are satisfied with present-day arrangements with their sponsors and complaints are few and far between.
The members are contented to get new pans, paint, regular tune-

ups, new uniforms, free transportation—and the pride in knowing that they are good enough to be singled out for sponsorship by a particular company.[13]

At the same time, sponsorship helped produce greater acceptance of the steelband movement in the society as a whole. Panmen realized that they gained further respectability by identifying with prominent businesses and by distancing themselves from the fighting of the street world.

However, there were also suspicions and resentments concerning sponsorship. Panmen were well aware that sponsorship arrangements greatly favored the businesses. As early as 1964 the writer Eric Roach reported:

> What does the band get out of it and what does the firm?
>
> Some steelbandsmen feel the bands are being exploited.
>
> That the firms are getting all the gravy for something like a $30-a-month retainer fee and a fixed sum paid to the band whenever it appears in public in the sponsor's name.
>
> They feel that this is nothing compared with what sponsors receive in free advertisement whenever and wherever the band appears in public, especially at competitions, festivals and promenade concerts, before thousands of people.
>
> Besides the band, being a household word, automatically makes the sponsor's name a household word.
>
> "The sponsors really can't pay for this sort of advertisement," one panman said recently.[14]

Panmen were also attuned to the PNM government's political interests in sponsorship. In the mid-1960s, for example, Owen Serrette was playing with Ebonites and was contemplating a move to Harmonites, a band that had recently obtained Joseph Charles Bottling Works (the manufacturers of Solo beverages) as a sponsor. He relates how the PNM facilitated sponsorship arrangements in order to maintain the allegiance of the panmen and their communities:

> My own view is that Eric Williams, when he came in, he came in on mass support. On support of the grass-roots. And he recognized the strength of the steelband as far as grass-roots support was concerned. Because, at that time, you could say that steelbands were really community steelbands. . . . It started with the introduction of getting sponsorship for steelbands. . . . Well, it was politically motivated, if

you want to say. Because I remember as far back as 1966 when I was thinking of moving across to Solo Harmonites. One of the things that people in Ebonites used to say: "Well, that's politics to go in that, you know.". . . So there was actually in the minds of the steelbandmen and people that this sponsorship thing was a political thing.[15]

In response to the concern over the politics of sponsorship during this period, NATTS set up a special committee to investigate the motivations of individuals who obtained sponsors for steelbands.[16]

Though sponsorship brought certain benefits to the panmen, it also had a detrimental effect on steelbands' utilization of their own resources. In particular, bands began to depend less on their members who could tune pans and arrange music. Michael "Penta" Cupidore, who played with Shell Invaders during much of the 1960s, explains:

Sponsorship bring the whole steelband into a new era. It formed chroming pans,[17] paying tuners, paying arrangers. But I think those were some of the negative things about sponsorship. Because the bands that got sponsored, if there was somebody arranging the music in that band, they were left out. Because we can afford somebody more. So that person just die a natural death. If you were the tuner, you die a natural death, too. . . . You just an ordinary person in the band. And that was some of the things. Because the sponsors were pulling the shots now. You have to come up to the top. You want better tuners. You want better arrangers. This is the amount of money. But the steelbands theyself—the pan players who was in these bands for years—they never inherit anything from sponsorship. . . . [18]

Until the advent of sponsorship, most grass-roots steelbands had their own tuners and arrangers. But this practice became less common as businesses began to encourage their sponsored bands to place more emphasis on making a good impression in major competitions. Businesses were very concerned with large competitions since these events provided the most exposure in terms of advertising and public relations. Thus bands were given funds to find the best tuners and arrangers available. Soon the top tuners in Trinidad experienced a great increase in demand for their pans and were able to become full-time professionals. At the same time, some formally trained or highly skilled musicians from outside the steelband world were able to earn extra money arranging music for steelbands. As these trends continued, many tuners and arrangers within bands had fewer opportunities to develop their own abilities.

Sponsorship also greatly increased the cost of producing a steelband. In order to obtain better publicity, sponsors were willing to expand their budgets for bands. As a result, the most popular tuners and arrangers were able to charge more and more money for their services. This had an adverse effect on the unsponsored bands who continued to constitute the majority of the movement. Kendall Lewis of Merrytones recalls that unsponsored bands in the 1960s found it increasingly difficult to compete. They simply did not have the money to purchase pans and hire arrangers at the standards being set by the top sponsored bands, and many eventually folded up in frustration.[19] In short, sponsorship created a new ranking of steelbands. A band's success was now to a considerable extent determined by whether it was sponsored and by the size of its budget. In order to survive and obtain prestige, smaller bands scrambled to find businesses who would sponsor them.

In general, panmen resented the fact that sponsorship eroded their control over their own bands—bands that they had developed for years. The most blatant change was that sponsored bands lost their own identity. The names of businesses were tacked onto band names and eventually some bands were colloquially referred to by their sponsors' names alone (for example, "Solo" instead of "Solo Harmonites"). Pans, signs, flags, and jerseys now also bore the names and/or colors of the sponsors. In addition, sponsors often influenced band decisions, either through subtle pressures or forthright demands, and could even claim credit for their bands' successes. In short, sponsored bands were no longer fully expressions of their own resources and of their respective communities. The whole experience of producing a steelband and competing with others was now mediated not only by the state but by the corporate sector.

In a scene in his novel *The Dragon Can't Dance,* Earl Lovelace offers a sense of the impact of sponsorship on steelbands and of the conflicting responses of the panmen. Fisheye, the badjohn of the novel, is outraged when Desperadoes appear on the streets for Carnival one year as a sponsored band:

For Desperadoes was the baddest band in the island, the band where the people was one. When they appeared on the road with new pans and emblem and waving a new flag: Sampoco Oil Company Gay Desperadoes,[20] well, he nearly went out his head. Gay? *Gay* Desperadoes. That was the end. And instead of the little fellars pushing the pans, you had the sponsors: the sponsor's wife and the sponsor's daughter and the sponsor's friends, a whole section of them, their faces reddened by the excitement and the sun, smiling and jumping out of time, singing, All Ah We Is One.[21]

Then when Casablanca, Rising Sun, and Tokyo obtain sponsors, Fisheye begins to worry that the members of his own band, Calvary Hill, might be looking for one. He approaches Reds:

'Reds, I hope you-all ain't thinking about getting sponsor in this band.'
'How you mean?'
'I mean Reds, this band is we band. This is the Calvary Hill people band; man we ain't want to be no Gay Calvary Hill or anything like that just to get a few free jerseys and some fresh paint on the pans.'
'Nobody can't take away the band, man,' Reds said.
Reds couldn't see. To him it was just like the project work, the Crash Programme. We support them, they support we.
'You see Desperadoes? You see Tokyo? You see Sun Valley?'
'I ain't see no difference. Is just that they looking newer and they playing in concerts and the fellars from the band getting work. That is all I see.'[22]

But Fisheye remains unconvinced and decides to start fighting again at Carnival because he knows that sponsors do not permit violence. He "wanted an army of warriors to take back the bands, to take back the streets and alleys, the hills and the lanes from Fuller Brothers and Sampoco Oil, and Cicada Cigarettes."[23]

The Steelband and the Black Power Protests of 1970

In early 1970 grass-roots Africans in Port of Spain did in fact take over the streets in militant protest. It was the most dramatic display of resistance to the socioeconomic order since the strikes and riots of 1937. At the vanguard of these protests was the National Joint Action Committee (NJAC), a loose coalition of students from the University of the West Indies, radical trade unionists, activists, and the urban unemployed. Essentially, NJAC leaders condemned the PNM for its failure to develop a meaningful independence for Trinidad and Tobago. They argued that the present government in effect perpetuated the colonialism of the past, since the nation remained highly dependent on foreign capital.

Multinationals, the local white elite, and the PNM leadership were held responsible for producing an economic system that was not responsive to local needs and that did not benefit the population as a whole. There was also a sense that the PNM had not been successful at fostering a truly independent cultural identity for the nation.

To a degree, NJAC's arguments were similar to a critique of post-independence Trinidad that had been developed by leftist intellectuals such as Lloyd Best and James Millette, an economist and a historian at the University of the West Indies. Both had been members of the radical New World Group, which was based at the UWI campus in Jamaica and included, among other figures, the Guyanese historian/activist Walter Rodney. Best and Millette contended that the PNM's development strategy based on incentives for foreign investment (the "Puerto Rican model") in fact created underdevelopment. Thus they advocated full-scale localization of the economy. NJAC leaders adopted this analysis of Trinidad's economic relations but phrased it explicitly in terms of the concept of Black Power, as it had been articulated by Rodney in the Caribbean and by activists such as the Trinidadian-born Stokely Carmichael in the United States. From NJAC's perspective, Trinidad was being strangled by a "White Power Structure" that included not only foreign and local white businessmen but their collaborators: "Afro-Saxons."

In early 1970 NJAC leaders were able to mobilize the support of primarily young grass-roots Africans from urban areas. This sector had become increasingly disenchanted with the government's programs. Eight years after political independence unemployment remained high, living conditions poor, and color discrimination a reality. To the urban poor, "Black Power" appeared to offer an alternative. However, in his analysis of the 1970 protests, Herman Bennett notes:

> Whereas radical intellectuals and university students sought to eradicate dependent relations, the urban dispossessed wanted to improve their material conditions. The prevailing ideology of Black Power was important to the urban poor but employed only insofar as it articulated their social grievances.[24]

The first Black Power demonstration occurred on February 26, 1970, in response to the treatment of several West Indian students at the Sir George Williams University in Montreal, Canada. Protesters moved through the streets of downtown Port of Spain under the watchful eye of the police and stopped periodically to deliver speeches against the Canadian High Commission, foreign banks, the Chamber of Commerce, local businesses, and the Catholic church. During the following weeks there were several other major demonstrations, including a march from Port of Spain into the sugar cane county of Caroni under the banner, "Indians and Africans Unite Now" (NJAC conceptualized "Black Power" as inclusive of Africans and Indians). Meanwhile, there was extensive fire-bombing of businesses in downtown Port of Spain, and NJAC held an ongoing "People's Parliament" in Woodford Square which featured speeches and cultural shows (including African drumming, calypso, pan, and Indian music). The demonstrations finally came to an end on April 21, when the government declared a state of emergency in response to the planning of a general strike by Black Power groups and various trade unions. A disillusioned section of the Trinidad Defense Force subsequently rebelled, but the mutiny was contained and order was gradually restored to the nation in the course of the following months.

Clearly NJAC fell short of developing widespread support for a transformation of Trinidadian society. The fact that the organization focused its concerns around the idea of Black Power alienated most Indians, who did not perceive themselves as "black," while its militant tactics troubled the majority of middle class Africans who were fearful of any form of major disruption. Nonetheless the uprising did bring new attention to the dynamics of racism and neo-colonialism. In the following years employment discrimination based on color decreased and the government initiated plans to place more of the economy under local control.[25]

The Black Power protests also highlighted the position of the steelband movement in the nation's economy and political life. By 1970 panmen had begun to seriously question their relations with the state and with sponsoring businesses. There was a sense that the government's programs and the sponsors' contributions had failed to improve appreciably the pan life. Thus many panmen were receptive to the idea of Black Power and some, especially those from the poorer neighborhoods on the eastern side of Port of Spain, actively participated in the rallies and demonstrations. Even before the protests began, Eric Williams realized that he was losing support among panmen, a sector of the grassroots class on whom he could traditionally count for strong allegiance. In January 1970 he began a tour of panyards in an effort to reaffirm his relationship with the movement.[26] Then, in the midst of the Black Power uprising, he initiated a series of meetings with steelband leaders to discuss the movement's chronic problems and to develop solutions. Among the proposals suggested were a steelband research council, a steelband co-operative, government assistance in helping unsponsored bands find sponsors, and greater projection of steelband music on radio and television.[27]

In the course of Williams's steelband conferences, Geddes Granger, the leader of NJAC, accused the Prime Minister of "using the steelbandsmen" in the current crisis and added that "Crash programmes will not fool anyone."[28] Though steelband leaders continued to negotiate with the PNM government, they also held a meeting with NJAC to discuss common goals. George Goddard, the President of NATTS at the time, states that he initiated this meeting in response to rumors that the Prime Minister was using him and the steelband movement as a whole against NJAC.[29] The agreements reached between the two organizations were reported in the *Guardian*:

> Government will be asked to hand out annual grants to the National Association of Trinidad and Tobago Steelbandsmen (NATTS) of a sum not less than $250,000 for the purpose of developing the steelbands, and thereby creating opportunities for steelbandsmen. . . .
>
> The Association dispelled the rumours that there was a plan afoot to organise anti-Black Power activities among steelbandsmen, since it was felt that the Association could not divorce or dissociate itself from the Black Power movement, whose aims and objects were similar to those of the Association.
>
> The Association's spokesman, Mr. Goddard, gave the assurance that all members would be circularised, warning them of non-participation, should any section of the community attempt to organise any anti-Black Power activities among steelbandsmen.
>
> The Association delegation agreed with leaders of the Black Power movement that sponsorship of steelbandsmen was inimical to the interest of steelbandsmen because of its dehumanising effect on its members as musicians. . . .
>
> The commercial tag which steelbandsmen were required to carry on their uniforms and instruments, which "was not in keeping with the dignity of reputable musicians," coupled "with the large profits to the sponsors by way of advertisement," also came up for discussion.
>
> The meeting agreed that financial consideration of a not inconsiderable amount should be made annually by the sponsors through the appropriate Government Ministry to the Steelband Association to be used for the development of the Association.
>
> The business section of the community should not be concerned only with personal advertisement, but concerned with the greater

good—the development of the steelbands and steelbandsmen, and thereby assisting in the creation of a better Trinidad and Tobago, the meeting agreed.[30]

The statement concerning anti-Black Power activities in the steelband movement appears in part to have been a reference to Desperadoes, the powerful steelband from Laventille with whom Williams had a special relationship. Pan researcher Jeffrey Thomas points out that by 1970 there was serious dissent within NATTS and that Rudolph Charles, the leader of Desperadoes, independently approached Williams with his own suggestions for the steelband movement.[31] The day after the NATTS-NJAC meeting, Desperadoes issued a statement to the press saying that they would no longer allow themselves to be attacked by Black Power advocates. They commented that they had been accused of "sending threatening letters to NJAC leaders; of being anti-Black Power, and of receiving a 'bribe' of $20,000 from Government." The so-called "bribe" was an eight-week course at a music school in the United States, which, Desperadoes stated, they received because of their musicianship. The band also noted that they had greatly contributed to the cause of Black Power.[32]

On the same day that Desperadoes issued their press statement, the *Guardian* attacked the NATTS and NJAC leaders for their remarks concerning sponsorship:

Even the most cynical among us will agree that sponsorship which came into the steelband movement a few years ago arrested a decline that was setting in and succeeded in elevating the steelband to a level which would not yet have been possible had steelbandsmen been left entirely up to themselves.

In addition, the *Guardian* dismissed the suggestion by NATTS and NJAC that sponsors' funds be pooled and distributed to all steelbands through the government and the steelband association. The newspaper was sympathetic with the advertising and public relations benefits of sponsorship and stated that the new proposal was "impracticable and unrealistic."[33]

Shortly after the NATTS-NJAC meeting, George Goddard spoke at NJAC's "People's Parliament" in Woodford Square. According to Richard Forteau, a steelband leader from Laventille, Goddard realized that his service as government steelband advisor was assisting the PNM more than the panmen themselves. So he decided to inform the gathered crowd in Woodford Square of all of the proposals that he had made to the government and of the government's failure to enact these proposals. In addition, he asserted that the sponsorship of bands was not motivated solely by a desire to develop pan music and that panmen were being exploited. During this period Goddard also stated to the press that Williams intended "to divide and rule the steelband movement."[34]

According to Melville Bryan, an officer of NATTS at the time, the association remained officially neutral in relation to NJAC. After a history of attempted manipulation by some members of the PNM, it was unwilling to establish an affiliation with any political organization.[35] However, as the Black Power protests developed, NATTS was increasingly perceived as aligned with NJAC. It is widely reported by panmen that Williams then began a campaign to destroy NATTS and remove Goddard from his position as leader of the steelband movement. He accomplished his goal by encouraging certain staunch PNM members associated with steelbands to rally the support of panmen dissatisfied with NATTS and form a new organization which became known as the "Steelband Improvement Committee."

The growth of the Steelband Improvement Committee coincided with the PNM's campaign for re-election in early 1971. During this period the party struggled to regain some of the support that it had lost from grass-roots Africans. Selwyn Ryan comments that

> Williams tried hard to look less "Afro-Saxon" by abandoning the proverbial coat and tie in favor of an open shirt and neckkerchief. During the carnival season he visited a large number of steelband yards and calypso tents and generally tried to project an image that was "blacker" culturally than had been the case since Independence. The popular view was that Williams was "playing mas"(i.e., masquerading) for the benefit of the electorate.[36]

In addition, the PNM government published a report that it had assisted over fifty steelbands. Goddard condemned this report (and the panyard excursions) after several of the listed steelbands complained to NATTS that they had received no assistance. A few weeks later Goddard was dismissed from his position as government steelband advisor.[37] He then sent a letter to Williams concerning the Steelband Improvement Committee's recruitment of bands:

> It has been brought to my attention that there are certain gentlemen in your employ who are going around to the leaders and members of steelbands claiming that they were sent by you to get the signatures of

steelbandsmen to form a new steelbandsmen body because your government has no confidence in me, and as a result would have no dealing with the Association of Steelbandsmen of which I am the
President-General.[38]

In June Goddard finally resigned as the leader of NATTS. The Steelband Improvement Committee gained the support of an increasing
number of bands and in October became the official steelband association under the name of "Pan Trinbago."[39] Pan Trinbago remained
closely tied to the PNM, which had won the 1971 elections, partly because of an election boycott by most of the other political groups in the
nation. In early 1973 the government sponsored a three-day National
Consultation on the Steelband which was chaired by Williams and attended by representatives of 93 bands. Goddard commented, "What
good is going to emerge from this conference, heaven (if not hell),
alone knows," since for years the government had failed to act on recommendations made by panmen and various steelband committees.[40]
The conference did at least provide panmen with another opportunity
to call the attention of the government and the public to the problems
that they continued to face. Among the issues discussed were sponsorship, funding for unsponsored bands, exploitation of steelbands, and
the need for trade courses to help panmen find jobs.[41] Though the government did not fulfill many of the promises that it made at the conference, it did initiate a course on business procedures to help panmen
improve the management of their bands.

On the whole, the early years of Pan Trinbago's existence were quite
tumultuous. Panmen gradually became convinced that the organization
was being manipulated by the PNM and that its executive officers were
using their positions to advance their political careers rather than to
serve the steelband movement. Dissent and divisiveness continued until
the latter 1970s, at which point Melville Bryan, George Goddard, and
Arnim Smith assumed leadership of the association. These individuals
and other pan leaders were then able to steer the association in a direction independent of the PNM and increase its stability and effective-
ness.

By the end of the decade, Pan Trinbago was engaged in an ongoing
confrontational relationship with the state. Panmen believed that the
government had essentially failed in terms of any productive policy for
the steelband and that the association had to fight constantly to protect
and further its interests. Selwyn Tarradath, the current Public Relations
Officer of Pan Trinbago, attributes this combative orientation toward

politicians (and other individuals outside the movement) to George Goddard:

> George Goddard was the man. The chief man. The man who was responsible for this. He was always a good defender of the steelband movement. And I think Arnim Smith fell into that role. . . . And it's coming from the class that they came from. . . . That they always felt that pressure, then, that's up there. These people up there always looking to exploit us and use us. And we have this thing that they want and we have to defend it. . . . This is something they always believed in—in the worth of the steelband.[42]

The steelband movement's independence was significantly limited, however, by the fact that it continued to receive a large amount of funding from the government. In the years after 1973 this funding actually increased, due to the growing oil revenues that the government enjoyed as a result of the OPEC embargo. The oil boom in Trinidad also enabled more businesses to sponsor steelbands and to raise substantially the amounts of their contributions. Perhaps self-sufficiency was not a realistic option for the steelband movement, given the large number of bands and their immense size and the country's small population and limited resources. Even in 1970 when steelband and Black Power leaders were highly critical of the movement's relationships with the state and the corporate sector, they did not call for an end of funding from these sources. Instead, they advocated types of funding that would allow the movement to build itself in its own interests rather than provide political support for the PNM and advertising for businesses. At the end of the decade steelband leaders were still pursuing these goals.

Carnival, Panorama, and Steelband Festivals

Though state and corporate support of the steelband movement was seriously questioned by panmen in the post-independence era, this support did have a significant impact on the public's perceptions of the movement. The official promotion of pan as a national music and the association of bands with leading businesses increased the movement's status in the society. At the same time, steelband fighting waned and panmen continued to develop their musical skills. All of these trends impressed the public and further attenuated the remaining misgivings about the steelband. In fact, during the 1960s pan became immensely popular. Many Trinidadians (particularly youths) took pride in steel-band music and enjoyed it at a range of occasions.

The growing national acceptance of the steelband, however, did not sever the movement's ties with the street world. The macho, saga boy image of the panman and the loyalties to neighborhood bands remained and continued to attract youths to the movement. Like his precursor in the 1940s, the saga boy of the 1960s was a sharp dresser, physically fit, and out to attract women. But now those panmen who were saga boys were more often middle class than grass-roots and their women were high-school students, secretaries, and clerks. The epitome of saga boy bands of this era was Starlift, which was based in the predominantly middle class neighborhood of Woodbrook. Selwyn Tarradath, who was a member of Starlift during this period, recalls the scene:

> Most of the young fellows then who were out on the streets—don't mind if you would be middle class and so on and you're from a good home . . . the pan thing had a tremendous attraction to us. The whole steelband image, the aura, the rebel image . . . it was a strong attraction. I want to be in a band. I want to be associated with this band. . . . When you beat pan and you come back to school, you're a hero. . . . I got status.

He continues:

> During the '60s a lot of college boys—and not just ordinary college boys—popular college boys took to the steelband movement. The girls began to follow. The girls from the correspondence schools. . . . The popular fellows. The fellows who are out there. The fellows in the parties. The fellows who playing sports: football, cricket, and so on. They associate themselves with the steelband. Carnival day, they in a band playing. So you find the girls who want to be with the popular boys would be in a steelband playing [masquerade], too. . . . You'd find them in Invaders, in Starlift . . . Highlanders, Dem Fortunates, Dem Boys, All Stars.[43]

For J'Ouvert, steelbands continued to come out with their bomb tunes and competed on the streets in informal and formal competitions. On Monday afternoon they often played a simple mas such as jeans and jerseys. Their main masquerade presentations were saved for Tuesday. Sailor mas remained popular as did American Indian, African, and Mexican portrayals; and some steelbands continued to experiment with unique themes like those portrayed by the historical masquerade bands. In 1963, for example, Silver Stars played "Gulliver's Travels" and won the coveted "Band of the Year" title. By the 1960s large numbers of people were choosing to play mas with steelbands, and bands such as All Stars, Invaders, City Syncopators, and Dem Boys had sailor masqueraders numbering in the thousands. Michael Cupidore recollects the enthusiastic support that steelbands received during this period:

> Carnival Monday, the steelbands would come out and play mas. Well we had one band from Belmont called Dem Boys. I think they had the biggest crowd behind a steelband up 'til today. Because when Dem Boys come out on a Monday evening [afternoon], they had all the girls. And all the young people playing with Dem Boys from Belmont. . . . We had band like Starlift. When Starlift come out on a Monday evening, Starlift had all the young ladies and the youth. The youth. Starlift was big. Steelbands was nice in those times. Nice. And people was glad. It used to be an honor to push a pan in a band—push a rack. Say: "Well, boy, I going with Starlift and help push the band and thing."[44]

These large followings enabled steelbands to earn a substantial amount of money from Carnival since they collected a band fee from each masquerader. Steelbands were also in high demand at fetes throughout the Carnival season, and these appearances provided them with another important source of revenue.

In addition to playing on the streets and in fetes, steelbands began participating in a new Carnival event in 1963: Panorama. Panorama was a nation-wide steelband competition that NATTS and the government Carnival Development Committee organized on the model of previous Carnival steelband competitions. As early as 1949 a champion steelband was selected at the Carnival Sunday night show at the Queen's Park Savannah. Beginning in 1958 the competition was held on the Friday night before Carnival, and the following year it was given the name "Carnival Bacchanal." Carnival Bacchanal was not terribly successful, due to the fact that the prizes were not substantial enough to attract the top steelbands.[45] But the government invested more money in Panorama, and this competition gradually became the preeminent showcase for steelbands—the occasion where bands proved their worth to each other and to the nation at large. Melville Bryan recalls:

> It was important, very important. . . . If you were a steelband at all, you had to go in. When you went, you were a steelband. And you gained a popularity there. Your standard was judged at the Panorama shows. . . .

The dream was—every steelbandsman wanted to go to the Big Yard [the Queen's Park Savannah]. This was the measure of his skill, his ability.[46]

Kendall Lewis adds:

Even from the beginning, Panorama was the steelbands' time to gallery [show off]. Because the whole focus was on steelband. So, even at the beginning, it was popular. But commercially, it wasn't that popular. In other words, not much business had got involved in it. . . . It started to grow. Because it started to grow in 1963, just one year after independence, when the country really started to grow as an independent country. And things started to open up in Trinidad. So Panorama grew with the nation, then. Every year the nation is one year, Panorama would be one year, too.[47]

Essentially, Panorama was an extension of the informal competition that occurred between steelbands on the streets. Initially, steelbands were judged while in motion for the preliminary round of the event. Each band pushed its mobile racks of pans off the streets and down a track through the Savannah, while judges assessed its performance of a current calypso at various points along the way. Meanwhile, large crowds of supporters followed their bands through the Savannah and cheered them on. For the finals, bands stopped on the Savannah stage and performed for the judges who were located there. The judges eventually found the crowds to be too distracting, and beginning in 1973 bands were judged alone on the Savannah stage without their followers for both the preliminary and final rounds of the competition.[48]

From the early days of Panorama, panmen realized that the event demanded more elaborate arrangements of calypsos than were currently being used on the streets and in fetes. Ray Holman, who was with Starlift at the time, recalls that arrangers initially could not figure out how to approach this new challenge. It was Anthony Williams of North Stars who led the way by creating more complex introductions for calypsos, by utilizing key modulations, and by experimenting with arpeggios. North Stars won the first Panorama with an arrangement of a calypso by Sparrow ("Dan Is the Man in the Van") and the second with a Kitchener calypso ("Mama Dis Is Mas"). Then Holman and Beverly Griffith of Desperadoes developed the use of theme and variation structures for calypsos, while Bobby Mohammed of Cavaliers worked with hard-driving rhythms in the bass section and Earl Rodney of Harmonites incorporated Latin rhythms.[49] Among the Panorama masterpieces of the 1960s were Mohammed's arrangement of Melody's "Mas," Griffith's rendition of Sparrow's "Obeah Wedding" ("Melda"), Rodney's version of Kitchener's "The Wrecker," and Holman's arrangement of Kitchener's "The Bull."

As Panorama developed, new pans were also introduced, such as Bertie Marshall's *double tenor* with a range slightly below that of the lead tenor. This was a versatile pair of pans that could be used for doubling the melody, for counter-melodies, or for strumming chords. Bands also expanded in size during the 1960s. By the latter part of the decade some bands were competing in Panorama with over one hundred players and were able to create a tremendously powerful sound.

Panorama's growth was interrelated with the development of sponsorship. Sponsors soon discovered that the enormous crowds the competition attracted provided an unparalleled opportunity for publicity. Since they began to channel much of their funding for bands into the preparation for Panorama, the event became as much a competition between businesses as a musical battle between bands. In a recent Pan Trinbago information booklet, Selwyn Tarradath describes the impact of sponsorship on Panorama:

> The Panorama show has become a monster which threatens to devour the very steelband movement from which it was conceived. The popularity of the Panorama competition encouraged the steelband sponsors to use it as one of their main vehicles for promotion and advertisement. Most of the annual budget was directed into this area to the neglect of others. The better the band did in the competition the more mileage for the sponsor, so no effort was spared to obtain good results. Tuners and arrangers were paid retainers' fees and as each band strived to keep an edge, the price of instruments sky-rocketed as did arrangers' fees.[50]

By the 1970s steelbands were devoting more energy to Panorama than to any other performance occasion. This trend was motivated not only by the sponsors' interests but also by the panmen's desire to obtain the prestige and prize monies that came with success in the competition. One result of this concentration on Panorama was a decline in the presence of steelbands on the streets for Carnival. Arrangements of Panorama calypsos became increasingly complex and required a great amount of time to learn. With bands focusing their practice sessions on these tunes, band supporters tended to spend less time in panyards during the Carnival season. A visit to a panyard now involved listening to intense drilling of difficult phrases from a Panorama tune rather than the concert of numerous calypsos that bands previously offered. At the same time, bands had less time to develop masquerades for Carnival. This shift of emphasis from street performance and masquerade to Panorama meant that fewer people played mas with steelbands, and some bands ceased coming out on the streets at all after J'Ouvert.

The decline of steelbands on the streets was also affected by Carnival trends that accompanied the oil boom. Large masquerade bands were investing greater sums of money in their portrayals, and steelbands found it difficult to compete with these bands. By the 1970s masquerade was also increasingly becoming the domain of women and the growing middle class. The oil boom opened up more employment for women, and they tended to spend their money on the more stylish and revealing costumes that were becoming popular with the large masquerade bands, rather than play in the traditional sailor outfits that were still common among steelbands. Carnival became an opportunity for women to display their bodies and their independence, and this could not effectively be accomplished in the male-dominated steelbands. At the same time, more middle class people (men and women) were playing mas, and they too preferred the more stylish and expensive costumes of the large masquerade bands. As a result of these trends, many grass-roots men lost interest in masquerade. Since they were the backbone of steelband mas in general and of sailor mas in particular, the steelbands suffered and the sailors, who had been such a lively presence on the streets for decades, became less common.[51]

Yet another factor in the decline of steelbands on the streets was a rise in the use of large amplification systems, again facilitated by oil boom money. When mounted on flatbed trucks, these systems were much more mobile in the crowded streets during Carnival than were steelbands, which had grown to mammoth sizes. Masquerade bands now found it easier to hire a deejay and/or an amplified brass band to provide music for their members. Furthermore, the steelbands could not compete with the high volume of amplified sound revelers now desired.

Though there were fewer steelbands on the streets during Carnival Monday and Tuesday, they by no means disappeared. Many steelbands continued to come out for these two days, without the large numbers of followers that they once enjoyed. In addition, steelbands continued to dominate the streets for J'Ouvert. Costs for J'Ouvert were minimal since revelers used inexpensive costumes or regular clothes. Moreover, the early Monday morning of Carnival had been an occasion for grass-roots rhythmic expression since the post-emancipation era, and the steelbands of the 1970s appear to have had little intention of relinquishing this tradition.

By the late 1970s and early 1980s, steelbands not only were withdrawing from Carnival masquerade but were playing at fewer fetes during the Carnival season. Because of their concentration on Panorama tunes, bands had less time to develop the necessary repertoires and did not want to lose the rehearsal time that a busy fete schedule required. As a result, steelbands actually began to turn down fete invitations. At the same time, fete promoters and the public began to prefer amplified brass bands and deejays, again because of the higher volume of sound that they provided. Promoters also resented the fact that steelbands tended to bring all their friends and family members with them when they performed. With decreasing fete opportunities, steelbands began to focus even more on Panorama.

In reference to these changing steelband performance patterns, Selwyn Tarradath concludes:

> The Panorama competition has become the biggest event in our annual entertainment calendar but the steelband has been forced to pay a high price to be King for a night. We have lost most of our traditional activities and sources of revenue.[52]

With the decline in income from masquerader fees and fetes, steelbands became increasingly dependent on the government's provision of appearance fees and prizes for Panorama. In fact, appearance fees became so important that steelbands actually boycotted Panorama in 1979 because of a dispute over the size of these payments. Selwyn Ryan reported:

> Pan Trinbago's spokesmen argued that Carnival was big business and lots of people were making a pile—hotels, liquor manufacturers and distributors, merchants, transport contractors, [masquerade] band organisers as well as all the smartmen and picaroons who use their wits to make money during the Carnival season.
>
> Everybody was making bread except the poor steelbandsm[e]n who all admit contribute mightily towards making Trinidad's Carnival the unique event that it is.
>
> Panmen feel that given the present status of the steelband movement, Carnival is the only time when they are in a position to make some of the money which is needed not only to pay panists, many of whom are unemployed or on Special Works, but also to meet the basic costs involved in producing a steelband—pans, wheels, pipe, canvas, tuners, arrangers, uniforms, etc.[53]

The following year the government provided the panmen with the fees
they demanded. Kendall Lewis, who was one of the leading proponents
of the boycott, comments that the action demonstrated the strength
and unity of Pan Trinbago and that, ever since, the public has realized
that the association must be taken seriously.[54]

While Panorama gradually became the premier steelband occasion in
the post-independence era, there were also two important series of
steelband festivals. 1962 was the last year that steelbands participated in
the Trinidad Music Festival, due to a misunderstanding at that year's
competition and a decision by the Trinidad Music Association that the
bands had outgrown the event.[55] In 1964 NATTS held its own Steelband
Music Festival at Queen's Hall, an elegant venue for the arts on the
edge of the Savannah. This competition was run by NATTS again in
1966 and 1968 and once by Pan Trinbago in 1973. In addition, steelband festivals commemorating independence were held in 1963, 1965,
1967, and 1972. While Panorama was devoted to calypso, steelbands
played both local and European classical music at the festivals. In their
preparation of classical pieces, a number of bands used formally trained
musicians from outside the movement as arrangers. For example, Jocelyn Pierre, Anthony Prospect, and Gerry Jemmott assisted Invaders,
Casablanca, and Trinidad All Stars respectively. Some panmen, such as
Anthony Williams of North Stars, also became very skillful at arranging
classical music.

There was much debate concerning whether adjudicators, test pieces,
and tunes of choice at these festivals should be local or foreign, and the
festivals in effect became a vehicle through which the newly independent nation reflected on its cultural identity. For the 1964 Steelband
Music Festival, both local and foreign adjudicators were employed.[56]
Then, in 1966, George Goddard stated that a foreign adjudicator would
be used that year, not because of any lack of confidence in local musicians but because the panmen felt that they benefited more from the
comments of musicians from overseas.[57] At the 1967 festival foreign adjudicators were again used; in 1968 there was a compromise, with Anthony Prospect and one foreign musician serving as judges. Finally, the
1973 festival was handled by one foreign adjudicator.

The selection of test pieces for the festivals reflects a similar pattern
of ambivalence. At the 1964 festival the test piece was locally composed:
Lennox Pierre's "Voice of the Panman." In 1966 there was one foreign
test piece (Mozart's "Eine Kleine Nachtmusik") and one local piece
(Anthony Prospect's "Intermezzo in E Flat"). However, one arranger
for this festival commented that Prospect's composition "sounded like

something from a Viennese operetta."[58] At the 1967 Independence Steelband Festival there was not only a British adjudicator but a German test piece: the Overture from Otto Nicolai's *The Merry Wives of Windsor*. Benjamin Britten's "Sunday Morning" was used in 1968, Anthony Prospect's "Maracas Bay" in 1972, and Schubert's "Marche Militaire" in 1973.

Steelbands selected both calypsos and foreign pieces for their tunes of choice at the Independence Steelband Festivals. At the Steelband Music Festivals, however, they favored European classical selections. In 1964, for example, Desperadoes played Strauss's "Emperor Waltz," Starlift performed Handel's "Hallelujah Chorus," and Savoys rendered Tchaikovsky's "Serenade for Strings." West Side won the competition with Strauss's "Roses from the South." In 1966 North Stars came in first with von Suppé's "Poet and Peasant Overture." However, an alternative to foreign music was offered that year by Silver Stars in their performance of Junior Pouchet's "On a Creole Melody." Trinidad All Stars won the 1968 festival with Mozart's "Minuet in E Flat" and a selection from Schubert's *Unfinished Symphony*. For the 1973 festival Pan Trinbago attempted to direct more attention to local music by requiring that bands play a calypso as one of their two tunes of choice.[59]

While there was a general consensus that panmen's musicianship continued to improve in the post-independence years, there was considerable controversy over whether European classics offered the best opportunity for the development of the steelband. In 1966, for example, this issue was debated at a panel discussion on the steelband by J. D. Elder and Anthony Williams. Elder argued that panmen should concentrate on creating music from indigenous traditions:

> By all means play the classics. . . . But what we want is the Trinidad image . . . the projecting of our own culture, not someone's else. If we are going to achieve a higher level musically, the basic raw material should be our folklore.

Williams countered:

> By interpreting the classics the steelband achieved many things. . . . We began to get ideas in modulations. . . . The classics play an important part in steelband development. Right now we are not mature enough to experiment in folklore, which is limited and simple.
>
> It is a case then of going to the masters to acquire knowledge, not so much a case of rejecting our own, which, like I said, offers no chal-

lenge. In time, we should be able to come back to our folklore and do a good job on it.[60]

In the years after the 1970 Black Power protests, criticism of foreign music and foreign adjudicators at steelband festivals became more intense. Some observers perceived the structure of the festivals as a dangerous legacy of colonialism. After attending the 1973 Steelband Music Festival, Fr. Terrence Julien, a local priest, contributed the following impressions to the *Trinidad Guardian*:

On Friday night I went to the Queen's Park Savannah to hear the finals of the Steelband Festival. I left halfway through, sick in my stomach at the most pathetic sight I have had to endure for years—the colonisation of the calypso and the steel pan. There before our very eyes were groups of performing Trinidadians, like so many classes, sitting a musical G.C.E., under the expert ears of examiner in chief—Professor Tom Manoff, of the Manhattan School of Music.

It is the most painful experience to have grown up during the movement for "political independence" and "massa dey done" and to have to face the sickening fact that the movement in our society is not towards independence through creativity but towards total enslavement through meticulous [aping].

I don't know which was more pathetic! The "conductors" or the "orchestras" trying to achieve the correct frenzy and mannerisms of Toscanini,—agonisingly wringing out from their classes the correct answers to the European Test piece. Or the bloodless abortion of the calypso-road-march as "symphonised" by these steel orchestras. . . .

Eleven years after our so-called "gaining of independence," we have as a test piece, for a Steelband Festival not a calypso, but a piece of English music! If the criterion for steelbandsmanship is now no longer calypso, and if the judge is no longer Trinidadian, but American or European musicologists, then we have once more entered the colonial syndrome where the original product of the colony is "refined" at home for transport to the metropolis.

What I am trying to say is that both the calypso and the steel pan have emerged from the slave plantation system of the Caribbean and were developed in the atmosphere of Trinidad Carnival.

There is no one in the world who can be a greater authority or judge of our original product, of our own creation, than people who have emerged from the same environment.

By ceding this birthright to European and American "authorities," we are allowing our people to be blinded to the fact that we created these two cultural elements and that their uniqueness and distinctiveness must be maintained as part of the foundation of our distinctive identity.

A people's distinctive identity and cultural creations are its basic independence, from which all other forms of independence flow and are maintained.[61]

The "symphonising" of calypsos to which Fr. Julien referred was a new practice in which calypsos were given more elaborate structures and played with greater variation in dynamics than was typical of their performance at Carnival. Fr. Julien went on to recommend that calypsos continue to be played with "dancing rhythms that you register in your body" and concluded that the Steelband Music Festival must become "an arena of creative expression, inspired by the events and experiences of Trinidad society."[62]

Steelband Recordings

Though there were ongoing controversies over the musical and economic dimensions of the steelband movement during the 1960s and early 1970s, the bands continued to receive widespread support from the public at competitions, fetes, clubs, and in Carnival street processions. A further indication of public enthusiasm was the extensive recording of pan music during this period. Appreciation of the steelband continued to revolve around live performances, but records were now available for radio and dance deejays, jukeboxes, and home phonographs.

It took a number of years for the recording industry to recognize the market for steelband music. Though some metallic percussion is present on a few calypso records from the 1940s, the first known recording of a steelband was not made until 1950 when an American tourist by the name of William Besser captured Invaders performing "Last Train to San Fernando" in a club in Port of Spain. This recording was never commercially released.[63] In conjunction with its trip to England in 1951, the Trinidad All Steel Percussion Orchestra (TASPO) recorded four 78-rpm discs for Vogue in Paris (V9017-V9020). Among the selections on these records are "Mango Walk," "Take Me," "Ramadin," and "Allies Quick-Step."[64] When TASPO left Paris for Trinidad, one of its members, Sterling Betancourt, returned to London. Between 1952 and 1956 Betancourt played ping pong on several 78s recorded for Melodisc and Lyragon with the Russell Henderson Band. Russell Henderson was a Trinidadian pianist whose small ensemble generally played conventional instruments, but at times performed as a steelband. Melodisc 1363, recorded in 1956, features the Henderson steelband playing "The Irish Washer Woman" and "Mambo Ping Pong."[65]

Meanwhile, recordings of steelbands were being made back in Trinidad. One important figure here was Eduardo Sa Gomes, who, in addition to owning music stores in Trinidad and other parts of the West Indies, had served as an agent for Decca and arranged for the recording of a number of calypsonians. By the early 1950s Sa Gomes was releasing pan records on his own label such as Casablanca's "In Ah Calabash" (Sagomes SG 101), Merry Makers' "Matilda" (SG 123), Katzenjammers' "Why Me Neighbour Vex with Me" (SG 118), and Boys Town's "Kitch Darling" (SG 127). In 1953 another local recording company was formed by Ross Russell of the Dial Recording Company (New York) and Aubrey Christopher of Christopher Bros. Cycle and Radio Service (Port of Spain).[66] Several steelband recordings were released on the firm's Calypso label: Finland's "Madeleine Oy" and "You Gonna Jump Up?" (Calypso 502), Johannesburg Fascinators' "Bo Bo Mambo" and "I Want Coconut Water" (Calypso 507), and Sun Valley's "Steel Band Clash" and "Never Love" (Calypso 513).

In 1956 the American Emory Cook arrived in Trinidad. Cook was a pioneer in high-fidelity technology, who during the 1950s and early 1960s recorded a wide range of music from various parts of the Caribbean.[67] His *Jump Up Carnival in Trinidad* (Cook 1072), recorded in 1956, includes unidentified steelbands on the street during Carnival performing "Back Bay Shuffle," "Puerto Rico Mambo," and Sparrow's "Jean and Dinah." In the course of the next several years, Cook released a number of steelband albums and singles which featured such bands as Katzenjammers, Merry Makers, Southern Symphony, Casablanca, Boys Town, Tropical Harmony, and Silvertones.

During the 1960s the recording of pan increased significantly and records were more widely distributed. RCA made a number of recordings of major steelbands from the early to mid 1960s. Albums featured such bands as Dixieland (RCA LPB-1076), Ebonites (RCA LPB-3002), North Stars (RCA LPB/LPS-3009 and LPSD-3035), Invaders (RCA LPB-3021), Desperadoes (RCA LPS-3033), and Silver Stars and Starlift (RCA LPS-3042). Around 1959 Telco, a local firm, recorded a single of Invaders (Telco 1000). Telco, along with other local companies such as Tropico and Antillana, went on to release numerous steelband singles and albums during the 1960s and 1970s. Among the most frequently recorded bands were All Stars, Silver Stars, Harmonites, Starlift, Desperadoes, and Gay Flamingoes.

The musical selections included on this array of steelband recordings provide a sense of developments in the aesthetic preferences of panmen and their audiences from the late 1950s into the 1970s. Calypsos of course were regularly featured throughout the period. Road marches and other compositions by Sparrow and Kitchener were particular favorites. For example, Anthony Williams's Panorama victory arrangements of Sparrow's "Dan Is the Man in the Van" and Kitchener's "Mama Dis is Mas" for North Stars can be heard on an RCA single (7-2151) and album (LPSD-3035). European classical music was also regularly recorded by steelbands during the 1960s and 1970s. There were bomb tunes such as All Stars' renditions of Beethoven's "Minuet in G" (RCA 7-9017) and Liszt's "Liebesträume" (RCA 7-9016). Favorites in festival or concert music ranged from North Star's performance of Strauss's "Voices of Spring" in 1962 (RCA LPB/LPS-3009) to All Stars' interpretation of Tchaikovsky's "1812 Overture" in 1974 (CTS-222).

In the area of foreign popular music, Latin selections were commonly performed in the late 1950s and early 1960s. For example, Boystown recorded "Mambo San Fernando" (Cook 901), Southern Symphony rendered "Cha Cha Cha Boom" (Cook CC 5900), and Ebonites recorded "Silencio" (RCA 7-2012). Throughout the 1960s songs from musicals were popular, such as Invaders' "Tonight" and "Student Prince" (RCA LPB-3021) and Desperadoes' "Selections from 'Sound of Music'" (Tropico TSI-2006). From the mid-1960s to the early 1970s, there was also interest in Beatles tunes such as Harmonites' "Yesterday" (Telco TW-3325) and Starlift's "Penny Lane" (CIBC-101). By the early 1970s, though, panmen were turning to soul and funk for their foreign popular music selections. For example, Fonclaire recorded "Do Your Thing" (Tropico TSI-2032) and "Ain't No Sunshine" (Tropico TSI-2039), while Tokyo played "The Caterpillar" and "Killing Me Softly" (Compas Records CRS-0001).[68]

The substantial release of steelband recordings in the post-independence period unfortunately resulted in relatively little income for the panmen. Though audio recording and commercial record distribution have contributed to the professionalization of many musical traditions around the world, this did not occur in the case of the steelband. In Trinidad there was a large number of panmen competing in a small market, and revenues from sales abroad were generally limited. Furthermore, Trinidadians have always preferred to hear steelbands in live performance. Pan has traditionally been conceived of as linked to Carnival festivity, an experience that is not easily captured in sound recordings.[69]

The Steelband and Independence

The steelband's rise to prominence in the 1960s was interrelated with Trinidad and Tobago's emergence as an independent nation. The PNM government was already courting the pan movement in the late 1950s, and after independence was able to develop its plans more fully. The steelband was displayed at official occasions, festivals, and concerts as a symbol of indigenous creativity and national identity. In addition, official support of steelbands was perceived as a means of channeling community pride into national pride. Since the PNM essentially conceived of itself as synonymous with the nation, it could interpret clientelistic relationships with steelbands and communities as nation-building. In other words, it could justify the steelband's role in strengthening its political network as a strengthening of the country as a whole.

At the same time, steelband sponsorship provided businesses with a means of publicly identifying themselves with the nation and demonstrating their willingness to participate in national development. Indeed, over the years the corporate sector's growth was manifested in a greater number of large and impressive steelbands.

As the steelband movement underwent further institutionalization, Trinidadians and Tobagonians increasingly embraced the music. During the 1960s steelbands were truly in their glory. They ruled the fetes and moved through the streets at Carnival with hundreds and even thousands of revelers responding to their music. The immense sailor bands that the panmen led seemed to embody the vitality and enthusiasm that initially accompanied independence. There was also greater identification with the steelband among the diverse sectors of the population. Though the majority of panmen continued to be of African descent, many steelbands in the 1960s included members of other ethnic groups. Furthermore, middle class youths were joining steelbands in increasing numbers. Middle and upper class condemnation of the movement waned as well and was replaced by a growing sense of appreciation of the music. More and more the steelband was promoted as something Trinidadian in which anyone could participate. Perceptions of inclusiveness, together with a vibrancy and openness to new possibilities, made the steelband popular and persuasive as a national symbol in the aftermath of independence.

By 1970, however, the steelband was losing some of its power as a symbol of independence. Many people, especially the younger generation, had become disillusioned with the nation and the promises of independence, and their criticism of the country's political and economic system was accompanied by a questioning of the steelband. The steelband appeared to be not only an expression of local creativity and independence but of dependency on the state, on businesses, and on the European musical tradition and its exponents. In short, the potential of the steelband seemed mired in neo-colonialism. Many panmen struggled to free the steelband from political and commercial manipulation and to seek other avenues for its development. But some became disenchanted with the pan life, dropped out, and searched for new symbols and activities. Kendall Lewis relates:

A lot of people turned to drumming and all kind of thing. . . . Because that was, let us say, the restless period in Trinidad. There were a lot of pan people who went into African drumming because that was part of the revolution: to find they roots. NJAC was built on a sort of roots kind of message. So you find a lot of people went NJAC. And a lot of people who were even more radical went into NUFF [National Union of Freedom Fighters]. And they started fighting on the hills and some robbing banks under the name of "Freedom Fighters" and all kind of thing. . . . There were a lot of pan people who would have got involved in that. . . .Then Rasta [Rastafari] movement came in at that same period. So there were a lot disenchanted, too, with that, so they went into Rastas. They didn't come out to fight no politics. They had their own little—well we call it spiritualism.

Then there were a lot of people who were in bags. You know about the bag people? Well it started in Diego Martin. A lot of people just turned—the '70s was something else—they just turned to bag. And they dress bag. . . . Those crocus bags and those sugar bags. . . . And they would walk with shepherd stick or whatever. . . . You know the calypsonian Shorty? Well they use bag. And they would be on the hills. And you'd see them walking: fifteen of them or so.

All of this was a spin-off of the '70 revolution. Everybody was, you know, disenchanted. They just had to turn to something. . . .

So a lot of these people who withdrew were pan people. And they never went back into pan. Some of them come back. Some of them never came back. But there were a lot of withdrawals in the '70s. So and that era coupled with the steelband turmoil of the times. But the whole country was in turmoil in terms of that restlessness. The '70s was a period of restlessness. Just as the steelband was restless, the whole country. . . . [70]

As discussed earlier, there also was a decline in the social uses of pan during the 1970s. Due to the growth of Panorama, the increasing appropriation of masquerade by women and the middle class, and the growing preference for amplified sound, steelbands were no longer in as high demand for Carnival street masquerades and fetes. This reorientation of Carnival and the steelband was to a significant extent shaped by the oil boom. Sponsors poured money into Panorama for advertising, working women and the middle class bought expensive costumes, and the technology of amplification became the rage. These trends were part of the larger pattern of mass consumption that the oil boom inspired. During the mid- to late 1970s, the disposable income of many Trinidadians increased dramatically, and they tended to focus their spending on foreign products and trips overseas. This emphasis on consuming new goods and experiences appears to have resulted in some neglect of the steelband. In addition, the oil boom had an impact on the panmen's economic situation: many found employment with the government's expanded Special Works program and some with state or private firms. With jobs and more cash for other forms of recreation, panmen tended to spend less time in their panyards.

By the end of the 1970s, the steelband had arrived at a curious position. It had become widely accepted by the public and evoked considerable national pride. At Panorama and other steelband occasions, enthusiasm for the music was as strong as ever. But the steelband no longer had as pervasive a presence in the society as during the 1960s. This lack of performance opportunities produced much bitterness among panmen, and they continued to question the nature of the support that they received from the government, the sponsors, and the public. Essentially, panmen wanted the chance to earn money from playing pan rather than having to subsist on hand-outs from the state and the corporate sector. But the role and character of the arts in the new nation were still unresolved, as was the direction of the nation itself. Dependent relationships proved to be exceedingly difficult to escape. While the nation as a whole struggled with the economic and cultural consequences of neo-colonialism, the steelband movement raised issues about the development of local forms of artistic expression and public commitment to and financing of such expression. In this sense, the debates and negotiations over the steelband during the 1960s and 1970s were manifestations of the larger dilemmas of independence and the definition of a national identity in Trinidad and Tobago.

Chapter Five
The Steelband Movement in Contemporary Trinidad and Tobago

The steelband movement today remains a vital and influential part of the artistic life of Trinidad and Tobago. Though an economic recession during the past decade and a half has posed many hardships, bands continue to thrive in communities throughout the nation, from the crowded neighborhoods of La Cour Harpe and John John in Port of Spain to peaceful villages like Belle Garden and Black Rock on the coasts of Tobago. All along the Eastern Main Road, from Port of Spain to the Atlantic Ocean, there are towns with prominent steelbands: Barataria, San Juan, St. Augustine, Tunapuna, Arima, and Sangre Grande. Pan music can also be heard in Enterprise and Couva, deep in the sugar cane region of central Trinidad, and in southern oil field towns such as San Fernando, Siparia, and Point Fortin. Performance settings vary widely: from concert nights at Queen's Hall to huge competitions in the Jean Pierre Complex to Carnival celebrations on neighborhood streets. A number of schools include steelbands in their music programs, churches sometimes use them in worship, and clubs and malls occasionally hire them to entertain their patrons. Government ministers regularly proclaim their visions for the movement and its importance to the nation's economy and cultural identity, while the officers of Pan Trinbago, the steelband association, attempt to convert state and corporate interest in pan into material benefits for panmen and panwomen. Through it all, the steelband continues to capture the imagination of artists and writers. It appears in sculptures, paintings, and postage stamps; in editorials, essays, and poetry. Calypsos, in particular, chronicle the many dimensions of the steelband experience: "Pan Night and Day," "Mystery Band," "Whey I Band," "Mr. Panmaker," "The Hammer," "Pan in Danger," "Pan Rising."

The present chapter outlines the various contours of the steelband movement in contemporary Trinidad. Most of the observations are derived from fieldwork conducted between October 1987 and April 1989, though occasional references are made to more recent developments. My main objective is to describe the pan life at present, the relationships between steelbands and communities, the role of Pan Trinbago in steelband negotiations, and the preparation for and characteristics of steelband performances. In Chapter 6, I offer an interpretation of the current manifestation of the pan movement in terms of perceptions of ethnicity, class, and nationhood and the dynamics of creativity, festivity, and social change.

Any understanding of the contemporary steelband movement requires some consideration of recent economic and political developments in Trinidad and Tobago. The recession that now grips the country has resulted in an exceptionally high unemployment rate among panmen, and funding of the movement by businesses and the state has not kept pace with inflation. So, while communities continue to produce steelbands, they do so against considerable odds. Moreover, there is a growing sense of frustration among pan musicians: a feeling that opportunities for a better life have vanished and a belief that their well-being has been sacrificed by a nation preoccupied with other concerns.

The roots of the current recession lie in the decline of the oil industry, the most important sector of Trinidad's economy. Petroleum production began to decrease in 1979, and during the early 1980s the price of oil on the world market dropped as well. In the following years there was a collapse of the nation's economy in general, with substantial loss of jobs in both the public and private sectors. While the unemployment rate was 7 percent in 1981, by 1986 it had reached 17 percent. As a result of this recession, Trinidadians have had to adjust to a much more restricted lifestyle than that to which they had become accustomed during the oil boom years.

The recession also eroded the PNM's long-standing popularity. By the time of the 1986 general elections, a new party had been formed: the National Alliance for Reconstruction (NAR). The NAR was a merger of the Organization for National Reconstruction, an essentially middle class and business party, and the National Alliance, itself a merger of the United Labour Front, which had wide support from rural Indians, the Democratic Action Committee, which had a strong following in Tobago, and the Tapia House Movement, a party led by progressive intellectuals.

The PNM entered the 1986 elections with far fewer resources than it had during the oil boom period. Selwyn Ryan notes that the "collapse of the petrodollar economy" meant that "there was little money available as there had been in 1976 and 1981 to bribe the underclass electorate in the urbanized East-West Corridor [Port of Spain and its environs]."[1] Kevin Yelvington points out that the PNM thus campaigned on the basis of its past achievements, while the new NAR lambasted the government on corruption, economic mismanagement, and the declining standard of living.[2] The NAR, under the leadership of A. N. R. Robinson, won by a landslide: 33 seats in the House of Representatives to the PNM's 3. Unlike the PNM, which remained a primarily grass-roots and middle class African party, the NAR was able to gain support from the range of ethnic groups and classes in the nation. It tried to devise an economic policy with elements that would appeal to different classes and also promoted multiculturalism in contrast to the PNM's melting pot theory.[3] In addition, it promised a new beginning for a population that had grown weary of thirty years of PNM rule. It was the electorate's desire for change, more than anything else, that brought about the NAR's victory.

The victory was soon followed, however, by signs of serious conflict within the new government. When cabinet ministers who had previously belonged to the United Labour Front began publicly criticizing their own government, the crisis was perceived by many people as having an ethnic dimension. By February 1988 Prime Minister Robinson had dismissed the dissenting ministers. These individuals went on to form a caucus within the NAR, which in 1989 was transformed into a full-fledged political party—the United National Congress (UNC). Though the UNC had aspirations of being national in scope, its supporters were primarily of Indian descent.

Internal fragmentation, however, was just one of the problems facing Robinson and the NAR. The economic decline continued and in 1988 the government stated that 22 percent of the population was unemployed and that nearly half of these individuals were under the age of 25. It was also announced that 25 percent of the population lived below the poverty line.[4] In order to deal with its mounting financial woes, the government applied to the International Monetary Fund, devalued the Trinidad and Tobago dollar, advocated privatization of state companies, toyed with the idea of opening Export Processing Zones to attract foreign investors, and enacted stringent budgetary measures. In response to this course of action, Kenrick Rennie, the president of the public servants' union, stated that "Robinson's ideological perspective is not geared for the development of the poor and working people but for international finance capital and the local comprador (overseer) class."[5]

Though the NAR originally attracted support that cut across class lines, it was increasingly perceived as a party that favored big business and the wealthy. More and more, Robinson was described as remote from the people and oblivious to the suffering that his economic policies created. Disillusionment with the NAR became widespread: there was a sense that the party had failed to deliver on its election promises. Living conditions continued to deteriorate, crime escalated, and a growing number of people prepared to emigrate. In downtown Port of Spain, young people lingered in the streets, looking for money or action. Sidewalk vendors virtually blocked the doors to stores in their desperation for sales, while the homeless struggled to get what they could. Trade unions staged protests and issued demands, and a sense of rage permeated debates among the crowds in Woodford Square.

The most dramatic manifestation of this discontent was an attempted coup in July 1990 led by Imam Yasin Abu Bakr of the Jamaat-al-Muslimeen, a primarily African Muslim group. The Muslimeen set fire to the police headquarters, stormed the Red House, where they held Robinson and several other ministers hostage, and took over the state-owned television station. Six days of arson, looting, and violence followed before the rebels were apprehended and order was restored. During the subsequent months Trinidadians attempted to fathom the significance of the insurrection, since they generally perceive their society as being relatively free of major political violence.

Disillusionment with the NAR and utter frustration over the lack of any signs of economic recovery contributed to the return to power of the PNM in the 1991 general elections. The NAR won only the two seats in Tobago, so the UNC became the new opposition party. During its campaign the PNM promoted its image as a populist and compassionate party, but once in office it essentially continued NAR policies of retrenchment, privatization, and pursuit of overseas investment. Trinidad's economy has remained depressed, though recently there have been improvements in some sectors.[6]

Panmen and Panwomen

Pan continues to be predominantly an art form of young grass-roots African men. Though steelbands often include some individuals of Indian, Chinese, Syrian, European, or "mixed" ancestry, approximately 90 percent of adult pannists (male and female) are of African descent.[7] Generally they range in age from the late teens to early thirties. This is the period in life during which men in particular have the fewest obligations and most enjoy the dynamics of street life. By the time they reach their early thirties, concern with having a steady income to support families usually begins to outweigh devotion to playing pan. However, some panmen in their late thirties and forties (or even older) remain actively involved in the movement. Often they no longer perform but function in leadership positions in bands and Pan Trinbago or work as musical arrangers and pan tuners. These older panmen are vital to the transmission of musical skills to the younger generation and provide youths with a sense of the steelband's history and importance.

Approximately 85 percent of pannists are grass-roots, and many of these have trade skills. The remaining 15 percent are middle class and work as civil servants, business persons, teachers, or other professionals. Due to the particularly severe impact of the recession on the grass-roots class and on younger people, approximately 75 percent of panmen are currently unemployed or marginally employed. Younger panmen generally live with family members upon whom they can depend to some degree for food and other necessities. Most, though, have to devise various means of hustling a living. Typically they do yard work and odd jobs, unload trucks for businesses, sell food and other goods on the street, or drive taxis. Income is also derived from various forms of gambling, such as buying lottery tickets, playing cards, or betting on horses at racing pools. All these methods of trying to make money are unreliable, so much ingenuity and diligence are required. For many panmen, every day involves considerable effort just to survive, and this sense of struggle is a recurring theme in conversations around panyards.

But if there are struggles, there are also limes and recreation: football and basketball, All Fours and draughts (card and board games), a beer at a local shop, or a circuitous drive around the country in search of friends and good times. Beach excursions, organized by bands, remain popular. On these occasions band members, relatives, and friends pack into maxi-taxis that are rented for the day. The maxis depart from the panyard loaded with ice coolers and containers of food, with sound systems blasting calypsos that are sometimes augmented by the band's rhythm section: drums, tambourines, cymbals, and pieces of metal. On an excursion I attended to the Vessigny beach in south Trinidad, repeated breakdowns of one of the maxis and rain pouring in through a broken window inspired a lavway from the passengers: "I goin to Vessigny but I eh [ain't] payin no money," and "I eh reach Vessigny but I done wet already." A spirit of *joie de vivre* prevails at most other social occasions as well. If panmen find themselves together at a wake, for example, there are bound to be animated discussions of pan history and prospects, along with the usual rounds of jokes and stories, as the raconteurs and their audiences, fortified with rum, coffee, Crix biscuits, and cheese, try to make it to daybreak.

And then there are the fetes. Though many bands have held fetes in their panyards over the years, none have surpassed Merrytones' extravaganzas during the late 1980s. By 1987 the band had finished building a new yard on the side of a wooded hill at the end of the Diego Martin Main Road. The imposing concrete "Pan Complex" attracted much attention and was frequently used for meetings by local community, religious, sports, and political organizations. The band also discovered that the yard could be a source of much-needed funds if it were used for entertainment. By 1988 band members or outside promoters were staging massive fetes almost every weekend, which featured the top deejays in the land, such as Papa Rocky, Dr. Hyde, and Star Child. For these events, the deejay's crew would arrive early in the day in a flatbed truck loaded with an enormous sound system. Hours were spent setting up and testing the system, and by late afternoon it could be heard throughout the surrounding area. At nightfall vendors arrived to set up food and drink stands and games of chance, and in the course of the evening hundreds of young men and women (both from the vicinity and from other parts of the island) began arriving to lime on the road outside the yard. By midnight many would pay the admission fee and go inside, where they spent several hours dancing to dub reggae (dancehall), American pop, and calypso. These popular fetes proved to be a relatively cheap form of entertainment for youths worn out by the recession, and provided work opportunities for Merrytones' members along with additional income for the band as a whole.

For the most part the pan life continues to revolve around male occupational pursuits and expressive styles associated with the streets. In addition, men still control pan affairs, from the management of bands to dealings with the government and with businesses. However, there has been a growing number of women playing pan since the 1970s, and today women make up approximately 15 percent of the membership of adult bands. Before the 1970s women rarely learned to play pan. Since panyards were an integral part of the male street world, they were to be avoided by any woman concerned with respectability. However, older panmen recall that even in the early days of the movement there were a few female players. During the 1950s at least two all-women steelbands were formed. Apparently the first was White Stars, which was organized in the early 1950s at the Girls' Industrial School, a correctional institution. The girls in this band were instructed by members of Casablanca. During this same period Hazel Henley, a school teacher, formed the Girl Pat Steel Orchestra, which consisted primarily of teachers, civil servants, and store clerks. This band received pans and some initial instruction from Ellie Mannette of Invaders and became accomplished enough to give numerous public performances.[8] The novelty of middle class women playing pan undoubtedly contributed to their popularity.

It was not until the 1970s, however, that women became a noticeable presence in steelbands. Their entry into the pan world was facilitated by the increasing economic and social independence of women since the 1960s, due to greater educational and occupational opportunities. Many women were staying in school longer, postponing marriage and childbearing, and developing careers. In short, women were assuming more control over their own lives and choosing to engage in a wider range of activities, including Carnival pursuits. As noted in Chapter Four, women were dominating masquerade by the 1970s and using it as an occasion to display their autonomy and sensuality. In playing pan many women, particularly those with middle class backgrounds, found a new avenue for utilizing skills acquired through music lessons and membership in choirs.

As steelbands increased their performance of European classical pieces, there was a growing demand for arrangers, conductors, and players with formal musical training. In Trinidad girls have traditionally had considerably more interest in music lessons than boys, who often perceive such instruction as another manifestation of the discipline and confinement of the home and the school. Many men who have formal musical knowledge acquired it through participation in police and military bands, and over the years a number of these individuals have played an active role in the steelband movement. However, panmen also increasingly turned to women in their search for formal musical expertise. For example, Jocelyn Pierre arranged "In a Monastery Garden" for Invaders for the 1960 Music Festival, and by the late 1960s Merle Albino-de Coteau was assisting Savoys with classical selections.[9] Since then several other prominent female musicians, such as Pat Bishop, Alma Pierre, Dawn Batson, and Gillian Nathaniel-Balintulo, have arranged for and conducted steelbands. At the same time, scores of women with formal musical backgrounds developed expertise as pan performers.

Women who were interested in becoming pannists tended to prefer the most respectable environments for developing pan skills. For example, a company band known as the Neal and Massy Trendsetters became an all-female organization during the 1970s. Many women also learned to play pan as students on the campus of the University of the West Indies. In 1973 they participated in the founding of Birdsong, a university band whose philosophy was in part an outgrowth of the Black Power movement which had blossomed on campus in 1970. Patricia Adams, a steelband arranger/instructor who was an original member of Birdsong, relates:

I would call us the people of the '70s. . . . We got together. The University, at that time, was still finding itself. Put it this way: you still had the intellectuals who wanted to explore their identity, for want of a better word. So there were movements. Birdsong Steelband was a group of the University community. You had lecturers, you had students, you had workers, you had people from the community—the area around. So that it was a unique kind of experience that was quite deliberate. And you also had a lot of females. And that was the first time, really, that you had that high percentage of female involvement in any steelband. . . .

Your competence, I think, had a lot to do with what position you eventually got. We had a lot of female section leaders, and that is where your authority came from. You had to be able to play to be a section leader. . . .

It was a democratic kind of organization. A lot of steelbands are not all that democratic. But Birdsong being founded when it was . . . we always had a voice because of how the band came about. And because we were the ones with the skills, we were in the positions and we maintained that.[10]

Similarly, Maureen Clement Moe, a pan instructor and soloist, recalls that what she liked about Birdsong was that "women were able to make decisions" and "were seen as important members of the band."[11] So, in contrast to the traditional steelbands with their authoritarian male structures and street ambiance, Birdsong provided an environment in which women could gain respect for both their musical and leadership abilities. The success of women in this band inspired many other women to become involved in the pan movement.

Certainly the most important factor in the entry of women into steelbands was the initiation of pan instruction in some of the nation's secondary schools. There had been occasional pan lessons in a few schools at least since the 1960s, but such programs became much more common in the 1970s. Apparently the first school band of any size and longevity was formed in 1974 at St. Francois Girls' College in Belmont. The school obtained some pans and brought in McDonald Redhead of Power Stars to offer instruction. Allison Dyer (who is currently the leader of a small all-female band called In Focus) recalls that she and a group of other students jumped at the opportunity, since their parents would not have permitted them to learn to play pan in a panyard.[12] Gradually more schools developed steelbands, especially after Pan Trinbago's introduction of a Schools' Panorama in the late 1970s and a Schools' Steelband Music Festival in 1981. Today there are over twenty school bands in Trinidad and Tobago. Though pan is still not an official part of the school curriculum, there is a feeling among many educators that children should be encouraged to learn to play the nation's indigenous instrument. There is also a belief that pan instruction helps create a sense of discipline among students and provides them with a constructive activity.

Currently girls make up the majority of the members of school steelbands. Some observers attribute this to the tendency of girls to engage in more extra-curricular activities in general than boys and to remain more dedicated to these activities. Another possibility is that boys prefer to learn to play pan in the male and street-oriented adult bands. In any case, a considerable number of the players in school bands eventually graduate to adult bands, and this helps to account for the growing number of women in these bands since the 1970s.

Initially some panmen were reluctant to allow women to join their bands. For years they had conceptualized pan and panyards as their own domain, and they were worried that the presence of women in the yards might disrupt the bands and threaten their control of the tradition. Moreover, there was a sense that women would not fully appreciate and respect the movement and its history of struggle.[13] Dawn Batson, a pan arranger/instructor who has worked with Pamberi and other bands, relates how some panmen perceived the situation:

> Well, you were fighting for this instrument. You were actually forming this instrument from nothing. And there is always a belligerent attitude of protectionism toward this instrument. And you're ready to strike out. So that you had this almost like a gang kind of setting. And, as you know, very few women are in gangs. So any person coming into that, whether it be male or female, was looked on like an outsider. And you had to really prove yourself. Not only in terms of playing, though playing was very important, but in terms of being able to protect the honor, so-called, of the band.

She continues:

> . . . they were afraid that women might not be able to cope with the mores of a panyard. Because some of them felt that it was being taken away from them. And I think this was a very, very important point. Because some people still feel that a pannist is a person who has grown up in the panyard, gone straight with the panyard education or whatever, and stays in that general area. And they don't like people from outside coming to, say, take away. They have this feeling that it is

theirs. And they don't want outsiders coming in. Whether you're coming in to help or whatever you say you're doing. They don't want that type of contamination, if that's not too strong a word. Fewer now feel that way. But I think as the women prove themselves as players, arrangers, whatever, the argument that they can't cope was thrown out the window. . . . [14]

When women began joining steelbands during the 1970s, they often met some resistance not only from panmen but from their own parents. Though the steelband movement was widely accepted in the society by the 1970s, it was still not considered entirely respectable for women to play pan. Essentially, women negotiated respectability by joining bands on their own terms: they focused on the music itself, avoided liming, and adhered to a sense of decorum and order. Furthermore, the establishment of steelbands in schools, where there was supervision by teachers, provided girls with a socially acceptable means of attaining proficiency in pan.

The growing presence of women in steelbands in turn has gradually changed the way Trinidadians perceive the movement. The macho image of the panman and the idea of pan as a flamboyant male activity continue, but are now tempered by the prominence of many highly skilled and dedicated panwomen. There is a sense that women are beginning to domesticate pan somewhat and are giving it even greater respectability. The fact that many panwomen are middle class and employed has strengthened these perceptions. Again, Maureen Clement Moe notes the early influence of Birdsong in this regard:

The fact that women got into pan and didn't get into trouble. . . . When I came into Birdsong, they must have had about eight women already. And they were visible and they were the kind of women that everybody wants their child to be like. So, that was good. Visible, educated, middle class, working. That is the kind of woman everybody wants their child to be like. So they see that these people are in the panyard and they're still successful. Nothing bad happened to them. . . . Maybe there's something to this thing after all. And they're playing good music. Birdsong used to have a lot of people watching. Endless people watching the band. And people saw that they really came to play music. . . .

I think it raised the esteem of the panman quite a lot when those kind of women were accepted in the panyard and produced music of the caliber with the men. So it raised in society's eyes the standard of the panmen to now be pannists.[15]

In becoming pannists themselves, instead of simply band supporters and masqueraders, women have embraced the instrument as their own and are helping to chart the direction of the movement. In particular, they are demonstrating the value of musical literacy and the application of such knowledge to arranging and rehearsing. At the same time, in assuming the roles of teachers, arrangers, conductors, performers, and even band officers, they are transforming public perceptions of the social basis of the music. Though unemployed panmen based in the world of the street still make up the bulk of the steelband movement, there is increasing recognition of the contributions of panwomen who, though devoted to pan, also identify with the world of the home, the school, and the office.

Steelbands and Communities

One indication of the steelband movement's vitality is the sheer number of bands: over 100 in a nation with a population of only some 1.2 million. Included in this number are over 50 large adult bands, many of which have more than 80 members. The rest fall into three categories: school bands, *pan-around-the-neck bands,* and small *stage sides.* The pan-around-the-neck ensembles are smaller than the regular bands and consist of individuals who carry their pans suspended from the neck in the old-time manner. They began to appear in the early 1970s, partially as a tribute to past practice and partially as an effort to streamline the process of producing a steelband for the Carnival season. The small stage sides are another means of avoiding the cumbersome size of the standard steelband. These ensembles usually consist of under ten members and generally perform at clubs, hotels, and fetes.

Most steelbands are located in towns, and the highest concentration is in greater Port of Spain (from Diego Martin in the west to Morvant Junction in the east). This region includes approximately 20 large adult bands, 15 pan-around-the-neck ensembles, 13 school bands, and 5 small stage sides. The large adult bands in this area are the focus of the following discussion.

In Port of Spain steelbands are a prominent feature of the public sphere, since their yards are generally located on major streets and are immediately visible to passersby. Most yards consist of open space along with one or more buildings or shelters for rehearsals and for the storage of pans and equipment. When a band is rehearsing for Panorama with its full membership, its pans are mounted on its mobile metal racks outside in the yard. In addition to being sites for rehearsals, panyards serve as venues for band meetings, for the maintenance of pans and racks, and for liming. Though much of this activity occurs at night, there are often some panmen around during the day, especially when bands are preparing for competitions or concerts. Because yards are located next to streets they also attract people from surrounding areas. Men and occasionally women regularly pass through yards to see what is happening and to visit with friends. Meanwhile, panmen are well-positioned to observe and engage in activity on the street. In short, panyards are key spaces for neighborhood interaction.

Most steelbands continue to be associated with particular communities. Typically, the core of a band's players and supporters will live in the neighborhood around the band's yard. However, bands also include members and supporters from outside their communities. Some especially successful and popular bands, though based in specific communities, attract players and supporters from throughout the nation and are often referred to as "national bands." For example, Desperadoes is deeply attached to the community of Laventille but also has members and followers from locations all over Trinidad. Similarly, while the majority of Tokyo's top players are from John John, the majority of its total membership is from outside the neighborhood. The memberships of steelbands reflect population movements as well. Often individuals will continue to play with or follow the band in the community where they grew up, even after they move to new locations. Over the past thirty years, for example, many people from the neighborhood of Woodbrook have moved to suburbs of Port of Spain, but they continue to perform with or support Invaders and Starlift, two popular Woodbrook bands.

Unlike some Carnival masquerade bands, steelbands are not divided along class lines. Virtually all steelbands (with the possible exception of Starlift) have predominantly grass-roots memberships. However, bands do vary to some extent in their percentages of middle class members. On the whole, bands on the west side of Port of Spain tend to have more middle class players than those on the east side, due to the relatively higher income levels of the west side neighborhoods. Though steelbands are primarily a grass-roots phenomenon, they attract supporters from all classes. Top bands such as Desperadoes, Renegades, Trinidad All Stars, and Phase II have vast followings from throughout the nation which cut across class and ethnic boundaries.

Though theoretically anyone can attempt to join any steelband, bands generally recruit their players along friendship and kinship lines. Brothers and sisters, cousins, and fathers and sons are often found in the same band. Similarly, individuals often join a steelband through the suggestions of a friend or a neighborhood acquaintance. In recent years school bands have become another important source of players for adult bands through what are essentially symbiotic relationships. An adult band will allow a nearby school group to come and practice on its pans during the day, and a few of its members will often offer the students some instruction. Eventually some of the more accomplished young pannists will join the adult band. For example, the success of the Wood-Trin school band during the 1980s was partially due to its association with Invaders, and Invaders in turn was strengthened by a number of Wood-Trin players.

Every steelband has a formal organizational structure. At the helm of the organization is a committee of officers which is elected by the band's general membership. Among the typical positions are captain, vice-captain, secretary, treasurer, public relations officer, trustee, and a representative who voices the opinions of the "floor members." In addition, many bands have a manager who handles the purchasing of pans and other materials and makes arrangements for performances. The hierarchy of pannists in a band also reflects their musical skill and commitment. Every band has a stage side, which usually includes twenty to thirty of its best players. These individuals must be willing to devote a considerable amount of time to the band, since the stage side rehearses and performs at various occasions throughout the year. A band's *road side*, on the other hand, includes the stage side pannists and other individuals who only play with the band for Panorama and Carnival.

One of the primary concerns of the officers and floor members of every steelband is the procurement of necessary funds. With the nation's economic decline, this has become a particularly challenging task. Just as panmen often talk about their personal lives in terms of struggle, they view steelband activities as a constant hustle for survival. The cost of running a steelband of acceptable quality is extremely high. For example, some bands spend as much as $80,000-90,000 TT to attend one Panorama alone.[16] As much as $30,000 of this may go to an arranger, with the remainder being used for such expenses as new pans, rack construction and maintenance, and band jerseys. Some of these expenses are recouped through government assistance and prizes for bands participating in the event. In 1988, for example, if a band made it all the way to the finals of the competition, it received $13,250 in flat fees and $16,000 to $26,000 in prize monies. Similarly, there are fees and prizes for the Steelband Music Festival, but they too only partially cover the costs of competing. In addition to performing in competitions, bands sometimes give concerts but these occasions usually provide little or no income.

This dire economic situation partially explains why sponsorship remains a reality in the steelband world. Some companies supplement their bands' performance income with enough money for them to meet many of their expenses (though there has been some tightening of budgets with the recession). As discussed in the previous chapter, these relationships have certain consequences: a sponsoring firm often owns its band's pans, may make management suggestions, uses the band for advertising and public relations, and may request that the band occasionally perform at company functions. Businesses often claim that the expenses and headaches of steelband sponsorship far outweigh any benefits for themselves.[17] Panmen generally feel that companies are more than amply rewarded for their contributions. The advertising and public relations benefits certainly cannot be denied. In the late 1980s, for example, Carib Tokyo played an integral role in the advertising war between the Caribbean Development Company (the brewer of Carib beer) and the National Brewing Company (the brewer of Stag beer). In some cases, the benefits are more subtle. In 1988 a popular band lost its sponsor and was quickly picked up by a major conglomerate. There were some suspicions in the pan world that this move was politically motivated. The conglomerate had become a symbol of the corporate control of the nation, and steelband sponsorship was a means through which it could attempt to improve its public image.

At present, it is primarily the largest and most popular steelbands that have sponsors. The majority of bands in Trinidad and Tobago, especially those outside Port of Spain, have no formal relationships with businesses. Periodically, these unsponsored bands receive small grants from the government. For the most part, however, they have to depend on their own initiative to survive. Generally they try to obtain donations of money and materials from businesses and individuals in their communities; some occasionally hold fundraisers such as barbecues and fetes. Since their financial needs are so great, most of these bands would not decline a sponsorship offer. However, they also take a certain pride in being independent and point out that sponsorship tends to erode a band's relationship with its community. When a band becomes sponsored, its members and community supporters soon begin to depend on the company to cover most of its expenses. An unsponsored band, on the other hand, constantly draws on its own resources and on those of its community. Members and supporters are more likely to contribute labor, materials, and funds to improve the band and increase its chances in competitions. The band's achievements can then be fully attributed to the talents and work of its players and community.

Though both unsponsored and sponsored steelbands have limited financial resources, their members still expect to receive some money in return for the tremendous amount of time they devote to preparing for performances. Each year, particularly after Panorama, many bands do give their players token payments (often under $200). With the recession, however, some bands are so strapped for funds that even such small payments are impossible.[18]

Panmen also look to their bands for access to various opportunities. For years, many panmen obtained temporary government jobs and public housing units through their bands. Clientelistic relationships with the PNM administration were particularly strong on the east side of Port of Spain, and the two electoral districts in this area were among the three that the PNM won in the 1986 elections. In 1988 the NAR government began phasing out the PNM labor scheme but then initiated a program of its own. After the PNM returned to power in 1991, it replaced the NAR's initiative with yet another program. These various labor schemes have all been an effective means of patronage for grassroots constituents, including panmen. Though steelbands continue to seek jobs and other types of assistance from the government, they do not always provide overt political support in return. In fact some bands are now fairly cynical about the overtures of politicians and attempt at least to appear politically neutral.

The funds and opportunities steelbands control, as well as the power hierarchies among players, create recurring patterns of internal conflict. It is not uncommon for the floor members of a band to be dissatisfied with and to have little trust in their officers, even though these individuals are democratically elected. There may be a feeling that the officers are not effectively carrying out their duties, that they are using the band for personal aggrandizement, and that they are perhaps even stealing band funds. For example, whenever an officer makes a large personal purchase of some sort, he immediately opens himself up to suspicion. Given this general distrust, officers often do not last very long in their posts. However, there are also a number of strong leaders who have been able to withstand attacks and effectively run their bands for extended periods of time.[19]

Controversies in steelbands often erupt in the aftermath of competitions, particularly if a band does not do as well as expected (which is almost always the case). Officers may then blame floor members for the band's failure and floor members may blame the officers. One of the key words in these disputes is "discipline." Pannists are constantly concerned with a sense of discipline in their yards: respect for authority, decency toward peers, regular and punctual attendance at rehearsals, accurate learning of music, and completion of band chores. Officers generally scold floor members for their poor discipline, while floor members criticize officers for not properly enforcing discipline.

Controversies also typically accompany the selection of musical arrangers. Since winning or at least doing well in a competition is of primary importance, much discussion is devoted ahead of time to the selection of the most promising arranger. Some bands have their own arrangers whom they use consistently from year to year. Others hire outside arrangers for specific competitions. During the past several years a number of the top arrangers have been hired by more than one band for Panorama, even though these bands compete against each other. After the competition is over there is inevitably the question of whether an arranger gave his best to a particular band. Sometimes a band feels cheated if a competitor using the same arranger fared better. The band may then scramble to find a new arranger for the following year, an effort that often creates more disappointment. The decision about which arranger to use is further complicated if various players in a band have loyalties to different arrangers. Also, the fact that these top arrangers are paid high fees for their services is a source of considerable discontent among the players who receive little or nothing for their own labor.

Recurring steelband conflicts have been heightened in recent years by the recession. For younger panmen with a source of food and no children, unemployment provides more time to rehearse and lime in the panyards. However, most panmen have to spend a great deal of time hustling money for food and other necessities. Thus they may not have enough time or energy to attend practices regularly. In addition, they have become increasingly dissatisfied with the small amount of pay they receive from their bands. Along with arguing with officers for more money, they sometimes seek out schemes for siphoning funds from their bands.

When a band's conflicts become too intense, it may temporarily or permanently break up. By and large though, most bands are able to survive a considerable amount of turmoil. *Bacchanal* or *confusion* (local terms for such conflict) is usually taken in stride and even appreciated for its humorous qualities. Furthermore, steelband conflicts are counteracted by the sheer commitment of pannists to their respective bands. Pannists devote an immense amount of time to their bands and are often willing to sacrifice family and work obligations, especially during the preparation for competitions. For unemployed panmen in particular, their band becomes a focus for collective action and creative expression. In opposition to the centrifugal force in a steelband, there is a striving for unity and solidarity. Members work together in learning music, accomplish band tasks as a group, and assist each other personally whenever possible. Most important, musical performances become a collective achievement of excellence. Countless hours are devoted to perfecting pieces of music that, when successfully rendered, produce a tremendous sense of pride. This devotion seems to be at least partially motivated by the fact that pannists perceive steelband performance as a creative process that they themselves initiate and control.

Nestor Sullivan, the captain of Pamberi, provides a clear sense of this commitment to and unity within steelbands:

> I think the fact that you're involved in pan and it's largely . . . the collective wisdom of the members of the band which guides it. And there's not much external influences. You find that you get more satisfaction doing something like that. When a band does well in Panorama, . . . they can lay back and say: "Well this is mine." That a kind of satisfaction you don't get if you're doing an eight to four job. Or you're working in a store, selling for somebody, and so on. That is largely your success. And you and your equals. There not no boss over you with no thing and so on. You're not being exploited, I mean in the sense that a profit is being made and you're not getting all of that profit. Not like that.
>
> And then, of course, the chemistry of steelband, that is, the human chemistry. Now you're playing in an orchestra. So what you doing on this pan complementing on another pan. So . . . the social interaction and that kind of vibes it does have with players and so on—that's a thing you don't enjoy in society.[20]

Dawn Batson expresses similar sentiments about why pannists are so devoted to their music:

> I think it's because you're generating within yourself a sense of pride and that you are working at something that you love, that you enjoy. And you're accomplishing something. You're working with others. . . . Because men and women work days and nights on end really, really hard just for one competition. Maybe you're thrown out after that. . . . It's something you choose to do. You're not told. You're not forced into it. And you gain the sense of accomplishment which is not readily available otherwise.[21]

Clive Bradley, a top arranger who has worked with Desperadoes and a number of other bands, suggests that pannists' commitment to their music is also inspired by a desire to realize and display their unique abilities:

Now these guys, every year they complain after Carnival: "Boy, I haven't made any money." But they come back next year because it's the only thing they have. These people would grow up and die without anybody seeing them. The steelband gives them a chance to do something. To be seen. To do something different that nobody else can do. This is what the steelband is to a lot of people. The money part of it, they know they're not going to make any money.[22]

The public accomplishments of steelbands in turn help generate a sense of solidarity and pride within their communities. In many communities in Trinidad and Tobago, steelbands are the most prominent organizations, though in some areas sports teams, Best Village groups, or other performing ensembles are equally or more important. Steelbands are appreciated for their contributions to community life. They perform at local functions, allow other organizations to use their yards for meetings, and provide a form of constructive activity for youths. It is their musical achievements, however, that most inspire their supporters. The excellence of a steelband is perceived as symbolic of the excellence or potential of the people of its community. The band helps establish the community's identity in the national sphere, and its followers share in its successes. Richard Forteau, a founder of Laventille Sounds Specialists from Eastern Quarry, relates how his band builds this sense of community identity while striving for musical perfection:

There are lots of people who live right within Trinidad and Tobago then and, if you tell them about Eastern Quarry, they ask you well where that is. And we are there to get our name out. . . . The only thing that allows people in Trinidad and Tobago to know there is an Eastern Quarry is Sounds Specialists. And while we go as "Laventille Sounds Specialists," I always have the announcer [at competitions] say: "Laventille Sounds Specialists from Eastern Quarry." 'Cause there is where we're from. And people have to know that. . . . And if we have to sell that part, this is what we intend to do then. To let people know then that we are knocking on the doors. . . . And we're not going to give up at all until successful.[23]

Like Laventille Sounds Specialists in Eastern Quarry, Merrytones are the most prominent institution in Green Hill Village. Residents from the area attend the band's functions and rehearsals, cheer it on at competitions, and follow it on the streets for Carnival. In reference to this local support and pride, Sylvan Salandy, the band's captain, states:

I guess it's a communal sense—knowing that our village . . . could go into town and play well enough to win. Say a band like Invaders . . . we could go into town and beat them in a competition. And it's like Diego Martin go in there to beat Woodbrook. So everybody get involved. So I guess that what really have the community tied up in the band: the fact that we could go away from our community and do well on a national scale.[24]

Pan Trinbago and the State

Most steelbands are based in particular communities and spend much of their time attending to their own affairs. However, the bands are all confronted with similar problems and they join together to pursue common interests through Pan Trinbago. As mentioned in the previous chapter, a new leadership assumed power of this association in the late 1970s and was able to wrest it from the control of the PNM government. Arnim Smith retained the post of president for a number of years and is credited with developing more political power for the organization in its negotiations with the government and other bodies. When Smith retired from office at the end of 1988, he was replaced by Owen Serrette, the well-established leader of Harmonites.

Though Pan Trinbago has a few paid staff positions, most of its officers work on a volunteer basis. The primary sources of funding for its programs are government subsidies, band membership fees, and revenues from its "Champs in Concert," a popular post-Carnival show that features the top steelbands, calypsonians, and masqueraders of the season. Pan Trinbago officers and their assistants coordinate or collaborate in most steelband affairs at the national level: pan competitions, steelband participation in major public events, overseas tours, pan in the schools, educational programs, projection of steelband music in the media, and research on the production and standardization of pans.

Government funding and administration of steelband affairs is handled through the ministry for culture and through the National Carnival Commission. On the whole, Pan Trinbago's relationship with the state has been somewhat strained. During the late 1980s many panmen felt that the NAR government was more concerned with tourism and benefits for the business community and the state than with the needs of steelbands. Steelband leaders Nestor Sullivan and Anthony Reid, for example, argued that the immense amount of money generated by Carnival was ending up in the hands of infrastructure providers and vendors rather than going to panmen and other Carnival artists. They suggested that, if Carnival were to benefit the people of Trinidad and Tobago as a whole, it should be run by artists instead of civil servants.[25]

Controversy over the management of Carnival was particularly prominent in late 1987 when the government proposed moving some of the major Carnival events from the Queen's Park Savannah to the National Stadium. This suggestion provoked a tremendous uproar from the nation, and Pan Trinbago became the most vocal opponent. The proposed change was interpreted as a desire by the government to take Carnival away from the masses, who traditionally converge in the open Savannah, and contain it in a stadium where it would be more appealing to local and foreign paying patrons. There were also suspicions that the Trinidad Turf Club, an upper class horse racing organization that rented the Savannah, was promoting the relocation of Carnival events. In an interview with the *Daily Express*, Arnim Smith stated emphatically that moving Carnival events would create class barriers. "The people who have struggled over the years to bring Carnival to where it is today," he said, "nobody thinks about them anymore." Smith also stated that "If Government is serious about [C]arnival let them serve notice to the Trinidad Turf Club to move out of the Savannah and build a permanent Carnival site there."[26] Three weeks later the government announced that all Carnival events would be held in the Savannah after all. Criticism of the proposed changes continued, however, and was even expressed in a popular calypso by Singing Francine: "Cultural Controversy." The calypso was a favorite with panmen, and they invited Francine to make a special guest appearance at their Champs in Concert show.

While Pan Trinbago collaborates with the National Carnival Commission for Panorama and other Carnival events, they work closely with the private sector in the staging of the Steelband Music Festival. The only steelband festivals of the 1970s occurred in 1972 and 1973. In 1980, at the height of the oil boom, the festival was revived; it has been held ever since on a biennial basis.[27] The first year it was sponsored by the Kirpalani Group of Companies and was managed jointly by Kirpalani staff and Pan Trinbago. This arrangement was repeated in 1982. In an effort at self-reliance, Pan Trinbago coordinated the 1984 festival, though they received financial and managerial assistance from the government, Kirpalani, and other firms.[28] In 1986 the Royal Bank took over the sponsorship of the festival and assisted Pan Trinbago with its management.

The 1988 Steelband Music Festival was again a collaboration between Pan Trinbago and the Royal Bank. An added attraction that year was the decision to make the competition international in scope, since a number of steelbands from other countries expressed interest in participating. The Festival was officially launched with much fanfare at the Royal Bank's downtown office, six months before opening night. Panmen, Royal Bank executives, and the press were all present and among the speakers was Ken Gordon, Minister of Industry, Enterprise, and Tourism. Gordon commended Pan Trinbago for thinking in international terms and asserted that he wanted to make pan the "centerpiece of our overseas tourist thrust." In addition to using the Festival to attract tourists to Trinidad, he suggested that "We must now aggressively plan on marketing pan to the world and as we do so review the once loudly proclaimed plans to make it a thriving industry."[29] Panmen and other interested parties had long discussed the possibility of mass-producing pans for the international market, and Gordon hoped that the Festival would give further impetus to these plans. He also proposed that a portion of the finals be televised internationally. So from the start, the Festival was conceived not only as an artistic event but as a means of earning foreign exchange for the recession-strapped nation.

Though only two foreign steelbands actually attended the Festival, there was wide participation from local bands. The level of performance was very high, the event was well-managed, and there was considerable local media coverage. However, many panmen felt that Royal Bank maintained too high a profile and that Pan Trinbago was surrendering control of what should be their own affair. Furthermore, it did not appear that many tourists attended. In any case, panmen argued that they derived no economic benefits from the Festival. Several months later many bands were still attempting to obtain funds to cover their debts.

The economic problems that perpetually plague the steelband movement are at the heart of most of the negotiations in which Pan Trinbago is engaged. The association constantly explains that official promotion of the steelband as a national art and symbol has not resulted in a decent livelihood for panmen. This disjunction between the success of pan as an art form and the economic position of the artists was summed up by Black Stalin several years ago in his calypso "Pan Gone": while everyone is talking about the heights that the steelband has reached, the panmen are still *scrunting* (struggling to make ends meet).[30] The financial plight of the panmen is partially due to the fact that there are only a limited number of occasions at which Trinidadians are accustomed or willing to pay to listen to steelband music. At the same time, the demand for steelband recordings is relatively small. Given these realities, Pan Trinbago continues to request financial support from the state and the corporate sector and justifies this support in terms of the contributions that steelbands make to the society, such as attracting tourists, promoting artistic expression, and providing a constructive activity for youths. In recent years Pan Trinbago has negotiated with the new PNM government for the payment of funds that the NAR administration had promised for major steelband programs. There is hope that such support will help the pan movement to position itself more effectively to exploit the growing international market for steelband instruments and music.

Panorama and Carnival

Though there is little or no economic incentive for playing pan, pannists remain devoted to their bands and to the perfection of their musical skills. Their efforts are focused on public performances, and success at these occasions is the primary goal of all steelbands. There bands experience a sense of achievement and establish reputations in the eyes of each other and the public at large. In preparation for performances, pannists marshall all of their available resources and make a range of organizational and aesthetic decisions that are calculated to bring victory. Even at occasions where there is no formal competition, bands work very hard to impress their audiences and to outplay each other. Victories are followed by celebration and boasting, defeats by a careful review of errors and the formulation of a strategy for the next musical encounter.

The first major event for steelbands each year is Panorama. Since this competition is just one highlight of the Carnival season, it is best understood in the context of the other activities that occur during this festive time of the year. Though the Carnival season officially does not open until after New Year's Day, preparation by a range of Carnival artists begins long before this.

Soon after Ash Wednesday, masquerade bandleaders and designers start planning their themes and costumes for the following Carnival. Eventually they initiate efforts to obtain the variety of necessary materials from local and foreign sources. By the latter part of the year bands start holding their *launchings* at which drawings of costumes are displayed to the public for the first time. Then the bands' craftsmen and seamstresses begin the actual production of the costumes. After New Year's this process intensifies and *mas camps* (masquerade band headquarters) are filled with workers until the wee hours of the morning. Particular attention is given to the costumes for the kings and queens of bands. These costumes, along with those of other special figures, are judged at a multi-round competition that is held in the Queen's Park

Savannah before the arrival of Carnival. Whole bands are then judged on Carnival Monday and Tuesday for the "Band of the Year" title and other awards.

During the weeks before Carnival, prospective masqueraders visit various camps where they inspect the costume drawings and decide in which band they will play that year. They then purchase costumes that often cost over $500 TT each. Large bands in Port of Spain have hundreds or even a few thousand masqueraders and thus are substantial business as well as creative enterprises. Unlike steelbands they are not community-based but are made up of players from all over the city, from elsewhere in Trinidad, and even from overseas. Some, however, have certain images related to class and color and attract members along these lines.

Another major sphere of activity during the Carnival season is calypso. Soon after one Carnival is over, calypsonians begin composing calypsos for the next. Some of these songs provide commentary on current political events, social trends, or scandals, while others deal with male-female relationships or with Carnival arts and festivity. In the course of the year the top calypsonians record a few of their pieces, and by the following January these recordings are regularly played on the local radio stations and on stereo systems in maxi-taxis. Once the calypsos are released, there is much discussion about their wit, insight, and musical quality, and some of the more daring ones generate considerable controversy.

Immediately after New Year's the calypso tents (halls) open in downtown Port of Spain, and patrons jam themselves into the tightly packed seating for evenings of intimate entertainment. Each tent has a resident brass band and a roster of calypsonians who perform their compositions throughout the Carnival season. Also present is the tent's emcee, who is responsible not only for introducing the performers but for maintaining a continuous delivery of jokes and banter between selections. The featured calypsonians all cultivate unique and generally flamboyant images, and their performances are carefully crafted dramas in which they act out the lyrics of their songs through appropriate dress, body movement, and gesture. Sometimes props and additional actors or dancers are also utilized. Audiences voice their approval of a calypsonian by the number of times they call him or her back onstage to deliver another verse of a selection. In addition to the informal musical battles in tents each night, calypsonians formally compete for the Calypso Monarch title and various other honors.

In 1988 Cro Cro won the calypso crown by singing "Corruption in Common Entrance," in which he argued that preference was being given to upper class and lighter skinned students in the assignment of places in the best secondary schools, and "Three Bo Rat," in which he critiqued the in-fighting that plagued the NAR Government. During this same season, Protector's "We Talking Change" questioned the NAR's slogan of "One Love" in a country with so much suffering, while Black Stalin's "We Can Make It If We Try" guided people away from emigration and toward local action. On a lighter side, David Rudder celebrated the delights of the "Bacchanal Lady," Crazy offered his mechanical services to a woman whose car was broken ("Drive It"), and Drupatee recounted how "Mr. Bissessar" revved up a Carnival fete when he started jamming with his tassa drum. On the topic of Carnival arts, Gypsy lamented the lack of appreciation for calypsonians in spite of their many contributions to society ("Respect the Calypsonian"), Chalkdust reflected on the decline of the slower and slyer style of calypso ("Calypso Cricket"), Kitchener reminisced about his love for pan during his boyhood days ("The Pan in Me"), and Commentor, in the costume of the Carnival Midnight Robber, warned of the domination of local culture by U.S. mass media ("Satellite Robber").

Along with visiting calypso tents and mas camps, many Trinidadians devote a considerable amount of time during the Carnival season to fetes. Fetes are held virtually every night of the week and include both private affairs in homes and clubs and enormous public events in parking lots. Much food and drink is available, and people dance through the night with friends and family members to the sounds of all the latest calypsos. Generally the music is provided by deejays, though the larger fetes also feature brass bands. In past years steelbands regularly performed at these occasions, but they are rarely hired at present.

The steelbands, however, are extremely busy during the Carnival season, and their activity is another focus of the public's interest. Preparation for Panorama begins toward the end of the previous year. Each band determines how many of its pans will need to be replaced before the competition and then makes arrangements with one or more tuners. Among the best-known tuners are Lincoln Noel, Bertie Marshall, Leo Coker, Bertram Kellman, Herman Guppy Brown, Kelvin "Zuzie" St. Rose, and Roland Harrigan. These individuals are in high demand and are generally able to make a living off tuning pans, while many other tuners work only on a part-time basis. Some tuners hire assistants to help with basic tuning processes such as sinking pans into the correct concave shapes and grooving individual sections for notes. Since each tuner uses slightly different techniques, bands generally try to hire the same ones from year to year in order to maintain some degree of consistency in their pans.[31]

Bands also line up arrangers before the Carnival season begins. As was already discussed, many bands employ independent arrangers and the most popular of these, such as Len "Boogsie" Sharpe, Jit Samaroo, Clive Bradley, Ray Holman, and Ken "Professor" Philmore, often secure more than one contract. As the Carnival season approaches, arrangers begin listening intently to the new calypsos and select some with which to work. Among the popular tunes of the 1988 season were Tambu's "This Party Is It," David Rudder's "Panama," and Kitchener's "The Pan in Me." In 1989 Baron's "Somebody" was a favorite with steelbands. A few steelband arrangers compose their own calypsos. For example, Ray Holman wrote "My Band" for Tokyo for the 1988 Panorama, and Boogsie Sharpe's primary band, Phase II, won the competition that year with his "Woman Is Boss." (The phenomenon of arrangers writing their own tunes for Panorama dates to 1972, when Holman composed "Pan on the Move" for Starlift.)

By January 2 rehearsals begin and pannists drift into their yards, frequently wearing old band jerseys. Some of the road side players, who perform only for Panorama, have not been seen since the previous year. There is always a great deal of excitement in the air as each band regroups and looks forward to learning its new Panorama tune. Meanwhile, there is much speculation about which arrangers and tunes other bands are using and about any internal conflicts that they may be experiencing.

Ideally, an arranger will try out at least two or three calypsos with a band before selecting one as the Panorama tune. The learning process is extremely slow and arduous since it is carried out almost entirely by ear. (Some arrangers write down melodic lines and chord progressions for their own usage.) An arranger begins by teaching musical phrases to the top players in each section of pans in a band. These players in turn teach the phrases to others in their sections. Next the phrases are drilled over and over again, both by sections independently and by the whole band, until they are committed to memory. This process is then repeated phrase by phrase through the entire arrangement of the calypso. Sometimes the arranger works on new material with the top players separately, while another individual rehearses the rest of the band. The objective is for every pannist to perform every note precisely as given. There is no improvisation. Rehearsals typically last for four or five hours and are held almost every night of the week.

A Panorama arrangement is a very complex piece of music and when completed is approximately ten minutes long. Essentially it is an elaboration on the possibilities inherent in the calypso form and rhythm, though some elements of jazz, North American pop, Latin American music, or European classical music are often incorporated.[32] The orchestra used for Panorama is immense (often including 80-100 members) and the various sections of pans all play specific roles. Generally tenors carry the melody; double tenors and double seconds double the melody, perform a counter-melody, or play chords; guitars, four-pans, and cellos play chords and short runs; and tenor basses (consisting of four pans each) and basses (consisting of six, nine, or twelve pans each) provide a foundation for the rhythmic and harmonic structure of the piece.[33] The orchestra also includes an *engine room* (rhythm section), consisting of traps sets, *timbalitas* (timbales), *tumbas* (congas), tambourines, *scratchers* (scrapers), cowbells, and irons. This section both maintains the underlying beat and generates dense polyrhythms. The irons (old brake drums) are particularly important. Often two or three of these repeat a steady rhythm while a "cutter" sounds an irregular counter-rhythm.

Arrangers tend to select calypsos with catchy melodies, harmonic complexity, and rhythmic drive. Over the past decade there has been a decided preference for *soca* music, a style of calypso that developed during the 1970s and features a strong, highly syncopated bass line. In terms of linear structure, a Panorama tune consists of an introduction, a verse, a chorus, variations on the verse and chorus, repeats, and an ending. Bridges are also used. Typical elements of arrangements include counterpoint or the interweaving of different melodic lines, shifting of the primary melody to different sections, call and response between sections, key modulations, fast runs, polyrhythms, a brisk tempo, and brief diminuendos followed by dramatic crescendos.

Though learning a Panorama tune is a very tedious process, many listeners are attracted to panyards during the weeks of rehearsals. In fact, panyards (like mas camps, calypso tents, and fete locations) become important social centers. Supporters of a band often lime in its yard for much of each evening, enjoying the music and the refreshments (such as beer, oranges, and peanuts) that are available for purchase. In the course of the season they become increasingly familiar with the nuances of their band's Panorama tune. At the same time, general pan enthusiasts visit from yard to yard to see how their favorite bands are progressing and to make predictions about the upcoming competition. If a band is playing mas for Carnival, drawings of its costumes will be on display as well.

While rehearsals usually occur at night, during the day panmen accomplish other tasks necessary to prepare their bands for the competition. Pans must be cleaned, polished, or painted, and the mobile racks on which they are mounted are repaired, painted, and sometimes decorated. Tuners also come to the yards to *blend* (tune) all of the pans that will be used in the competition.

Panorama itself is a multi-day event spread over the two-week period preceding Carnival. Preliminary rounds are currently held in the Queen's Park Savannah and in Shaw Park in Tobago, followed by regional finals in the Savannah and in Skinner Park in San Fernando. National semi-finals and finals are then held in the Savannah. Weeks in advance government workers prepare the Savannah for this competition and other Carnival events. An enormous stage is constructed in front of a permanent "Grand Stand," while a temporary "North Stand" is built on the opposite side of the stage. A dirt road (known as "the stretch") connects the stage with the street on the edge of the Savannah, and some bleachers are built along this route. Numerous enclosed booths are also constructed in the surrounding area and are rented to beverage and food vendors.

In terms of its scope and emotional appeal, Panorama is truly a national occasion. Its stature in Trinidad is equivalent to that of the World Series in the United States. In fact, it closely resembles a major sporting event: the focus is on competition and there are immense crowds with passionate loyalties toward particular bands. For weeks ahead of time fans debate the prospects of different bands, while the daily newspapers provide reports, opinions, and data similar to sports statistics. In addition, Trinidad's several lively tabloids offer gossip on conflicts and scandals in the various bands. The competition itself then receives continuous live television and radio coverage, with panels of commentators.

The preliminary round of Panorama for bands from northern and eastern Trinidad begins on the Sunday morning two weeks before Carnival. The night before, most bands start hauling their racks and pans down to the Savannah arena on large flatbed trucks. (The government covers all pan transport costs for Panorama and reportedly spends over a half million dollars every year on this alone.) A few bands, such as Desperadoes, traditionally set up encampments in the Savannah a day or two ahead of time.[34]

By early Sunday morning the Savannah is bustling with activity. Steelbands fill the area and many are busy holding last-minute rehearsals. Crowds of people begin to congregate: some groups stake out seats in the stands while others listen to the bands practice or simply mill around. The atmosphere is unmistakably one of Carnival festivity. People are here with friends and family to have a good time—to *free up* to the sounds of pan. For some the music is what is important, while others are more concerned with the general revelry of the occasion. Dress is casual, though stylish, and jerseys bearing the names of steelbands or lines from current calypsos are common. Many women wear tight and revealing clothing (cycle shorts were the rage in 1989), since Panorama and Carnival are times to *gallery* (show off) and be admired. In addition, there is heavy consumption of alcohol (mainly rum and beer) and food. Some people bring their own food, such as containers of *pelau*—a spicy stew of meat, rice, peas, and other vegetables. Vendors also offer a wide variety of foods such as chicken and shark sandwiches, *roti* (a dough casing stuffed with curried meat or shrimp, chickpeas, and potato), *souse* (pig's feet), boiled corn, coconuts, oranges, peanuts, and snow-cones.

By mid-morning the first bands scheduled to play line up along the stretch and out onto the street, which is temporarily closed to traffic. As the contest begins, the massive bands move slowly down the stretch like military regiments and wait for their turn to compete. By this point the stretch is jammed with people, and a band's supporters carefully push its racks through the crowds. The band itself continues to play its tune over and over again, while its supporters *jump up*[35] to the rhythm of the music and often sing along. Since everyone has been playing or listening to the tune for weeks, it becomes a sort of aural symbol of the band and the community. It is also a battle cry with which the band maintains enthusiasm and prepares itself for the contest. When a band's turn to perform arrives, members and supporters roll its racks up a ramp onto the stage and into positions that have been worked out ahead of time. This is a complicated process and can take at least fifteen minutes. To keep the crowd entertained, a recording of the band's musical selection (as originally performed by the calypsonian) is played over a huge sound system in the stands. In the meantime the band's followers often wander around the stage until they are forced off by officials.

The entry of a steelband onto the stage is a spectacular sight, and the audience particularly looks forward to the arrival of the most famous bands. Earl Lovelace provides a wonderful sense of Desperadoes' entry into the arena:

> To see them at the preliminaries of Panorama, organising their pans is a ceremony all its own. They come onto the savannah stage with a shaggy solidity, their captains bulky in khaki overalls, folded towels on their shoulders, some of them in dark shades and thick soled army boots, ambling with controlled nonchalance as if they had marched through the centuries of fire out of which pan emerged. And then, with their pans assembled, and silenced by the signal to commence playing, they stand, embraced and shaded and surrounded by the

magnificent architecture of their pans, dressed as for those wars long ended, as if they were waiting for the war to begin.[36]

Once a steelband is ready to play, an announcer states who they are, where they are from, how many players they have, their selected tune, and its composer and arranger. The band then launches into its ten-minute performance for the judges and audience, with its supporters jumping up on the wings of the stage. The pannists play frantically, dancing in place as they execute each note. As the performance progresses, their exuberance and the power of the music continue to build. Other key performers on the stage are the flag women, a reinterpretation of the tradition of flagmen who still lead steelbands through the streets at Carnival. Each band has at least one flag bearing its name and one or more banners that further state its identity and resources: captain, arranger, tuner(s), musical selection, and composer. The women who carry these flags and banners embody Carnival revelry and sensuality. They wear tight-fitting outfits and are experts at *wining*, a dance style involving gyrating the hips while lowering the body toward the ground. During their band's performance, they circle around the stage in order to create a festive mood and increase the band's appeal. In his calypso "Flag Woman," Kitchener describes how the movements of these popular artistes help to inspire the band and elicit a response from even the most staid members of the audience.[37] Though women are favorites in this role, some bands continue to use a flagman onstage who often has experience in twirling the flag in the traditional street manner.

A band's time onstage is its long-awaited moment of glory. If each band is an expression of its community, the culmination of this expression occurs in the Savannah where pannists display their skills before thousands of spectators and the television cameras. Here a band and its followers assert and affirm their identity in front of the nation. However, the name of the band's sponsor is also prominent on pans, jerseys, banners, and signs attached to racks. Even the many unsponsored bands are vehicles for advertising, since they generally receive free jerseys, banners, and signs from businesses such as the Carib brewery and add their own names to these. Thus Panorama performances contain multiple messages: some about festivity, creativity, and community identity, and others referring to corporate paternalism and Carnival consumption.

Audience responses to these performances vary between the Grand Stand and the North Stand. The Grand Stand is considered to be the more respectable place to sit. There people enjoy and move with the music, but usually keep to their seats. The North Stand, on the other hand, is *madness*. Those who prefer this perspective on Panorama arrive early in the morning with their coolers of beer and bottles of rum and are already in a very festive mood by the time the first band reaches the stage. As the bands play, they dance on their chairs, shout, and sing along. In addition, metal objects and the stand itself are used to create a percussive din that continues unabated the entire day. The level of revelry has become so intense over the years that in 1989 the authorities decided not to install chairs at all for the preliminaries. In the North Stand, and in the Grand Stand as well, people cheer ecstatically when their favorite bands enter and leave the stage and at high points in their performances.

In the course of the day, band after band moves onto the stage, performs, and exits on the other side where they load their racks of pans on the waiting trucks. When the sun sets, floodlights are used to illuminate the stage. In 1988, 32 bands performed and the event did not end until approximately 2:30 a.m., providing the audience with close to fifteen hours of pan.

After the preliminaries the successful bands return to their yards for more late-night rehearsals in preparation for the regional finals and national semi-finals. Written comments from the judges are used to improve performances, and arrangers add new material to the tunes as the bands move to further stages in the competition. No band wants to come out with all its "fireworks" right away. At the national finals on the Saturday night before Carnival, the top twelve bands from the semi-finals compete against the reigning champion. All of the contestants try to reach their performance peak at this point. Winning—even placing well in the finals—brings tremendous prestige and all participants receive cash prizes. Here bands maintain or enhance their reputations, and this helps them obtain new members and opportunities in the upcoming year. Bands that are eliminated early in the competition suffer and often lose a few of their players.

After the Panorama finals, pannists are finally able to get some rest. The main event of Sunday night is the Dimanche Gras show in the Savannah, which includes the calypso finals, the masquerade king and queen finals, and a variety of special performances. On Sunday there are also many all-night fetes, with deejays and brass bands supplying the music.

Then, after weeks of preparation, performances, and feting, Carnival itself arrives. Officially Carnival Monday and Tuesday are not holidays, but few people go to work. Much of downtown Port of Spain is closed off to traffic, and myriads of outdoor bars are set up with large sound systems blasting calypsos to attract customers. Like Panorama, Carnival is a national event.[38] During the Carnival season there is extensive media coverage of masquerade bands and calypsonians (as well as steelbands), and Carnival itself is televised live. One has the option of participating in the festival at various levels. The most actively involved are the pannists, calypsonians, brass band musicians, masquerade artists, and thousands of masqueraders. Then there are the crowds of people who jump up or lime on the streets throughout Monday and Tuesday. Others prefer to stay at home and watch the spectacle on television, while some people have little or no interest in it at all.

The opening of Carnival is J'Ouvert, which begins on Monday at 2:00 a.m. At this point, people begin to wander out from the all-night fetes into the streets. Spirits are particularly high and the whole town is transformed by revelry. Some people simply jump up on the streets in casual or old clothes, while others play mas. There are various types of devils, such as Jab Molassis (covered with black grease) and blue devils (covered with a blue dye). Mud mas, in which people coat their bodies with wet clay, is also common. One local interpretation of this masque is that it represents zombies who have come back from the earth. Devil mas and mud mas are both often accompanied by metal percussion instruments such as brake drums, biscuit tins, and other containers. Also popular at J'Ouvert is ol' mas, which, as mentioned earlier, involves dressing up in old and ludicrous clothes and using props and signs to make satirical statements on local politics or other current events. In addition to these traditional forms of masquerade, some J'Ouvert bands have recently been coming out with simple costumes on themes like those portrayed by the large mas bands of Monday afternoon and Tuesday.

Though deejays and brass bands accompany some masqueraders, J'Ouvert is the part of Carnival in which steelbands continue to have a strong presence. Steelbands are everywhere, and it is possible to stand in the middle of Port of Spain before the sun rises and hear a beautiful cacophony of pan from all directions. The bands inch slowly through the dark and crowded streets with their flagmen and followers. In past years bands used their mobile racks, while now most rest their pans on flatbed trucks or other vehicles. Though bands used to play bomb tunes for J'Ouvert, Panorama selections are generally performed at present. Revelers around the bands jump up with much passion and wine aggressively against each other. Many are simply dressed in old clothes, though some bands include masqueraders. In 1988, for example, Merrytones played devils and created a genuinely macabre effect. A number of individuals from their community covered themselves with black

grease and some wore horns and carried pitch forks. One dragged another along by a chain. The most impressive of the group was a master
of traditional devil body movements: he maintained a glazed look in his
eyes, ran about in a frenzied manner, gyrated his shoulders, and lunged
his head forward in random directions.

J'Ouvert is essentially a continuation of the Canboulay tradition of
the nineteenth century, in which there was a focus on vigorous percussion, demonic and threatening masques, and ludicrous parody. (Note
the similarity between Merrytones' presentation in 1988 and the description of the 1847 Carnival, cited in Chapter One, in which a band of
masqueraders in black varnish dragged one member along by a chain.)
It is in the darkness and dawn of J'Ouvert that the underworld dimension of Carnival is manifested: grim and sinister characters, dirty and
coarse costumes, and aggressive verbal and physical action.

In contrast to this diabolical revelry, the masquerades of Monday afternoon and Tuesday occur in bright sunlight and are full of splendor.
Exquisite costumes are made of fine and fancy materials in an array of
brilliant colors. The themes portrayed by the masquerade bands vary
widely. In 1989, for example, there was "Heromyth" by Wayne Berkeley's band, "War Dance" (an American Indian mas) by Raoul Garib,
"Polynesia" by Edmund Hart, and "Japanorama" by Max Awon. The
threatening side of Carnival was represented as well in Peter Minshall's
"Santimanitay" (*sans humanité*—"without mercy"), which portrayed a variety of malevolent figures and forces. In addition, the veteran Jason
Griffith continues to bring out spectacular fancy sailor bands, and in
1989 presented "Alkebulan, Reflection of a Sailor's Vision" (portraying
sailors ashore in Africa). Music for these and the many other masquerade bands is supplied by brass bands and/or deejays. On both Monday
and Tuesday the masqueraders move slowly through the crowded
streets and generally parade through the Queen's Park Savannah and
other locations where their portrayals are judged. They jump up and
wine throughout the two days, but often save their best performances
for when they cross the judging points. Television cameras are focused
on the Savannah stage and it is here that gallerying reaches a climax.[39]

On Monday afternoon the steelbands generally rest but some appear
on the streets for Tuesday. Occasionally they present masquerades and
sailors remain a favorite. In 1988, for example, Desperadoes played
"USS Despers on Shore Leave" which included sailors, firemen with
beards and stokers, and even a model boat. Steelbands, however, are
more likely to be on the streets during Monday and Tuesday nights. On
Monday night there are a few small pan contests, organized by Pan Trinbago and sponsored by the Carib brewery and other firms, which pro-

vide a diversion for the large crowds of people playing fashionable night mas or simply roaming the streets. The most popular of these events is a bomb competition. Though steelbands now spend most of the Carnival season learning their Panorama tunes, they often still find some time to work out arrangements of foreign tunes in calypso rhythm. Some of the bombs performed in 1988 were Bach's "Air on the G String," the Beatles' "Yesterday," Madonna's "La Isla Bonita," Atlantic Star's "Always," and the themes from *Dr. Zhivago* and *The Young and the Restless* (an American soap opera that is immensely popular in Trinidad).

Tuesday night is known as *Las Lap* and is a traditional time to have one last jump-up behind a steel or brass band. Though some people still follow bands through the streets, others simply dance to the recorded music that blasts from the stationary sound systems associated with bars. Pan enthusiasts often attend yet another steelband competition, this one sponsored by Berger Paints. At midnight the lengthy season of festivity is officially over and the weary revelers begin wandering home.

The Trinidad Carnival is in essence a tremendous outburst of creative expression in music, body movement, language, and material art. Participants want both to "free up" and to be innovative—to move beyond the recurrent structures of experience. In masquerade they explore the entire natural, cultural, and imaginary world; in calypso they comment on the shifting characteristics of their own lives. The steelband, in turn, remains vital both because its percussive sounds are a powerful inspiration for festivity and because its uniqueness makes it a central symbol of the process in which the Carnival tradition has been localized. Panorama is certainly the most popular of all the Carnival competitions. Commitments to calypsonians and mas bands are generally not as strong as steelband loyalties. All the competitions generate a great deal of interest, but at Panorama community pride is at stake. The victories and defeats of steelbands, as played out on the Panorama stage, evoke community-wide celebration or dejection and echo people's trials and potential.

For decades local observers of Carnival have reiterated a belief that the festival "breaks down social barriers" and produces a sense that "All ah we is one." People are in fact more accommodating during Carnival. Many revelers pay less attention to prevailing social rules and are willing to drink and wine with others on the streets, with little concern for who they are or where they come from. But ultimately Carnival does not so much "bring the society together" as temporarily compress it. In sharing the same public spaces, people are forced to encounter each other in ways that differ from the customary interactions of the rest of the year. Of course some people attempt to avoid such direct encounters by attending fetes or playing in mas bands that cater to certain social groups. Still, the overwhelming spectacle of Carnival as it is experienced on the streets and broadcast by television creates a heightened awareness of the nation's diverse population. This awareness is articulated most explicitly in calypsos, which routinely illustrate and critique class, color, ethnic, and gender differences and sometimes evoke as much anger as laughter. But masquerade provides a similar medium of expression as people take off their clothes, try on other identities, and confront each other in the blazing sun. If Carnival is a national fete, it is one in which the society's fractures and dissonance, as well as its liaisons and desire for unity, are revealed in all of their nuances.[40]

The Steelband Music Festival

After Panorama and Carnival, the Steelband Music Festival (also called "Pan is Beautiful") is the next most important occasion for pan performance in Trinidad. This multi-round competition is held every other year, generally in October, and requires far more preparation than Panorama, since each band must learn three pieces of music: a test piece, a calypso, and a tune of choice. Rehearsals begin months in advance and are held several nights a week. Because of the amount of time involved and the complexity of the different genres of music, only the most skilled and dedicated pannists participate in this event. Some bands are unable or choose not to attend at all, and those that do compete usually have sides of under fifty players.

In preparing for the Festival, steelbands give special attention to the selection of their tunes of choice. Generally they turn to music of the European classical tradition since orchestral scores are readily available. In addition, the performance of classical pieces is perceived to be particularly demanding and the most effective way of impressing the adjudicators. Over the years pannists have shown a decided preference for music from the Romantic period because of its complexity, richness, and drama. This pattern continued in the 1988 Festival. For example, Desperadoes (the victors) played Tchaikovsky's "Marche Slave," Trinidad All Stars selected Tchaikovsky's "Capriccio Italien," Harmonites rendered the Overture from Wagner's *Rienzi*, Pamberi performed the Overture from Wagner's *The Flying Dutchman*, and both Merrytones and Tropical Angel Harps chose the Fourth Movement of Rimsky-Korsakov's *Scheherazade*. Pieces from the Baroque and Classical periods have also been played regularly at past Festivals but are less popular now, since they are thought to be insufficiently adventurous.

A desire for new and innovative music has led some bands to begin experimenting with twentieth-century compositions. For example, Pamberi performed part of Copland's *Billy the Kid* in 1984 and an excerpt from Stravinsky's *The Rite of Spring* in 1986. At the 1988 Festival, Renegades performed "Mars" from Holst's *The Planets,* Phase II chose Gershwin's *Rhapsody in Blue,* and Our Boys played part of Copland's *Appalachian Spring.* In 1988 there was one selection from the jazz tradition as well: Billy Strayhorn's "Take the A Train," rendered by Bidco Invaders from Guyana. Occasionally local compositions are used as tunes of choice. Desmond Waithe, a music teacher and arranger, interpreted Sparrow's "The Slave" for Nutones in 1980; and Boogsie Sharpe has composed several pieces over the years, such as "The Three Seasons," which was performed by Skiffle Bunch in 1988. In 1988 a number of contestants in the soloist category of the Festival also played original selections, and the test pieces for both regular and pan-around-the-neck bands were locally composed.

Some steelbands have at least one member who can read music and arrange a classical piece for pan, while others employ music teachers or other formally trained musicians.[41] Long in advance of the Festival, a band's arranger and leaders begin listening to possible tunes of choice. Once they have made a selection, they obtain the full orchestral score for the piece. The arranger then begins assigning the musical parts of the various orchestral instruments to the different pans. Since there is not an exact equivalency in ranges, each type of pan often plays the parts of multiple orchestral instruments in the course of the arrangement. In Kendall Lewis's arrangement of *Scheherazade* for Merrytones, tenor pans played first violin, second violin, flute, oboe, clarinet, and trumpet parts. Double tenors and double seconds substituted for the first violins, second violins, violas, oboes, clarinets, trumpets, trombones, and the harp. The quadrophonic played second violin, viola, and trombone parts. Guitars, four-pans, and cellos replaced violas, cellos, and trombones. And tenor basses and basses played contrabass, bassoon, and tuba parts. All the original percussion instruments in the composition were also used by Merrytones, including the gong, which was struck only once.

A few arrangers write out the various parts for pannists who can read music, but most of the learning process occurs by ear. A piece is taught phrase by phrase and drilled for months until every note is played correctly. Toward the end of the rehearsal season, arrangers focus on details of phrasing and dynamics. Meanwhile, bands learn the festival test piece (for which there is a score) and work out arrangements of their calypsos.

The Festival itself is a unique adaptation of a European classical music concert or competition. Approximately eight regular bands compete at a time. Since the process of setting up pans requires a great deal of effort, the event is held at the Jean Pierre Complex, a sports facility with an outdoor court large enough to accommodate all the contestants scheduled for each night. Pans are mounted on individual stands and arranged in a manner that resembles the layout of a European orchestra. In front of each band is a conductor's podium and a table and chairs for the adjudicators. Since the Festival is held at night, the court is flood-lit and the chromed and brightly polished pans glisten. Potted plants are placed in the center of the court and colorful banners and flags are suspended on the sides. The atmosphere is one of formality: members of the audience dress up for the occasion and are subdued. While waiting for the competition to begin, they chat with each other and read their printed programs.

The event opens with a performance of the national anthem on tenor pan. A few introductory comments are then made by representatives of Pan Trinbago and the government. Eventually the adjudicators are introduced and escorted onto the court; in 1988 one was from Trinidad, another from England, and a third from the United States. A standard format is followed throughout the evening. After a band is announced, its members walk single file onto the court and take their positions behind their pans. They wear elegant dress pants and shirts or skirts and blouses. The band's conductor (usually the arranger) is then escorted to the podium. After the band and conductor bow in unison to the adjudicators, they begin their first selection which is almost always the test piece. At the conclusion of this piece, there is a pause during which the adjudicators write down their comments. Next the band usually plays its tune of choice, followed by its calypso. For the performance of the test piece and tune of choice, the pannists are tense and focused on the conductor. A conductor is not usually used for the calypso, and at this point they loosen up and move in rhythm with the music in a manner reminiscent of Panorama. A similar pattern is apparent in the audience's responses during the performances: while they are restrained for the test piece and tune of choice, they begin to move with the calypso and a few even get up from their seats. All of the music, though, is much appreciated and the audience applauds when each band comes onto the court and at the conclusion of each selection.

At the end of the evening, there is a long wait for the adjudicators to finish their deliberations. Once they are ready, all of the bands are called back onto the court. The judges then carefully read their comments and scores for every selection by every band. Afterwards the bands receive written copies of these remarks and study them in preparation for further rounds in the competition.

By the time of the finals the contestants have been narrowed down to eight regular bands, three pan-around-the-neck sides, and five soloists.[42] This night is a truly grand affair and is televised live. The stadium is packed and special seats on the edges of the court are reserved for dignitaries and for guests of Pan Trinbago and the sponsor. Everyone is dressed more formally and many of the pannists are now in suits and ties. The evening opens with a ceremonial display of all of the Festival participants on the court: bands, soloists, adjudicators, and Pan Trinbago's and the sponsor's personnel. After a performance of the national anthem, there are speeches by Pan Trinbago officers. In 1988 there was also a dedication of the Festival to the deceased George Goddard, the great leader of the steelband movement from the 1950s through the 1970s. After this opening ceremony, the most intense competition of the Festival begins, with all of the contestants attempting to top their previous performances.

When the Steelband Music Festival is compared with Panorama, a number of sharp contrasts are apparent. At Panorama steelband music is part of the general experience of Carnival revelry, while at the Festival the focus is on pan alone. The Festival is essentially a celebration of the pan as an instrument and is an opportunity to explore its possibilities. There is also more concern that competition contribute to the development of musical skills, and the importance of evaluation is made explicit in the practice of having the adjudicators actually read their comments to the contestants. Because of this focus on musical perfection, the Festival is a real pannists' affair. Many pannists consider victory here to be more prestigious than at Panorama. While bands expand in size for Panorama, only the best players participate in the Festival. In addition, there is much discussion among pannists about the different bands' performances and how they compare with the highlights of past years. In short, the Festival is an occasion at which the pan community evaluates itself, while providing entertainment for the pan enthusiasts who make up the audience.

The contrast between the Festival and Panorama can also be considered in terms of stage and street orientations. Along the continuum of steelband performance settings in Trinidad, Carnival most fully embodies the street orientation with its fluidity of movement, informal encounters, and revelry. Similarly, Panorama reflects a street orientation: the stage is literally an extension of the street and crowds of revelers follow their favorite steelbands in the same way that they do at Carnival. At the Festival, on the other hand, there is clearly a stage orientation. Instead of a parade of bands through open space, there is a static display of pans in orchestral formation within a contained venue. A sense of formality prevails. In contrast to the casual dress, heavy drinking, and general revelry of Panorama, the audience dresses smartly and is relatively sedate. The pannists in turn replace their band jerseys with suits. Audience responses to the bands also differ. At Panorama there is a sense of participation in the music: people dance, cheer, and even create percussion instruments of their own. At the Festival, on the other hand, the audience engages in distanced appreciation and evaluation, and for the most part shows its approval in polite applause.

These street and stage performance orientations are related to notions of reputation and respectability and to some degree parallel verbal performance styles in the West Indies as described by Roger Abrahams. Abrahams discusses how men, in the world of the road or street, achieve reputations through aggressive, witty, and competitive usage of Creole English. This performance style reaches a peak during street festivities such as Carnival. In contrast to the sense of license in the street is the concern with respectability, order, and decorum in the home and other indoor settings. This concern is prominent at special family occasions, such as *thanksgivings*, where there is formal and elaborate oratory in local standard English.[43]

In the case of steelband performances, calypso, with its thoroughly local expressive qualities, corresponds to Creole English. At street occasions such as Carnival and Panorama, bands achieve reputations through aggressive and spirited performances of calypsos in an atmosphere of license and revelry. Competition and reputation-seeking also occur at the Steelband Music Festival, but within the context of respectability. Here steelband interpretations of European classical music are prominent, just as there is an emphasis on local standard English at indoor ceremonial events. Decorum and solemnity prevail in the overall organization of the Festival, and in the execution and evaluation of classical selections and the test piece.

The Festival and Panorama also differ in terms of the statements that they make about national identity. Panorama is local in orientation. It is devoted exclusively to calypso and is an integral part of the process in which Carnival has developed as a local celebration. The Festival, however, combines local practices with a cosmopolitan orientation. Pannists conceive of the competition as a chance to explore different musical traditions and discover new ways of using the pan. Though some critics continue to argue that they should not play European music, pannists pay little attention to these suggestions. Generally they perceive pan both as Trinidadian and as something that has transcended the local tradition to become part of the international music scene. This orientation is also apparent in Pan Trinbago's continued use of foreign as well as local adjudicators and in their decision to open the 1988 Festival to foreign bands.

The international scope of the competition in 1988 sparked much interest among pannists and was commended by the press. The *Trinidad Guardian* stated:

A new vision and, hopefully, a new era seem to be opening up for our steelband. The objective is nothing less than the dynamic and fruitful realisation of steelband music's global potential. . . . how fitting it is that the country which gave sweet steelband music to the world should now be staging the world's first steelband festival![44]

The *Daily Express* commented:

Today, the steelband movement is the institution of which Trinidadians are most proud and the instrument, itself, has won wide acceptance among the family of instruments that bring music to the world. . . .

The steelpan has long ceased to be a Trinidadian instrument, restricted to Trinidad and Trinidadians. Trinidadians who yearn for those days do themselves and their beloved instrument a disservice not unlike that done by people who preach in every speech and every article, that it is the 20th century's only new instrument.

We no longer have to prove anything to anybody about pan. It has long proven itself, and Pan Trinbago, by throwing open the Festival to all-comers has shown itself to be conscious of that truth.[45]

The Festival and Panorama thus represent two different visions of Trinidadian identity. Panorama affirms indigenous cultural traditions and experiences and their importance for formulating a sense of nationhood. The Festival, on the other hand, represents Trinidad as a cosmopolitan nation—as a people who participate in transnational arts. These local and cosmopolitan orientations are examples of what Clifford Geertz refers to as "essentialism" and "epochalism" in the nationalist movements of the postwar world. After colonies have achieved independence, ideologizing shifts from opposition to colonial power to definitions of national identity. Geertz suggests that nations emphasize, to varying degrees, "The Indigenous Way of Life" (essentialism) and "The Spirit of the Age" (epochalism):

To stress the first of these is to look to local mores, established institutions, and the unities of common experience—to "tradition," "culture," "national character," or even "race"—for the roots of a new
identity. To stress the second is to look to the general outlines of the
history of our time, and in particular to what one takes to be the overall direction and significance of that history.[46]

In Trinidad and Tobago there has been promotion of both essentialism
and epochalism, and Panorama and the Steelband Music Festival are
two of the nation's artistic events that enable people to explore these
complementary conceptions of themselves.[47]

Though there is an emphasis on cosmopolitanism in the Steelband
Music Festival, the event also has a local dimension. European classical
music and the European concert setting are in fact perceived by
Trinidadians not as entirely foreign but as integral parts of their own experience. They are traditions that Trinidadians have perpetuated and
reworked to suit their own sensibilities and aesthetics. This process of
localization is particularly apparent at the Festival where steelbands re-
create European classics and give them a new sound. In addition, calypso is an important part of the Festival. When steelbands launch into
their exuberant arrangements of calypsos, they temporarily evoke the
spirit of Carnival and affirm the distinctively local qualities of the pan
tradition.

The Steelband in Other Street and Stage Settings

A European-to-local style-switch is also apparent in the structure of Independence Day celebrations in Trinidad. For Independence Day in
1988, large crowds of people gathered in the Queen's Park Savannah
for the official ceremony at 8:00 a.m. In formation on the grounds were
the nation's various armed and unarmed service contingents—the regiment, the coast guard, the police, the fire service, and medical/rescue
groups. Music was provided not by steelbands but by the police and regiment marching bands. The ceremony opened with the national anthem. Then President Noor Hassanali was driven around the grounds
in a Land Rover to inspect the service groups. During this procedure
the bands played two current calypsos in march rhythm. Following the
inspection there was a formal march of the groups in front of the President and the Grand Stand, while the bands performed a few more selections in march rhythm, including a British military tune and a sea

chantey. The ceremony ended at approximately 9:00 a.m. with a 21-gun salute and a repeat of the national anthem.

Following this display of military order, the crowds rushed outside the Savannah to prepare for the traditional jump-up that occurs as the bands and service groups parade through the streets to the St. James police barracks. At this point the musicians began to perform calypsos in calypso rhythm and with much verve. The streets were filled with people along the entire route of the parade, and the event assumed something of a Carnival atmosphere.

Ethnomusicologist Morton Marks argues that style-switching of this type is common in the popular music events of peoples of African descent in the New World. Musical performances that begin with a European orientation often gradually take on African characteristics such as polyrhythm, call and response, and manipulation of pitch and timbre. These shifts, Marks suggests, often express statements about cultural identity.[48]

In the case of Independence Day celebrations in Trinidad, the shift from European march style to local calypso style creates a sense of freeing-up for the spectators and seems to encapsulate symbolically the nation's transition from colonialism to independence. The steelband, as a primary symbol of independence and local identity, is also prominently featured in the celebrations. By late afternoon on Independence Day in 1988, several steelbands began proceeding from the Memorial Park (near the Savannah) to Woodford Square in the downtown area.[49] There was a distinct feeling of Carnival festivity as bands played calypsos and people jumped up around them. In the meantime a number of other bands set up their pans in Woodford Square and performed calypsos (as well as other selections) for the assembled crowd.[50]

This final event in Woodford Square is an example of what are locally known as *blocos* (*blocoramas* —block parties) or *pan jams*. Steelbands first began holding blocos in the late 1960s; by the mid-1970s there were blocos virtually every weekend of the year. These events then began to die out, both because they were uneconomical and because they were sometimes exploited by promoters from outside the steelband movement. However, they continued to be held occasionally, and with the recession made something of a comeback, since they provided a free form of entertainment.

Though Pan Trinbago occasionally organizes blocos, most are held by individual steelbands. A host band issues an invitation to one or more guest bands. The guest bands' stage sides then travel to the host band's yard and set up their pans either there or in the adjacent street

area. Usually a sizable crowd of people from the surrounding community is attracted, as well as panmen from outside the neighborhood who
enjoy attending any steelband performance. The host band hopes to
earn some money from the affair by setting up a bar. It then compen-
sates the guest bands by covering their transportation expenses and supplying them with free drinks. Often blocos are connected with special
occasions. For example, Cordettes (from Sangre Grande) held a pan
jam with seven bands in celebration of their 25th anniversary in 1987.
On May 1, 1988, Tokyo and Pandemonium performed for the John
John Sports and Family Day in a basketball court near Tokyo's yard and,
for Father's Day that year, Blue Diamonds held a bloco on the street
outside their yard in eastern Port of Spain. Some bands, such as Renegades and Trinidad All Stars, often hold pan jams during the Carnival
season.

The format for blocos is always the same. After the sun goes down and
the bands have set up their pans, each takes a turn performing several
selections. While a band is playing, the audience crowds around it on all
sides. People may move with the music but rarely dance. Bloco performances are primarily for listening, and the audience shows its approval
by applauding at the end of each selection. Generally bands play a variety of calypsos and American pop tunes, though they occasionally include Latin or reggae selections. Panorama tunes are almost always
performed, along with other calypsos from the past few years. (At pan
jams during the Carnival season, calypsos are usually played exclusively.) Among the many American tunes in the repertoires of steelbands in 1988 were Lionel Richie's "Lady in Red," Stevie Wonder's
"Overjoyed," Marvyn Gaye's "Night Shift," Kenny Roger's "Lady," Linda
Rondstadt and James Ingram's "Somewhere Out There," and the swing
standard, "In the Mood." When a band has finished performing its selections, there is usually a brief intermission with music provided by a
deejay. Then the next band begins to play and everyone crowds around
it. Informal competition between bands is definitely a part of these occasions, and audience members evaluate the quality of the various performances.

Blocos are community events in a street setting: they are free of
charge and easily accessible to the residents around panyards. When
evening arrives and the bands begin to play, families and groups of
friends drift into the street to share in the entertainment. In addition to
being expressions of community solidarity, blocos help maintain good
relationships among bands by establishing a whole system of convivial
exchanges. When a band invites another to its yard, it can expect to
eventually receive an invitation in return. Bands perform for the benefit

of each other at blocos, and these performances are one of the few types in which all monies generated remain in the hands of the pannists.[51]

In addition to these neighborhood street events, the stage sides of steelbands sometimes play in concert settings outside their communities. In the past some bands regularly performed in hotels and nightclubs. At present only the Hilton Hotel routinely features pan in its floor shows, while a handful of clubs occasionally invite steelbands to perform. In Tobago, where there is a more developed tourist industry, a few hotels regularly employ steelbands.

Steelbands also occasionally give concerts in other types of settings. Since 1987 the Central Bank has held an annual series of late-afternoon pan concerts in its outdoor plaza in downtown Port of Spain in celebration of independence. Otherwise most concerts are organized by steelbands themselves. Certainly the epitome of concert or stage pan occurs at Queen's Hall where top bands periodically give performances. These are very formal and genteel affairs and attract primarily middle and upper class patrons. They are also impressive displays of the versatility of the pan and of virtuoso musicianship. A wide range of music is performed and pans are often combined with other instruments and with choirs.

Trinidad All Stars, for example, have been giving concerts in Queen's Hall for a number of years. Among the selections in their 1987 program were Strauss's "Tales from the Vienna Woods" and the "Battle Hymn of the Republic," performed with the Love Movement Choir. The band was also joined by a pianist (Gillian Nathaniel-Balintulo) and a clarinetist (Sergeant C. Ross) for a rendition of Gershwin's *Rhapsody in Blue*. Another highlight of 1987 was a joint Christmas concert by Desperadoes and the Lydian Singers. For this occasion, Desperadoes performed some items alone: Chopin's "Etude in A Flat" ("El Relicario"), Offenbach's "Orpheus in the Underworld," and five pieces from Saint-Saëns's *Carnival of the Animals*. In addition, there were carols in which voices were combined with pan and a performance of Handel's "Hallelujah Chorus" that incorporated trumpets and a saxophone as well. Even more innovative was a joint performance by Phase II and the Noble Douglas Dance Company in 1988 in which the two ensembles explored possibilities for combining pan with contemporary dance.[52]

Pan virtuosity is also much in evidence in "Pan Ramajay," an annual multi-round competition that was introduced in 1989 by the Exodus Steel Orchestra. This event is currently held in August at the National Flour Mills compound on Wrightson Road. Stage sides with no more than ten members each perform both a calypso and a tune of choice for the panel of judges and the enthusiastic audience of other pannists and pan fans. The idea behind this competition was to highlight the unique musical skills and sound of small ensembles. In contrast to the huge bands and tight arrangements of Panorama, Pan Ramajay places emphasis on improvisation ("ramajaying") and the subtle interaction between band members. Though some critics of the event have noted that there is often little actual improvisation in the pannists' solos, there is much room for display of imaginative arrangements and technical skills. Furthermore, in 1993 a soloist category was added to the competition in which each contestant pulls the name of a calypso out of a hat and is required to improvise on this selection with a conventional rhythm section.[53]

Over the years virtuoso pan soloists have become increasingly prominent in the steelband movement. Among the top artists of today are Robert Greenidge, Rudy "Tulef" Smith, Len "Boogsie" Sharpe, Othello Molineaux, Ken "Professor" Philmore, Earl Rodney, Earl Brooks, Annise "Halfers" Hadeed, Sydney Joseph, Clive Telemaque, Selwyn Springer, and Liam Teague. Several of these individuals live abroad, at least for part of the year, and have made major contributions to the internationalization of pan. Most are active in both calypso and pop music. They often arrange Panorama tunes and other pieces for steelbands and sometimes perform with calypsonians on recordings and in tents. Boogsie Sharpe, Ken Philmore, Earl Brooks, and Sydney Joseph have also appeared as soloists on Pan Assembly's calypso and pop recordings where they are backed by conventional instruments. A few of these virtuosos have worked with foreign popular music stars. Robert Greenidge, for example, has recorded with musicians such as John Lennon, Ringo Starr, Taj Mahal, Grover Washington, Ralph MacDonald, Barry Manilow, Jimmy Buffett, and Earth, Wind and Fire.[54]

Pan soloists have found jazz to be a particularly rich medium for improvisation and experimentation. In support of this interest, a series of Pan Jazz Festivals has been held since 1986 at various venues in Port of Spain. The festivals feature groups that include a pannist as well as ensembles from other jazz traditions. Over the years most of the soloists mentioned above have appeared, as have ensembles led by local artists such as Andre Tanker, Michael "Toby" Tobias, Clive Alexander (Zanda), Michael Boothman, Raf Robertson, and Mungal Patasar (a sitarist). Among the many foreign guests have been American pannist Andy Narell, the West Indies Jazz Band (led by Luther François of St. Lucia, with Annise Hadeed on pan), the Courtney Pine Jazz Reggae Band, Dizzy Gillespie and the Arturo Sandoval Group, the Paquito d'Rivera Quintet, the Hilton Ruiz Latin Jazz Allstars, the Gonzalo Mico Quartet, the Tania Maria Septet, the Tommy Flanagan Trio, the Stanley

Turrentine Quintet, the Freddie Hubbard Quintet, the Wynton Marsalis Quartet, the Roy Hargrove Quintet, and the Alain-Jean Marie Quartet.

Though pan soloists usually have associations with particular steelbands, they basically lead independent careers and are often professionals or semi-professionals. This is an entirely different type of existence from that of most panmen. The great majority of panmen not only are underemployed but earn little or no money from pan. For them playing pan is something that is done in a panyard, and they conceive of themselves as members of bands that are based in communities. Their musicianship for the most part is focused on competitions, Carnival, and neighborhood events. Top pan soloists, however, operate outside steelbands and communities and in a number of cases even outside Trinidad. From their perspective the pan is not simply a component of a large steel orchestra which engages in competitions, but a unique instrument which can be combined with any other instrument and used in any type of musical setting. In short, they are part of the process in which the pan is taken beyond distinctively local experiences of the street, the community, and Carnival.

Ian Jones, a Trinidadian pannist, arranger, and composer who emigrated to Canada, suggests that the virtuosity of individual pannists is vital to international acceptance of the instrument:

> Pan has been marketed as a band rather than an instrument. We have concentrated on what is an ethnic format. The steel orchestra is the format in which pan developed in Trinidad and how it remains among Caribbean people abroad. But that isn't necessarily how the rest of the world will accept it.

Jones adds that, though large steelbands will continue to exist in West Indian contexts, he is interested in exploring "the magic of pan as an instrument which is capable of taking its rightful place among the world's instruments."[55]

At present cosmopolitan pan soloists are still only a very small minority. For most people, pan involves large bands that are rooted in local cultural practices. Even with the recession, exorbitant costs, and few lucrative performance opportunities, large bands remain active. In the end, most pannists are less interested in having economically viable ensembles than in creating magnificent orchestras with tremendous musical richness and power. It is the sheer size of steelbands that makes them so awesome as they move through the streets at Carnival or onto the Panorama stage. Furthermore, steelbands are inclusive organizations. Panyards are open to everyone, and novices are encouraged to develop their musical skills and to become band members. Wide participation is in fact emphasized much more than individual virtuosity. Pannists strive for individual excellence but with the aim of perfecting the band as a whole. Playing pan is perceived as a group activity, and for the most part it is steelbands rather than individual pannists that achieve musical reputations in Trinidad. Thus communities continue to build large bands, and through collective effort hope to become victorious in the national arena.[56]

Chapter Six
The *Steelband*: Cultural Creativity and the Construction of Identities

In his essay entitled "History, Fable and Myth in the Caribbean and the Guianas," the Guyanese novelist Wilson Harris calls for a history of the region that moves beyond the chronicling of imperialism to include "inner time" and "the arts of the imagination." One of the folk arts that Harris uses to disclose the West Indian experience more fully is the limbo. He suggests that this dance, which Africans may have first performed during the Middle Passage, was "a certain kind of gateway or threshold to a new world," and represented "the renascence of a new corpus of sensibility that could translate and accommodate African and other legacies within a new architecture of cultures." In addition, he states, "It is my view—a deeply considered one—that this ground of accommodation, this art of creative coexistence—pointing away from apartheid and ghetto fixations—is of utmost importance and native to the Caribbean, perhaps to the Americas as a whole."[1]

The present study of the steelband movement has been an effort to demonstrate the importance of the musical imagination in the creation of Trinidad and Tobago as a nation. Over the years musical performances have been a salient means by which the various sectors of the society have negotiated their co-existence. The steelband is essentially a culmination of a long process of musical creolization, a process in which diverse musical traditions have been locally re-created. Among the many sources of steelband music are Afro-Trinidadian tamboo bamboo, metallic percussion, and Orisha drumming; the calypso tradition of vocals and string-band accompaniment, which itself is a creole synthesis of African, French, Spanish, and British musical elements; Indo-Trinidadian tassa drumming; European marching band and classical traditions; Afro/Latin American dance rhythms and tunes; and North American popular songs and jazz. Clearly, the panmen's musical sensibility has been open and inclusive: they have continually drawn on the entirety of their experience to fabricate a new and distinctively local music.

This localizing dimension of creolization is sometimes referred to by scholars of the Caribbean as "indigenization." For example, John Stewart, in his ethnographic and fictional account of Trinidadian village life, describes indigenization as the process by which people create themselves in the place in which they find themselves. From this perspective he suggests that cultural pluralism in the Caribbean is best understood, not as an explanation of the contemporary social order, but as a historical condition which people attempt to transcend through cultural strategies such as syncretism, accommodation, and acculturation. Stewart notes that one manifestation of indigenization in Trinidad is that "typical" "African" and "Indian" behavior patterns are increasingly perceived by locals less as ethnic properties than as actions that anyone may employ in appropriate situations.[2]

Concepts of cultural pluralism and integration have been for years a central theme of studies of Trinidad and of the West Indies as a whole. From the 1950s until his death in 1993, M. G. Smith, one of the Caribbean's most illustrious anthropologists, persistently described the region as consisting of "plural societies."[3] Though he revised his analytical framework over the years, Smith basically defined a plural society as one in which the population is sharply divided into different groups, each with its own values and institutions. Such a society generally is controlled by a dominant minority group and is characterized by dissension and conflict. Though Smith's work offered an important alternative to functionalist interpretations of Caribbean societies that emphasized normative consensus, his model could not adequately account for the extensive cultural interaction and change that are undeniably a part of Caribbean life. The actual dynamics of cultural creativity have been the basis of the creolization model of Caribbean society alluded to above. One of the most prominent creolization theorists, historian/poet Kamau Brathwaite, stresses that creolization should be understood not as

> a 1:1 give and take act of gift or exchange, resulting in a new or altered product, but as a process, resulting in subtle and multiform orientations from or *towards* ancestral originals. In this way, Caribbean culture can be seen in terms of a dialectic of development taking place within a seamless guise or continuum of space and time; a model which allows for blood flow, fluctuations, the half-look, the look both/several ways; which allows for and contains the ambiguous, and rounds the sharp edges off the dichotomy.[4]

Far from being homogeneous, the Caribbean creole society is a multiplicity of intersecting realities, driven by both centrifugal and centripetal forces. The members of such a society find themselves in the crosscurrents of many cultural traditions and develop identities both in terms of ethnic images and notions of a shared, trans-ethnic nation. As early as the 1950s, anthropologist Daniel Crowley noted these patterns in Trinidad which he described as "plural acculturation" and "differential acculturation." Plural acculturation is the process in which members of each ethnic group learn some of the practices of other groups, while differential acculturation is the acceptance or rejection of other practices to suit particular objectives. Crowley argued that "differential acculturation and the existence of aspects of the Creole culture as 'common denominators' between groups are the means by which this complex society has preserved desirable segments of each cultural entity without fragmenting the society to the point of dissolution."[5]

Patterns of differentiation and convergence remain central to Trinidadian society today and the steelband, along with other prominent expressive forms, plays an important role in the ongoing discourse over national identity. For many Trinidadians the steelband is an indigenous creation that transcends ethnic heritages. Though it was originally developed by Afro-Trinidadians and was most firmly rooted in Afro-Trinidadian folk music, the scope of the music was expanded to encompass other cultural traditions, and some members of other ethnic groups eventually participated in the movement. At present pannists do not perceive their music as ethnic and almost never talk about it in ethnic terms. For them steelbands are expressions of geographic communities and of the nation as a whole. Perceptions such as these are also fairly common in the society in general. Many people, regardless of ethnic background, conceive of pan as a unique local art and a central symbol of national identity. This attitude is consistent with the vision of Trinidad as a creolized society—a vision that was the official policy of the PNM government from the mid-1950s to the mid-1980s.

Perceptions of pan as a national art persist in spite of the fact that the great majority of pannists are of African descent. Few Indians play in steelbands, even though the Indian and African populations in Trinidad are roughly equal in size. Similarly, steelband music is basically a synthesis of African- and European-derived traditions with relatively little Indian input. These characteristics are significant to some Indians. For such individuals pan is not a national music but an Afro-Trinidadian music in which they have little interest and with which they do not identify. Similar sentiments exist towards calypso and Carnival, which are also heavily promoted as national symbols.

In short, some Indians reject the idea of a creolized society: they feel that creolization means that they will be forced to give up distinctively Indian cultural practices and adopt "national" practices which they perceive as essentially Afro-Trinidadian. In the Trinidadian political arena, where ethnic identity is integrally related to claims of political power, to surrender cultural uniqueness is to relinquish a vehicle for political gains. For years Indians have felt that they have been relegated to the status of second-class citizens and excluded from full participation in the society. During the first three decades of PNM rule, Africans controlled the government, the public service, and the state-owned industries, and Indian arts and festivals received little official support. While there were signs of change with the election of the multiethnic National Alliance for Reconstruction in 1986, this party eventually fragmented and in 1991 the PNM returned to power. This ongoing experience of limited access to political power has heightened an already strong sense of ethnic consciousness among Indians, though their cultural practices as a whole are actually quite diverse, with significant differentiation along religious lines and varying degrees of creolization among different segments of the population.[6]

Indians often advocate a multicultural model of Trinidadian society in which value is placed on all ethnic groups perpetuating their own traditions while also identifying with the nation as a whole. This concept of the nation is based on an assumption that ethnic pride combined with mutual respect will help produce a strong and harmonious society. For example, Indrani Rampersad, a community activist, suggests:

> The evolution of our national cultural identity will only be facilitated by the freedom of expression of all the ethnic groups in their diversity, and the adoption of the policy of 'unity in diversity.'
>
> A national culture cannot be one of sterile homogeneity, given our historical and social realities.[7]

Many Indians are willing to accept Carnival, steelband, and calypso as national symbols but argue that the government should equally promote Indian practices such as Hosay, tassa drumming, *Divali* (a Hindu festival), and *Eid-ul-Fitr* (a Muslim observance), which have also become integral parts of the Trinidadian milieu. The NAR administration, in keeping with its official policy of multiculturalism, did in fact offer land and funds to Hindus and Muslims for their festivals.[8]

African responses to Indian cultural practices range from adoption to indifference to outright rejection. On the one hand, there are traditions such as the Muslim observance of Hosay which, in the Port of Spain neighborhood of St. James, has been transformed into a street festival that attracts huge crowds of Africans as well as Indian Muslims and Hindus. The tassa drum ensembles that accompany the street processions include both Indians and Africans, and a number of Africans and Indians who have grown up in St. James and in nearby Woodbrook have regularly played in both tassa ensembles and steelbands. A similar phenomenon is Indian or "chutney" soca, in which both Indian and African calypsonians perform soca tunes that incorporate Indian musical and lyrical elements. Activities such as these represent accommodation between Africans and Indians and cultural convergence.

On the other hand, there is often African resistance to Indian cultural endeavors that are perceived to have political consequences. In the late 1980s, for example, Indians advocated the construction of an Indian Cultural Centre, which the government of India had offered to fund. Many Africans criticized the idea because it promoted distinctively Indian cultural traditions. The criticism basically stemmed from a perception that Indians tend to be "clannish" and that their desire to preserve their culture perpetuates ethnic divisions and tensions. Such attitudes are sometimes related to fears of an Indian "takeover" of the country. There is already some uneasiness about Indian economic power and a belief that, if Indians became the dominant political group, they would favor themselves and discriminate against Africans.[9]

Issues such as these are regularly debated on the streets and in columns and letters in newspapers. For example, Ronald John, a contributor to the *Trinidad Guardian,* stated during the Indian Cultural Centre dispute that

> To my mind, one love [the slogan of the NAR] will remain a farce, will forever be unattainable in this plural society of ours where separatist attitudes are continually nurtured.
>
> Acceptance of the Indian Cultural Centre will surely assist in propagating already established separatist institutions such as Mastan[a] Bahar [a televised Indian talent competition], the annual East Indian Pageant, and the National Council of East Indian Culture. . . .
>
> The essential point a lot of people are scared to make is that many prominent East Indians refuse to accept the concept of an emerging callaloo[10] culture.
>
> This is probably so because steelband, calypso and Carnival with their mainly African base are now the vanguard of this coming together.

Steelband, calypso and Carnival are the only unique creations of
these islands and a lot of individualists have refused to accept this as
the true reason why all racial groups have responded to it.[11]

John goes on to point out that not all Carnival bandleaders, calypsonians, and pannists are of African descent.

A week and a half later, a letter appeared in the *Guardian* from a
Ronald Jagroop in response to John:

It seems to me that Mr John would like to see all "subcultures" in
our cosmopolitan country lose their identity by merging with what he
seems to think is the dominant culture.

As a member of that ethnic group whose culture he apparently
wishes to see disappear, I feel very threatened by what could only be
interpreted as a sinister desire to impose one culture on the population of Trinidad and Tobago. . . .

Does the fact that a handful of East Indians have successfully participated in certain Carnival activities mean that the cultures are
being integrated? Does the fact that a number of Afro-Trinidadians
sing East Indian songs indicate integration? . . .

Finally, Mr John, would you be prepared to accept a callaloo culture based on tassa and phagwa [a Hindu festival] instead of on steelband, calypso and carnival? If not, why not?[12]

What is clearly at issue in such debates is not only different visions of
a national identity but the whole process of ethnic ascription. Ethnic
categories are of course always social constructions: cultural practices
are not inherently "African" or "Indian" but are labeled as such in the
context of particular social situations and historical conventions, as well
as in accordance with individual perceptions and agendas. Furthermore, decades of social interaction and mutual cultural influence between peoples identified as different ethnic groups in Trinidad have in
some manner altered all cultural practices. In spite of ongoing change,
Trinidadians, to varying degrees, create a sense of cultural traditions
that are defined in terms of categories such as "African" and "Indian."
The assertion of such traditions provides a sense of history and ethnic
identity and, as already noted, is an integral part of the competition for
political power in Trinidad.

In contrast to this multicultural conception of Trinidad is the vision
of a creolized nation. "Creolization," however, is a complex, polysemous
term in Trinidad. It is sometimes used to refer to the process in which
different ethnic groups influence each other culturally to the extent

that a new culture is created. This then raises the question of whether the new culture transcends ethnic ascriptions altogether or whether it is possible to trace ethnic "components" in the "blend." Though this sense of "creolization" is certainly present in Trinidad, the term is also sometimes employed to refer to the "Africanization" of other ethnic groups. Historically, Africans have expected Indians to become more like themselves, but they have seen this more as a matter of becoming "Trinidadian" than of becoming "African." Many Indians, however, resist any notion that they should surrender their unique cultural practices or identity.

These creolist and pluralist perspectives are poles in the ongoing debate over the status and significance of the steelband in Trinidad, and from time to time an incident occurs that displays the two perspectives in a particularly salient way. In June 1994, for example, the ministries for culture and education, along with Pan Trinbago, announced a pilot project in which selected schools would use pans as the medium for instruction in music theory (schools generally use the recorder and piano for this purpose). Following the announcement, Satnarine Maharaj, Secretary-General of the Sanatan Dharma Maha Sabha (a Hindu organization), criticized the exclusive selection of the pan for the project and argued for the inclusion of the harmonium, an instrument used in some forms of Indian music. When the Minister of Education, Augustus Ramrekersingh, agreed to this request, Pan Trinbago issued a statement that described Maharaj's motivations as racist and divisive and criticized the minister for succumbing so easily to his demands. In short, Pan Trinbago argued that the pan was an indigenous instrument that belonged to all Trinidadians regardless of ethnicity. Maharaj in turn accused Pan Trinbago of racism and cultural chauvinism and condemned the organization as a drain on taxpayers' money.[13]

Given debates of this sort, it is obvious that pan is a contested national symbol which is continually subject to negotiation. On the one hand, it marks division and tension: it is perceived by some Indians as Afro-Trinidadian and as symbolic of an effort by Africans to impose their culture on the rest of the nation. On the other hand, many people (including a number of Indians) view the steelband as an indigenous art which can help draw the nation's diverse groups together and express a sense of common identity. This politically charged significance of the steelband differentiates it from relatively uncontested national symbols such as parang music. Parang, a popular string band and vocal music with roots in Venezuela, is perceived as "Spanish" in Trinidad. As anthropologist Aisha Khan points out, "Spanish" is an ethnic category that generally refers to "mixtures" and does not correspond to any demarcated ethnic group. As "Spanish," parang is a national music which presents no cultural/political threat and thus can easily be appreciated by all segments of the population.[14]

Along with its complex ethnic/national symbolism, the steelband also has multifaceted class significance. Pan originated in the late 1930s as a grass-roots music which was, at least implicitly, a form of resistance to the socioeconomic order. By the late 1940s and 1950s, however, it was attracting middle class support and participation. It would be incorrect to interpret this middle class interest as simply an example of what Raymond Williams describes as the ongoing incorporation of emergent working class cultural practices by the dominant culture in a class-stratified society.[15] The 1950s in Trinidad was a period of changing relations of power. A nationalist middle class was seeking political power and utilized grass-roots cultural forms such as the steelband in its own resistance to the colonial order. Pan did not so much become integrated into the status quo as it was part of the change of the status quo. Moreover, pan's growing stature was not merely the result of a middle class initiative to accept and promote grass-roots culture. Since the late 1930s grass-roots Trinidadians had been aggressively asserting their interests in the society, and eventually panmen themselves desired to be part of the mainstream. By the early 1950s they were thinking of pan more in terms of expanded opportunities than as a form of combativeness or resistance.

Basically, the 1950s brought collaboration between the African middle and grass-roots classes, and this collaboration contributed to the rise of both the PNM and the steelband movement. Once the PNM obtained power, pan was officially promoted as a national symbol and was used to cultivate clientelistic relationships. By the mid-1960s the government was encouraging businesses to sponsor steelbands as an indication of their willingness to participate in national development. So with the institutionalization of pan came a diversification of influences over its control.

At present the steelband has ambiguous class significance. To some extent it is part of the mainstream. There are a growing number of middle class pannists, a strong interest in steelband music among all classes in the society, and continued state and corporate support of the movement. Thus pan cuts across class lines: it is a means by which members of all classes can achieve a sense of national identity. At the same time, pan continues to be based in grass-roots communities. The great majority of pannists are grass-roots and, though bands are influenced by the state and by businesses, they are primarily shaped by their own members.

A question that remains is whether the steelband currently is part of a culture of resistance, such as the type described by Michael Lieber in his ethnography of the street world of Port of Spain. Many of the men whom Lieber studied were unemployed and engaged in hustles. He describes their street-based lifestyles as focused on flexibility, sociability, and aestheticism and interprets these styles as forms of resistance to the mainstream culture with its values of employment, economic success, family, and respectability. Lieber emphasizes that the men consciously chose these street styles: they enjoyed the freedom of designing their own lives as opposed to being constrained by regimented and unsatisfying jobs and family commitments.[16]

The individuals Lieber discusses have much in common with most panmen, in that panmen have also developed a unique street-based lifestyle. At the heart of this style is aestheticism. For panmen, playing pan is a focal activity and a key means of self-identification and expression. Such an approach to life does contrast with middle class respectability. Furthermore, steelbands, as street organizations, exist partially outside the dominant institutional structure of the society. Through steelbands, grass-roots communities set their own goals and organize themselves for creative action. There is also a widespread feeling among panmen that their life is one of struggle. To some extent this is a struggle for tangible forms of appreciation of pan and for continued grass-roots control of the movement. In a broader sense the struggle is against a whole socioeconomic order in which panmen feel their life possibilities are limited.

Though the steelband movement is based in the street world, it is difficult to describe it as a form of opposition to the mainstream, since it is so widely accepted in the nation and receives such extensive support from the state and the corporate sector. Most panmen do not see their music as really resisting anything in the local society. In fact they would rather see pan more fully integrated into mainstream cultural activities. Similarly most panmen do not appear to reject middle class life: they would prefer to find good jobs and become economically successful. Ideally they would like to make pan a full-time occupation—a way of earning a respectable livelihood.

In summary, just as pan carries ambiguous ethnic/national and class/national significance, it cannot be interpreted as exclusively oppositional or mainstream. It involves expressions of both national consensus and of grass-roots, street-based assertion and struggle.

Additional insights into the steelband's complex significance can be gained by juxtaposing the movement with another passion in Trinidad and Tobago: basketball. Though basketball is foreign in origin and pan is indigenous, there are some distinct parallels between the social uses of the two traditions. In their ethnography of basketball leagues in Trinidad and Tobago, Jay and Joan Mandle state that the members are primarily men (though women are also active players) and that they are generally between the ages of 18 and 30. The basketballers are almost exclusively grass-roots Africans and a large percentage of them are unemployed. The spectators at games are primarily grass-roots Africans as well. According to the authors, ethnic and class divisions are central to the nation's social structure, and the social characteristics of the sport reflect these divisions.[17]

The Mandles stress the intense commitment of basketballers and note that the sport has become "an important—even central—structural focus to their lives." The leagues are "a community in which they initiate and influence what goes on" and "where they can be valued and appreciated for their skills and contributions." In short, basketball is an "empowering" activity for a people at the bottom of a class-stratified society.[18] Along with examining the organization of leagues, the authors address the issue of clientelism. They describe how the basketballers look to the government and its basketball representatives for assistance. Clientelistic relationships, however, are incomplete because the patrons are unable to fully satisfy the basketballers' needs. The Mandles also argue that clientelism does not really exist in this situation because the basketballers are not passive but are committed to and capable of managing their affairs on their own.[19]

Obviously, panmen and basketballers are drawn from precisely the same sector of the population. Furthermore, both steelbands and basketball teams and leagues are creative and successful grass-roots organizations, involve intense commitment, and are a means whereby their members achieve a sense of status and power in the society. An important difference is that clientelism is quite developed in the case of the steelband movement. Steelbands, however, are strong and assertive organizations, which suggests that passivity is not a necessary characteristic of clientelism. In fact it is precisely the strength and influence of steelbands that make them attractive targets for clientelistic relationships. Perhaps such relationships with basketball teams and leagues are undeveloped because these relatively new organizations have not yet proven themselves as effective vehicles for mobilizing political support.

The steelband movement also differs from basketball in terms of being more of a national activity. While basketball is almost entirely a grass-roots African affair, pan draws some players and many fans from the various ethnic groups and classes in the society. In this sense it is somewhat closer to cricket or football, sports that involve all sectors of the nation.

The significance of cricket in Trinidad, and in the West Indies as a whole, has been thoroughly illustrated by C. L. R. James in *Beyond a Boundary*. James examines cricket as an expressive form that embodies elements of West Indian social structure and history. In colonial Trinidad, the focus of his discussion, the top cricket clubs were divided along lines of class and color. Keen rivalries existed between the clubs and their matches became occasions in which social tensions were dramatically acted out. According to James, "the cricket field was a stage on which selected individuals played representative roles which were charged with social significance."[20] In addition to expressing local conflicts, cricket mirrored the transition to independence from Britain. The great cricketers between World War I and World War II, particularly Learie Constantine, became symbols of the nationalist aspirations of the West Indian people. Constantine's tremendous achievements on the cricket field, combined with his outspokenness on social and political issues, made him a West Indian hero. James goes on to suggest that the style and daring quality of West Indian cricket reflected the transition to independence and describes how the 1960 appointment of Frank Worrell as the first black captain of a West Indian Test team was a victory that summed up the nationalist fervor of the period.

Thus for James cricket is a vehicle for investigating the complexities of colonialism and decolonization in Trinidad and the West Indies in general. "What do they know of cricket who only cricket know?" he asks. "West Indians crowding to Tests bring with them the whole past history and future hopes of the islands."[21] Though cricket was a game of the metropole, West Indians made it their own and used it as a means of defining and asserting their identity in the international arena.[22]

In the course of the present study, I have suggested that the steelband, like cricket, expresses basic patterns of social relations and social change in Trinidad. The steelband emerged in the midst of the class conflict of the late 1930s and 1940s, and this conflict was dramatically acted out in pan performances on the streets and in the hostile reaction to these performances by the middle and upper classes. By the early 1950s middle class (and light-skinned) youths were also forming steelbands. Though at times there was some tension between middle class and grass-roots panmen, their bands did not regularly engage in competitions that reflected class tensions in a manner similar to cricket matches. Since the 1960s steelbands have generally not had memberships that are divided along class and color lines. As in earlier years, class and ethnic conflicts in the society have been played out not in band competitions but in terms of the uses and interpretations of pan. Particularly prominent have been debates over proper respect for and promotion of the steelband, grass-roots control of the movement, and the issue of whether pan is really a national art.

Pan and cricket have also been important expressions of nationalist aspirations, though in different ways. Cricket was a British game that West Indians localized by integrating it into their island societies and developing their own style of play. Pan, on the other hand, was an indigenous creation. Accomplishments in both pan and cricket, however, helped inspire nationalist sentiments during the period of decolonization and, since independence, both have continued to be important national activities which evoke passionate commitments.

In their efforts to construct national identities, Caribbean societies have all had to come to terms with populations that are multiethnic and class-stratified. The process in which the steelband movement has embodied and displayed class and ethnic conflicts and accommodations is also apparent in the development and symbolism of many other Caribbean musical styles. Moreover, the steelband's importance in Trinidad as a vehicle of decolonization is paralleled by the manner in which other Caribbean nations have drawn on musical styles to define independent identities within the global order.

In the anglophone Caribbean, Jamaica has become Trinidad's chief rival in the production and dissemination of new musical performance styles. The development of reggae is in some ways similar to the story of the steelband, though reggae has had a much more dramatic worldwide impact. By the late 1950s, youths in the grass-roots neighborhoods of urban Jamaica had created a music known as "ska," which was essentially a localization of American R&B songs. Ska underwent rhythmic changes during the 1960s to become "rock steady" and eventually reggae, a style that incorporated both R&B/soul elements and Afro-Jamaican rhythms and instrumental techniques. Since reggae and its precursors were associated with a grass-roots, street-based culture and with the Rastafari movement, they were widely condemned by the Jamaican mulatto middle class which was committed to a more European-oriented cultural style.

By the early 1970s, however, black nationalist sentiments were becoming more widespread in Jamaica and reggae, along with Rastafari, was increasingly embraced by middle class youths. At the same time, reggae was assuming substantial political significance. In her analysis of Jamaican electoral politics, Anita Waters describes how the middle class leaders of Jamaica's political parties began utilizing reggae music and

Rastafari symbols as a means of identifying with the grass-roots class and mobilizing votes. The progressive People's National Party, in particular, drew on the protest dimensions of reggae and Rastafari to critique Jamaica's neocolonial socioeconomic order.[23] As the 1970s progressed, reggae achieved international fame and became a central symbol for the nation as a whole.

Issues of class and African-derived musical traditions have also been part of the dynamics of national identity formation in the Dominican Republic. In her examination of Dominican popular music since the demise of the Trujillo regime in 1961, Deborah Pacini Hernández describes how social and political conflicts have been symbolically expressed through different musical styles.[24] In the post-Trujillo era, musical styles associated with different classes began to compete in the marketplace. The *orquesta merengue,* which was associated with the urban middle and upper classes, received considerable financial support and media coverage, while the guitar-based *bachata* music of the rural poor and urban migrants was marginalized. At the same time, merengue competed with foreign musical styles, especially salsa, which symbolized a pan-hispanophone Caribbean identity. Nationalist promotion of merengue, however, made it the dance music of choice in the Dominican Republic by the mid-1980s. Merengue also figured in a discourse that was developing concerning the content of Dominican national culture, particularly its African components which had been rejected or ignored for years. A group of musicians and researchers reevaluated the nation's musical heritage and began to emphasize the rural and African roots of the merengue. Pacini Hernández notes that asking "where did merengue come from?" was another way of asking "where did we Dominicans come from, and who are we?"[25]

The development of dance bands in twentieth-century Haiti, as described by Gage Averill, provides another example of the dimensions of class, ethnicity, and color in Caribbean musical styles.[26] Averill notes a deep Haitian concern with cultural authenticity that is manifested in efforts to define traditions that are indigenous and truly embody the national experience. From 1915 to 1934 the United States occupied Haiti and supported governments run by a mulatto elite. During this period the proponents of the *noiriste* or *indigène* movement began to argue that Afro-Haitian peasant culture, particularly Vodou, represented the "soul of the nation." Through this ideology the black elite (which was primarily middle class) was able to establish a political alliance with the black masses. In the postwar years the black middle class assumed power and a new dance music, known as Vodou-jazz, developed. Vodou-jazz bands, particularly the famous Jazz des Jeunes, performed a fusion of swing,

Haitian *méringue,* and Vodou rhythms. Averill relates that the music of Jazz des Jeunes "was considered a weapon of struggle against a Europhile elite."[27]

The Duvalier era was dominated by another dance music, *konpa-dirèk,* which was based on the Dominican merengue. During this period of repressive dictatorship, there seems to have been less concern with assertion of an indigenous identity and more interest in seeking an escape through music. Averill argues that konpa-dirèk represented the triumph of an ideology of middle class consumerism over the ideology of negritude. With the departure of Jean-Claude Duvalier in 1986, however, Haitian dance music has been reinvigorated by new styles: *musik rasin* and *novel jénérasyon.* The music of bands playing in these styles is characterized by a revival of Haitian folk traditions, international eclecticism, technological experimentation, and greater expression of Haitian political conditions.[28]

Broad similarities in the development of reggae, merengue, Haitian dance music, and the steelband (as well as calypso) suggest some basic patterns in Caribbean music and nationhood. For much of the history of the post-Columbian Caribbean, grass-roots African-based musical traditions were denigrated due to the pervasive influence of Eurocentric ideologies. But as nationalist movements emerged at different times and places throughout the Caribbean, local African-derived musical styles were reevaluated and affirmed as expressions of national identities. Often this affirmation was linked to an attempt by a nationalist middle class to forge a political alliance with a grass-roots class. The process in which musicians have both interpreted indigenous musical traditions and incorporated foreign musical elements in their development of national styles has, in turn, reflected broader concerns with local and cosmopolitan definitions of national identities.

In the case of the steelband, reevaluation of the music has been interrelated with the cultural change that has accompanied decolonization. Pan originated as a Carnival street music and this performance orientation has been reproduced up to the present. But by the late 1940s and 1950s pan was also being performed at other festive occasions, in formal competitions, and in indoor concerts and shows. By the 1960s and 1970s it was assuming a significant role in the official occasions of the state and in churches and schools. This continuity and change in performance contexts has been paralleled by continuity and change in steelband symbolism. Early panmen and sympathetic members of the grass-roots class interpreted the music in terms of festivity and community power and identity. On the other hand, the middle and upper classes (and many members of the grass-roots class) initially interpreted it in terms of a colonial discourse on noise and disruption. Notions of festivity, community, and disruption continue up to the present, but since the late 1940s pan has also been viewed in the context of a nationalist discourse on local arts and identity.

These developments illustrate the interrelatedness of cultural assumptions and practical action in initiating cultural change. As Trinidadians began to conceive of pan in new ways, they started to employ it in new occasions. At the same time, the appearance of steelbands in new social settings transformed people's interpretations of the music. Re-conception and new performance practices were accompanied by an influx of new pannists into the movement: members of the middle class and of other ethnic groups and, by the 1970s, women. The expansion of the movement was in turn linked to an expansion of audiences and the solidification of relationships with the state and the corporate sector.

Though changes in the steelband movement and its significance have been substantial, decolonization in Trinidad and the music's achievement of national status are ongoing processes. Pan is still not embraced by the entire population, nor does it have the institutional infrastructure that would be necessary to support a large number of professional artists. On the thirtieth anniversary of independence in 1992, the new PNM government officially declared the pan the national instrument of Trinidad and Tobago.[29] Many Trinidadians and Tobagonians believed that such a declaration was long overdue, since pan had for years been such a central part of their expressive life. But official proclamations in themselves change little. Today it is often felt that pan is still becoming a fully national music.

Emotional commitments to pan in Trinidad, however, are extensive. Most steelband performance occasions, especially Panorama and Carnival, assume virtually ritual significance. Unlike reggae or Guadeloupian and Martinican zouk, which depend heavily on recordings for their dissemination, pan is primarily a music of live performance. Steelband recordings are appreciated but pan enthusiasts generally want to be at the scene of the action. Pan is still deeply rooted in the Carnival experience of dramatic presentation and communal celebration. People desire to be enveloped by the pan sound—not only actually to feel the rhythms and hear the range of voices in the orchestras but to immediately connect with the music's creators. Pan is a participatory music performed by bands with large numbers of members who represent communities, both geographic and sentimental. At steelband occasions, communities publicly display themselves, compete with each other, and affirm a sense of worth. In addition, the experience of the conventional cadences of the calypso form by performers and audiences seems to evoke a familiar way of moving and being in Trinidad and, beyond this, a whole heritage rooted in the island.

Earlier in the chapter I discussed certain messages that the steelband has carried concerning ethnic and class differentiation and integration. At performance occasions, however, other dimensions of steelband symbolism prevail. In listening to bands strive to execute complex musical arrangements without flaw, many Trinidadians re-encounter and appreciate qualities that are believed to be key aspects of their national experience: local creativity, struggle and achievement, and festivity.

The fact that the steelband was invented in Trinidad is a source of tremendous pride. Trinidadian youths discovered a new way of making music, and in a relatively short period of time developed their pans into instruments suitable for playing a wide range of musical styles. This feat is often perceived by Trinidadians as one important representation of their imagination and resourcefulness and of the whole process in which they have created themselves as a people. In a similar vein, pan is often discussed as representative of local culture in general. Pannists and supporters, in particular, tend to believe that a threat to the steelband movement is a threat to Trinidadian culture as a whole. Currently there is much concern with foreign cultural domination, and the pan is affirmed not only as a means of identifying the nation in the international arena but as an instrument for resisting the impact of foreign media. For example, Selwyn Tarradath, the Public Relations Officer of Pan Trinbago, states:

> All we have is our culture at this point in time. . . . And the steelband is the standard bearer. It is what people could identify with Trinidad and Tobago. It's what we could say: "Well, look, this is what we have given the world.". . . We had a little teaspoon of oil—we thought it was a big thing. The oil market dry up. We see we're high and dry with nothing.
> . . . we are about to be submerged by American culture. More and more now with this cable TV and satellite and everything. You find that soon we'll be a nation of—all our young people will be young Americans. So the culture, steelband and calypso especially, is what we have to ward off them.[30]

Yet the steelband is by no means a complete rejection of foreign cultures. Throughout the history of the movement, there has been not only a development of the calypso form but a reinterpretation of foreign musical styles. This ongoing interplay between local and cosmopolitan orientations in the steelband world has in turn reflected more general debates over the definition of Trinidadian identity. A major issue here is how a small nation can participate in contemporary transnational activities and cultural exchanges while still maintaining its unique traditions and a sense of itself.

Related to the notion of local creativity is a conception of struggle and achievement. As noted earlier, panmen perceive the steelband movement's struggle for acceptance and respect as linked to their personal struggle for survival and success. At the same time, many people view steelband history as somehow representative of the general struggle of nation-building. From this perspective the sacrifices and accomplishments of the panmen evoke a sense of the nation's efforts to achieve political, economic, and cultural independence.

The present study has been an attempt to further reveal this symbolism of creativity and struggle. I have argued that the emergence of the steelband in the late 1930s and its subsequent development have paralleled the emergence and development of Trinidad and Tobago as a nation. Certainly the steelband has reflected shifting ethnic and class relations and ideas of national identity. At the same time, it has been a dynamic force in the creation of a new society. In the late 1930s and 1940s, the steelband was one vehicle of the grass-roots assertion that hastened the demise of colonialism. During the late 1940s and 1950s, it was a means by which nationalists mobilized middle class and grass-roots support in the transition to independence. Since independence, pan has helped shape a sense of national consciousness, while also perpetuating feelings of solidarity in many grass-roots communities. Finally, the steelband, throughout its history, has been a factor in the localization of perceptions, values, notions of respectability, and social occasions.

Over the years it has been in performances that pan has made its most dramatic impact. Innovations in the actual use of the steelband have led people to think about the music and themselves in new ways, and such reorientations have allowed for social change. It is significant that most steelband performance occasions have a festive character. Pan originated as a Carnival music and gradually was incorporated into a wide range of public and private festive events. Festivity is certainly the most immediate and tangible dimension of steelband symbolism in that pan almost always evokes a spirit of revelry or well-being. When the tenor pans soar over the rich harmonies of the mid-range pans, the rolling cadences of the basses, and the piercing rhythms of the irons, performers and audiences together transcend the limits of day-to-day life. Festivity, however, involves much more than license and exuberance. At festive moments Trinidadians and Tobagonians imaginatively explore their experience and various visions of themselves. The pan, as an indigenous instrument of festivity, is one vital means by which the nation creates, contemplates, and celebrates itself.

Suggested Listening

Steelband recordings from the 1950s and 1960s are difficult to find. Fortunately, the Smithsonian Institution's Center for Folklife Programs and Cultural Studies is currently preparing to re-release material from Emory Cook's Caribbean collection, including pan recordings from Trinidad. The Center can be contacted at 955 L'Enfant Plaza, SW, Suite 2600, Washington, DC 20560 (Tel: 202-287-3251).

Numerous good pan recordings have appeared over the past ten years. Sanch Electronix has issued cassettes of the varied repertoires of many of the top steelbands in Trinidad and also has a "Panyard Series," which features bands performing Panorama tunes in their yards during the Carnival season. Also available from Sanch are a few pan jazz recordings: *Jazz 'n' Steel* (Sanch 8806), which includes the Rudy Smith Trio and the Annise Hadeed Quartet, and *Pan Jazz Conversations* (Sanch 9105 and 9206), which feature an ensemble led by Clive Alexander and Annise Hadeed. *Cuatro 'n' Steel* (Sanch 9306) presents Rudy Smith in the context of a parang ensemble. For a sampling of Pan Ramajay, see *Pan Ramajay '93* (Sanch 9302). Sanch Electronix can be contacted at 16 Riverside Road, Curepe, Trinidad, W.I. (Tel: 809-663-1384).

A number of Sanch's recordings have been released on compact disc by Delos International as part of their "Caribbean Carnival Series" and are distributed in North America by A&M Records. Delos has CDs featuring individual bands, such as Desperadoes' *The Jammer* (DE 4023), and compilation recordings, such as *Carnival Jump-Up: Steelbands of Trinidad & Tobago* (DE 4014). Rudy Smith and Annise Hadeed's *Jazz 'n' Steel* (Sanch 8806) is available from Delos as *Jazz 'n' Steel from Trinidad and Tobago* (DE 4013), while most of the selections on Clive Alexander and Annise Hadeed's *Pan Jazz Conversations* (Sanch 9105) can be found on Delos's CD of the same name (DE 4019). Delos International can be contacted at Hollywood & Vine Plaza, 1645 North Vine St., Suite 340, Hollywood, CA 90028.

Pan Assembly cassettes and CDs, featuring pan virtuosos such as Boogsie Sharpe, Robert Greenidge, Ken Philmore, Earl Brooks, and Sydney Joseph, can be obtained from Carotte at 144 Eastern Main Road, Petit Bourg, Trinidad, W.I. Jazz pannist Othello Molineaux can be heard on a compact disc entitled *It's About Time* from Big World Music (2010). Big World Music's address is P.O. Box 128, 315 Empire Blvd., Brooklyn, NY 11225.

Selections from the 1988 and 1992 Steelband Music Festivals are available on cassette as *Pan Is Beautiful V* (Trini-T TTC801, TTC802, and TTC803) and *Pan Is Beautiful VI* (Trini-T TTC931 and TTC932). Trini-T can be reached at P.O. Box 3290, Diego Martin, Trinidad, W.I. Selections from the 1988 Festival can also be obtained on a compact disc from Flying Fish entitled *Steelbands of Trinidad and Tobago: The Heart of Steel* (FF 70522). Flying Fish Records' address is 1304 W. Schubert, Chicago, IL 60614.

American pannist Andy Narell has done much to help popularize the instrument. An example of his work is *Down the Road* on Windham Hill Records (1934-10139-2).

For a comprehensive pan discography, see Jeffrey Thomas, *Forty Years of Steel: An Annotated Discography of Steel Band and Pan Recordings, 1951-1991* (Westport, Conn.: Greenwood Press, 1992). Thomas's well-indexed book covers both steelbands and soloists in Trinidad and in other countries. Information on steelband recordings and other pan affairs can also be obtained from *Pan-Lime*, a monthly newsletter published by Panyard, Inc., 1206 California Ave., Akron, OH 44314 (Tel: 800-377-0202).

Notes

Introduction

1. The island of Trinidad lies 7 miles off the coast of Venezuela, while the smaller island of Tobago is 19 miles to the northeast of Trinidad. The two islands form the single nation-state of Trinidad and Tobago. Almost all my research was conducted in Trinidad and, for the most part, Trinidad is the subject of my discussion. Thus I generally employ the term "Trinidadian" rather than "Trinidadian and Tobagonian."

2. For years "Negro" was the most common local term for persons of entirely or primarily African descent. This term is still used but "African" is now preferred by many people. "Afro-Trinidadian" is also sometimes employed. In this study I use the terms "African" and "Afro-Trinidadian" interchangeably. Trinidadians also utilize a variety of color distinctions such as "dark," "brown," "red," and "whitish" or "fair-skinned." In earlier years people with complexions from the middle to lighter end of this spectrum were referred to as "colored."

3. George "Sonny" Goddard, *Forty Years in the Steelbands: 1939–1979* (London: Karia Press, 1991). Some other examples of this literature are Bertie Marshall, "The Bertie Marshall Story: Pan Is Mih Gyul," *Tapia* 2 (1972): installments in issues 1–10; Ellie Mannette, "The Story of Pan," *The Sun* (1986): nine weekly installments, 21 March - 16 May; Donald Seon, *South Panmen* (San Fernando, Trinidad: Donald Seon, 1979); Lennox Pierre, "From Dustbins to Classics," *Independence Supplement of the Sunday Guardian* (26 August 1962), pp. 107–110; Anthony E. Rouff, *"Authentic" Facts on the Origin of the Steelband* (St. Augustine, Trinidad: Bowen's Printery, 1972); Anthony M. Jones, *Steelband: The Winston "Spree" Simon Story* (Barataria, Trinidad: Educo Press, 1982); Percival Borde, "The Sounds of Trinidad: The Development of the Steel-Drum Bands," *Black Perspective in Music* 1 (1973): 45–49; and Landeg E. White, "Steelbands: A Personal Record," *Caribbean Quarterly* 15, no. 4 (1969): 32–39. Panman narratives also form the basis of a series of articles written by Kim Johnson entitled "From Body Music to Sweet Pan," *Sunday Express* (17 January, 24 January, 31 January, 7 February, 21 February 1993).

4. Jacob D. Elder, "Color, Music and Conflict: A Study of Aggression in Trinidad with Reference to the Role of Traditional Music," *Ethnomusicology* 8 (1964): 128–136; idem., "Evolution of the Traditional Calypso of Trinidad and Tobago: A Socio-historical Analysis of Song-Change" (Ph.D. dissertation, University of Pennsylvania, 1966); idem., *From Congo Drum to Steelband: A Socio-historical Account of the Emergence and Evolution of the Trinidad Steel Orchestra* (St. Augustine, Trinidad: University of the West Indies, 1969); Errol Hill, *The Trinidad Carnival: Mandate for a National Theatre* (Austin: University of Texas

Press, 1972); Lloyd Braithwaite, "The Problem of Cultural Integration in Trinidad," *Social and Economic Studies* 3, no. 1 (1954): 82–96.

5. General analytical overviews of the steelband movement include Jeffrey R. Thomas, "A History of Pan and the Evolution of the Steel Band in Trinidad and Tobago" (M.A. thesis, Wesleyan University, 1985); and William R. Aho, "Steelband Music in Trinidad and Tobago: The Creation of a People's Music," *Latin American Music Review* 8 (1987): 26–58. Analytical examinations of particular aspects of the movement include Judith Ann Weller, "A Profile of a Trinidadian Steel-Band," *Phylon* 22 (1961): 68–77; Jeffrey Thomas, "The Changing Role of the Steel Band in Trinidad and Tobago: Panorama and the Carnival Tradition," *Studies in Popular Culture* 9, no. 2 (1986): 96–108; Ancil A. Neil, *Voices from the Hills: Despers and Laventille* (n.p.: A. A. Neil, 1987); and Selwyn Tarradath, "Race, Class, Politics and Gender in the Steelband Movement," in *Social and Occupational Stratification in Contemporary Trinidad and Tobago,* ed. Selwyn Ryan (St. Augustine, Trinidad: Institute of Social and Economic Research, University of the West Indies, 1991), pp. 377–384.

6. For musicological commentary on the steelband, see G. A. Prospect, *Treatise on the Steelband of Trinidad and Tobago* (Port of Spain: G. A. Prospect, 1970); and Peter Seeger, "The Steel Drum: A New Folk Instrument," *Journal of American Folklore* 71 (1958): 52–57. For a comprehensive discography, see Jeffrey Thomas, *Forty Years of Steel: An Annotated Discography of Steel Band and Pan Recordings, 1951–1991* (Westport, Conn.: Greenwood Press, 1992). For a detailed listing of contestants and their musical selections in various steelband competitions in Trinidad from 1963 to 1993, see Gideon Maxime, *41 Years of Pan* (Trinidad: n.p., n.d.).

7. Marshall Sahlins, *Islands of History* (Chicago: University of Chicago Press, 1985); Renato Rosaldo, *Culture and Truth: The Remaking of Social Analysis* (Boston: Beacon Press, 1989).

8. Victor Turner, *Dramas, Fields and Metaphors: Symbolic Action in Human Society* (Ithaca, N.Y.: Cornell University Press, 1974); Roger D. Abrahams, *The Man-of-Words in the West Indies: Performance and the Emergence of Creole Culture* (Baltimore: Johns Hopkins University Press, 1983).

9. For anthropological perspectives on the history of urban musical performance styles and their symbolic dimensions, see Morton Marks, "Uncovering Ritual Structures in Afro-American Music," in *Religious Movements in Contemporary America,* ed. Irving I. Zaretsky and Mark P. Leone (Princeton, N.J.: Princeton University Press, 1974), pp. 60–134; José E. Limón, "Texas Mexican Popular Music and Dancing: Some Notes on History and Symbolic Process," *Latin American Music Review* 4 (1983): 229–246; David B. Coplan, *In Township Tonight! South Africa's Black City Music and Theatre* (London: Longman, 1985); and Christopher Alan Waterman, *Jùjú: A Social History and Ethnography of an African Popular Music* (Chicago: University of Chicago Press, 1990). A useful theoretical model for examining the social negotiation of musical meanings is provided by Richard Middleton in "Articulating Musical Meaning/Re-Constructing Musical History/Locating the 'Popular,'" *Popular Music* 5 (1985): 5–43; and "Popular Music, Class Conflict and the Music-Historical Field," in *Popular Music Perspectives 2: Papers from the Second International Conference on Popular Music Studies* (Göteborg, Sweden: International Association for the Study of Popular Music, 1985), pp. 24–46. For a general discussion of social struggle over forms of popular culture, see Stuart Hall, "Notes on Deconstructing 'the Popular,'" in *People's History and*

Socialist Theory, ed. Raphael Samuel (London: Routledge and Kegan Paul, 1981), pp. 227–240.

10. Though I occasionally refer to negotiations over the steelband as "social dramas," I do not argue that these dramas have the four distinct stages outlined by Turner in *Dramas, Fields and Metaphors.*

11. Edward Brathwaite, *The Development of Creole Society in Jamaica: 1770–1820* (Oxford: Clarendon Press, 1971); idem., *Contradictory Omens: Cultural Diversity and Integration in the Caribbean* (Mona, Jamaica: Savacou Publications, 1974). For other perspectives on creolization and cultural creativity in the Caribbean, see Sidney W. Mintz, *Caribbean Transformations* (New York: Columbia University Press, 1989 [1974]); Roger D. Abrahams and John F. Szwed, eds., *After Africa: Extracts from British Travel Accounts and Journals* (New Haven, Conn.: Yale University Press, 1983); Abrahams, *The Man-of-Words in the West Indies*; Lee Drummond, "The Cultural Continuum: A Theory of Intersystems," *Man* 15 (1980): 352–374; and Mervyn C. Alleyne, "A Linguistic Perspective on the Caribbean," in *Caribbean Contours,* ed. Sidney W. Mintz and Sally Price (Baltimore: Johns Hopkins University Press, 1985), pp. 155–179. For a critique of the concept of creolization, see O. Nigel Bolland, "Creolization and Creole Societies: A Cultural Nationalist View of Caribbean Social History," in *Intellectuals in the Twentieth-Century Caribbean,* vol. 1, ed. Alistair Hennessy (London: Macmillan Caribbean, 1992), pp. 50–79. Bolland stresses that creolization is not simply a matter of "blending" but of cultural transformations shaped by the contradictions and conflicts of colonial societies.

12. Raymond Williams, *Marxism and Literature* (Oxford: Oxford University Press, 1977), pp. 108–114.

13. In this study, classes are conceived of as groups distinguishable by both economic interests and cultural characteristics. The "grass-roots class" includes skilled and unskilled manual workers, small farmers, and street vendors. The "middle class" includes professionals, white-collar workers, small and moderate-sized business persons, and moderate-sized landowners. (Highly skilled and successful manual workers can also be considered "middle class.") The "upper class" includes large business persons and large landowners. For similar outlines of class structures in Trinidad, Guyana, and Jamaica, see Percy Hintzen, *The Costs of Regime Survival: Racial Mobilization, Elite Domination and the Control of the State in Guyana and Trinidad* (Cambridge: Cambridge University Press, 1989); and Carl Stone, *Democracy and Clientelism in Jamaica* (New Brunswick, N.J.: Transaction Books, 1980). I use the term "grass-roots class" throughout this study. "Working class" is inappropriate because of high rates of unemployment and self-employment in Trinidad. "Grass-roots class" also does not have the negative connotations of "lower class." A further justification for the term is that grass-roots people perceive themselves as a distinct group in the society and are perceived as such by the middle and upper classes.

14. A "French Creole" is any locally born individual of entirely or primarily European ancestry.

15. Two general histories of Trinidad are Bridget Brereton's *A History of Modern Trinidad: 1783–1962* (Kingston: Heinemann Educational Books [Caribbean] Ltd., 1981); and Eric E. Williams's *History of the People of Trinidad and Tobago* (Port of Spain: PNM Publishing Co., 1962). For overviews of nineteenth-century Trinidad, see Donald Wood, *Trinidad in Transition* (London: Oxford University Press, 1968); and Bridget Brereton, *Race Relations in Colonial*

Trinidad: 1870–1900 (Cambridge: Cambridge University Press, 1979). Two particularly insightful discussions of twentieth-century Trinidad are Selwyn D. Ryan, *Race and Nationalism in Trinidad and Tobago: A Study of Decolonization in a Multiracial Society* (Toronto: University of Toronto Press, 1972); and Ivar Oxaal, *Black Intellectuals and the Dilemmas of Race and Class in Trinidad* (Cambridge, Mass.: Schenkman Pub. Co, 1982). The population statistics cited are from *South America, Central America and the Caribbean 1993,* "Trinidad and Tobago" (London: Europa Publications Limited, 1993), pp. 577, 582.

16. Three relevant critiques of the concept of culture are Drummond, "The Cultural Continuum," pp. 352–353; Ulf Hannerz, "The World in Creolization," *Africa* 57 (1987): 546–559, at pp. 550–552; and Rosaldo, *Culture and Truth,* pp. 20, 208. Drummond suggests utilizing creole linguistics, rather than structural linguistics, as a means of describing cultures and of developing a theory of culture. He argues that a culture is an "intersystem" or cultural continuum characterized by internal variation and change instead of uniform rules or invariant properties. Though cultural continua exist in all societies, they are particularly apparent in polyethnic societies like those found in the Caribbean. Drummond illustrates his argument with examples derived from his fieldwork in Guyana. Hannerz also draws on creole linguistics to discuss a world in creolization, that is, a world characterized by intensifying global cultural flow. Due to the "uneven flow of communications and the diversity of experiences and interests," there is a "differentiation of perspectives" among the members of any given society. Rosaldo suggests that a culture is not a self-contained, coherent whole but "a more porous array of intersections where distinct processes crisscross from within and beyond its borders." Borderlands, in turn, "should be regarded not as analytically empty transitional zones but as sites of creative cultural production that require investigation."

17. Cf. Daniel Crowley, "Plural and Differential Acculturation in Trinidad," *American Anthropologist* 59 (1957): 817–824.

18. For a historical discussion of nations as cultural creations, see Benedict R. O'G. Anderson, *Imagined Communities: Reflections on the Origin and Spread of Nationalism* (London: Verso, 1983). For a useful overview of the literature on this topic, see Robert J. Foster, "Making National Cultures in the Global Ecumene," *Annual Review of Anthropology* 20 (1991): 235–260.

19. C. L. R. James, *Beyond a Boundary* (Durham, N.C.: Duke University Press, 1993 [1963]).

20. Edward Kamau Brathwaite, "Caribbean Man in Space and Time," *Savacou* 11/12 (1975): 6.

21. Some recent examples of the growing scholarship on Caribbean musical traditions are Gordon Rohlehr, *Calypso & Society in Pre-Independence Trinidad* (Port of Spain: Gordon Rohlehr, 1990); Donald R. Hill, *Calypso Calaloo: Early Carnival Music in Trinidad* (Gainesville: University Press of Florida, 1993); Keith Q. Warner, *Kaiso! The Trinidad Calypso: A Study of the Calypso as Oral Literature* (Washington, D.C.: Three Continents Press, 1985); Hollis Urban Lester Liverpool, *Kaiso and Society* (Diego Martin, Trinidad: Juba Publications, 1990); Anita M. Waters, *Race, Class, and Political Symbols: Rastafari and Reggae in Jamaican Politics* (New Brunswick, N.J.: Transaction Books, 1985); Erna Brodber, "Black Consciousness and Popular Music in Jamaica in the 1960s and 1970s," *Nieuwe West-Indische Gids* 61 (1987): 145–160; Jocelyne Guilbault, *Zouk: World Music in the West Indies* (Chicago: University of Chicago Press, 1993); Gage Averill, "Haitian Dance Bands, 1915–1970: Class, Race, and Authenticity," *Latin American*

Music Review 10 (1989): 203–235; Jorge Duany, "Popular Music in Puerto Rico: Toward an Anthropology of Salsa," *Latin American Music Review* 5 (1984): 186–216; Deborah Pacini Hernández, "*La lucha sonora*: Dominican Popular Music in the post-Trujillo Era," *Latin American Music Review* 12 (1991): 105–123; and Kenneth M. Bilby, "The Caribbean as a Musical Region," in *Caribbean Contours*, Mintz and Price, pp. 181–218.

Chapter 1: Festive and Musical Traditions

1. For a brief description of the French aristocratic tradition in Trinidad, see Andrew Pearse, "Carnival in Nineteenth Century Trinidad," *Caribbean Quarterly* 4 (1956): 176–177.

2. For a first-hand account of African dances and drumming in pre-emancipation Trinidad, see Mrs. A. C. Carmichael, *Domestic Manners and Social Conditions of the White, Coloured, and Negro Population of the West Indies*, vol. 2 (New York: Negro Universities Press, 1969 [1833]), pp. 205–206, 284–285, 288–297. For additional descriptions of pre-emancipation dancing and drumming and the European responses, see Jacob D. Elder, "Evolution of the Traditional Calypso of Trinidad and Tobago: A Socio-historical Analysis of Song-Change" (Ph.D. dissertation, University of Pennsylvania, 1966), pp. 83-88; and Gordon Rohlehr, *Calypso & Society in Pre-Independence Trinidad* (Port of Spain: Gordon Rohlehr, 1990), pp. 3–5, 8–13.

3. Quoted in Rohlehr, *Calypso & Society*, pp. 12–13.

4. For descriptions of the Christmas season and the militia, see Carmichael, *Domestic Manners*, pp. 75–76, 288–297; Pearse, "Carnival," pp. 179–185; and Errol Hill, *The Trinidad Carnival: Mandate for a National Theatre* (Austin: University of Texas Press, 1972), p. 13.

5. Peter Marsden, *An Account of the Island of Jamaica* (Newcastle, 1788), and Cynric R. Williams, *A Tour Through the Island of Jamaica* (London, 1826), in *After Africa: Extracts from British Travel Accounts and Journals*, ed. Roger D. Abrahams and John F. Szwed (New Haven, Conn.: Yale University Press, 1983), pp. 229–230, 249–250.

6. For accounts of the discovery of the African regiments, see V. S. Naipaul, *The Loss of Eldorado: A History* (Harmondsworth: Penguin Books Ltd., 1969), pp. 291–299; and Lionel Mordaunt Fraser, *History of Trinidad*, vol. 1 (London: Frank Cass & Co. Ltd., 1971 [1891]), pp. 267–272 (song quotation at p. 270).

7. Roger Bastide, *African Civilizations in the New World* (New York: Harper and Row, 1971), pp. 9–11.

8. Ibid., pp. 9–10, 94–95; Judith Bettelheim, "Carnaval in Cuba: Another Chapter in the Nationalization of Culture," *Caribbean Quarterly* 36, nos. 3&4 (1990): 29–31; Thurlow Weed, *Letters from Europe and the West Indies* (Albany, N.Y., 1866), in *After Africa*, Abrahams and Szwed, p. 273.

9. H. H. Breen, *St. Lucia: Historical, Statistical, and Descriptive* (London, 1844), in *After Africa*, Abrahams and Szwed, pp. 263–268.

10. For several accounts of "set girls" in Jamaica, see Abrahams and Szwed, *After Africa*, pp. 234, 240, 242–243, 247–248, 251–254, 276–277.

11. See Bastide, *African Civilizations*, pp. 144, 177, 181.

12. Bettelheim, "Carnaval in Cuba," p. 30.

13. For examinations of Carnival in nineteenth-century Trinidad, see Hill, *The Trinidad Carnival*; Pearse, "Carnival"; Kim Johnson, "The Social Impact of

Carnival," in *The Social and Economic Impact of Carnival*, seminar held at the University of the West Indies, St. Augustine, Trinidad, November 24–26, 1983 (St. Augustine, Trinidad: Institute of Social and Economic Research, University of the West Indies, 1984), pp. 174–187; Jacob D. Elder, "Color, Music and Conflict: A Study of Aggression in Trinidad with Reference to the Role of Traditional Music," *Ethnomusicology* 8 (1964): 130–131; idem., "Evolution of the Traditional Calypso," pp. 94–109; Donald Wood, *Trinidad in Transition* (London: Oxford University Press, 1968), pp. 243–247; and Bridget Brereton, *Race Relations in Colonial Trinidad: 1870–1900* (Cambridge: Cambridge University Press, 1979), pp. 169–175.

14. Quoted in Pearse, "Carnival," p. 184.

15. A nineteenth-century priest's account of an emancipation celebration that included a communion ritual provides additional evidence of a connection between the Canboulay bands and the pre-emancipation regiments (see Hill, *The Trinidad Carnival*, pp. 30–31).

16. Quoted in Pearse, "Carnival," pp. 185, 187.

17. Barrack yards are spaces in the interiors of city blocks in which there are long multi-room dwellings with one family living in each room.

18. For discussions of the jamette world, see Pearse, "Carnival," pp. 191–193; Brereton, *Race Relations*, pp. 122–126, 166–171; and David V. Trotman, *Crime in Trinidad: Conflict and Control in a Plantation Society, 1838–1900* (Knoxville: University of Tennessee Press, 1986), pp. 167–169, 267–268.

19. Trotman, *Crime in Trinidad*, p. 169.

20. Ibid., p. 182.

21. Rohlehr, *Calypso & Society*, pp. 16, 53. For further discussion of stickfighting, see Jacob D. Elder, "Kalinda: Song of the Battling Troubadours of Trinidad," *Journal of the Folklore Institute* 3 (1966): 192–203.

22. For accounts of the 1881 Carnival riot and the aftermath, see J. N. Brierley, *Trinidad: Then and Now* (Port of Spain: Franklin's Electric Printery, 1912), pp. 318–330; and Brereton, *Race Relations*, pp. 171–175. It should be noted that the Peace Preservation Ordinance applied to Indian festivals and drumming as well. A riot resulted in 1884 when the police attempted to control the celebration of *Hosay*, a Muslim observance that by the late nineteenth century was already attracting Hindu Indians and Africans (see Elder, "Evolution of the Traditional Calypso," pp. 106–107; and Trotman, *Crime in Trinidad*, pp. 269–270).

23. Africans increasingly spoke English by the end of the nineteenth century.

24. For descriptions of the middle and upper classes' return to the street Carnival and of their "improvement" efforts, see Pearse, "Carnival," pp. 190, 193; Hill, *The Trinidad Carnival*, pp. 45–46; Brereton, *Race Relations*, pp. 173–174; Rohlehr, *Calypso & Society*, pp. 13–14, 26; and Donald R. Hill, *Calypso Calaloo: Early Carnival Music in Trinidad* (Gainesville: University Press of Florida, 1993), pp. 44–63. The most comprehensive treatments of calypso in colonial Trinidad are Rohlehr's *Calypso & Society* and Donald Hill's *Calypso Calaloo*. Rohlehr traces the various verbal and musical traditions present in nineteenth-century Trinidad and suggests that the calypso grew out of the stickfighting "milieu of confrontation and mastery, of violent self-assertion and rhetorical force; of a constant quest for a more splendid language, and excellence of tongue" (p. 54). Hill examines how tent calypso was the musical expression of the new middle class Carnival, linked to "a commercial, industrializing Trinidad" (pp. 213–214).

25. F. A. Crichlow, "Carnival Magic Grips City," *Sunday Guardian* (3 March 1946), p. 16. The clash which Crichlow describes involved a band from Belmont, with Miler the Mighty as its champion, and a band from Corbeaux Town, led by Fitzie Banrye. Crichlow relates:

> The decade-long feud between these rival bands was always revived in blood every Carnival period. Clash they would, and clash they did. Neither foot nor mounted police dared to venture among the milling, chanting thousands, hypnotised by the display of power and the ever-present blood-lust, for these two leaders were the greatest fighters in the land. At once, a 50-foot ring was formed. On the periphery the opposed bamboo-beaters and chanters thundered out their defiant notes, steel triangles and shouts adding to the awful din.

After the champions fought, a full-scale battle between the two bands broke out:

> . . . the opposing bands came together. Stickmen streamed with blood. Band supporters now resorted to broken bottles, bricks and stones. Hundreds took part in the great struggle.

26. One form of bele was a community-based social dance presided over by a king and queen. Two other forms involved religious practices (see Andrew Pearse, "Aspects of Change in Caribbean Folk Music," *International Folk Music Journal* 7 [1955]: 29–36). Orisha is a Yoruban religion in Trinidad that also includes elements of Catholicism and other spiritual beliefs. At feasts (ceremonies), drumming is an integral part of the process in which participants are possessed by deities. Shango is a prominent deity in the Trinidadian pantheon. For an examination of Yoruban verbal, musical, and ritual traditions and influences in Trinidad, see Maureen Warner-Lewis, *Guinea's Other Suns: The African Dynamic in Trinidad Culture* (Dover, Mass.: Majority Press, 1991).

27. Hill, *The Trinidad Carnival*, p. 45.

28. J. H. Kwabena Nketia, *The Music of Africa* (New York: Norton, 1974), p. 76; Luis Felipe Ramón y Rivera, "Venezuela: Folk Music," in *The New Grove Dictionary of Music and Musicians*, vol. 19, ed. Stanley Sadie (London: Macmillan Publishers Limited, 1980), p. 612; Harold Courlander, *The Drum and the Hoe: Life and Lore of the Haitian People* (Berkeley: University of California Press, 1960) pp. 196, 198; and Abrahams and Szwed, *After Africa*, pp. 42–43.

29. Hill, *The Trinidad Carnival*, p. 47; Lennox Pierre, "From Dustbins to Classics," *Independence Supplement of the Sunday Guardian* (26 August 1962), pp. 107–108; and Anthony Prospect, personal interview, Champs Fleur, Trinidad (14 November 1988).

30. *Trinidad Guardian* (5 February 1920), quoted in Hill, *The Trinidad Carnival*, p. 47.

31. Victor Wilson, personal interview, Newtown, Trinidad (22 March 1988).

32. Alfred Mayers, personal interview, Point Cumana, Trinidad (21 February 1989).

33. Andrew Carr, "Jour Ouvert: An Aspect of Trinidad Carnival," in *Down Town Carnival Competition Programme* (n.p., 1965); and Hill, *The Trinidad Carnival*, p. 86. A Soucouyant is an old woman who sheds her skin, flies through the night as a ball of fire, and sucks blood from her victim. La Diablesse attracts

men in her appearance as a beautiful woman, but is really a female devil who has one foot and one cloven hoof. Loup Garou is a figure among whose magical powers is the ability to change shape. Papa Bois is an old man who is considered father of the forest.

34. *Port-of-Spain Gazette* (18 February 1920), p. 9; (5 March 1935), p. 7; Wilson, personal interview (22 March 1988); and Hill, *The Trinidad Carnival*, p. 47.

35. Nketia, *The Music of Africa*, p. 72–74; Courlander, *The Drum and the Hoe*, p. 208; Annette C. Macdonald, "The Big Drum Dance of Carriacou," *Revista/Review Interamericana* 8 (1978/1979): 572; Abrahams and Szwed, *After Africa*, pp. 233, 304–307; Judith Bettelheim, "Carnaval and Festivals in Cuba," in *Caribbean Festival Arts: Each and Every Bit of Difference*, ed. John W. Nunley and Judith Bettelheim (Seattle: University of Washington Press, 1988), pp. 139–140; and Dena J. Epstein, *Sinful Tunes and Spirituals: Black Folk Music to the Civil War* (Urbana: University of Illinois Press, 1977), p. 43.

36. Quoted in Pearse, "Carnival," p. 184; Elder, "Evolution of the Traditional Calypso," pp. 157, 160–161.

37. Hill, *The Trinidad Carnival*, p. 48; Crichlow, "Carnival Magic," p. 16; Prince Batson, lecture on the steelband, Trinidad Public Library, Port of Spain, Trinidad (31 October 1988); and idem., personal interview, Barataria, Trinidad (27 March 1989).

38. Nydia Daniel, personal communication, St. James, Trinidad (29 September 1988).

39. Hill, *The Trinidad Carnival*, p. 13. Naval representations have appeared elsewhere in the West Indies as well. For example, Roger Abrahams mentions the Barbados Landship Association, whose processions included officers and other personnel, model ships, and the observation of strict naval decorum (Roger D. Abrahams, "The Shaping of Folklore Traditions in the British West Indies," *Journal of Inter-American Studies* 9 [1967]: 478). Matthew Lewis describes a Blue set girls procession in Jamaica in the early nineteenth century which consisted of a young woman masquerading as Britannia, the Blue King in a full British admiral's uniform, the Blue Queen and other royal personnel, and a "'Nelson's car,' being a kind of canoe decorated with blue and silver drapery, and with 'Trafalgar' written on the front of it" (Matthew Gregory Lewis, *Journal of a West Indian Proprietor* [London, 1834], in *After Africa*, Abrahams and Szwed, pp. 242–243).

40. Hill, *The Trinidad Carnival*, pp. 93–94.

41. Batson, personal interview (27 March 1989).

42. Jason Griffith, personal interview, Belmont, Trinidad (7 April 1989); Jerry Serrant, personal interview, Port of Spain, Trinidad (18 April 1989). For further descriptions of the various types of sailor masquerades, see Daniel J. Crowley, "The Traditional Masques of Carnival," *Caribbean Quarterly* 4 (1956): 200–204; and Jerry Serrant, *Kings of the Fancy Sailors: The Saga of Jason Griffith's Old-Fashioned Sailors* (n.p., 1988).

43. *Port-of-Spain Gazette* (11 February 1930), p. 4.

44. *Port-of-Spain Gazette* (9 February 1930), p. 13.

45. Other New World Carnivals have also been characterized by ethnic and class differentiation and negotiation, cultural multiplicity and creolization, and concerns with "improvement" and public order. For historical discussions of Carnival in Brazil, Venezuela, Cuba, and the United States, see Maria Julia Gold-

wasser, "Carnival," in *The Encyclopedia of Religion*, vol. 3, ed. Mircea Eliade (New York: Macmillan, 1987), pp. 98–104; Robert H. Lavenda, "The Festival of Progress: The Globalizing World and the Transformation of the Caracas Carnival," *Journal of Popular Culture* 14 (1980): 465–475; Bettelheim, "Carnaval in Cuba," pp. 29–41; and Samuel Kinser, *Carnival American Style: Mardi Gras at New Orleans and Mobile* (Chicago: University of Chicago Press, 1990).

Chapter 2: The Emergence of the Steelband

1. Lennox Pierre, "From Dustbins to Classics," *Independence Supplement of the Sunday Guardian* (26 August 1962), p. 108; George "Sonny" Goddard, *Forty Years in the Steelbands: 1939–1979* (London: Karia Press, 1991), pp. 30–33.
2. Oscaret Claude, "Evolution, History and Future of the Steel Band," *Trinidad Guardian* (2 March 1946), p. 4.
3. Alfred Mayers, personal interview, Point Cumana, Trinidad (21 February 1989).
4. Victor Wilson, personal interview, Newtown, Trinidad (22 March 1988).
5. *Port-of-Spain Gazette* (9 February 1937), p. 6.
6. *Port-of-Spain Gazette* (11 February 1937), p. 7; *Trinidad Guardian* (9 February 1937), pp. 1, 4.
7. *Port-of-Spain Gazette* (2 March 1938), p. 7; *Trinidad Guardian* (3 March 1938), p. 3; *Port-of-Spain Gazette* (21 February 1939), p. 6.
8. *Port-of-Spain Gazette* (7 February 1940), p. 7.
9. *Port-of-Spain Gazette* (15 February 1940), p. 7. If Decca produced a record of a steelband from this trip, no known copy exists today. However, the company did release a dance band rendition of "Run Your Run Hitler" which includes metallic percussion (Decca 17348). This selection was recorded in Trinidad on February 8, 1940, by an ensemble referred to as the "Sa Gomes Rhythm Boys with Cambulay." I am grateful to Don Hill for providing me with a copy of this recording.
10. *Trinidad Guardian* (8 February 1940), p. 9.
11. *Port-of-Spain Gazette* (25 February 1941), p. 2; *Trinidad Guardian* (27 February 1941), p. 5; *Port-of-Spain Gazette* (27 February 1941), p. 2.
12. Pierre, "From Dustbins to Classics," p. 108; Goddard, *Forty Years in the Steelbands,* pp. 30–33.
13. Goddard, *Forty Years in the Steelbands,* pp. 37–38, 41.
14. Mayers, personal interview (21 February 1989).
15. Pierre, "From Dustbins to Classics," p. 108; Lennard Morris, "Tamboo Bamboo," in *Steelband Interviews II* (n.d.), National Cultural Council Collection, Ministry of Community Development, Culture, and Women's Affairs, Belmont, Trinidad. The calypsonian Raphael De Leon (Roaring Lion) states that he saw Alexander's Ragtime Band at Christmas, 1939, and that it inspired him to write a calypso for the 1940 Carnival season. The calypso describes how the band paraded the streets on Christmas night with bottle and spoon and biscuit pan (Goddard, *Forty Years in the Steelbands,* p. 25).
16. Jacob D. Elder, "Color, Music and Conflict: A Study of Aggression in

Trinidad with Reference to the Role of Traditional Music," *Ethnomusicology* 8 (1964): 134.

17. Jerry Serrant, personal interview, Port of Spain, Trinidad (7 March 1989).

18. See Claude, "Evolution, History and Future of the Steel Band," p. 4; Errol Hill, *The Trinidad Carnival: Mandate for a National Theatre* (Austin: University of Texas Press, 1972), p. 48; and Frankie Belle, "Steelband 1936–1986" (1985), manuscript in "History of Steelband" file, National Heritage Library of Trinidad and Tobago, Port of Spain, Trinidad.

19. Anthony E. Rouff, *"Authentic" Facts on the Origin of the Steelband* (St. Augustine, Trinidad: Bowen's Printery, 1972), p. 2; Bertie Marshall, "The Bertie Marshall Story: Pan Is Mih Gyul," *Tapia* 2, no. 2 (1972): 3. Professor Wilfred Cartey, who grew up in John John, also recalls this pastime (personal communication, 5 September 1988). A "steel" is an instrument used to sharpen butcher knives.

20. Wilson, personal interview (22 March 1988).

21. McKeller Sandiford, personal interview, Port of Spain, Trinidad (15 March 1989).

22. Wilson, personal interview (22 March 1988); Prince Batson, lecture on the steelband, Trinidad Public Library, Port of Spain, Trinidad (31 October 1988).

23. Rouff, *"Authentic" Facts,* pp. 4–6.

24. One band that was particularly famous for its buglers was Casablanca. Some members of this band grew up in a nearby orphanage and learned to play the bugle there.

25. Sandiford, personal interview (15 March 1989); Anthony Prospect, personal interview, Champs Fleur, Trinidad (14 November 1988).

26. Batson, public lecture (31 October 1988); idem., personal interview, Barataria, Trinidad (27 March 1989); George Yeates, personal interview, Belmont, Trinidad (2 March 1989); Leo Alfred, personal interview, Port of Spain, Trinidad (31 March 1988). East Dry River is the part of Port of Spain on the east side of the East Dry River. It includes such neighborhoods as Belmont, Gonzales, La Cour Harpe, Laventille Hill, and John John. Hell Yard is on the west bank of the river in downtown Port of Spain. Western Port of Spain is to the west of the downtown area and includes the neighborhoods of Woodbrook, Newtown, St. Clair, St. James, and Cocorite.

27. Batson, personal interview (27 March 1989).

28. Noorkumar Mahabir, "Influence of Tassa Drums on Carnival and Steelband," *Daily Express* (17 February 1984), p. 13, (18 February 1984), p. 23. It should be noted that pans were also based on musical principles similar to those of the xylophone, and the xylophone may have been another influence on the early steelband. Xylophones are found throughout much of Africa, both as solo instruments and in ensembles. One type used in the western and central regions of the continent has multiple wooden keys which are graded in size and produce a series of tones. The keys are suspended over gourd resonators and are struck with two sticks which have soft material on the ends. Some gourd xylophones in Africa are mounted on frames, while others are suspended around the neck [J. H. Kwabena Nketia, *The Music of Africa* (New York: Norton, 1974), pp. 77, 81–84; Gerhard Kubik and James Blades, "Marimba," in *The New Grove Dictionary of Music and Musicians,* vol. 11, ed. Stanley Sadie (London: Macmillan Publishers Limited, 1980), pp. 681–683; Dena J. Epstein, *Sinful Tunes and Spirituals: Black Folk Music to the Civil War* (Urbana: University of Illinois Press), pp.

55–57]. Knowledge of xylophones was brought by Africans to the New World and, during the slavery period, versions of the instrument were reported in Barbados, St. Vincent, Jamaica, Suriname, and Virginia (Epstein, *Sinful Tunes and Spirituals*, pp. 57–58). Traditional types are still played in Brazil, Columbia, Ecuador, Nicaragua, Guatemala, Mexico, and Cuba where they are often known as *marimbas*. In Guatemala the marimba is the national instrument. There, at least one form is played with sticks that are wrapped with varying amounts of rubber, according to whether they are used for treble or bass keys. The marimba was first manufactured as a modern orchestral instrument in the United States in 1910 [Kubik and Blades, "Marimba," pp. 682–683; Linda L. O'Brien, "Guatemala: Folk Music," in *The New Grove Dictionary*, vol. 7, Sadie, pp. 776–777; George List, "Columbia: Folk Music," in *The New Grove Dictionary*, vol. 4, Sadie, p. 574].

29. Rouff, *"Authentic" Facts*, pp. 4–7, 10; Ellie Mannette, "The Story of Pan," *The Sun* (21 March 1986), p. 9, (4 April 1986), p. 9; Neville Jules, "The History of Pan," *Down Town Mas* (1984): 15; idem, personal interview, Brooklyn, New York (10 April 1991).

30. Anthony Williams, personal interview, Laventille, Trinidad (23 June 1988); idem., personal interview, Laventille, Trinidad (4 October 1988); Jules, "The History of Pan," p. 15.

31. Mannette, "The Story of Pan," (21 March 1986), p. 9; Lennox Pierre, lecture on the steelband, Oilfield Workers Trade Union Hall, Port of Spain, Trinidad (2 November 1988); Batson, lecture on the steelband (31 October 1988).

32. Jeffrey R. Thomas, "A History of Pan and the Evolution of the Steel Band in Trinidad and Tobago" (M.A. thesis, Wesleyan University, 1985), pp. 132–133; Williams, personal interview (4 October 1988); Mannette, "The Story of Pan," (21 March 1986), p. 9; Jules, personal interview, (10 April 1991).

33. Lennox Pierre, "History and Development of Steelband," video tape of lecture delivered at West Indian Reference Section, Central Library of Trinidad and Tobago, Belmont, Trinidad (St. James, Trinidad: Educational Television Unit, Ministry of Education, 1987).

34. Jules, personal interview (10 April 1991).

35. Ibid.; Prince Batson, personal interview, Port of Spain, Trinidad, (31 October 1988).

36. Leo Warner, personal interview, Belmont, Trinidad (10 May 1988).

37. Hill, *The Trinidad Carnival*, p. 52.

38. Selwyn D. Ryan, *Race and Nationalism in Trinidad and Tobago: A Study of Decolonization in a Multiracial Society* (Toronto: University of Toronto Press, 1972), pp. 47–57. For additional commentary on the 1930s, see Bridget Brereton, *A History of Modern Trinidad: 1783–1962* (Kingston: Heinemann Educational Books [Caribbean] Ltd., 1981); Roy E. Thomas, ed. *The Trinidad Labour Riots of 1937: Perspectives 50 Years Later* (St. Augustine, Trinidad: Extra-Mural Studies Unit, University of the West Indies, 1987); Kelvin Singh, *Race and Class Struggles in a Colonial State: Trinidad 1917–1945* (Mona, Jamaica: The Press—University of the West Indies, 1994); Arthur Calder–Marshall's journalistic study, *Glory Dead* (London: Michael Joseph, 1939); and Ralph de Boissière's historical novel, *Crown Jewel* (London: Pan Books, 1981 [1952]). For a discussion of how calypsonians perceived the social conditions and events of this period, see Gordon Rohlehr, *Calypso & Society in Pre-Independence Trinidad* (Port of Spain: Gordon

Rohlehr, 1990).

39. Brereton, *A History of Modern Trinidad,* p. 184.

40. Michael Anthony, *Port-of-Spain in a World at War, 1939–1945* (Port of Spain: Ministry of Sport, Culture and Youth Affairs, n.d.), p. 43. In addition to Anthony's overview of the war years, see Brereton, *A History of Modern Trinidad,* pp. 189–192; and Singh, *Race and Class Struggles.* Ralph de Boissière's second novel, *Rum and Coca-Cola* (London: Allison and Busby, 1984 [1956]), and Samuel Selvon's first novel, *A Brighter Sun* (London: Allan Wingate, 1952), offer vivid portrayals of the period. For the perspectives of the calypsonians, see Raymond Quevedo, *Atilla's Kaiso: A Short History of Trinidad Calypso* (St. Augustine, Trinidad: Department of Extra Mural Studies, University of the West Indies, 1983); and Rohlehr, *Calypso & Society.*

41. Lloyd Braithwaite, "Social Stratification in Trinidad," *Social and Economic Studies* 2, nos. 2 & 3 (1953): 133–134; Wenzell Brown, *Angry Men, Laughing Men: The Caribbean Caldron* (New York: Greenberg, 1947), p. 247.

42. Quevedo, *Atilla's Kaiso,* p. 75.

43. Ibid., p. 76–77.

44. Ibid., p. 72; Anthony, *Port-of-Spain in a World at War,* pp. 64–65.

45. Braithwaite, "Social Stratification in Trinidad," pp. 77–78, 134.

46. Alfred, personal interview (31 March 1988); Vernon Mannette, personal interview, Woodbrook, Trinidad (4 December 1988).

47. Wellington Bostock, personal interview, Port of Spain, Trinidad (23 February 1989).

48. Mayers, personal interview (21 February 1989).

49. Alfred, personal interview (31 March 1988).

50. The writer Patrick Leigh Fermor visited Trinidad after the war and, in *The Traveller's Tree: A Journey Through the Caribbean Islands* (London: John Murray, 1950), provides an account of his trip to Hell Yard:

We all four took a taxi to the street called Piccadilly, on the other side of the dry river, and our new acquaintance led us down an alley-way between heavily populated wooden houses, over a wall and into a large pit built in a bay of the embankment. It was full of young Negroes hammering out, on extraordinary instruments, the noise I had heard. When we appeared with his friend, the leader rose, shook hands, and gave us four little rum kegs to sit on, and went on playing.

The leader, or Captain, was a Negro in his early twenties called Fish Eyes Rudolf Olivier. His face, of which the most notable feature were two great bulging eyes, was full of humor and sensibility and remarkably attractive. When the din had stopped, he made some introductions. 'This is Neville Jules, my second-in-command, and this is my managing director, O. Rudder.' The ease of his manner was admirable. 'Now I'll show you our yard.' He led the way into the centre with the air of a country magnate flinging open the double doors of the ballroom.

It was a piece of waste land, a-flutter with clothes lines, jammed between the embankment and the backs of houses, and the only way in and out was by climbing the six-foot wall we had just negotiated. The band was a little group of young men from the neighborhood who had installed themselves here and turned it into a stronghold. A blue banner, embroidered with the name of the group, was stuck in the ground, and, beyond the minstrels, half a dozen familiars were playing gin-rummy on a plank between two kegs. . . .

The instruments that produced the music looked at first like the rusty spare parts of motor cars, and on closer inspection that is exactly what some of them proved to be (pp. 170–171).

Leigh Fermor goes on to describe the band's pans and a rendition of "Ave Maria." His observations on Trinidad also include a detailed description of a saga boy dress style (pp. 175–176).

51. Jules, personal interview (10 April 1991).

52. Batson, personal interview (27 March 1989).

53. *Port-of-Spain Gazette* (17 February 1942), p. 2; ibid. (5 January 1944), p. 3; Serrant, personal interview (7 March 1989).

54. MacDonald Kinsale, personal interview, Morvant, Trinidad (20 March 1989). In *Forty Years in the Steelbands*, pp. 42–43, George Goddard states that Red Army was not formed until V-J Day and that it was Alexander's Ragtime Band that painted its pans with hammers and sickles for V-E Day. This does not entirely conflict with Mack Kinsale's story since Red Army drew on some of the membership of Alexander's Ragtime Band.

55. *Trinidad Guardian* (9 May 1945), p. 1; *Port-of-Spain Gazette* (9 May 1945), p. 1.

56. *Trinidad Guardian* (18 August 1945), p. 1.

57. *Trinidad Guardian* (5 January 1946), p. 1; ibid. (8 January 1946), p. 1; John G. La Guerre, "The General Elections of 1946 in Trinidad and Tobago," *Social and Economic Studies* 21, no. 2 (1972): 189. For additional accounts of Trinidad in the postwar years, see Brereton, *A History of Modern Trinidad;* Braithwaite, "Social Stratification in Trinidad"; Brown, *Angry Men, Laughing Men*; and Leigh Fermor, *The Traveller's Tree.*

58. Batson, personal interview (27 March 1989); Kinsale, personal interview (20 March 1989).

59. *Trinidad Guardian* (5 March 1946), pp. 1–2.

60. *Trinidad Guardian* (6 March 1946), p. 1.

61. *Trinidad Guardian* (18 February 1947), p. 5; (18 February 1947), p 1.

62. Due to the war, British and American military uniforms were banned from Carnival in 1940 and 1941 respectively (Rohlehr, *Calypso & Society,* p. 335). In 1946 uniforms were again permitted "so long as they are modified so as not to represent the identical outfit now used by the forces" (*Trinidad Guardian* [26 February 1946], p. 1).

63. Jason Griffith, personal interview, Belmont, Trinidad (7 April 1989); Warner, personal interview (10 May 1988).

64. *Trinidad Guardian* (11 February 1948), p. 2.

65. Ibid.; Alfred, personal interview (31 March 1988).

66. Jerry Serrant, personal interview, Port of Spain, Trinidad (19 September 1988).

67. Williams, personal interview (4 October 1988).

68. *Trinidad Guardian* (7 August 1946), pp. 1, 7.

69. Warner, personal interview (10 May 1988); Wilson, personal interview (22 March 1988); Alfred, personal interview (31 March 1988).

70. Goddard, *Forty Years in the Steelbands,* p. 42.

71. *Port-of-Spain Gazette* (5 March 1946), p. 1; Rouff, *"Authentic" Facts*, pp. 11–12.

72. Williams, personal interview (4 October 1988).

73. *Trinidad Guardian* (19 December 1946), p. 7; Kinsale, personal interview (20 March 1989).

74. *Sunday Express* (21 February 1993), Living Section, p. 2.

75. Gordon Rohlehr, personal communication (17 April 1989).

76. Lennox Pierre, personal interview, Port of Spain, Trinidad (12 July 1988).

77. *Trinidad Guardian* (6 February 1947), p. 4.

78. *Trinidad Guardian* (20 February 1947), p. 1; (6 August 1947), p. 5.

79. *Trinidad Guardian* (29 December 1948), pp. 1–2.

80. Ibid., p. 1.

81. Mannette, personal interview (4 December 1988). For coverage of the Invaders-Casablanca feud, see *Trinidad Guardian* (15 September 1949), p. 3; (28 October 1949), p. 7; (10 December 1949), p. 5; (10 January 1950), p. 1; and (11 January 1950), p. 1.

82. *Trinidad Guardian* (16 September 1949), p. 6.

83. *Trinidad Guardian* (1 March 1946), p. 5.

84. *Trinidad Guardian* (18 February 1947), p. 6; *Sunday Guardian* (27 February 1949), p. 8; *Trinidad Guardian* (6 February 1948), p. 6.

85. *Trinidad Guardian* (8 December 1945), p. 2.

86. *Trinidad Guardian* (6 June 1946), p. 4; (30 May 1946), p. 4.

87. *Trinidad Guardian* (12 June 1946), p. 3.

88. *Trinidad Guardian* (13 June 1946), p. 4.

89. Bertie Marshall, "The Bertie Marshall Story: Pan Is Mih Gyul," *Tapia* 2, no. 2 (1972): 3.

90. Kinsale, personal interview (20 March 1989).

91. Sandiford, personal interview (15 March 1989).

92. See Keith Smith, ed., *Sparrow: The Legend* (n.p.: Inprint, n.d.).

93. *Trinidad Guardian* (12 May 1945), p. 2; (18 August 1945), p. 2.

94. Jacob Elder, personal communication (16 November 1988).

95. Lytton Stewart, personal interview, Mt. Pleasant, Tobago (17 November 1988); *Trinidad Guardian* (2 March 1946), p. 5.

96. Stewart, personal interview (17 November 1988); George Richardson, personal interview, Plymouth, Tobago (17 November 1988).

97. Elder, personal communication (16 November 1988); Richardson, personal interview (17 November 1988).

98. There was heavy migration to Trinidad from a range of islands in the West Indies during the war years, and the return of migrants to their homes after the war appears to have been an important means by which the steelband spread through the Caribbean. For example, pan was introduced to Antigua around 1946 by some Antiguans who had been living in Trinidad. Among the early bands on this island were Hell's Gate, Brute Force, and Red Army (Rick Howard, "Is Antiguan Pan Ready to Rebound?," *Pan* 1, no. 1 [1985]: 15–17). Meanwhile, Trinidadians themselves took their pans to other islands. For example, Trinidadians working for an oil company in Aruba celebrated V-E Day there with pans (*Trinidad Guardian* [31 May 1945], p. 2). In 1946 five Trinidadian crew members of a schooner in port at St. Lucia took their pans out on the streets to celebrate the eve of Empire Day and managed to incite "mob violence" among their singing and dancing followers. The Trinidadians were ad-

vised by the police on proper behavior in St. Lucia and their pans were seized (*Sunday Guardian* [26 May 1946], p. 9). Red Army's tour to British Guiana in December 1946 may also have been the first time pans were heard in this territory.

99. The spiritual significance of drumming may also have continued in pan. Trinidadians sometimes describe pan as having a religious dimension.

100. Peter J. Wilson, "Reputation vs. Respectability: A Suggestion for Caribbean Ethnology," *Man* 4 (1969): 70–84; idem., *Crab Antics: The Social Anthropology of English-Speaking Negro Societies of the Caribbean* (New Haven, Conn.: Yale University Press, 1973). In the 1950s Andrew Pearse suggested a perspective on Trinidadian society that in some respects parallels Wilson's framework. Pearse described a "superstructure" which consists of "the interwoven administrative, legal, economic and religious institutions stemming from the colonising power (or its predecessor) and supported by it." Existing within this system are the "folk"—"the major part of whose culture has been transmitted to them from sources other than those of the superstructural institutions." Pearse also commented that the jamettes "represented the reversal of the values of respectability and a flamboyant rejection of the norms of the superstructure" ("Carnival in Nineteenth Century Trinidad," *Caribbean Quarterly* 4 [1956]: 190–192).

101. Roger D. Abrahams, "Reputation vs. Respectability: A Review of Peter J. Wilson's Concept," *Revista/Review Interamericana* 9 (1979): 448–453; idem., *The Man-of-Words in the West Indies: Performance and the Emergence of Creole Culture* (Baltimore: Johns Hopkins University Press, 1983); Jean Besson, "Reputation and Respectability Reconsidered: A New Perspective on Afro-Caribbean Peasant Women," in *Women and Change in the Caribbean*, ed. Janet H. Momsen (Bloomington: Indiana University Press, 1993), pp. 15–37.

102. Stuart Hall and Tony Jefferson, eds., *Resistance Through Rituals: Youth Subcultures in Post-War Britain* (London: Hutchinson, 1976). In *Subculture: The Meaning of Style* (New York: Methuen, 1979), Dick Hebdige gives special attention to how the startling, fabricated character of youth cultural styles disrupts symbolic systems and thus presents a challenge to the dominant cultural order. For a critical perspective on the Birmingham school's research in this area, see Gary Clarke, "Defending Ski-Jumpers: A Critique of Theories of Youth Subcultures," in *On Record: Rock, Pop, and the Written Word*, ed. Simon Frith and Andrew Goodwin (New York: Pantheon Books, 1990), pp. 81–96.

Chapter 3: The Institutionalization of the Steelband

1. Bridget Brereton, *A History of Modern Trinidad: 1783–1962* (Kingston: Heinemann Educational Books [Caribbean] Ltd., 1981), p. 143.

2. Ibid., pp. 161, 167.

3. Selwyn D. Ryan, *Race and Nationalism in Trinidad and Tobago: A Study of Decolonization in a Multiracial Society* (Toronto: University of Toronto Press, 1972), pp. 38.

4. C. L. R. James, *Minty Alley* (London: New Beacon Books Ltd., 1975 [1936]).

5. Brereton, *A History of Modern Trinidad*, pp. 240–241. In addition to Brereton's general history of Trinidad, see Ryan, *Race and Nationalism in Trinidad and Tobago*, and Ivar Oxaal, *Black Intellectuals and the Dilemmas of Race and Class in Trinidad* (Cambridge, Mass.: Schenkman Publishing Co., 1982), for in-depth studies of the development of nationalism and the transition to independence.

In *Urban Nationalism: A Study of Political Development in Trinidad* (Gainesville: University of Florida Press, 1988), Alvin Magid provides a detailed account of nationalism in Port of Spain in the late nineteenth and early twentieth centuries. See Bruce King, ed., *West Indian Literature* (Hamden, Conn.: Archon Books, 1979) for essays dealing with literary movements and figures in Trinidad, including novelists who began publishing in the 1950s such as Samuel Selvon, Michael Anthony, and V. S. Naipaul. For various perspectives on social structure and ethnic relations in Trinidad during the period of decolonization, see Lloyd Braithwaite, "Social Stratification in Trinidad," *Social and Economic Studies* 2, nos. 2&3 (1953): 5–175; idem., "The Problem of Cultural Integration in Trinidad," *Social and Economic Studies* 3, no. 1 (1954): 82–96; Daniel J. Crowley, "Plural and Differential Acculturation in Trinidad," *American Anthropologist* 59 (1957): 817–824; idem., "Cultural Assimilation in a Multiracial Society," *Annals of the New York Academy of Sciences* 83, no. 5 (1960): 850–854; Vera Rubin, "Culture, Politics and Race Relations," *Social and Economic Studies* 11 (1962): 433–455; and Daniel A. Segal, "'Race' and 'Colour' in Pre-Independence Trinidad and Tobago," in *Trinidad Ethnicity*, ed. Kevin Yelvington (London: Macmillan Caribbean, 1993), pp. 81–115. For a sceptical view on national consciousness in Trinidad at mid-century, see V. S. Naipaul's *The Middle Passage* (New York: Vintage Books, 1981 [1962]), pp. 40–85.

6. Spiritual Baptist churches range from those that are essentially Protestant to ones that have substantial Orisha influence. The religion was prohibited in Trinidad from 1917 until 1951.

7. Initially, Gomes wrote this column under the pseudonym of "Ubiquitous." By 1949, however, he was using his own name.

8. *Sunday Guardian* (16 June 1946), p. 4B.

9. *Sunday Guardian* (20 November 1949), p. 16.

10. *Sunday Guardian* (27 November 1949), p. 6.

11. *Sunday Guardian* (4 December 1949), p. 6.

12. *Sunday Guardian* (15 February 1948), p. 13. See Gomes's autobiography, *Through a Maze of Colour* (Port of Spain: Key Caribbean Publications Ltd., 1974), pp. 95–100, for additional impressions of the steelband movement.

13. *Trinidad Guardian* (13 June 1946), p. 4.

14. *Trinidad Guardian* (22 June 1946), p. 6.

15. During this same period calypso music was also increasingly appreciated and researched as a local art. For a discussion of this interest and the resistance to government censorship of calypso, see Gordon Rohlehr, *Calypso & Society in Pre-Independence Trinidad* (Port of Spain: Gordon Rohlehr, 1990), pp. 385–400.

16. Lennox Pierre, "History and Development of Steelband," video tape of lecture delivered at West Indian Reference Section, Central Library of Trinidad and Tobago, Belmont, Trinidad (St. James, Trinidad: Educational Television Unit, Ministry of Education, 1987); Errol Hill, *The Trinidad Carnival: Mandate for a National Theatre* (Austin: University of Texas Press, 1972), p. 49.

17. Beryl McBurnie, personal interview, St. James, Trinidad (17 March 1988). McBurnie's interest in folklore was also encouraged by Carlton Comma, a librarian at the Trinidad Public Library who had studied at the Hampton Institute in the United States. For an overview of McBurnie's career and contribution to the arts in Trinidad, see Molly Ahye, *Cradle of Caribbean Dance: Beryl McBurnie and the Little Carib Theatre* (Trinidad and Tobago: Theatre Heritage Cultures Ltd., 1983).

18. *Sunday Guardian* (16 June 1946), p. 4B. For further description of this event, see *Trinidad Guardian* (8 June 1946), p. 4.

19. "Talking Drums," program for the formal opening of the Little Carib Theatre (25 November 1948), National Heritage Library of Trinidad and Tobago, Port of Spain, Trinidad.

20. McBurnie, personal interview (17 March 1988).

21. Vernon Mannette, personal interview, Woodbrook, Trinidad (4 December 1988); Alfred Mayers, personal interviews, Point Cumana, Trinidad (22 December 1988 and 21 February 1989).

22. *Trinidad Guardian* (7 February 1950), p. 5.

23. W. Austin Simmonds, *Pan: The Story of the Steelband* (Maraval, Trinidad: BWIA International, n.d. [1959]), p. 13. See also *Trinidad Guardian* (21 February 1950), p. 11.

24. *Trinidad Guardian* (31 May 1951), p. 10.

25. Pierre, "History and Development of Steelband"; idem., "From Dustbins to Classics," *Independence Supplement of the Sunday Guardian* (26 August 1962), p. 108.

26. Pierre, "History and Development of Steelband"; idem., lecture on the steelband, Oilfield Workers Trade Union Hall, Port of Spain, Trinidad (2 November 1988).

27. *Trinidad Guardian* (22 September 1949), p. 7.

28. *Sunday Guardian* (25 September 1949), p. 13.

29. *Sunday Guardian* (27 November 1949), p. 1. One of the organizations represented on the committee, the Trinidad and Tobago Folklore Society, had been formed just two months earlier. Its management committee included Eric Williams, Albert Gomes, H. O. B. Wooding, Lennox Pierre, Dom Basil Matthews, Beryl McBurnie, and C. R. Ottley (see *Sunday Guardian* [2 October 1949], p. 3).

30. Minutes of the Steel Band Committee meeting, Red House, Port of Spain, Trinidad (8 December 1949). I owe special thanks to steelband researcher Jeffrey Thomas for providing me with copies of the minutes of this meeting and of the two Steel Band Committee meetings cited below.

31. *Trinidad Guardian* (4 January 1950), p. 2.

32. Minutes of the Steel Band Committee meeting, Trinidad Public Library, Port of Spain, Trinidad (12 January 1950); Minutes of the Steel Band Committee meeting, Red House, Port of Spain, Trinidad (18 January 1950).

33. *Sunday Guardian* (22 January 1950), p. 16.

34. Though accounts of steelband history generally credit the Steel Band Committee's efforts as being the first attempt to unite the panmen, there is some evidence that similar efforts were made almost a year earlier by an individual named Harold Blake. Blake recently passed on some manuscript material to Pan Trinbago (the current steelband association) that suggests that he had organized a meeting at the Government Training College in March 1949 which was attended by representatives of some twenty steelbands. Among the speakers at the meeting were Henry Hall (the principal of the College), Albert Gomes, and Blake himself. Blake claims that by June 1949 the bands had formed a Steel Band Music Association of Trinidad and Tobago with patrons such as Gomes, Farquhar, McBurnie, and H. O. B. Wooding. Later that year, when he heard about the Steel Band Committee, Blake wrote the Colonial Secretary about his association. The letter was forwarded to the Steel Band Committee and dis-

cussed at their first meeting. The Committee decided to write Blake and express their appreciation of his efforts (Minutes of the Steel Band Committee meeting [8 December 1949]). What is not clear at present is how much attention the steelbands gave to this association. Given the fact that there was a considerable amount of steelband violence in late 1949 and early 1950, it appears that the organization was short-lived and not very effective.

35. *Trinidad Guardian* (16 February 1950), p. 3; (21 February 1950), p. 1; (2 March 1950), p. 1.

36. *Trinidad Guardian* (7 March 1950), p. 2.

37. *Trinidad Guardian* (21 March 1950), p. 5. For Albert Gomes's impressions of the Steel Band Committee's efforts to resolve band conflicts, see *Sunday Guardian* (2 April 1950), p. 16.

38. *Trinidad Guardian* (7 April 1950), p. 3.

39. *Trinidad Guardian* (14 April 1950), p. 3.

40. *Trinidad Guardian* (13 May 1950); p. 6. For reports on the organization of steelbands in southern Trinidad, see ibid. (15 April 1950), p. 5; and (18 April 1950), p. 3.

41. Jerry Serrant, personal interview, Port of Spain, Trinidad (8 June 1988).

42. Mayers, personal interview (21 February 1989).

43. Leo Warner, personal interview, Belmont, Trinidad (3 May 1988); McKeller Sandiford, personal interview, Port of Spain, Trinidad (15 March 1989); John E. Slater, *The Advent of the Steel Band and My Life and Times with It* (n.p., n.d.), p. 19.

44. Mannette, personal interview (4 December 1988); Leo Alfred, personal interview, Port of Spain, Trinidad (31 March 1988); Oscar Pile, lecture on the steelband, Trinidad Public Library, Port of Spain, Trinidad (31 October 1988).

45. *Sunday Guardian* (29 April 1951), p. 6. Antigua also planned to send a steelband to the festival (see *Trinidad Guardian* [20 January 1951], p. 1).

46. Anthony Williams, personal interview, Laventille, Trinidad (23 June 1988).

47. Pierre, "History and Development of Steelband."

48. These selections are listed on a program for a TASPO concert at the Globe Cinema, Port of Spain, on June 25, 1951. A copy of the program is in Pan Trinbago's archives, Port of Spain, Trinidad.

49. *Trinidad Guardian* (20 June 1951), p. 2.

50. *Sunday Guardian* (13 May 1951), p. 16.

51. *Trinidad Guardian* (31 May 1951), p. 6; *Sunday Guardian* (17 June 1951), p. 6.

52. Anthony Williams, personal interview, Laventille, Trinidad (4 October 1988).

53. *Sunday Guardian* (1 July 1951), p. 9.

54. *Trinidad Guardian* (7 July 1951), p. 1.

55. Ibid., p. 5.

56. Ibid.

57. *Trinidad Guardian* (28 July 1951), p. 1.

58. *Trinidad Guardian* (5 September 1951), p. 10.

59. Pierre, "History and Development of Steelband."

60. For additional reports on TASPO's preparation in Trinidad and appearances in Britain, see the following issues of the *Guardian*: 23 February 1951, 17

April 1951, 22 April 1951, 3 May 1951, 6 May 1951, 20 May 1951, 29 May 1951, 13 June 1951, 4 July 1951, 15 July 1951, 3 August 1951, 4 August 1951, 9 August 1951, 14 August 1951, and 25 August 1951.

61. Junior Pouchet, personal interview, Woodbrook, Trinidad (2 February 1989).

62. Ray Holman, personal interview, Woodbrook, Trinidad (13 December 1988).

63. Curtis Pierre, personal interview, Port of Spain, Trinidad (14 January 1992). For a description of Dixieland's membership and activities around 1960, see Judith Ann Weller, "A Profile of a Trinidadian Steel-Band," *Phylon* 22 (1961): 68–77.

64. Mayers, personal interview (21 February 1989).

65. Pouchet, personal interview (2 February 1989).

66. "Stromboli," in *Steelband Interviews II* (n.d.), National Cultural Council Collection, Ministry of Community Development, Culture, and Women's Affairs, Belmont, Trinidad.

67. Pouchet, personal interview (2 February 1989).

68. Ibid.

69. Mayers, personal interview (21 February 1989); Holman, personal interview (13 December 1988).

70. Holman, personal interview (13 December 1988).

71. Anthony Williams, personal interview, Laventille, Trinidad (23 September 1988).

72. *Trinidad Guardian* (5 March 1952), p. 7; (7 March 1952), p. 7.

73. *Trinidad Guardian* (12 March 1952), p. 1.

74. Ibid.

75. Williams, personal interview (4 October 1988).

76. Anthony Williams, "Excerpts from Anthony Williams' History of the Steelband, 1946–1962," in *Steel Pan: Trinidad & Tobago's Gift to the World*, (n.p., n.d.), p. 18; *Sunday Guardian* (26 February 1956), p. 12.

77. *Trinidad Guardian* (17 March 1956), p. 2; (20 March 1956), p. 11.

78. *Sunday Guardian* (25 March 1956), p. 6.

79. Pierre, personal interview (14 January 1992).

80. Williams, personal interview (4 October 1988).

81. *Sunday Guardian* (25 March 1956), p. 6.

82. A brass band is a dance band that includes not only brass instruments but reeds, stringed instruments, and a rhythm section. These bands also accompany calypsonians and perform on the streets for Carnival.

83. Owen Serrette, personal interview, Port of Spain, Trinidad (14 December 1988).

84. Williams, personal interview (23 September 1988). Jeffrey Thomas states that the first double seconds were conceived by Ernest Ferreira of Dixieland and tuned by Percy Thomas of Katzenjammers. Their instrument consisted of two single seconds welded together and included a total of 23 notes (*Forty Years of Steel: An Annotated Discography of Steel Band and Pan Recordings, 1951–1991* [Westport, Conn.: Greenwood Press, 1992], p. xvi).

85. Williams, personal interview (4 October 1988).

86. Sandiford, personal interview (15 March 1989).

87. See George "Sonny" Goddard, *Forty Years in the Steelbands: 1939–1979*

(London: Karia Press, 1991), p. 49.

88. *Trinidad Guardian* (6 June 1953), p. 1.

89. *Trinidad Guardian* (9 June 1953), p. 7. For other reports on the Coronation Carnival, see *Sunday Guardian* (7 June 1953), p. 1; and *Trinidad Guardian* (9 June 1953), p. 2; (10 June 1953), p. 1. The estimated two hundred injuries for the event may have been an exaggeration (see *Sunday Guardian* [5 July 1953], p. 7; and *Trinidad Guardian* [22 July 1953], p. 6).

90. Curtis Pierre quoted in William R. Aho, "Steelband Music in Trinidad and Tobago: The Creation of a People's Music," *Latin American Music Review* 8 (1987): 41; *Trinidad Guardian* (9 June 1953), p. 6; *Port-of-Spain Gazette* (13 June 1953), p. 4.

91. *Trinidad Guardian* (23 June 1953), p. 6.

92. *Sunday Guardian* (5 July 1953), p. 7.

93. Williams, personal interview (4 October 1988); idem., "Excerpts from Anthony Williams' History of the Steelband," p. 18; Pierre, "From Dustbins to Classics," p. 110.

94. Prince Batson, personal interview, Port of Spain, Trinidad (31 October 1988); Jerry Serrant, personal interview, Port of Spain, Trinidad (19 September 1988). Occasionally, steelbands played foreign tunes and commercial jingles in calypso rhythm as road marches for their masqueraders. This generated considerable controversy among aficionados of Carnival music during the 1950s (see Rohlehr, *Calypso & Society*, pp. 437–442).

95. *Sunday Guardian* (16 February 1958), p. 20.

96. Williams, personal interview (4 October 1988).

97. In reference to bomb tunes, Bertie Marshall of Highlanders comments: "For myself, I have always enjoyed interpreting classical tunes. I felt when I was arranging a particular classic that I was imposing myself on the composer. It was taking the foundation he had built for his tune and building an entirely new house" ("The Bertie Marshall Story: Pan Is Mih Gyul," *Tapia* 2, no. 7 [1972]: 10).

98. *Trinidad Guardian* (26 January 1959), p. 9.

99. Leo Warner, personal interview, Belmont, Trinidad (10 May 1988).

100. Williams, personal interview (4 October 1988); Mayers, personal interview (21 February 1989).

101. Oxaal, *Black Intellectuals,* p. 96.

102. In addition to Ivar Oxaal's examination of the People's National Movement, see Ryan, *Race and Nationalism in Trinidad and Tobago,* and Brereton, *A History of Modern Trinidad.* For a collection of and commentary on Williams's speeches, see Selwyn R. Cudjoe, ed., *Eric E. Williams Speaks: Essays on Colonialism and Independence* (Wellesley, Mass.: Calaloux Publications, 1993).

103. George Yeates, personal interview, Belmont, Trinidad (2 March 1989).

104. Susan E. Craig, *Community Development in Trinidad and Tobago, 1943–1973: From Welfare to Patronage* (Mona, Jamaica: Institute of Social and Economic Research, University of the West Indies, 1974), p. 34.

105. Bertie Marshall, "The Bertie Marshall Story: Pan Is Mih Gyul," *Tapia* 2, no. 4 (1972): 4.

106. *Trinidad Guardian* (23 February 1957), p. 2.

107. Rohlehr, *Calypso & Society,* p. 447. For additional discussion of the Downtown vs. Savannah Carnival opposition, see ibid., pp. 401–408, 425. See also Albert Gomes's analysis of the 1957 Downtown-Savannah conflict in the *Sunday*

Guardian (3 March 1957), p. 24. Gomes comments that: "The Savannah cele-brations have always been regarded with suspicion and even hostility by those purists and die-hards, who see in the orientation towards St. Clair [the nearby elite neighborhood] a sinister threat of slow emasculation that ultimately will transform the Bacchanalian ritual into polite school-graduation pantomime. There is a powerful class motivation in this criticism." However, Gomes also notes that the residents of St. Clair probably would not protest if more down-towners came to the Savannah because "on Carnival days the interesting phe-nomenon is that St. Clair strives valiantly to emulate the orgiastic gyrations of down-town across-the-bridge and on-top the hill."

108. *Sunday Guardian* (3 March 1957), p. 8; Rohlehr, *Calypso & Society,* pp. 401, 425.

109. Franz Fanon, *The Wretched of the Earth* (New York: Grove Press, 1963), p. 170 (see also pp. 47–48, 121–124, 133, 169). For general discussions of national-ism in the anglophone Caribbean, see Gordon K. Lewis, *The Growth of the Modern West Indies* (New York: Monthly Review Press, 1968); and Wendell Bell, "Equality and Social Justice: Foundations of Nationalism in the Caribbean," *Caribbean Studies* 20, no. 2 (1980): 5–36. In recent years greater attention has been given to nationalism and culture in West Indian societies. See, for example, Brackette F. Williams, *Stains on My Name, War in My Veins: Guyana and the Politics of Cultural Struggle* (Durham, N.C.: Duke University Press, 1991).

110. Braithwaite, "The Problem of Cultural Integration in Trinidad," p. 90; Barbara E. Powrie, "The Changing Attitude of the Coloured Middle Class To-ward Carnival," *Caribbean Quarterly* 4 (1956): 231.

111. Braithwaite, "The Problem of Cultural Integration in Trinidad," pp. 90–91.

Chapter 4: The Steelband in the Post-Independence Era

1. *Trinidad Guardian* (30 August 1962), pp. 1–2. For accounts of the build-up to Independence Day, see the following issues of the *Guardian*: 15 July 1962, 5 August 1962, 9 August 1962, 10 August 1962 and 26–31 August 1962.

2. Carl Stone, *Democracy and Clientelism in Jamaica* (New Brunswick, N.J.: Transaction Books, 1980), pp. 93, 95. For a discussion of clientelism in Trinidad, see Percy C. Hintzen, *The Costs of Regime Survival: Racial Mobilization, Elite Domination and Control of the State in Guyana and Trinidad* (Cambridge: Cam-bridge University Press, 1989).

3. Susan E. Craig, *Community Development in Trinidad and Tobago, 1943–1973: From Welfare to Patronage* (Mona, Jamaica: Institute of Social and Economic Re-search, University of the West Indies, 1974), p. 40.

4. Scott B. MacDonald, *Trinidad and Tobago: Democracy and Development in the Caribbean* (New York: Praeger, 1986), p. 148.

5. *Daily Mirror* (24 March 1965), p. 17; *Trinidad Guardian* (16 August 1965), p. 9.

6. George "Sonny" Goddard, *Forty Years in the Steelbands: 1939–1979* (London: Karia Press, 1991), pp. 109, 115, 130–136, 154–155, 168–169; Junior Pouchet, personal interview, Woodbrook, Trinidad (2 February 1989).

7. *Trinidad Guardian* (29 January 1973), p. 1, 9; Goddard, *Forty Years in the Steelbands,* p. 178. For a review of one of the Carols and Classics on Steel con-

certs, see *Trinidad Guardian* (21 December 1967), p. 6.

8. Pouchet, personal interview (2 February 1989). At times, the Esso band used the name "Esso Southern Symphony." In 1959, for example, Cook Records recorded a few singles of the band under this name (CC 5848, CC 5849, and CC 5900).

9. *Trinidad Guardian* (3 February 1960), p. 5; (1 March 1966), p. 7.

10. See Selwyn D. Ryan, *Race and Nationalism in Trinidad and Tobago: A Study of Decolonization in a Multiracial Society* (Toronto: University of Toronto Press, 1972), pp. 409–412.

11. Anthony Williams, personal interview, Laventille, Trinidad (4 October 1988).

12. Pouchet, personal interview (2 February 1989).

13. *Trinidad Guardian* (1 March 1966), p. 7.

14. *Evening News* (9 September 1964), p. 4.

15. Owen Serrette, personal interview, Port of Spain, Trinidad (14 December 1988).

16. *Trinidad Guardian* (20 January 1965), p. 6.

17. Steelbands began chroming their higher range pans in the early 1970s in order to better preserve the metal and to give them a more impressive appearance.

18. Michael Cupidore, personal interview, St. James, Trinidad (20 December 1988).

19. Kendall Lewis, personal interview, Diego Martin, Trinidad (27 October 1988).

20. Sampoco Oil Company Gay Desperadoes is a fictitious name for Coca Cola Gay Desperadoes.

21. Earl Lovelace, *The Dragon Can't Dance* (Harlow: Longman, 1981), p. 68.

22. Ibid., pp. 68–69.

23. Ibid., p. 70.

24. Herman L. Bennett, "The Challenge to the Post-Colonial State: A Case Study of the February Revolution in Trinidad," in *The Modern Caribbean,* ed. Franklin W. Knight and Colin A. Palmer (Chapel Hill: University of North Carolina Press, 1989), p. 134.

25. For discussions of the Black Power movement in Trinidad, see Ryan, *Race and Nationalism in Trinidad and Tobago,* pp. 365–373, 425–428, 454–469; James Millette, "The Black Revolution in the Caribbean," in *Is Massa Day Dead? Black Moods in the Caribbean,* ed. Orde Coombs (Garden City, N.Y.: Anchor Books, 1974), pp. 47–66; Ivar Oxaal, *Black Intellectuals and the Dilemmas of Race and Class in Trinidad* (Cambridge, Mass.: Schenkman Publishing Co., 1982), pp. 195–279; and Bennett, "The Challenge to the Post-Colonial State," pp. 129–146. For a review of the poetry of disillusionment and discontent that was written in Trinidad during the 1960s and 1970s, see Gordon Rohlehr, "My Strangled City," in *My Strangled City and Other Essays* (Port of Spain: Longman Trinidad Limited, 1992), pp. 168–269. Included in Rohlehr's essay is an analysis of "Pan Run" (Parts I and II), poems about the violent birth of pan and the rage of the panman written by Black Power leader Abdul Malik while he was in prison for his role in the 1970 uprising. For an analysis of the language and themes of the calypsos of this period, see Keith Q. Warner, *Kaiso! The Trinidad Calypso: A Study of the Calypso as Oral Literature* (Washington, D.C.: Three Continents Press, 1985).

26. See *Trinidad Guardian* (25 January 1970), p. 1.

27. *Trinidad Guardian* (22 March 1970), p. 1; *Sunday Guardian* (5 April 1970), p. 2; ibid. (12 April 1970), p. 1; and *Trinidad Guardian* (24 April 1970), p. 9.
28. *Trinidad Guardian* (26 March 1970), p. 1.
29. Goddard, *Forty Years in the Steelbands,* p. 196.
30. *Trinidad Guardian* (2 April 1970), p. 1.
31. Jeffrey R. Thomas, "A History of Pan and the Evolution of the Steel Band in Trinidad and Tobago," (M.A. thesis, Wesleyan University, 1985), p. 195. See also Goddard, *Forty Years in the Steelbands,* pp. 192–195.
32. *Trinidad Guardian* (3 April 1970), p. 1.
33. *Trinidad Guardian* (3 April 1970), p. 8. In this editorial the *Guardian* also noted that, of the 130 steelbands in the country, just under 60 were sponsored. See ibid. (15 April 1970), p. 11, for a detailed review of financial arrangements between sponsors and steelbands during this period.
34. Richard Forteau, personal interview, Port of Spain, Trinidad (16 December 1988); Goddard, *Forty Years in the Steelbands,* p. 197; *Sunday Guardian* (5 April 1970), p. 2.
35. Melville Bryan, personal interview, Port of Spain, Trinidad (29 March 1989).
36. Ryan, *Race and Nationalism in Trinidad and Tobago,* p. 482.
37. *Trinidad Guardian* (10 February 1971), p. 1; Goddard, *Forty Years in the Steelbands,* p. 203.
38. *Trinidad Guardian* (22 March 1971), p. 1.
39. Goddard, *Forty Years in the Steelbands,* pp. 204–205; Thomas, "A History of Pan," pp. 207–208.
40. *Trinidad Express* (19 January 1973), p. 15.
41. *Trinidad Guardian* (30 January 1973), pp. 1, 6; (1 February 1973), p. 1.
42. Selwyn Tarradath, personal interview, Petit Valley, Trinidad (27 February 1989).
43. Ibid.
44. Cupidore, personal interview (20 December 1988).
45. See *Sunday Guardian* (16 February 1958), p. 2; *Trinidad Guardian* (30 January 1959), p. 2; and *Trinidad Express* (18 January 1968), p. 2.
46. Bryan, personal interview (29 March 1989).
47. Kendall Lewis, personal interview, Diego Martin, Trinidad (12 April 1989).
48. Keith Smith, "Panorama: The Past, the Future, the Unclear Present," *Tapia* 3, no. 8 (1973): 3.
49. Ray Holman, personal interview, Woodbrook, Trinidad (13 December 1988).
50. Selwyn Tarradath, *Pan Trinbago's Information Booklet* (n.p., 1987).
51. For a recent discussion of men and women in Carnival, see Molly Ahye, "Carnival, the Manipulative Polymorph: An Interplay of Social Stratification," in *Social and Occupational Stratification in Contemporary Trinidad and Tobago,* ed. Selwyn Ryan (St. Augustine, Trinidad: Institute of Social and Economic Research, University of the West Indies, 1991), pp. 399–416. For an analysis of how women's sexuality in Carnival is exploited in Trinidad's consumer culture, see Kim Johnson, "The Social Impact of Carnival," in *The Social and Economic Impact of Carnival,* seminar held at the University of the West Indies, St. Augustine, Trinidad, November 24–26, 1983 (St. Augustine, Trinidad: Institute of Social and Economic Research, University of the West Indies, 1984), pp. 197–201. For

various perspectives on Trinidad during the oil boom years, see Selwyn Ryan, ed., *Trinidad and Tobago: The Independence Experience, 1962–1987* (St. Augustine, Trinidad: Institute of Social and Economic Research, University of the West Indies, 1988); idem., *Social and Occupational Stratification;* and MacDonald, *Trinidad and Tobago.*

52. Tarradath, *Pan Trinbago's Information Booklet.*

53. *Sunday Express* (25 February 1979), p. 4.

54. Kendall Lewis, personal interview, Diego Martin, Trinidad (19 July 1988).

55. For a discussion of the steelbands' departure from the festival, see Goddard, *Forty Years in the Steelbands,* pp. 116–119.

56. Ibid., p. 125.

57. *Trinidad Guardian* (4 August 1966), p. 3.

58. Landeg E. White, "Steelbands: A Personal Record," *Caribbean Quarterly* 15, no. 4 (1969): 32.

59. For the above details on the steelband festivals, see the following issues of the *Guardian*: (7 April 1964), p. 2; (2 July 1964), p. 3; (4 August 1966), p. 3; (5 August 1966), p. 9; (9 August 1966), p. 2; (10 August 1966), p. 9; (29 June 1967), p. 9; (6 July 1967), p. 1; (19 September 1968), p. 1; and (18 November 1973), p. 6. See also *Evening News* (2 August 1967), p. 1; *Trinidad Express* (8 June 1972), p. 28; and ibid. (24 August 1973), p. 3. Recordings of selections from the 1964 Steelband Music Festival were released by Tropico (LPB 3024 and TSI–3029).

60. *Trinidad Guardian* (23 November 1966), p. 18.

61. *Trinidad Guardian* (13 December 1973), p. 15.

62. Ibid. For a critique of the colonial character of steelband festivals by Pete Simon, see *Sunday Guardian* (3 February 1974), p. 5.

63. The Besser recording can be heard on the compact disc that accompanies Donald R. Hill's *Calypso Calaloo: Early Carnival Music in Trinidad* (Gainesville: University Press of Florida, 1993). Examples of earlier records that include metallic percussion are Atilla the Hun and His Tamboo Bamboo Band's "Fire Brigade" (Decca 17389, recorded 1938); Houdini's "Mama, Call the Fire Brigade" (Bluebird B-10647, recorded 1940); and the Sa Gomes Rhythm Boys' "Run Your Run Hitler" (Decca 17348, recorded 1940). I am grateful to Don Hill for copies of these recordings and of a number of the other pan recordings from the 1950s mentioned below.

64. Jeffrey Thomas, *Forty Years of Steel: An Annotated Discography of Steel Band and Pan Recordings, 1951–1991* (Westport, Conn.: Greenwood Press, 1992), pp. 142–143.

65. See ibid., pp. 12, 112, 136; and Kim Johnson, "Russell Henderson—Pan Jazz Pioneer," *Sunday Express* (3 November 1991), Living Section, pp. 7–8.

66. For information on Eduardo Sa Gomes and Aubrey Christopher, see Gordon Rohlehr, *Calypso & Society in Pre-Independence Trinidad* (Port of Spain: Gordon Rohlehr, 1990), pp. 148–151, 523–524.

67. Thomas, *Forty Years of Steel,* p. xii. Thomas notes that Cook's first steelband recording was made in Antigua in 1955 and featured Hell's Gate, Brute Force, and Big Shell.

68. I owe many thanks to the National Broadcasting Service in Trinidad for allowing me to review their extensive record collection and to compile discographic data. Readers seeking a comprehensive discography of pan music should consult Thomas, *Forty Years of Steel.*

69. Historically, calypsonians have benefited somewhat more from record-

ings than panmen. For a discussion of the recording of calypso from the early part of the century through the 1940s, see Hill, *Calypso Calaloo.* Hill discusses the recording of calypsonians both in Trinidad and abroad and notes that, between 1912 and 1945, some 300 78-rpm discs were produced (p. 140). There was also extensive recording of West Indian dance bands during this period. In addition to his analysis of phonograph recordings, Hill examines the international popularization of calypso through vaudeville-type shows, radio, and movies. Substantial recording of calypsonians and dance bands continued in the post-indepedence period, though the international presence of Trinidadian music declined.

70. Lewis, personal interview (12 April 1989).

Chapter 5: The Steelband in Contemporary Trinidad and Tobago

1. Selwyn Ryan, "Political Change and Economic Reconstruction in Trinidad and Tobago," *Caribbean Affairs* 1, no. 1 (1988): 132–133.

2. Kevin A. Yelvington, "Vote Dem Out: The Demise of the PNM in Trinidad and Tobago," *Caribbean Review* 15, no. 4 (1987): 12, 29.

3. Ibid., pp. 31–32.

4. *Daily Express* (14 April 1988), p. 1; *Sunday Express* (3 July 1988), p. 18.

5. *Sunday Express* (1 January 1989), p. 35.

6. For overviews of economic and political developments in Trinidad and Tobago during the 1980s and early 1990s, see Selwyn Ryan, ed., *Trinidad and Tobago: The Independence Experience, 1962–1987* (St. Augustine, Trinidad: Institute of Social and Economic Research, University of the West Indies, 1988); idem., *Social and Occupational Stratification in Contemporary Trinidad and Tobago* (St. Augustine, Trinidad: Institute of Social and Economic Research, University of the West Indies, 1991); idem., *The Muslimeen Grab for Power: Race, Religion and Revolution in Trinidad and Tobago* (Port of Spain: Inprint Caribbean, 1991); Scott B. MacDonald, *Trinidad and Tobago: Democracy and Development in the Caribbean* (New York: Praeger, 1986); and *South America, Central America and the Caribbean 1993,* "Trinidad and Tobago" (London: Europa Publications Limited, 1993), pp. 577–592.

7. All numeric estimates in this chapter concerning steelbands and their members are based on data gathered between 1988 and 1989.

8. Sylvia Gonzalez, *Steelband Saga: A Story of the Steelband—The First 25 Years* (Port of Spain: Ministry of Education and Culture, 1978), pp. 27–29. For additional details on the members of Girl Pat and other early panwomen, see Kim Johnson, "Women in Pan," *Sunday Express* (15 May 1994), Section 2, pp. 1, 3.

9. Selwyn Tarradath, "Race, Class, Politics and Gender in the Steelband Movement," in *Social and Occupational Stratification,* Ryan, p. 382; Merle Albino-de Coteau, personal interview, Belmont, Trinidad (14 November 1994).

10. Patricia Adams, personal interview, Trincity, Trinidad (8 November 1994).

11. Maureen Clement Moe, personal interview, Trincity, Trinidad (8 November 1994).

12. Allison Dyer, personal interview, Port of Spain, Trinidad (22 December 1988).

13. This issue has also been raised in relation to school children. On October 25, 1987, for example, Trinidad's Radio 610 broadcast a steelband forum in

which one participant questioned whether children being taught pan in schools (as opposed to panyards) would learn about the steelband struggle.

14. Dawn Batson, personal interview, Barataria, Trinidad (24 November 1988).

15. Moe, personal interview (8 November 1994). For additional commentary on women in pan, see *Sunday Express* (26 February 1984), p. 23. Included in this article are remarks by Geraldine Connor, who has arranged for Invaders and for Ebony in London, and by Elaine Brown, who was associated with the Neal and Massy Trendsetters.

16. In 1988 the Trinidad and Tobago dollar was devalued from a fixed rate of $3.60 = $1.00 U.S. to $4.25 = $1.00 U.S. In 1993 the dollar was floated and currently has an exchange rate of approximately $5.85 = $1.00 U.S.

17. For comments on steelband sponsorship by various company public relations officers, see *People* [Trinidad] (January 1983), pp. 21, 23–24.

18. In recent years some panmen have been playing with more than one band for Panorama in order to make more money and to increase their chances of performing in the prestigious finals of the competition.

19. One of the most-admired steelband leaders ever was the late Rudolph "The General" Charles of Desperadoes. Charles, who appeared at Panorama in army fatigues, was known for his serious and strict leadership style and his absolute devotion to pan. When he died in 1985, his body was placed in a "chariot pan casket" (made from two chromed bass pans) and carried from Desperadoes' panyard on top of Laventille Hill to the Catholic cathedral in downtown Port of Spain. Thousands of mourners attended his funeral, and his contribution to pan was later immortalized in David Rudder's calypso "The Hammer." For reminiscences of Charles and descriptions of his funeral, see Ancil A. Neil, *Voices from the Hill: Despers and Laventille* (n.p.: A. A. Neil, 1987).

20. Nestor Sullivan, personal interview, San Juan, Trinidad (30 March 1989).

21. Batson, personal interview (24 November 1988).

22. Clive Bradley, personal interview, Diego Martin, Trinidad (23 February 1988).

23. Richard Forteau, personal interview, Port of Spain, Trinidad (16 December 1988).

24. Sylvan Salandy, personal interview, Diego Martin, Trinidad (31 May 1988).

25. Sullivan, personal interview (30 March 1989); Anthony Reid, speech delivered at Pan Trinbago's 1988 awards ceremony, Seamen and Waterfront Workers Trade Union Hall, Port of Spain, Trinidad (30 March 1988).

26. *Daily Express* (31 October 1987), p. 9; (27 October 1987), p. 5.

27. No Festival was held in 1990, due to a state of emergency which remained in effect for several months after the attempted coup.

28. See *Daily Express* (21 September 1984), p. 3; and ibid. (8 October 1984), p. 17.

29. *Sunday Guardian* (3 April 1988), p. 11.

30. See Louis Regis, *Black Stalin: The Caribbean Man* (Borde Narve Village, Trinidad: Jordan's Printery, n.d.), p. 79.

31. There is much debate in the steelband world about the standardization of pans. Standardization would entail all tuners using the same *styling* or layout of notes for a particular type of pan. Some pans are already close to being standardized, while for others there are still multiple stylings. Standardization

would obviously facilitate pan instruction and performance and the possibility of the mass production of pans. However, tuners often state that they are still experimenting with different stylings and that standardization at present would be premature. For diagrams of some of the contemporary pan stylings, see Jeffrey R. Thomas, "A History of Pan and the Evolution of the Steel Band in Trinidad and Tobago" (M.A. thesis, Wesleyan University, 1985).

32. Clive Bradley, for example, comments that he has learned a lot from listening to jazz, Muzak, and movie soundtracks (personal interview [23 February 1988]).

33. Some bands also use other pans such as the *quadrophonic,* a set of four pans with a very wide range.

34. Over the past few years there have been some changes in the format of the Panorama preliminaries. In 1995 bands from all regions of Trinidad competed together in the Savannah on Saturday and Sunday. For Panorama transport costs, see *Trinidad Guardian* (4 February 1988), p. 9.

35. "Jumping up" is a type of dance that involves rocking back and forth on either leg while gyrating the shoulders. In its more ecstatic form, the arms are raised up and down above the head.

36. Earl Lovelace, "The Spirit of Pan," *Daily Express* (17 February 1985), p. 1.

37. See *Trinidad and Tobago Carnival and Calypsoes, 1976* (n.p., 1976), p. 12.

38. Though the most spectacular celebration occurs in Port of Spain, there are Carnival festivities throughout Trinidad and Tobago.

39. After the 1988 Carnival there was much condemnation in the press of the "immorality" and "obscenity" of women's dancing as they crossed the Savannah stage. For an analysis of the 1988 Carnival, and of wining in particular, see Daniel Miller, "Absolute Freedom in Trinidad," *Man* 26 (1991): 323–341.

40. For another perspective on the contemporary Carnival, see John Stewart, "Patronage and Control in the Trinidad Carnival," in *The Anthropology of Experience,* ed. Victor M. Turner and Edward M. Bruner (Urbana: University of Illinois Press, 1986), pp. 289–315. Stewart suggests that the politicizing of Carnival and the emphasis on official competitions has led many Trinidadians to become disenchanted with the festival. For a comparison of the values and aesthetics of Carnival with those of Christmas, see Daniel Miller, *Modernity, an Ethnographic Approach: Dualism and Mass Consumption in Trinidad* (Oxford: Berg, 1994), pp. 82–134. An excellent fictional account of the Carnival experience is provided by Earl Lovelace in *The Dragon Can't Dance* (Harlow: Longman, 1981).

41. In 1988, for example, Valley Harps used Anthony Prospect (a past director of the police band), Desperadoes employed Pat Bishop (a choir director), Invaders used Louise McIntosh (a music teacher), and Trinidad All Stars hired Gillian Nathaniel-Balintulo (a concert pianist).

42. These numbers refer to the 1988 Festival when the preliminary round for soloists was held in an indoor venue and the final round in the stadium. In the 1994 Festival, ten soloists were selected for the finals and both rounds of the competition were held inside. The competition for pan-around-the-neck bands is regularly held in the stadium.

43. Roger D. Abrahams, *The Man-of-Words in the West Indies: Performance and the Emergence of Creole Culture* (Baltimore: Johns Hopkins University Press, 1983). Thanksgivings are parties given after difficult experiences.

44. *Trinidad Guardian* (4 April 1988), p. 8.

45. *Daily Express* (16 August 1988), p. 8.

46. Clifford Geertz, "After the Revolution: The Fate of Nationalism in the New States," in *The Interpretation of Cultures* (New York: Basic Books, 1973), p. 240.

47. Essentialism and epochalism in Trinidad have been expressed not only in the steelband movement but in other art forms since the postwar years. For example, Hans Guggenheim provides an in-depth discussion of localists and cosmopolitans in the visual art world during Trinidad's transition to independence (the late 1950s and early 1960s). He describes how the localists focused on the Trinidadian folk culture and milieu, had a naturalistic style, and were concerned with projecting a traditional value system. On the other hand, the cosmopolitans worked with abstract styles and were interested in creating a modern, progressive image of Trinidad which reflected internationalization and Westernization ("Social and Political Change in the Art World of Trinidad during the Period of Transition from Colony to New Nation" [Ph.D. dissertation, New York University, 1968], pp. 47–51, 164). Guggenheim also examines how politicians manipulated art to represent conceptions of Trinidadian identity and notes that the localists and cosmopolitans were allied with different factions of the PNM.

48. Morton Marks, "Uncovering Ritual Structures in Afro-American Music," in *Religious Movements in Contemporary America*, ed. Irving I. Zaretsky and Mark P. Leone (Princeton, N.J.: Princeton University Press, 1974), pp. 60–134.

49. In earlier years Independence Day celebrations included steelband performances at various locations in Port of Spain. In 1987, the 25th anniversary of independence, Pan Trinbago began organizing a steelband parade on the street.

50. This account of Independence Day in Trinidad differs from Thomas Hylland Eriksen's description of the event as an empty ritual of little personal importance ("Formal and Informal Nationalism," *Ethnic and Racial Studies* 16 [1993]: 5). In his discussion of Trinidad and Mauritius, Eriksen makes a distinction between formal nationalism, linked to the apparatus of the nation-state, and informal nationalism, associated with collective celebrations and sports competitions. In the case of Trinidad, this distinction seems to overlook the extent to which Independence Day has been carnivalized by the people and events like Carnival have been formalized by the state.

51. During the 1990s there has again been a decline in the number of blocos, mainly because of the costs involved. However, other pan events have appeared that are in some ways similar to blocos. Since 1989 the Borough of Point Fortin has been holding "Pan on the Move" in conjunction with its anniversary celebrations in May. In this street competition each band plays a current calypso, a calypso from ten years earlier, and a bomb tune. The event has been attracting numerous steelbands from around the island and massive crowds. In the course of the past few years, the towns of Tunapuna and Sangre Grande have also held pan competitions.

52. Catholic, Anglican, and Pentecostal churches are other indoor settings in which steelbands and individual pannists perform. Pan in church dates to 1965. Initially there was some resistance to this practice, and George Goddard did not hesitate to send a letter and a recording to the Pope in an effort to obtain his support. In his response, the Pope thanked Goddard for his "devoted message" and "thoughtful gesture" and stated that the matter would be considered (*Trinidad Express* [12 December 1967], p. 1). See also *Daily Mirror* (19 April 1965), p. 7; and *Trinidad Guardian* (30 August 1965), p. 1.

53. For two critiques of Pan Ramajay, see *Sunday Express* (7 June 1992), p. 8; and *Sunday Guardian* (7 June 1992), p. 24.

54. *Trinidad Guardian* (26 February 1984), p. 5.

55. Ian Jones interviewed by Lennox Grant, "Pan and Ian," *Trinidad and Tobago Review* 5, no. 3 (1981): 21.

56. See "Suggested Listening," following Chapter 6, for a select discography of steelband recordings from the 1980s and 1990s, including tapes and compact discs of Panorama, the Steelband Music Festival, Pan Ramajay, and pan soloists.

Chapter 6: Cultural Creativity and the Construction of Identities

1. Wilson Harris, "History, Fable and Myth in the Caribbean and the Guianas," *Caribbean Quarterly* 16, no. 2 (1970): 6, 8.

2. John O. Stewart, *Drinkers, Drummers, and Decent Folk: Ethnographic Narratives of Village Trinidad* (Albany: State University of New York Press, 1989), pp. 21–22, 219–220.

3. For a collection of M. G. Smith's early discussions of the plural society thesis, see *The Plural Society in the British West Indies* (Berkeley: University of California Press, 1965). One of his last statements on the topic was "Plural and Social Stratification," in *Social and Occupational Stratification in Contemporary Trinidad and Tobago,* ed. Selwyn Ryan (St. Augustine, Trinidad: Institute of Social and Economic Research, University of the West Indies, 1991), pp. 3–35.

4. Edward Kamau Brathwaite, "Caribbean Man in Space and Time," *Savacou* 11/12 (1975): 7. See also idem., *Contradictory Omens: Cultural Diversity and Integration in the Caribbean* (Mona, Jamaica: Savacou Publications, 1974).

5. Daniel Crowley, "Plural and Differential Acculturation in Trinidad," *American Anthropologist* 59 (1957): 823–824.

6. For a range of discussions of Indian cultural patterns and Indian-African relations in Trinidad, see I. J. Bahadur Singh, ed., *Indians in the Caribbean* (New Delhi: Sterling Publishers, 1987); Selwyn Ryan, ed., *Trinidad and Tobago: The Independence Experience, 1962–1987* (St. Augustine, Trinidad: Institute of Social and Economic Research, University of the West Indies, 1988); idem., *Social and Occupational Stratification;* and Kevin Yelvington, ed., *Trinidad Ethnicity* (London: Macmillan Caribbean, 1993). A comparative perspective on Trinidad can be obtained through consideration of historical and ethnographic data from Guyana which also has a large Indian population. For a recent examination of African-Indian cultural negotiations in this nation-state, see Brackette F. Williams, *Stains on My Name, War in My Veins: Guyana and the Politics of Cultural Struggle* (Durham, N.C.: Duke University Press, 1991). Williams explores how Africans and Indians establish claims to the "ownership" of Guyanese cultural practices and to relative social status in the context of colonial/post-colonial hegemonic assumptions about the contributions and place of different ethnic groups in the society.

7. *Trinidad Guardian* (13 April 1988), p. 16.

8. See Ralph Premdas, "Ethnic Conflict in Trinidad and Tobago: Domination and Reconciliation," in *Trinidad Ethnicity,* Yelvington, p. 158.

9. Ralph Premdas argues that disagreement between African and Indian cabinet ministers over the Indian Cultural Centre contributed to the break-up of the NAR government (ibid., pp. 149, 153–154, 158).

10. Callaloo is a dish consisting of dasheen bush, okra, coconut cream, pumpkin, and salt meat or crab. It is often used as a metaphor for the blending of cultures in Trinidad.

11. *Trinidad Guardian* (13 February 1988), p. 14.

12. *Trinidad Guardian* (23 February 1988), p. 8.

13. *Trinidad Guardian* (10 June 1994), p. 14; (14 June 1994), p. 14; (16 June 1994), pp. 1, 11; (17 June 1994), p. 3; and *Trinidad Express* (17 June 1994), pp. 7, 9. For additional commentary on the pan-harmonium dispute, see *Sunday Express* (19 June 1994), pp. 8, 25.

14. Aisha Khan, "What Is 'a Spanish'? Ambiguity and 'Mixed' Ethnicity in Trinidad," in *Trinidad Ethnicity*, Yelvington, pp. 194–195. Khan notes, however, that there are limits to the acceptance of a "mixed" national culture: "Trinidad, though a self-proclaimed 'callaloo' society, cannot *unequivocally* or *uniformly* embrace an ideology of a "mixed" national identity, given the concern over potential cultural oblivion that competing ethnic groups allegedly risk" (ibid., p. 189). Similar ethnic concerns are prevalent in Guyana. In her discussion of past negotiations over the ethnic/national significance of the Guyanese Tadjah festival (which parallels Hosay in Trinidad), Brackette F. Williams states: "Until everyone and everything was simply Guyanese it was too risky for anyone to claim simply to be Guyanese" ("Nationalism, Traditionalism, and the Problem of Cultural Inauthenticity," in *Nationalist Ideologies and the Production of National Cultures*, ed. Richard G. Fox [Washington, D.C.: American Anthropological Association, 1990], p. 127).

15. Raymond Williams, *Marxism and Literature* (Oxford: Oxford University Press, 1977), pp. 124–126.

16. Michael Lieber, *Street Life: Afro-American Culture in Urban Trinidad* (Cambridge, Mass.: Schenkman Publishing Co., 1981). For insightful discussions of similar grass-roots male cultural styles in Suriname and Jamaica, see Gary Brana-Shute, *On the Corner: Male Life in a Paramaribo Creole Neighborhood* (Assen, the Netherlands: Van Gorcum, 1979); and Diane J. Austin, *Urban Life in Kingston, Jamaica: The Culture and Class Ideology of Two Neighborhoods* (New York: Gordon and Breach Science Publishers, 1984).

17. Jay R. Mandle and Joan D. Mandle, *Grass Roots Commitment: Basketball and Society in Trinidad and Tobago* (Parkersburg, Iowa: Caribbean Books, 1988).

18. Ibid., pp. 18–19.

19. Ibid., pp. 49–67.

20. C. L. R. James, *Beyond a Boundary* (Durham, N.C.: Duke University Press, 1993 [1963]), p. 66.

21. Ibid., p. 233.

22. There have been a number of studies of the social and cultural dimensions of West Indian cricket since James's seminal book. For example, Orlando Patterson describes the Test match in the West Indies as "a collective ritual, a social drama in which almost all of the basic tensions and conflicts in the society are played out symbolically" ("The Ritual of Cricket," in *Caribbean Essays*, ed. Andrew Salkey [London: Evans Brothers Limited, 1973], p. 109). He argues that a Test match against England, when it is going well for the West Indian team, has three basic symbolic functions: 1) it enables West Indians to work out their ambivalent relationship with British culture by beating the colonizers at their own game, 2) it resolves class conflict by providing the masses with a means of expressing class hostility in the context of play, and 3) it is an occasion at which the lower class transcends its many internal conflicts and experiences a sense of

class solidarity (ibid.: 112–114). Also relevant to the present study is Richard D. E. Burton's examination of West Indian cricket in relation to Carnival and street life. Burton suggests that cricket, an embodiment of English respectability, was refashioned in the West Indies into a street-based activity similar to Carnival with an emphasis on style, aggression, and reputation-seeking ("Cricket, Carnival and Street Culture in the Caribbean," *British Journal of Sports History* 2, no. 2 [1985]: 179–197). Another useful perspective on cricket is provided by Frank E. Manning in his interpretation of matches in Bermuda in terms of black consciousness, economic dependency, and local politics ("Celebrating Cricket: The Symbolic Construction of Caribbean Politics," *American Ethnologist* 8 [1981]: 616–632). A recent study of the significance of cricket in Trinidad is Kevin A. Yelvington's article on the West Indies vs. India Test series in 1976. Yelvington examines Indo-Trinidadian support for the Indian team in the context of ethnic relations and the 1976 elections in Trinidad ("Ethnicity 'Not Out': The Indian Cricket Tour of the West Indies and the 1976 Elections in Trinidad and Tobago," *Arena Review* 14, no. 1 [1990]: 1–12).

23. Anita M. Waters, *Race, Class, and Political Symbols: Rastafari and Reggae in Jamaican Politics* (New Brunswick, N.J.: Transaction Books, 1985). For a synopsis of the development of reggae, see Peter Manuel, *Popular Musics of the Non-Western World: An Introductory Survey* (New York: Oxford University Press, 1988), pp. 75–78. See also Erna Brodber, "Black Consciousness and Popular Music in Jamaica in the 1960s and 1970s," *Nieuwe West-Indische Gids* 61 (1987): 145–160.

24. Deborah Pacini Hernández, "*La lucha sonora*: Dominican Popular Music in the post-Trujillo Era," *Latin American Music Review* 12 (1991): 105–123.

25. Ibid., p. 116.

26. Gage Averill, "Haitian Dance Bands, 1915–1970: Class, Race, and Authenticity," *Latin American Music Review* 10 (1989): 203–235; idem., "'Toujou Sou Konpa': Issues of Change and Interchange in Haitian Popular Dance Music," in *Zouk: World Music in the West Indies*, Jocelyne Guilbault (Chicago: University of Chicago Press, 1993), pp. 68–89. See also Daisann McLane, "The Haitian Beat Thrives in Times of Suffering," *New York Times* (8 March 1992), Section 2, pp. 31–32.

27. Averill, "Haitian Dance Bands," p. 219.

28. For another discussion of music and identity in the French Creole-speaking Caribbean, see Guilbault, *Zouk*. Guilbault describes how zouk was transformed from a youth music to a symbol of national identity and pride in the French overseas *départements* of Guadeloupe and Martinique. In order to achieve international commercial success, zouk artists have had to develop a music that includes both distinctively local musical elements and an "international sound" associated with Euro-American musical conventions (p. 150). Guilbault notes that this contradiction is interrelated with "the ambiguous position in which Guadeloupians and Martinicans find themselves in relation to their own identity" (p. 176).

29. *Trinidad Guardian* (31 August 1992), p. 1.

30. Selwyn Tarradath, personal interview, Petit Valley, Trinidad (27 February 1989).

Bibliography

Personal Interviews Cited

Adams, Patricia. Trincity, Trinidad (8 November 1994).
Albino-de Coteau, Merle. Belmont, Trinidad (14 November 1994).
Alfred, Leo. Port of Spain, Trinidad (31 March 1988).
Batson, Dawn. Barataria, Trinidad (24 November 1988).
Batson, Prince. Port of Spain, Trinidad (31 October 1988).
———. Barataria, Trinidad (27 March 1989).
Bostock, Wellington. Port of Spain, Trinidad (23 February 1989).
Bradley, Clive. Diego Martin, Trinidad (23 February 1988).
Bryan, Melville. Port of Spain, Trinidad (29 March 1989).
Cupidore, Michael. St. James, Trinidad (20 December 1988).
Dyer, Allison. Port of Spain, Trinidad (22 December 1988).
Forteau, Richard. Port of Spain, Trinidad (16 December 1988).
Griffith, Jason. Belmont, Trinidad (7 April 1989).
Holman, Ray. Woodbrook, Trinidad (13 December 1988).
Jules, Neville. Brooklyn, New York (10 April 1991).
Kinsale, MacDonald. Morvant, Trinidad (20 March 1989).
Lewis, Kendall. Diego Martin, Trinidad (19 July 1988).
———. Diego Martin, Trinidad (27 October 1988).
———. Diego Martin, Trinidad (12 April 1989).
Mannette, Vernon. Woodbrook, Trinidad (4 December 1988).
Mayers, Alfred. Point Cumana, Trinidad (22 December 1988).
———. Point Cumana, Trinidad (21 February 1989).
McBurnie, Beryl. St. James, Trinidad (17 March 1988).
Moe, Maureen Clement. Trincity, Trinidad (8 November 1994).
Pierre, Curtis. Port of Spain, Trinidad (14 January 1992).
Pierre, Lennox. Port of Spain, Trinidad (12 July 1988).
Pouchet, Junior. Woodbrook, Trinidad (2 February 1989).
Prospect, Anthony. Champs Fleur, Trinidad (14 November 1988).
Richardson, George. Plymouth, Tobago (17 November 1988).
Salandy, Sylvan. Diego Martin, Trinidad (31 May 1988).
Sandiford, McKeller. Port of Spain, Trinidad (15 March 1989).
Serrant, Jerry. Port of Spain, Trinidad (8 June 1988).
———. Port of Spain, Trinidad (19 September 1988).
———. Port of Spain, Trinidad (7 March 1989).
———. Port of Spain, Trinidad (18 April 1989).
Serrette, Owen. Port of Spain, Trinidad (14 December 1988).
Stewart, Lytton. Mt. Pleasant, Tobago (17 November 1988).
Sullivan, Nestor. San Juan, Trinidad (30 March 1989).

Tarradath, Selwyn. Petit Valley, Trinidad (27 February 1989).
Warner, Leo. Belmont, Trinidad (3 May 1988).
———. Belmont, Trinidad (10 May 1988).
Williams, Anthony. Laventille, Trinidad (23 June 1988).
———. Laventille, Trinidad (23 September 1988).
———. Laventille, Trinidad (4 October 1988).
Wilson, Victor. Newtown, Trinidad (22 March 1988).
Yeates, George. Belmont, Trinidad (2 March 1989).

Other Unpublished Material

Batson, Prince. Lecture on the steelband. Trinidad Public Library, Port of
    Spain, Trinidad (31 October 1988).
Belle, Frankie. "Steelband 1936–1986" (1985). Manuscript in "History of Steel-
    band" File. National Heritage Library of Trinidad and Tobago, Port of Spain,
    Trinidad.
Blake, Harold A. Manuscript material concerning a steelband association
    (n.d.). Pan Trinbago, Port of Spain, Trinidad.
Elder, Jacob D. "Evolution of the Traditional Calypso of Trinidad and Tobago:
    A Socio-historical Analysis of Song-Change." Ph.D. dissertation, University of
    Pennsylvania, 1966.
Guggenheim, Hans. "Social and Political Change in the Art World of Trinidad
    during the Period of Transition from Colony to New Nation." Ph.D. disserta-
    tion, New York University, 1968.
Harris, John. "The PNM Government and the Steelband Movement from 1956
    to the Present." Undergraduate thesis, University of the West Indies - St. Au-
    gustine, 1975.
Little Carib. "Talking Drums." Program for the formal opening of the Little
    Carib Theatre (25 November 1948). National Heritage Library of Trinidad
    and Tobago, Port of Spain, Trinidad.
Pierre, Lennox. "History and Development of Steelband." Video tape of lec-
    ture delivered at West Indian Reference Section, Central Library of Trinidad
    and Tobago, Belmont, Trinidad (1987). Educational Television Unit, Min-
    istry of Education, St. James, Trinidad.
———. Lecture on the steelband. Oilfield Workers Trade Union Hall, Port of
    Spain, Trinidad (2 November 1988).
Pile, Oscar. Lecture on the steelband. Trinidad Public Library, Port of Spain,
    Trinidad (31 October 1988).
Reid, Anthony. Speech delivered at Pan Trinbago's 1988 awards ceremony.
    Seamen and Waterfront Workers Trade Union Hall, Port of Spain, Trinidad
    (30 March 1988).
Remy, Jeannine Irene. "A Historical Background of Trinidad and Panorama
    Competitions with an Analysis of Ray Holman's 1989 Panorama Arrangement
    of 'Life's Too Short.'" Ph.D. dissertation, University of Arizona, 1991.
Saldenha, Robert. "The Innovations of Anthony Williams, and How They Revo-
    lutionized the Steelband, Steelband Music and Carnival." Undergraduate
    thesis, University of the West Indies - St. Augustine, 1984.

Steel Band Committee. Minutes of meeting held at Red House, Port of Spain, Trinidad (8 December 1949).

———. Minutes of meeting held at Trinidad Public Library, Port of Spain, Trinidad (12 January 1950).

———. Minutes of meeting held at Red House, Port of Spain, Trinidad (18 January 1950).

Steelband Interviews II (n.d.). National Cultural Council Collection. Ministry of Community Development, Culture, and Women's Affairs; Belmont, Trinidad.

Thomas, Jeffrey R. "A History of Pan and the Evolution of the Steel Band in Trinidad and Tobago." M.A. thesis, Wesleyan University, 1985.

Wilson, Rhonda. "The Organizational Development of the Steelband Movement from 1950-1977." Undergraduate thesis, University of the West Indies - St. Augustine, 1978.

Newspapers

Daily Express
Port-of-Spain Gazette
Sunday Express
Sunday Guardian
Trinidad Express
Trinidad Guardian

Books, Articles, and Pamphlets

Abrahams, Roger D. *The Man-of-Words in the West Indies: Performance and the Emergence of Creole Culture*. Baltimore: Johns Hopkins University Press, 1983.

———. "Reputation vs. Respectability: A Review of Peter J. Wilson's Concept."*Revista/Review Interamericana* 9 (1979): 448–453.

———. "The Shaping of Folklore Traditions in the British West Indies." *Journal of Inter-American Studies* 9 (1967): 456–480.

Abrahams, Roger D., and John F. Szwed, eds. *After Africa: Extracts from British Travel Accounts and Journals*. New Haven, Conn.: Yale University Press, 1983.

Aho, William R. "Steelband Music in Trinidad and Tobago: The Creation of a People's Music." *Latin American Music Review* 8 (1987): 26–58.

Ahye, Molly. "Carnival, the Manipulative Polymorph: An Interplay of Social Stratification." In *Social and Occupational Stratification in Contemporary Trinidad and Tobago,* edited by Selwyn Ryan, pp. 399–416. St. Augustine, Trinidad: Institute of Social and Economic Research, University of the West Indies, 1991.

———. *Cradle of Caribbean Dance: Beryl McBurnie and the Little Carib Theatre.* Trinidad and Tobago: Theatre Heritage Cultures Ltd., 1983.

Alleyne, Mervyn C. "A Linguistic Perspective on the Caribbean." In *Caribbean Contours,* edited by Sidney W. Mintz and Sally Price, pp. 155–179. Baltimore: Johns Hopkins University Press, 1985.

Anderson, Benedict R. O'G. *Imagined Communities: Reflections on the Origin and Spread of Nationalism.* London: Verso, 1983.

Anthony, Michael. *Port-of-Spain in a World at War, 1939–1945.* Port of Spain: Ministry of Sport, Culture and Youth Affairs, n.d.

Austin, Diane J. *Urban Life in Kingston, Jamaica: The Culture and Class Ideology of Two Neighborhoods.* New York: Gordon and Breach Science Publishers, 1984.

Averill, Gage. "Haitian Dance Bands, 1915–1970: Class, Race, and Authenticity." *Latin American Music Review* 10 (1989): 203–235.

————. "'Toujou Sou Konpa': Issues of Change and Interchange in Haitian Popular Dance Music." In *Zouk: World Music in the West Indies,* Jocelyne Guilbault, pp. 68–89. Chicago: University of Chicago Press, 1993.

Bahadur Singh, I. J., ed. *Indians in the Caribbean.* New Delhi: Sterling Publishers, 1987.

Bastide, Roger. *African Civilizations in the New World.* New York: Harper and Row, 1971.

Bell, Wendell. "Equality and Social Justice: Foundations of Nationalism in the Caribbean." *Caribbean Studies* 20, no. 2 (1980): 5–36.

Bennett, Herman L. "The Challenge to the Post-Colonial State: A Case Study of the February Revolution in Trinidad." In *The Modern Caribbean,* edited by Franklin W. Knight and Colin A. Palmer, pp. 129–146. Chapel Hill: University of North Carolina Press, 1989.

Besson, Jean. "Reputation and Respectability Reconsidered: A New Perspective on Afro-Caribbean Peasant Women." In *Women and Change in the Caribbean,* edited by Janet H. Momsen, pp. 15–37. Bloomington: Indiana University Press, 1993.

Bettelheim, Judith. "Carnaval and Festivals in Cuba." In *Caribbean Festival Arts: Each and Every Bit of Difference,* edited by John W. Nunley and Judith Bettelheim, pp. 137–146. Seattle: University of Washington Press, 1988.

————. "Carnaval in Cuba: Another Chapter in the Nationalization of Culture." *Caribbean Quarterly* 36, nos. 3&4 (1990): 29–41.

Bilby, Kenneth M. "The Caribbean as a Musical Region." In *Caribbean Contours,* edited by Sidney W. Mintz and Sally Price, pp. 181–218. Baltimore: Johns Hopkins University Press, 1985.

Bolland, O. Nigel. "Creolization and Creole Societies: A Cultural Nationalist View of Caribbean Social History." In *Intellectuals in the Twentieth-Century Caribbean,* vol. 1, edited by Alistair Hennessy, pp. 50–79. London: Macmillan Caribbean, 1992.

Borde, Percival. "The Sounds of Trinidad: The Development of the Steel-Drum Bands." *Black Perspective in Music* 1 (1973): 45–49.

Bowles, Paul. "Calypso—Music of the Antilles." *Modern Music* 17 (1940): 154–159.

Braithwaite, Lloyd. "The Problem of Cultural Integration in Trinidad."*Social and Economic Studies* 3, no. 1 (1954): 82–96.

————. "Social Stratification in Trinidad."*Social and Economic Studies* 2, nos. 2&3 (1953): 5–175.

Brana-Shute, Gary. *On the Corner: Male Life in a Paramaribo Creole Neighborhood.* Assen, the Netherlands: Van Gorcum, 1979.

Brathwaite, Edward Kamau. "Caribbean Man in Space and Time." *Savacou* 11/12 (1975): 1–11, 106–108.

————. *Contradictory Omens: Cultural Diversity and Integration in the Caribbean.* Mona, Jamaica: Savacou Publications, 1974.

————. *The Development of Creole Society in Jamaica: 1770–1820.* Oxford: Clarendon Press, 1971.

Brereton, Bridget. *A History of Modern Trinidad: 1783–1962.* Kingston: Heinemann Educational Books (Caribbean) Ltd., 1981.

———. *Race Relations in Colonial Trinidad: 1870–1900.* Cambridge: Cambridge University Press, 1979.

Brierley, J. N. *Trinidad: Then and Now.* Port of Spain: Franklin's Electric Printery, 1912.

Brodber, Erna. "Black Consciousness and Popular Music in Jamaica in the 1960s and 1970s." *Nieuwe West-Indische Gids* 61 (1987): 145–160.

Brown, Wenzell. *Angry Men, Laughing Men: The Caribbean Caldron.* New York: Greenberg, 1947.

Burton, Richard D. E. "Cricket, Carnival and Street Culture in the Caribbean." *British Journal of Sports History* 2, no. 2 (1985): 179–197.

Calder-Marshall, Arthur. *Glory Dead.* London: Michael Joseph, 1939.

Cameron, N. E. "Harmony in Steel Bands." *New Commonwealth* (London) 30, no. 11 (1955): 18–19.

Carmichael, Mrs. A. C. *Domestic Manners and Social Conditions of the White, Coloured, and Negro Population of the West Indies,* vol. 2. New York: Negro Universities Press, 1969 [1833].

Carr, Andrew. "Jour Ouvert: An Aspect of Trinidad Carnival." In *Down Town Carnival Competition Programme.* N.p., 1965.

Clarke, Gary. "Defending Ski-Jumpers: A Critique of Theories of Youth Subcultures." In *On Record: Rock, Pop, and the Written Word,* edited by Simon Frith and Andrew Goodwin, pp. 81–96. New York: Pantheon Books, 1990.

Claude, Oscaret. "Evolution, History and Future of the Steel Band." *Trinidad Guardian* (2 March 1946), p. 4.

Cohen, Abner. "Drama and Politics in the Development of a London Carnival." *Man* 15 (1980): 65–87.

Coplan, David B. *In Township Tonight! South Africa's Black City Music and Theatre.* London: Longman, 1985.

Courlander, Harold. *The Drum and the Hoe: Life and Lore of the Haitian People.* Berkeley: University of California Press, 1960.

———. *Negro Folk Music, U.S.A.* New York: Columbia University Press, 1963.

Craig, Susan E. *Community Development in Trinidad and Tobago, 1943–1973: From Welfare to Patronage.* Mona, Jamaica: Institute of Social and Economic Research, University of the West Indies, 1974.

———. "Sociological Theorizing in the English-Speaking Caribbean: A view." In *Contemporary Caribbean: A Sociological Reader,* vol. 2, edited by Susan Craig, pp. 143–180. Trinidad: S. Craig, 1982.

Crichlow, F. A. "Carnival Magic Grips City." *Sunday Guardian* (3 March 1946), p. 16.

Crowley, Daniel J. "Cultural Assimilation in a Multiracial Society." *Annals of the New York Academy of Sciences* 83, no. 5 (1960): 850–854.

———. "Plural and Differential Acculturation in Trinidad." *American Anthropologist* 59 (1957): 817–824.

———. "Toward a Definition of 'Calypso.'" *Ethnomusicology* 3 (1959): 55–66, 117–124.

———. "The Traditional Masques of Carnival." *Caribbean Quarterly* 4 (1956): 194–223.

Cudjoe, Selwyn R., ed. *Eric E. Williams Speaks: Essays on Colonialism and Indepen-*

dence. Wellesley, Mass.: Calaloux Publications, 1993.

de Boissière, Ralph. *Crown Jewel*. London: Pan Books, 1981 [1952].

———. *Rum and Coca-Cola*. London: Allison and Busby, 1984 [1956].

Drummond, Lee. "The Cultural Continuum: A Theory of Intersystems." *Man* 15 (1980): 352–374.

Duany, Jorge. "Popular Music in Puerto Rico: Toward an Anthropology of Salsa." *Latin American Music Review* 5 (1984): 186–216.

Elder, Jacob D. "Color, Music and Conflict: A Study of Aggression in Trinidad with Reference to the Role of Traditional Music." *Ethnomusicology* 8 (1964): 128–136.

———. *From Congo Drum to Steelband: A Socio-historical Account of the Emergence and Evolution of the Trinidad Steel Orchestra*. St. Augustine, Trinidad: University of the West Indies, 1969.

———. "Kalinda: Song of the Battling Troubadours of Trinidad." *Journal of the Folklore Institute* 3 (1966): 192–203.

Epstein, Dena J. *Sinful Tunes and Spirituals: Black Folk Music to the Civil War*. Urbana: University of Illinois Press, 1977.

Eriksen, Thomas Hylland. "Formal and Informal Nationalism." *Ethnic and Racial Studies* 16 (1993): 1–25.

Espinet, Chas. S. "Trinidad's Tinpany." *Trinidad & Tobago Tourist Board Information Bulletin*, series F 91, no. 1 (1964).

Espinet, Chas. S., and Harry Pitts. *Land of Calypso: The Origin and Development of Trinidad's Folk Song*. Port of Spain: Guardian Commercial Printery, 1944.

Fanon, Frantz. *The Wretched of the Earth*. New York: Grove Press, 1963.

Foster, Robert J. "Making National Cultures in the Global Ecumene." *Annual Review of Anthropology* 20 (1991): 235–260.

Fraser, Lionel Mordaunt. *History of Trinidad*, vol. 1. London: Frank Cass & Co. Ltd., 1971 [1891].

Geertz, Clifford. *The Interpretation of Cultures*. New York: Basic Books, Inc., 1973.

Gibbs, John A. *The Unit Steel Band*. Hicksville, N.Y.: Exposition Press, 1978.

Goddard, George "Sonny." *Forty Years in the Steelbands: 1939–1979*. London: Karia Press, 1991.

Goldwasser, Maria Julia. "Carnival." In *The Encyclopedia of Religion*, vol. 3, edited by Mircea Eliade, pp. 98–104. New York: Macmillan, 1987.

Gomes, Albert. *Through a Maze of Colour*. Port of Spain: Key Caribbean Publications Limited, 1974.

Gonzalez, Sylvia. *Steelband Saga: A Story of the Steelband—The First 25 Years*. Port of Spain: Ministry of Education and Culture, 1978.

Guilbault, Jocelyne. *Zouk: World Music in the West Indies*. Chicago: University of Chicago Press, 1993.

Hall, Stuart. "Notes on Deconstructing 'the Popular.'" In *People's History and Socialist Theory*, edited by Raphael Samuel, pp. 227–240. London: Routledge and Kegan Paul, 1981.

Hall, Stuart and Tony Jefferson, eds. *Resistance Through Rituals: Youth Subcultures in Post-War Britain*. London: Hutchinson, 1976.

Hannerz, Ulf. "The World in Creolization." *Africa* 57 (1987): 546–559.

Hanson, Donald R., and Robert Dash. "The Saga of the Steelband." *Caribbean* 8, no. 8 (1955): 173, 176–177, 184.

Harris, Wilson. "History, Fable and Myth in the Caribbean and the Guianas." *Caribbean Quarterly* 16, no. 2 (1970): 1–32.

Hebdige, Dick. *Subculture: The Meaning of Style.* New York: Methuen, 1979.

Herskovits, Melville J. and Frances S. Herskovits. *Trinidad Village.* New York: Octagon Books, 1964 [1947].

Hill, Donald R. *Calypso Calaloo: Early Carnival Music in Trinidad.* Gainesville: University Press of Florida, 1993.

Hill, Errol. *The Trinidad Carnival: Mandate for a National Theatre.* Austin: University of Texas Press, 1972.

Hintzen, Percy C. *The Costs of Regime Survival: Racial Mobilization, Elite Domination and Control of the State in Guyana and Trinidad.* Cambridge: Cambridge University Press, 1989.

Holder, Geoffrey. "Drumming on Steel Barrel-Heads." *Music Journal* 13, no. 5 (1955): 9, 20, 24.

Howard, Rick. "Is Antiguan Pan Ready to Rebound?" *Pan* 1, no. 1 (1985): 15–17.

James, C. L. R. *Beyond a Boundary.* Durham, N.C.: Duke University Press, 1993 [1963].

———. *Minty Alley.* London: New Beacon Books Ltd., 1975 [1936].

Johnson, Kim. "From Body Music to Sweet Pan." *Sunday Express* (17 January, 24 January, 31 January, 7 February, 21 February 1993).

———. "Russell Henderson—Pan Jazz Pioneer." *Sunday Express* (3 November 1991), Living Section, pp. 7–8.

———. "The Social Impact of Carnival." In *The Social and Economic Impact of Carnival,* seminar held at the University of the West Indies, St. Augustine, Trinidad, November 24–26, 1983, pp. 173–207. St. Augustine, Trinidad: Institute of Social and Economic Research, University of the West Indies, 1984.

———. "Women in Pan," *Sunday Express* (15 May 1994), Section 2, pp. 1, 3.

Jones, Anthony M. *Steelband: The Winston 'Spree' Simon Story.* Barataria, Trinidad: Educo Press, 1982.

Jones, Ian. "Pan and Ian" (interviewed by Lennox Grant). *Trinidad and Tobago Review* 5, no. 3 (1981): 4–5, 21–22.

Jules, Neville. "The History of Pan." *Down Town Mas* (1984): 15–16.

Khan, Aisha. "What Is 'a Spanish'? Ambiguity and 'Mixed' Ethnicity in Trinidad." In *Trinidad Ethnicity,* edited by Kevin Yelvington, pp. 180–207. London: Macmillan Caribbean, 1993.

King, Bruce, ed. *West Indian Literature.* Hamden, Conn.: Archon Books, 1979.

Kinser, Samuel. *Carnival, American Style: Mardi Gras at New Orleans and Mobile.* Chicago: University of Chicago Press, 1990.

Kronman, Ulf. *Steel Pan Tuning: A Handbook of Steel Pan Making and Tuning.* Stockholm: Musikmuseet, 1991.

Kubik, Gerhard and James Blades. "Marimba." In *The New Grove Dictionary of Music and Musicians,* vol. 11, edited by Stanley Sadie, pp. 681–683. London: Macmillan Publishers Limited, 1980.

La Guerre, John G. "The General Elections of 1946 in Trinidad and Tobago." *Social and Economic Studies* 21, no. 2 (1972): 184–204.

Lavenda, Robert H. "The Festival of Progress: The Globalizing World and the Transformation of the Caracas Carnival." *Journal of Popular Culture* 14 (1980): 465–475.

Lee, Ann. "Class, Race, Colour and the Trinidad Carnival." In *Social and Occupational Stratification in Contemporary Trinidad and Tobago,* edited by Selwyn Ryan, pp. 417–433. St. Augustine, Trinidad: Institute of Social and Economic Research, University of the West Indies, 1991.

Leigh Fermor, Patrick. *The Traveller's Tree: A Journey through the Caribbean Islands.* London: John Murray, 1950.

Lewis, Gordon K. *The Growth of the Modern West Indies.* New York: Monthly Review Press, 1968.

Lieber, Michael. *Street Life: Afro-American Culture in Urban Trinidad.*Cambridge, Mass.: Schenkman Publishing Co., 1981.

Limón, José E. "Texas Mexican Popular Music and Dancing: Some Notes on History and Symbolic Process." *Latin American Music Review* 4 (1983): 229–246.

List, George. "Columbia: Folk Music." In *The New Grove Dictionary of Music and Musicians,* vol. 14, edited by Stanley Sadie, pp. 570–581. London: Macmillan Publishers Limited, 1980.

Liverpool, Hollis Urban Lester. *Kaiso and Society.* Diego Martin, Trinidad: Juba Publications, 1990.

Lovelace, Earl. *The Dragon Can't Dance.* Harlow: Longman, 1981.

———. "The Spirit of Pan." *Daily Express* (17 February 1985), pp. 1, 13, 29.

Macdonald, Annette C. "The Big Drum Dance of Carriacou." *Revista/Review Interamericana* 8 (1978/1979): 570–576.

MacDonald, Scott B. *Trinidad and Tobago: Democracy and Development in the Caribbean.* New York: Praeger, 1986.

Magid, Alvin. *Urban Nationalism: A Study of Political Development in Trinidad.* Gainesville: University of Florida Press, 1988.

Mahabir, Noorkumar. "Influence of Tassa Drums on Carnival and Steelband." *Daily Express* (17 February 1984), p. 13; (18 February 1984), p. 23.

Mandle, Jay R. and Joan D. Mandle. *Grass Roots Commitment: Basketball and Society in Trinidad and Tobago.* Parkersburg, Iowa: Caribbean Books, 1988.

Mannette, Ellie. "The Story of Pan." *The Sun* (nine weekly installments, 21 March - 16 May 1986).

Manning, Frank E. "Celebrating Cricket: The Symbolic Construction of Caribbean Politics." *American Ethnologist* 8 (1981): 616–632.

Manuel, Peter. *Popular Musics of the Non-Western World: An Introductory Survey.* New York: Oxford University Press, 1988.

Marks, Morton. "Uncovering Ritual Structures in Afro-American Music." In *Religious Movements in Contemporary America,* edited by Irving I. Zaretsky and Mark P. Leone, pp. 60–134. Princeton, N.J.: Princeton University Press, 1974.

Marshall, Bertie. "The Bertie Marshall Story: Pan Is Mih Gyul." *Tapia* 2 (installments in issues 1–10, 1972).

Maxime, Gideon. *41 Years of Pan.* Trinidad: n.p., n.d.

McLane, Daisann. "The Haitian Beat Thrives in Times of Suffering." *New York Times* (8 March 1992), Section 2, pp. 31–32.

Middleton, Richard. "Articulating Musical Meaning/Re-Constructing Musical History/Locating the 'Popular.'" *Popular Music* 5 (1985): 5–43.

———. "Popular Music, Class Conflict and the Music-Historical Field." In *Popular Music Perspectives 2: Papers from the Second International Conference on Popular Music Studies,* pp. 24–46. Göteborg, Sweden: International Association for the Study of Popular Music, 1985.

Miller, Daniel. "Absolute Freedom in Trinidad." *Man* 26 (1991): 323–341.

———. *Modernity, an Ethnographic Approach: Dualism and Mass Consumption in Trinidad.* Oxford: Berg, 1994.

Millette, James. "The Black Revolution in the Caribbean." In *Is Massa Day Dead?*

Black Moods in the Caribbean, edited by Orde Coombs, pp. 47–66. Garden City, N.Y.: Anchor Books, 1974.

Mintz, Sidney W. *Caribbean Transformations.* New York: Columbia University Press, 1989 [1974].

Naipaul, V. S. *The Loss of Eldorado: A History.* Harmondsworth: Penguin Books Ltd., 1969.

———. *The Middle Passage.* New York: Vintage Books, 1981 [1962].

Neil, Ancil A. *Voices from the Hills: Despers and Laventille.* N.p.: A. A. Neil, 1987.

Nketia, J. H. Kwabena. *The Music of Africa.* New York: Norton, 1974.

O'Brien, Linda L. "Guatemala: Folk Music." In *The New Grove Dictionary of Music and Musicians,* vol. 7, edited by Stanley Sadie, pp. 776–780. London: Macmillan Publishers Limited, 1980.

Oxaal, Ivar. *Black Intellectuals and the Dilemmas of Race and Classin Trinidad.* Cambridge, Mass.: Schenkman Publishing Co., 1982.

Pacini Hernández, Deborah. "*La lucha sonora:* Dominican Popular Music in the post-Trujillo Era." *Latin American Music Review* 12 (1991): 105–123.

Patterson, Orlando. "The Ritual of Cricket." In *Caribbean Essays,* edited by Andrew Salkey, pp. 108–118. London: Evans Brothers Limited, 1973.

———, ed. "Aspects of Change in Caribbean Folk Music." *International Folk Music Journal* 7 (1955): 29–36.

———. "Carnival in Nineteenth Century Trinidad." *Caribbean Quarterly* 4 (1956): 175–193.

Pearse, Andrew, ed. "Mitto Sampson on Calypso Legends of the Nineteenth-Century." *Caribbean Quarterly* 4 (1956): 250–262.

Pierre, Lennox. "From Dustbins to Classics." *Independence Supplement of the Sunday Guardian* (26 August 1962), pp. 107–110.

Powrie, Barbara E. "The Changing Attitude of the Coloured Middle Class Toward Carnival." *Caribbean Quarterly* 4 (1956): 224–232.

Premdas, Ralph. "Ethnic Conflict in Trinidad and Tobago: Domination and Reconciliation." In *Trinidad Ethnicity,* edited by Kevin Yelvington, pp. 136–160. London: Macmillan Caribbean, 1993.

Prospect, G. A. *Treatise on the Steelband of Trinidad and Tobago.* Port of Spain: G. A. Prospect, 1970.

Quevedo, Raymond. *Atilla's Kaiso: A Short History of Trinidad Calypso.* St. Augustine, Trinidad: Department of Extra Mural Studies, University of the West Indies, 1983.

Ramón y Rivera, Luis Felipe. "Venezuela: Folk Music." In *The New Grove Dictionary of Music and Musicians,* vol. 19, edited by Stanley Sadie, pp. 606–613. London: Macmillan Publishers Limited, 1980.

Regis, Louis. *Black Stalin: The Caribbean Man.* Borde Narve Village, Trinidad: Jordan's Printery, n.d.

Rennie, Bukka. *History of the Working Class in the Twentieth Century, Trinidad and Tobago.* Toronto: New Beginning Movement, 1974.

Rohlehr, Gordon. *Calypso & Society in Pre-Independence Trinidad.* Port of Spain: Gordon Rohlehr, 1990.

———. *My Strangled City and Other Essays.* Port of Spain: Longman Trinidad Limited, 1992.

Rosaldo, Renato. *Culture and Truth: The Remaking of Social Analysis.* Boston: Beacon Press, 1989.

Rouff, Anthony E. *"Authentic" Facts on the Origin of the Steelband.* St. Augustine,

Trinidad: Bowen's Printery, 1972.

Rubin, Vera. "Culture, Politics and Race Relations." *Social and Economic Studies* 11 (1962): 433–455.

Ryan, Selwyn. *The Muslimeen Grab for Power: Race, Religion and Revolution in Trinidad and Tobago.* Port of Spain: Inprint Caribbean, 1991.

———. *Race and Nationalism in Trinidad and Tobago: A Study of Decolonization in a Multiracial Society.* Toronto: University of Toronto Press, 1972.

———. "Political Change and Economic Reconstruction in Trinidad and Tobago." *Caribbean Affairs* 1, no. 1 (1988): 126–160.

———, ed. *Social and Occupational Stratification in Contemporary Trinidad and Tobago.* St. Augustine, Trinidad: Institute of Social and Economic Research, University of the West Indies, 1991.

———, ed. *Trinidad and Tobago: The Independence Experience, 1962–1987.* St. Augustine, Trinidad: Institute of Social and Economic Research, University of the West Indies, 1988.

Sahlins, Marshall. *Islands of History.* Chicago: University of Chicago Press, 1985.

Seeger, Peter. "The Steel Drum: A New Folk Instrument." *Journal of American Folklore* 71 (1958): 52–57.

———. *The Steel Drums of Kim Loy Wong.* New York: Oak Publications, 1964.

Segal, Daniel A. "'Race' and 'Colour' in Pre-Independence Trinidad and Tobago." In *Trinidad Ethnicity,* edited by Kevin Yelvington, pp. 81–115. London: Macmillan Caribbean, 1993.

Selvon, Samuel. *A Brighter Sun.* London: Allan Wingate, 1952.

Seon, Donald. *South Panmen.* San Fernando, Trinidad: Donald Seon, 1979.

Serrant, Jerry. *Kings of the Fancy Sailors: The Saga of Jason Griffith's Old-Fashioned Sailors.* N.p., 1988.

Simmonds, W. Austin. *Pan: The Story of the Steelband.* Maraval, Trinidad: BWIA International, n.d. [1959].

Simon, Pete. "Steelband." In *David Frost Introduces Trinidad and Tobago,* edited by Michael Anthony and Andrew Carr, pp. 99–111. London: A. Deutsch, 1975.

Singh, Kelvin. *Race and Class Struggles in a Colonial State: Trinidad 1917–1945.* Mona, Jamaica: The Press—University of the West Indies, 1994.

Slater, John E. *The Advent of the Steel Band and My Life and Times with It.* N.p., n.d.

Smith, Keith. "Panorama: The Past, the Future, the Unclear Present." *Tapia* 3, no. 8 (1973): 3.

Smith, Keith, ed. *Sparrow: The Legend.* N.p.: Inprint, n.d.

Smith, M. G. "Plural and Social Stratification," in *Social and Occupational Stratification in Contemporary Trinidad and Tobago,* ed. Selwyn Ryan, pp. 3–35. St. Augustine, Trinidad: Institute of Social and Economic Research, University of the West Indies, 1991.

———. *The Plural Society in the British West Indies.* Berkeley: University of California Press, 1965.

South America, Central America and the Caribbean 1993, "Trinidad and Tobago," pp. 577–592. London: Europa Publications Limited, 1993.

Stewart, John. *Drinkers, Drummers, and Decent Folk: Ethnographic Narratives of Village Trinidad.* Albany: State University of New York Press, 1989.

———. "Patronage and Control in the Trinidad Carnival." In *The Anthropology of Experience,* edited by Victor M. Turner and Edward M. Bruner, pp. 289–315. Urbana: University of Illinois Press, 1986.

Stone, Carl. *Democracy and Clientelism in Jamaica.* New Brunswick, N.J.: Transaction Books, 1980.

Tarradath, Selwyn. *Pan Trinbago's Information Booklet*. N.p., 1987.

———. "Race, Class, Politics and Gender in the Steelband Movement." In *Social and Occupational Stratification in Contemporary Trinidad and Tobago*, edited by Selwyn Ryan, pp. 377–384. St. Augustine, Trinidad: Institute of Social and Economic Research, University of the West Indies, 1991.

Thomas, Jeffrey. "The Changing Role of the Steel Band in Trinidad and Tobago: Panorama and the Carnival Tradition." *Studies in Popular Culture* 9, no. 2 (1986): 96–108.

———. *Forty Years of Steel: An Annotated Discography of Steel Band and Pan Recordings, 1951–1991*. Westport, Conn.: Greenwood Press, 1992.

Thomas, Roy E., ed. *The Trinidad Labour Riots of 1937: Perspectives 50 Years Later*. St. Augustine, Trinidad: Extra-Mural Studies Unit, University of the West Indies, 1987.

Trinidad and Tobago Carnival and Calypsoes, 1976. N.p., 1976.

Trotman, David V. *Crime in Trinidad: Conflict and Control in a Plantation Society, 1838–1900*. Knoxville: University of Tennessee Press, 1986.

Trouillot, Michel-Rolph. "The Caribbean Region: An Open Frontier in Anthropological Theory." *Annual Review of Anthropology* 21 (1992): 19–42.

Turner, Victor. *Dramas, Fields and Metaphors: Symbolic Action in Human Society*. Ithaca, N.Y.: Cornell University Press, 1974.

Warner, Keith Q. *Kaiso! The Trinidad Calypso: A Study of the Calypso as Oral Literature*. Washington, D.C.: Three Continents Press, 1985.

Warner-Lewis, Maureen. *Guinea's Other Suns: The African Dynamic in Trinidad Culture*. Dover, Mass.: The Majority Press, 1991.

Waterman, Christopher Alan. *Jùjú: A Social History and Ethnography of an African Popular Music*. Chicago: University of Chicago Press, 1990.

Waters, Anita M. *Race, Class, and Political Symbols: Rastafari and Reggae in Jamaican Politics*. New Brunswick, N.J.: Transaction Books, 1985.

Weller, Judith Ann. "A Profile of a Trinidadian Steel-Band." *Phylon* 22 (1961): 68–77.

White, Landeg E. "Steelbands: A Personal Record." *Caribbean Quarterly* 15, no. 4 (1969): 32–39.

Williams, Anthony. "Excerpts from Anthony Williams' History of the Steelband, 1946–1962." In *Steel Pan: Trinidad & Tobago's Gift to the World*, pp. 17–18. N.p., n.d.

Williams, Brackette F. "Nationalism, Traditionalism, and the Problem of Cultural Inauthenticity." In *Nationalist Ideologies and the Production of National Cultures*, edited by Richard G. Fox, pp. 112–129. Washington, D.C.: American Anthropological Association, 1990.

———. *Stains on My Name, War in My Veins: Guyana and the Politics of Cultural Struggle*. Durham, N.C.: Duke University Press, 1991.

Williams, Eric E. *History of the People of Trinidad and Tobago*. Port of Spain: PNM Publishing Co., 1962.

Williams, Raymond. *Marxism and Literature*. Oxford: Oxford University Press, 1977.

Wilson, Peter J. *Crab Antics: The Social Anthropology of English-Speaking Negro Societies of the Caribbean*. New Haven, Conn.: Yale University Press, 1973.

———. "Reputation vs. Respectability: A Suggestion for Caribbean Ethnology."

Man 4 (1969): 70–84.

Wood, Donald. *Trinidad in Transition.* London: Oxford University Press, 1968.

Yelvington, Kevin A. "Ethnicity 'Not Out': The Indian Cricket Tour of the West Indies and the 1976 Elections in Trinidad and Tobago." *Arena Review* 14, no. 1 (1990): 1–12.

————. "Vote Dem Out: The Demise of the PNM in Trinidad and Tobago." *Caribbean Review* 15, no. 4 (1987): 8–33.

————, ed. *Trinidad Ethnicity.* London: Macmillan Caribbean, 1993.

Index

Abrahams, Roger D., 5, 72–73, 210
Adams, Patricia, 179–80
Alexander's Ragtime Band, 35–36, 38, 58, 247 n.15, 251 n.54
Alfred, Leo "Little Drums," 39, 47, 50, 56, 58, 93
All Stars. *See* Trinidad All Stars
Anthony, Michael, 46
Arranging, steelband. *See* Steelband music, arranging of
Associations (New World African), pre-emancipation, 17–19
Atilla the Hun. *See* Quevedo, Raymond
Averill, Gage, 231–32

Bamboo percussion, 23. *See also* Tamboo bamboo
Bar 20 (steelband), 60
Basketball, 227–28
Bastide, Roger, 17
Batson, Dawn, 179, 181–82, 189
Batson, Prince, 27–29, 38–39, 41, 51, 113
Bennett, Herman L., 151
Besson, Jean, 73
Best, Lloyd, 151
Best, Stanley, 80–81
Betancourt, Sterling, 167
Birdsong, 179–80, 182
Bishop, Pat, 179, Fig. 8
Black Power protests (1970), 150–52; and the steelband, 152–55
Blake, Harold, 255–56 n.34
Blakie (Lord Blakie), 110
Blocoramas, 213–15
Bodu, Ignacio, 22
Bolland, O. Nigel, 241 n.11
Bomb tunes, 113–14, 205, 258 n.97
Bostock, Wellington "Blues," 48
Bradley, Clive, 189–190, 197, 265 n.32
Braithwaite, Lloyd, 3, 45, 47, 122–23
Brass bands, 55, 108, 162, 257 n.82
Brathwaite, Edward Kamau, 7, 11–12, 220
Brereton, Bridget, 79

Brown, Wenzell, 45
Bryan, Melville, 155–56, 159–160
Burton, Richard D. E., 269 n.22
Butler, Uriah "Buzz," 44, 78

Calypso: early forms of, 22, 25, 244 n.24, 262–63 n.69; during and after World War II, 46, 254 n.15, 262–63 n.69; contemporary, 195–96, 205–6; performed by steelbands (pre-Independence), 41, 56–57, 112–13, 167–68; performed by steelbands (post-Independence), 113, 160–61, 169, 197–98. *See also* Repertoires, steelband
Canboulay, 20–22, 25–26
Carmichael, Mrs. A. C., 16
Carnival: nineteenth-century, 19–23; early twentieth-century, 25–36, 51–52; post-World War II, 54–64, 69, 75, 81, 112–16, 120–21; post-Independence, 158–59, 161–62, 191–92, 194–96, 202–206; "improvement" efforts, 22, 29–31, 63–64
Carnival Development Committee (CDC), 120–21, 159
Carr, Andrew, 26, 83–84
Casablanca, 56–57, 62, 85–86, 89–91, 248 n.24
Charles, Rudolph, 154, 264 n.19, Fig. 7
Christmas, pre-emancipation, 15–18
Churches, steelbands in, 266 n.52
Cipriani, A. A., 77–78
Clashes, steelband. *See* Steelbands, clashes between
Class: concept of, 241 n.13; grass-roots, defined, 2, 241 n.13
Class relations: pre-Independence, 6–10, 44–45, 53–54, 77–78, 120–23; post-Independence, 150–52, 174–76; and the pre-World War II Carnival, 30–31; and the steelband (1940s), 62–68, 74–75; and the steelband (1950s), 76, 79, 90, 100–105, 110–12, 123–24; and the steelband (post-Independence), 170, 184,

This book was set in Baskerville and Eras typefaces. Baskerville was designed by John Baskerville at his private press in Birmingham. England, in the eighteenth century. The first typeface to depart from the oldstyle typeface design, Baskerville has more variation between thick and thin strokes. In an effort to insure that the thick and thin strokes of his typeface reproduced well on paper, John Baskerville developed the first wove paper, the surface of which was much smoother than the laid paper of the time. The development of wove paper was partly responsible for the introduction of typefaces classfied as modern, which have even more contrast between thick and thin strokes.

Eras was designed in 1969 by Studio Hollenstein in Paris for the Wagner Typefoundry. A contemporary script-like version of a sans-serif typeface, the letters of Eras have a monotone stroke and are slightly inclined.

Printed on acid-free paper.